AF361557

Papal Letters in the
Early Middle Ages

HISTORY OF MEDIEVAL CANON LAW

Edited by Wilfried Hartmann and Kenneth Pennington

---

*Canonical Collections of the Early Middle Ages
(ca. 400–1140): A Bibliographical Guide to the
Manuscripts and Literature*

Papal Letters in the Early Middle Ages

The History of Western Canon Law to 1000

*The History of Byzantine and
Eastern Canon Law to 1500*

*The History of Canon Law in the Age
of Reform, 1000–1140*

*The History of Medieval Canon Law in
the Classical Period, 1140–1234*

The History of Medieval Canon Law, 1234–1300

Doctrines of Canon Law, 1100–1298

*The History of Medieval Canon Law in the
Late Middle Ages*

*The History of Courts and Procedure in
Medieval Canon Law*

*A Guide to Medieval Canon Law Jurists
and Collections, 1140–1500*

Detlev Jasper and Horst Fuhrmann

Papal Letters in the Early Middle Ages

The Catholic University of America Press • Washington, D.C.

LIBRARY OF CONGRESS CATALOGING-IN-PUBLICATION DATA

Jasper, Detlev.
    Papal letters in the Early Middle Ages / Detlev Jasper and
Horst Fuhrmann.
        p. cm. — (History of medieval canon law)
    Includes bibliographical references and index.
    ISBN 0-8132-0919-6 (alk. paper)
    1. Letters, Papal—History—To 1500. 2. Canon law—
Sources. I. Fuhrmann, Horst. II. Title. III. Series.

LAW
262.99'1'0902—dc21
                                        00-059035

Contents

Foreword

The present volume of the History of Medieval Canon Law contains two essays on late antique and early medieval papal letters: Detlev Jasper describes the history of the transmission and spread of papal decretals from the beginning of the fourth to the end of the ninth century in the Latin West; Horst Fuhrmann tells the story of the Pseudo-Isidorian Forgeries, a collection of conciliar decrees and papal letters that were arranged chronologically. The most influential and important texts in this collection were forged papal decretals that were attributed to popes who reigned during the first four centuries of the Christian era.

Dating from the time of Pope Siricius (384–399) and afterward, we have papal letters that answered questions sent to Rome and that gave responses to legal problems. These decretals soon gained authority that rivaled conciliar canons. Together decretals and conciliar canons formed the foundation of early ecclesiastical law. Beginning in the fifth century, papal decretals were arranged in collections. These collections contained complete or partial texts of the decretals and the canons of church councils. They were arranged in chronological order at first, but later collections were arranged systematically, according to legal topics. In the middle of the ninth century, still unknown forger(s) from the ecclesiastical province of Reims composed sixty decretals that were attributed to early popes. These forger(s) were convinced that the Roman bishops had given legal rulings on questions touching the liturgy of the church, the regulation of clerical life, and the constitution of the church since the beginning of Christianity. They wrote letters that supported and provided evidence for their convictions.

Both essays offer readers materials that have not existed before in the scholarly literature. This is especially true of Jasper's history of the transmission and reception of papal decretals into canonical collections up to the time of Gratian in the twelfth century. His wide-ranging and comprehensive survey of the literature and, even more, his intimate knowledge of the manuscript tradition create a scholarly synthesis of this material that is completely new. One may count the earlier studies on papal legislation in the early Middle Ages on one hand. The majority of the newest essays, dictionary articles, and general essays in reference works deal almost exclusively with the period of the high Middle Ages, above all from the twelfth and thirteenth centuries (e.g. Gérard Fransen's masterly *Les décrétales et les collections de décrétales* [1972 and 1984]). Jasper, however, begins at the first stirrings of papal legislative consciousness in late antiquity. His essay will be required reading for anyone interested in the evolution of papal authority.

Horst Fuhrmann first published much of the material in his essay in the early seventies. His monumental, three-volume work of over eleven hundred pages, *Einfluß und Verbreitung der pseudoisidorischen Fälschungen* (1972–1974), set new standards for the study of early medieval legal collections when it was published. But his work has been readily available only to scholars who read German easily and consequently his conclusions have not entered the non-German-speaking worlds as pervasively as they should have. Although several short encyclopedia articles have given brief summaries of his work in English (Horst Fuhrmann, *New Catholic Encyclopedia* 5 [1967] 820ff and John van Engen, *Dictionary of the Middle Ages* 4 [1984] 124–127), his essay in this volume gives scholars the full scope and richness of his work with sufficient supporting detail.

Due to a series of problems, this volume has, unfortunately, spent many years in the editorial process—to the dismay of the authors, the editors, and the Press. The delay has hampered inclusion of the most recent literature, especially in the section on Pseudo-Isidore. Readers should take note, nonetheless, of the recent essay by Horst Fuhrmann in the *Deutsches Archiv* 55.1 (1999) 183–191 and of an article that will soon be printed in *Francia* (2001) by Klaus Zechiel-Eckes. Zechiel-Eckes will put forward new insights into the time when the forged letters in Pseudo-Isidore might have been composed, the place of composition, and the author of this great forgery.

The editors are indebted to Steven Rowan who translated Jasper's essay from German into English and to Mary Sommar who revised Rowan's translation with Jasper while working in the Monumenta Germaniae Historica in Munich. Timothy Reuter translated Fuhrmann's essay. Both editors spent a summer in Syracuse polishing the translation of both essays. They remain responsible for any infelicities that remain in the texts.

WILFRIED HARTMANN AND KENNETH PENNINGTON
Tübingen and Syracuse, April 2000

Abbreviations

Abh.	Abhandlungen
ACO	*Acta conciliorum oecumenicorum*
AHC	*Annuarium historiae conciliorum*
AHP	*Archivum historiae pontificiae*
AKKR	*Archiv für katholisches Kirchenrecht*
BDHI	*Bibliothek des Deutschen Historischen Instituts in Rom*
BEC	*Bibliothèque de l'École des Chartes*
BISM	*Bullettino dell'Istituto Storico Italiano per il Medio Evo e Archivio Muratoriano*
B.L.	British Library
BMCL	*Bulletin of Medieval Canon Law, New series*
B.N.	Bibliothèque Nationale
CCL	*Corpus Christianorum, Series latina*
CHR	*Catholic Historical Review*
Clavis	E. Dekkers-E. Gaar, *Clavis patrum latinorum*, ed. 2 (1961); ed. 3 (1995)
Clm	Codices latini Monacenses of the Bayerische Staatsbibliothek, Munich
CSEL	*Corpus scriptorum ecclesiasticorum latinorum*
DA	*Deutsches Archiv für Erforschung des Mittelalters*
DBI	*Dizionario biografico degli Italiani*
DDC	*Dictionnaire de droit canonique*
DHGE	*Dictionnaire d'histoire et de géographie ecclésiastiques*
DMA	*Dictionary of the Middle Ages*
EHR	*English Historical Review*
EOMIA	*Ecclesiae occidentalis monumenta iuris antiquissimi,* ed. C. H. Turner. 2 vols. Oxford 1899–1939

Ep(p).	Epistola(e)
Études Le Bras	*Études d'histoire du droit canonique dédiées à G. Le Bras.* 2 vols. Paris 1965
Fälschungen im Mittelalter 2	*Fälschungen im Mittelalter, 2: Gefälschte Rechtstexte: Der bestrafte Fälscher. Schriften der MGH 33.2;* Hannover 1988
HRG	*Handwörterbuch zur deutschen Rechtsgeschichte*
IRMAe	*Ius romanum medii aevi*
JE, JK, JL	Ph. Jaffé, *Regesta pontificum romanorum*, ed. secundam curaverunt S. Loewenfeld (JL: an.882–1198), F. Kaltenbrunner (JK: an.?–590), P. Ewald (JE: an.590–882). Leipzig 1885. Repr. Graz 1956
JEH	*Journal of Ecclesiastical History*
JTS	*Journal of Theological Studies*
lat.	<Codices> latini
LMA	*Lexikon des Mittelalters*
LThK	*Lexikon für Theologie und Kirche*
Maassen, Geschichte	F. Maassen, *Geschichte der Quellen und der Literatur des canonischen Rechts im Abendlande bis zum Ausgange des Mittelalters.* Graz 1870. Repr. Graz 1956
Mansi	*Sacrorum conciliorum nova et amplissima collectio,* ed. J. D. Mansi
MGH	*Monumenta Germaniae Historica*
MIC	*Monumenta iuris canonici*
MIÖG	*Mitteilungen des Instituts für österreichische Geschichtsforschung*
NA	*Neues Archiv der Gesellschaft für ältere deutsche Geschichtskunde*
NCE	*New Catholic Encyclopedia*
N.S.	New Series
ÖAKR	*Österreichisches Archiv für Kirchenrecht*
PL	Migne, *Patrologia latina*
Proceedings	*Proceedings of the International Congress of Medieval Canon Law*
QF	*Quellen und Forschungen aus italienischen Archiven und Bibliotheken*
RB	*Revue bénédictine*
RDC	*Revue de droit canonique*
RE	*Realencyklopädie für protestantische Theologie und Kirche,* 3rd ed.

RHD	*Revue historique de droit français et étranger*
RHE	*Revue d'histoire ecclésiastique*
SB	Sitzungsberichte
Settimane Spoleto	*Settimane di studio del Centro italiano di studi sull'Alto Medioevo*
SG	*Studia Gratiana*
TRE	*Theologische Realenzyklopädie*
TRG	*Tijdschrift voor rechtsgeschiedenis*
Vat.	Città del Vaticano, Biblioteca Apostolica Vaticana
ZKG	*Zeitschrift für Kirchengeschichte*
ZRG Kan. Abt.	*Zeitschrift der Savigny-Stiftung für Rechtsgeschichte,* Kanonistische Abteilung

The Beginning of
the Decretal Tradition

*Papal Letters from the Origin
of the Genre through the
Pontificate of Stephen V*

Detlev Jasper

Prefatory Remarks

A separate discussion of the papal letters written through the end of
the ninth century has not been customary in histories of medieval canon
law. Thus the present essay calls for a brief description of what it offers
the reader—and more importantly, what it does not offer. In contrast to
most handbooks and histories of canon law, which usually skim over the
beginning of the papal decretal tradition and the earliest decretal collections of the fourth and fifth centuries,[1] the following pages will try to
present a detailed discussion of the question, beginning with the first papal letters and continuing through their transmission and their reception
into the canonical tradition up to Gratian's *Decretum* (1140). This effort,
however, will be limited by the difficulties of accessing the widely scat-
tered literature and by the present unsatisfactory state of scholarship on
many issues.

1. See, for example, B. Kurtscheid, *Historia Iuris Canonici*, 2.1 (Rome 1941) 137ff., A. Van
Hove, *Prolegomena* (Commentarium Lovaniense in Codicem iuris canonici 1.1; 2nd ed.
Mechelen-Rome 1945) 136ff., A. Stickler, *Historia Iuris Canonici* (Turin 1950) 14ff., H.E. Feine,
Kirchliche Rechtsgeschichte (4th ed. Weimar 1964) 94f., A. García y García, *Historia del derecho
canónico* (Universidad Pontificia de Salamanca Instituto de Historia de la Teología Españo-
la, Subsidia 1; Salamanca 1967) 166ff., and J. Gaudemet, *Église et Cité: Histoire du droit canon-
ique* (Paris 1994) 46ff. With extensive bibliographies, J. Gaudemet, 'Kirchenrecht I', TRE 18
(1989) 719ff., and G. May, 'Kirchenrechtsquellen 2.1', TRE 19 (1990) 3ff. Basic tools for re-
searching papal letters are P. Jaffé, *Regesta pontificum Romanorum* (2nd ed. Leipzig 1885, repr.
Graz 1956) F. Kaltenbrunner, ed. (JK through Pelagius II, 578–590), P. Ewald (JE through
John VIII, 872–882), S. Loewenfeld (JL through Celestine III, 1191–1198), and additions in R.
Hiestand, *Initienverzeichnis und chronologisches Verzeichnis zu den Archivberichten und Vorarbeiten der Regesta pontificum Romanorum* (MGH Hilfsmittel 7; Munich 1983). For editions of
the earlier period through Gregory I (590–604), one still relies on P. Coustant, *Epistolae Romanorum Pontificum*, 1: *Ab anno Christi 67 usque ad annum 440* (Paris 1721; repr. Farnborough
1967) and the continuation by A. Thiel, *Epistolae Romanorum Pontificum genuinae*, 1: *A S. Hi-
lario usque ad Hormisdam ann. 461–523* (Braunsberg 1868). They no longer meet scholarly ex-
pectations, cf. K. Silva-Tarouca, 'Beiträge zur Überlieferungsgeschichte der Papstbriefe des
IV., V. u. VI. Jahrhunderts', *Zeitschrift für katholische Theologie* 43 (1919) 469f., 474ff., 479f.,
idem, 'Le antiche lettere dei papi e le loro edizioni', *La Civiltà Cattolica* 72 (1921) 327ff. The
survey in Stickler, *Historia* 308ff. should be consulted for further editions; the *Clavis Patrum
Latinorum* by E. Dekkers and A. Gaar (CCL; 3rd ed. Steenbrugge 1995) No. 1568ff. gives the
state of papal letters through Constantine I (708–715). Some new editions will be mentioned at the proper place. Earlier brief surveys and bibliographical citations for the papal
letters from Siricius to Gregory I are found in O. Bardenhewer, *Geschichte der altkirchlichen
Literatur* (2nd ed. Freiburg 1923) 3.591ff. (2nd ed. Freiburg 1924) 4.613ff. (Freiburg 1932)
5.278ff.; for the popes from Liberius to Leo I, B. Studer, 'Les pontifes romains de Sirice à
Léon le Grand', *Initiations aux Pères de l'Église IV: Les Pères latins*, ed. Angelo di Berardino
(Paris 1986) 735ff. A survey of editions and translations is found in G. Pentini and M.
Spadoni Cerroni, *Epistolari cristiani (secc. I–V) Repertorio bibliografico*, 2: *Epistolari latini
(secc.IV–V)* (Rome 1990).

The present work covers the period from the end of the fourth century to the end of the ninth century, i.e., from Siricius (384–399), whose pontificate undoubtedly produced the first known papal decretal (JK 255, February 10, 385), to Stephen V (885–891). A large lacuna in the history of the popes after the pontificate of Pope Stephen V in the *Liber Pontificalis* dictates that our survey should end with him.[2] Also, the canonists stopped including contemporary papal letters in their collections after Stephen's pontificate. This practice continued at least until Pope Leo IX (1049–1054).[3]

The obvious place to begin this discussion is with Pope Siricius' letters and decretals, because these decretals, which were issued mostly as *responsa*, reveal a new capacity of the popes to act as legislators. From the time of Siricius, popes claimed that their decretals were equal to conciliar decisions. Thus, gradually, a system of ecclesiastical law came into being that was founded on two elements: conciliar canons and papal rescripts.[4]

Our survey will start from research of Maassen on papal letters and decretals.[5] He limited himself to the canonical collections containing papal letters but later took into account papal letters in materials like the *Collectio Ratisbonensis* and the *Collectio Grimanica* of Leo I's letters, the register of Gregory the Great, the *Collectio pontificia* of Boniface's letters, and the *Codex Carolinus*.[6] Modern canonistic research was strongly influenced by Maassen (his *Geschichte* appeared in 1870), and by the exploration of the papal registers, especially the work of Paul Ewald on the reconstruction of Gregory the Great's register (published in *Neues Archiv* 3, 1878). This research inspired later scholars like Harold Steinacker, Otto Günther, Car-

---

2. L. Duchesne, *Le Liber Pontificalis* (Paris 1892) 2.196ff., and introduction vii–viii, H. Löwe, *Deutschlands Geschichtsquellen im Mittelalter: Vorzeit und Karolinger* (Weimar 1963) 4.462–463 and R. Davis, *The Lives of the Ninth-Century Popes (Liber Pontificalis)* (Translated Texts for Historians 20; Liverpool 1995) ix–xii. Stephen's biography breaks off after the first year of his pontificate. Papal biographies became sketchy after Stephen. The writing of detailed biographies began again in the twelfth century with the *Liber Pontificalis* of Petrus Guillermus (cf. Duchesne xxiv ff. and U. Přerovský, *Liber Pontificalis nella recensione di Pietro Guglielmo e del card. Pandolfo, glossato da Pietro Bohier* [SG 21–23; Rome 1978] 39ff. and the 'Liber Pontificalis of Tortona', *Liber Pontificalis prout exstat in codice manuscripto Dertusensi textum genuinum complectens hactenus ex parte ineditum Pandulphi scriptoris pontificis*, ed. J. March [Barcelona 1925]).

3. Cf. for example the index of sources in *Bonizo von Sutri, Liber de vita christiana*, ed. E. Perels (Texte zur Geschichte des römischen und kanonischen Rechts im Mittelalter 1; Berlin 1930) 360ff., on the *Collection in 183 Titles* of Santa Maria Novella, *Liber canonum diversorum sanctorum patrum sive Collectio in CLXXXIII titulos digesta* ed. J. Motta (MIC Series B, 7; Vatican City 1988) 327ff., on Polycarp cf. U. Horst, *Die Kanonessammlung Polycarpus des Gregor von S. Grisogono: Quellen und Tendenzen* (MGH Hilfsmittel 5; Munich 1980) 200ff. or on Gratian's *Decretum* ed. Friedberg, xxxi.

4. Cf. E. Schwartz, 'Die Kanonessammlungen der alten Reichskirche', ZRG Kan. Abt. 25 (1936) 20, repr. idem *Gesammelte Schriften* (Berlin 1960) 4.178.

5. Maassen, *Geschichte* 226ff.

6. See below, p. 104ff.

lo Silva-Tarouca, Eduard Schwartz, and Hubert Wurm to deepen our knowledge of the registers and papal letters with their work.[7] Later, unfortunately, scholars shifted their attention very quickly, and almost exclusively, to problems of paleography, diplomatics, and other ancillary disciplines. They concentrated on the appearance of the papal registers, their composition, and the functioning of the papal archives; to date there is no general agreement on these questions of indisputable importance, and interest in this research appears to have declined.[8] In keeping with the goal of this history to present primarily the transmission and reception of canonical texts, problems of paleography, diplomatics, and related disciplines will be dealt with only in passing.

To survey the reception of papal letters and decretals into the canonical jurisprudence, fourteen canonical collections between the *Collectio Anselmo dedicata* (late ninth century) and Gratian's *Decretum* (1140) will be explored. Our work will be based on the letters of twenty-five popes from Siricius to Stephen V included in these collections. A model for this research is the survey that Ernst Perels made in his investigation of the letters of Pope Nicholas I and their reception into canonical collections.[9]

7. P. Ewald, 'Studien zur Ausgabe des Registers Gregors I.', NA 3 (1878) 433ff. H. Steinacker, 'Die Deusdedithandschrift (Cod.Vat. 3833) und die ältesten gallischen libri canonum', MIÖG Ergänzungsband 6 (1901) 113ff., idem, 'Ueber das älteste päpstliche Registerwesen', MIÖG 23 (1902) 1ff., R. von Heckel, 'Das päpstliche und sicilische Registerwesen', *Archiv für Urkundenforschung* 1 (1908) 394ff., O. Günther, *Avellana-Studien* (SB Wien 134; Vienna 1896) and the introduction to his edition of the *Collectio Avellana, Epistulae imperatorum pontificum aliorum* (CSEL 35.1; Vienna 1895) lv ff.; C. Silva-Tarouca, 'Beiträge zur Überlieferungsgeschichte' and in his studies on the letters of Leo I and particularly idem, 'Nuovi studi sulle antiche lettere dei Papi', *Gregorianum* 12 (1931), which was published as a monograph in 1932 which will be cited, E. Schwartz in his introduction to the ACO volumes, particularly to his edition of the letters of Leo the Great, ACO 2.4 (Berlin 1932) and H. Wurm, *Studien und Texte zur Dekretalensammlung des Dionysius Exiguus* (Kanonistische Studien und Texte 16; Bonn 1939). Further efforts are mentioned by C. R. Cheney, *The Study of the Medieval Papal Chancery* (Glasgow University Publications, The Edwards Lectures 2; Glasgow 1966) 23ff. and in the instructive survey by O. Hageneder, 'Papstregister und Dekretalenrecht', *Recht und Schrift im Mittelalter* (Vorträge und Forschungen 23; Sigmaringen 1977) 320ff.

8. Cf. the summary of the research situation in D. Lohrmann, *Das Register Papst Johannes' VIII. (872–882)* (BDHI 30; Tübingen 1968) 95ff., 157ff., 225ff., who is particularly at odds with F. Bock, 'Bemerkungen zu den ältesten Papstregistern und zum "Liber diurnus Romanorum pontificum",' *Archivalische Zeitschrift* 57 (1961) 11ff.; cf. also the survey in O. Hageneder, 'Papstregister', LMA 6 (1993) 1687–1688. The most recent comprehensive attempt to interpret the policy of Gregory I (590–604) by using his register and rescript practices and to understand their function at the papal court was made by E. Pitz, *Papstreskripte im frühen Mittelalter* (Beiträge zur Geschichte und Quellenkunde des Mittelalters 14; Sigmaringen 1990) which should be compared with the criticisms of B. Maleczek-Pferschy, MIÖG 99 (1991) 505ff.

9. NA 39 (1914) 140ff. The following collections were examined: the *Collectio Anselmo dedicata:* J.-C. Besse, *Histoire des Textes du Droit de l'Église au Moyen-Age de Denys à Gratien: Collectio Anselmo dedicata: Étude et texte* (Paris 1960); Regino of Prüm, *Libri duo de synodalibus*

As ever, it is a great hindrance for such research that there are no reliable editions for most of the earlier papal letters.[10] For the writings of Siricius, Innocent I, Boniface I, Celestine I, Leo I (the decretals), Gelasius I, and the popes of the seventh century, we are still largely dependent on the editions of Coustant, the Ballerinis, Thiel or on reprints in Migne's Patrologia Latina.[11] The situation is better for the papal letters of the eighth and ninth century: for the most part there are good editions available in the Monumenta Germaniae Historica, Epistolae, volumes 3 through 7.[12]

causis, ed. F. G. A. Wasserschleben (Leipzig 1840); Burchard of Worms, *Decretum* PL 140.537ff. The *Collection in Seventy-Four Titles: Diversorum patrum sententie sive Collectio in LXXIV titulos digesta,* ed. J. Gilchrist (MIC Series B, 1; Vatican City 1973); Anselm of Lucca, *Collectio canonum,* ed. F. Thaner (Regensburg 1906–1915); for the portion of the collection not edited, 11.16–13.29, Vat. lat. 1363 (twelfth century) was used; Deusdedit, *Die Kanonessammlung,* ed. V. Wolf von Glanvell (Paderborn 1905); Bonizo, *Liber de vita christiana* ed. E. Perels; the *Collection in 183 Titles: Liber canonum diuersorum sanctorum patrum siue Collectio in CLXXXXIII titulos digesta,* ed. J. Motta (MIC Series B, 7; Vatican City 1988); *Collectio Britannica* based on London, B.L. Add. 8873; *Collectio Tripartita* based on Paris, B.N. lat. 3858B; Ivo, *Decretum* PL 161.59ff.; Ivo, *Panormia* PL 161.1041ff.; Gregory of San Grisogono, *Polycarpus,* see Horst, *Polycarpus,* and Gratian, *Decretum,* ed. Friedberg. As with Perels' list, I have provided information about the origins of the material and the extent of its reception and do not intend to explain the dependence of one collection on another. That task could not be done with the present editions.

10. P. Ewald, 'Die Papstbriefe der Brittischen Sammlung' NA 5 (1880) 290 and Schwartz, 'Kanonessammlungen' 20–21 n. 1 (*Gesammelte Schriften* 4, 179 n. 1) already complained of this.

11. Thanks to Eduard Schwartz's enormous energy, which appears in the volumes of ACO, there has been some improvement, cf. the survey of the papal letters edited by him in the ACO in the *Registerband* ACO 4.3.1, ed. R. Schieffer (Berlin 1974) 574ff., on which see the Schwartz edition of letters of Popes Simplicius, Felix III, and Gelasius, *Publizistische Sammlungen zum acacianischen Schisma* (Abh. München N.S. 10; Munich 1934). Among earlier scholarly editions worth mentioning are the papal letters from Zosimus (417–418) to Pelagius I (556–561) gathered in the *Liber auctoritatum Arelatensis ecclesiae,* ed. W. Gundlach (MGH Epp. 3; Berlin 1892) 1ff., the *Collectio Avellana,* ed. O. Guenther (CSEL 35.1.2; Vienna 1895–1898), the edition of the *Collectio Thessalonicensis,* ed. C. Silva-Tarouca (Rome 1937), and the more recent edition of the letters of Pope Pelagius I by P. M. Gassó and C. M. Batlle *Pelagii I papae epistulae quae aupersunt (556–561),* (Scripta et documenta in abbatia Montisserrati 8; Montserrat 1956). The letter register of Gregory the Great exists in two scholarly editions: P. Ewald and L. M. Hartmann (MGH Epp. 1–2; Berlin 1891–1899) and D. Norberg (CCL 140 and 140A; Turnhout 1982). On details, the survey in Clavis 1568ff. should be consulted.

12. Cf. the survey in Stickler, *Historia* 310.

PART I

Papal Letters and Decretals Written from the Beginning through the Pontificate of Gregory the Great (to 604)

I. Transmission and Reception of Decretals and Letters from Siricius (384–399) through Sixtus III (432–440)

1. The Papacy at the End of the Fourth Century

Cuthbert Hamilton Turner described the reign of Pope Damasus (366–384) as 'the period of the first definite self-expression of the papacy'.[13] And, indeed, Damasus' pontificate produced fundamental formulations of papal authority and power that have been transmitted to later epochs. In addition his pontificate marked a period in which the emperors issued a number of imperial constitutions granting the Church and the emerging papacy the freedom needed for their development. The Roman emperors Valentinian II, Gratian, Valens, and, after Valens' death at Adrianople in 378, Theodosius the Great all commanded that the procedure of ecclesiastical courts in matters of appeals be patterned after the civil law (*Codex Theodosianus* = CTh 16.2.23 of 376). Clergy of the rank of doorkeeper and above were free from taxation (CTh 13.1.11 of 379) and were no longer obliged to perform public service (CTh 16.2.24 of 377). The emperors promulgated comprehensive legislation against heretics that affected principally the Donatists (CTh 16.5.4 and 16.6.2 of 377–379). These constitutions were virtually a death sentence for those heretics, stripping them of all rights and property.[14] More significant in this context is the famous

---

13. Cf. C. H. Turner, 'The Organisation of the Church', *The Christian Roman Empire and the Foundation of the Teutonic Kingdoms* (The Cambridge Medieval History 1; 2nd ed. Cambridge 1924) 172.

14. Fundamental is K. L. Noethlichs, *Die gesetzgeberischen Maßnahmen der christlichen Kaiser des vierten Jahrhunderts gegen Häretiker, Heiden und Juden* (Cologne 1971) 99ff. Cf. as well R. Lorenz, *Das vierte bis sechste Jahrhundert (Westen)* 1.4 (Die Kirche in ihrer Geschichte; Göttingen 1970) 36; G. Gottlieb, *Ambrosius von Mailand und Kaiser Gratian* (Hypomnemata 40;

edict on the faith, *Cunctos populos,* which was issued on February 28, 380, in Thessalonika by Emperor Theodosius, who had not yet been baptized (CTh 16.1.2). This law was reinforced the same day by a penal sanction threatening to punish any violation as sacrilege (CTh 16.2.25).[15] In *Cunctos populos* the emperors declared that the faith bestowed by 'divine apostle' Peter on the Romans, which Pope Damasus and Peter, Bishop of Alexandria, embraced, was the Trinitarian confession, as formulated in Nicaea (325). This faith must be henceforward constitutionally binding.[16] The prominence of the Apostle Peter and the Roman Bishop Damasus as guarantors of orthodoxy received its classic formulation two years later in a Roman synodal canon, written in opposition to the First Council of Constantinople (381), in which Roman sensibilities had been injured by granting primatial honors to Constantinople as the New Rome.[17] This canon was used extensively in what is known as the *Praefatio longa* of the First Council of Nicaea (written in the first third of the fifth century), which begins the oldest Latin *Corpus canonum Africano-Romanum* and the *Quesnelliana* collection. It was also included in the widely distributed Pseudo-Gelasian *Decretum de libris recipiendis et non recipiendis* (early sixth century).[18] According to this work, the primacy of Rome over all other

Göttingen 1973) 52ff. and A. Lippold, *Theodosius der Große und seine Zeit* (2nd ed. Munich 1980) 129ff., 169. The laws of the Theodosian Code are translated into English and commented upon by P. R. Coleman-Norton, *Roman State and Christian Church: A Collection of Legal Documents to A.D. 535* (London 1966) 1.342ff.

15. This law opens the Code of Justinian, Cod. 1.1.1 *Corpus Iuris Civilis,* ed. P. Krüger (Berlin 1884) 2.5. W. Ensslin, *Die Religionspolitik des Kaisers Theodosius d. Gr.* (SB München Heft 2; Munich 1953) 5ff., 16ff. is fundamental. Cf. also A. Ehrhardt, 'The First Two Years of the Emperor Theodosius I', JEH 15 (1964) 1ff., C. Pietri, *Roma christiana: Recherches sur l'Église de Rome, son organisation, sa politique, son idéologie de Miltiade à Sixte III (311–440)* (Bibliothèque des Écoles Françaises d'Athènes et de Rome 224; Rome 1976) 849ff., Lippold, *Theodosius* 21ff., 123f., 169.

16. Besides the literature cited in the previous note, cf. E. Caspar, *Geschichte des Papsttums von den Anfängen bis zur Höhe der Weltherrschaft* (Tübingen 1930) 1.233; E. Schwartz, 'Zur Kirchengeschichte des 4. Jahrhunderts', *Zeitschrift für die neutestamentliche Wissenschaft 34* (1935) 196–197 (repr. *Gesammelte Schriften* [Berlin 1966] 4.88–89); and Schwartz, 'Über die Reichskonzilien von Theodosius bis Justinian', ZRG Kan. Abt. 11 (1921) 212 (repr. *Gesammelte Schriften* 4.115), which summarizes the motives of the emperor as follows: 'Here speaks the pious Spanish soldier, to whom the church established by the Apostle Peter is the protector of tradition'. W. Ullmann, *Gelasius I. (492–496): Das Papsttum an der Wende der Spätantike zum Mittelalter* (Päpste und Papsttum 18; Stuttgart 1981) 6ff. and K. M. Girardet, 'Gericht über den Bischof von Rom', *Historische Zeitschrift* 259 (1994) 6–7.

17. Cf. Caspar, *Papsttum* 1.247ff., E. Schwartz, 'Zum Decretum Gelasianum', *Zeitschrift für die neutestamentliche Wissenschaft* 29 (1930) 166ff., Pietri, *Roma christiana* 1.866ff., 881ff. and Ullmann, *Gelasius* 21–22.

18. Turner, EOMIA 1.155ff. in a parallel-column edition; see H. Mordek, 'Der römische Primat in den Kirchenrechtssammlungen des Westens vom IV. bis VIII. Jahrhundert', *Il primato del vescovo di Roma nel primo millennio: Ricerche e testimonianze: Atti del symposium storico-teologico Roma, 9–13 ottobre 1989,* ed. M. Maccarrone (Pontificio comitato di scienze

churches did not rest on synodal decrees, as did Constantinople's claims, but rather directly on the Word of the Lord in Matthew 16:18–19. But it was not simply its apostolic and biblical origins that distinguished the Roman Church. Rome was the sole apostolic foundation in the Western half of the Empire and could also claim double apostolicity through the martyrdoms of Peter and Paul within its walls, a privilege not granted to any other church. Consequently the order of the three 'Petrine sees' was established as: Rome, Alexandria, and Antioch. This ranking had been in effect since the third century due to the political and economic importance of these towns, but now it was justified on other grounds. The historical and chronological argument, that Antioch's Christian community was older than that of Rome, was overturned by the biblical and apostolic arguments.[19] In the wake of this development, papal statements increasingly used the title 'sedes apostolica' to refer to the Roman episcopal see.[20]

Damasus' successor, Siricius (384–399), developed this line of reasoning even further. In the introductory sentences of his first decretal to Bishop Himerius of Tarragona (JK 255), the identification of the Roman bishop with Peter is complete: the pope bears the burdens of all, 'quin immo haec (=onera) portat in nobis beatus apostolus Petrus, qui nos in omnibus, ut confidimus, administrationis suae protegit et tuetur heredes'.[21] Siricius adopted Paul's words that the Apostle had to bear 'solicitude for all churches' (2 Corinthians 11:28) and applied them to Rome.[22] He also used the metaphor of Rome as the head and the other congregations as members of the body.[23] The decretal of January 6, 386, to the African bish-

---

storiche: Atti e documenti 4; Vatican City 1991) 535ff., idem, 'Karthago oder Rom? Zu den Anfängen der kirchlichen Rechtsquellen im Abendland', *Studia in honorem eminentissimi Cardinalis Alphonsi M. Stickler* (Studia et textus historiae iuris canonici 7; Rome 1992) 367–368. On its adoption by the *Decretum Gelasianum,* cf. Schwartz, 'Decretum Gelasianum' 162ff. and Caspar, *Papsttum* 1.598–599 and 2.773–774.

19. Cf. Caspar, *Papsttum* 1.248ff., who stresses that in this case it was still concerned with assuring precedence, not in subordinating Alexandria and Antioch; M. Wojtowytsch, *Papsttum und Konzile von den Anfängen bis zu Leo I. (440–461)* (Päpste und Papsttum 17; Stuttgart 1981) 139ff. and Ullmann, *Gelasius* 21–22.

20. Cf. P. Batiffol, *Cathedra Petri: Etudes d'histoire ancienne de l'Église* (Unam Sanctam 4; Paris 1938) 151ff., Wojtowytsch, *Papsttum und Konzile* 138–139 with more literature, and M. Maccarrone, '"Sedes Apostolica"—"Vicarius Petri": La perpetuità del primato di Pietro nella sede e nel vescovo di Roma (secoli III–VIII)', *Il Primato del vescovo di Roma* 281ff.

21. PL 13.1133A; cf. Ullmann, *Gelasius* 27ff., who stresses the Roman-law component of this theology of Peter's heirs; J. Fellermayr, *Tradition und Sukzession im Lichte des römisch-antiken Erbdenkens* (Munich 1979) 347ff. and Maccarrone, '"Sedes Apostolica"' 288ff.

22. Cf., for example, Siricius, JK 255 PL 13.1138A, JK 263 PL 13.1164A, Zosimus, JK 342, Günther (CSEL 35) 115.17f., Boniface I, JK 364, Silva-Tarouca, *Collectio Thessalonicensis* 36.39, Celestine I, JK 375, Schwartz, ACO 1.2 (Berlin 1925–1926) 15.11, Leo I, JK 496, PL 54.1052B etc., cf. Caspar, *Papsttum* 1.261 and Pietri, *Roma christiana* 1518ff.

23. Cf., for example, Siricius, JK 255 c.15 (20), PL 13.1146A, Innocent I, JK 303, PL 20.527B,

ops (JK 258) reveals Siricius' no less famous dictum that Peter was the origin of the episcopal office and founder of the apostolic succession, a phrase which was often quoted, especially by Siricius' great successors Nicholas I (858–867) and Gregory VII (1073–1085).[24]

Scholars have established a close connection between the appearance of papal decretals and Gratian and Valentinian II's imperial rescript, *Ordinariorum*, from late 378 or early 379 (*Collectio Avellana* 13)[25] that granted the request of the Roman Synod of 378 for the 'official assistance' of the state in carrying out sentences.[26] This synod, presided over by Pope Damasus, assembled 'ad sublime sedis apostolicae sacrarium' for the establishment of rules governing judicial appeals in church courts. Whether the territory covered by *Ordinariorum* was limited to Italy or included the entire Western half of the Empire is disputed.[27] Neither position adequately explains certain phrases in the text, according to which, disobedient and stubborn Italian bishops were to be brought forcibly to Rome. In more distant places ('in longinquioribus partibus') the trial was to be handled by the appropriate metropolitan, but when a metropolitan was accused, he

Boniface I, JK 364, Silva-Tarouca, *Collectio Thessalonicensis* 35.11, Sixtus III, JK 396, Silva-Tarouca, 43.55 and 59, cf. on this Wojtowytsch, *Papsttum und Konzile* 139.

24. Ed. C. Munier, *Concilia Africae A. 345–A. 525* (CCL 149; Turnhout 1974) 59.25f., cf. also Innocent I, JK 286, PL 20.470A; JK 321, PL 20.583A; Boniface I, JK 364, Silva-Tarouca, *Collectio Thessalonicensis* 34.4–5; Nicholas I, Ep. 69 (JE 2783) MGH Epp. 6.385.2; Ep. 71 (JE 2785) 399.21; Ep. 88 (JE 2796) 474.28 and Gregory VII, Reg. 1.64, *Das Register Gregors VII.* ed. E. Caspar (MGH Epp. selectae 2; Berlin 1920) 93.27 and JE 4985 ed. L. Santifaller, *Quellen und Forschungen zum Urkunden-und Kanzleiwesen Papst Gregors VII.* (Studi e testi 190; Vatican City 1957) no. 136 p. 142, cf. on this issue Batiffol, *Cathedra Petri* 95ff. and Ullmann, *Gelasius* 24.

25. Cf. H. Getzeny, *Stil und Form der ältesten Papstbriefe bis auf Leo d. Gr.: Ein Beitrag zur Geschichte des römischen Primats* (Günzburg 1922) 37–38, 42–43; Caspar, *Papsttum* 1.215–216, J. Haller, *Das Papsttum: Idee und Wirklichkeit* (2nd ed. Urach 1950) 1.92–93. A more careful view in G. Roethe, 'Zur Geschichte der römischen Synoden im 3. und 4. Jahrhundert', *Geistige Grundlagen römischer Kirchenpolitik* (Forschungen zur Kirchen-und Geistesgeschichte 11; Stuttgart 1937) 108–109 and Wojtowytsch, *Papsttum und Konzile* 148–149.

26. The syndol petition is edited by M. Zelzer as Ep. 7 in the 'corpus' of the letters of Ambrose 'extra collectionem' (CSEL 82.3; Vienna 1982) 191ff., the imperial rescript, ibid., xciii ff. repeats the edition in the *Avellana* no. 13, 54ff. Both texts have often been analyzed. Besides the literature cited in the previous note,cf. Lorenz, *Jahrhundert* 36–37; Pietri, *Roma christiana* 741ff., 746ff., J. Martin, *Spätantike und Völkerwanderung* (Oldenbourg Grundriß der Geschichte 4; Munich 1987) 131f.; J. Gaudemet, *L'Église dans l'Empire Romain (IVe–Ve siècles)* (Histoire du Droit et des Institutions de l'Église en Occident 3; 2nd ed. Paris 1990) 241–242; F. Vittinghoff, 'Der Primatsanspruch des Bischofs von Rom—der Kampf um die Kirchenführung', *Handbuch der europäischen Wirtschafts-und Sozialgeschichte* (Stuttgart 1990) 1.297ff. and Girardet, 'Gericht' 5–6, 18ff.

27. Cf. the thorough treatment of Roethe, 'Synoden' 106ff., Lorenz, *Jahrhundert* 37; Vittinghoff, 'Primatsanspruch' 297, with n. 7 favors Italy as the area in which the decree was valid. Other scholars think the decree was valid in the whole Western half of the Empire: Caspar, *Papsttum* 1.215; Pietri, *Roma christiana* 746; Wojtowytsch, *Papsttum und Konzile* 148; Martin, *Spätantike* 131 and Girardet, 'Gericht' 5.

would be tried in Rome. The possibility of appeal to the Bishop of Rome or to a neighboring council was only permitted as a 'provocatio', that is, only when a case had already been brought to court. The defendant could reject the court on grounds of prejudice.[28] Any immediate impact of this rescript on formulations of papal authority is not known.[29] *Ordinariorum* did not, after all, describe actual judicial procedure: its theoretical outline of the legal system did not correspond to practice. Rather, it was a system toward which the Church worked. We may assume that the decree's impact was not immediate. In the end, its impact on procedure cannot be measured. In any case, Gratian's rescript helped to refortify the ties between Rome and the suburbicarian dioceses, which ties had become tenuous during the dogmatic struggles of the fourth century. These renewed connections would be 'of great importance for the development and expansion of papal thought and institutions',[30] as well as for closer ties between the Western metropolitans and their place of judgment, Rome.

2. The First Papal Decretals

2.1. The Characteristics of Papal Decretals

An impressive example of closer ties between Western metropolitans and Rome is offered by Pope Siricius' letter to Bishop Himerius of Tarragona from February 10, 385 (JK 255).[31] Technically a rescript, it is the first indisputable papal decretal (see below for definition).[32] Siricius answers

---

28. § 13 cf. E. Caspar, 'Der Prozeß des Papstes Damasus und die römisch-bischöfliche Gerichtsbarkeit', ZKG 47 (1928) 198ff. and idem, *Papsttum* 1.213, A. Steinwenter, 'Der antike kirchliche Rechtsgang und seine Quellen', ZRG Kan. Abt. 23 (1934) 50f., L. Wenger, *Die Quellen des römischen Rechts* (Vienna 1953) 293 and idem, 'Appellation', *Reallexikon für Antike und Christentum* 1 (1950) 569f.

29. Thus Getzeny, *Stil und Form* 38.

30. Roethe, 'Synoden' 109 who presents the evidence for his decision on p. 89ff., and Wojtowytsch, *Papsttum und Konzile* 148–149.

31. PL 13.1131ff. repeats Coustant's edition (*Epistolae* 623ff). A new edition of the decretal by K. Zechiel-Eckes, based on the all surviving texts will soon appear. The letter has often been interpreted, cf. Getzeny, *Stil und Form* 27ff., Caspar, *Papsttum* 1.261ff., Pietri, *Roma christiana* 1050ff., Wojtowytsch, *Papsttum und Konzile* 141ff., 199ff.

32. Below (p. 28ff.) I will treat more thoroughly the *Canones synodi Romanorum ad Gallos episcopos* usually attributed to Damasus and often considered the first papal decretal. Important evidence for this point of view is Jerome's assertion that he had helped Pope Damasus 'in the composition of ecclesiastical documents,' and that he had 'responded to synodal consultations from the East and the West' (Ep.123 c.9, rec. I. Hilberg, CSEL 56 [Vienna 1918] 82.14ff.) cf. Caspar, *Papsttum* 1.247 and 265 n.4; Pietri, *Roma christiana* 673–74; Wojtowytsch, *Papsttum und Konzile* 431 and J. Gaudemet, *Les Sources du droit de l'Église en Occident, du IIe au VIIe siècle* (Initiations au christianisme ancien 1; Paris 1985) 60–61. The presumption that the lack of decretals for Damasus is due only to chance, which is the position of Caspar and Wojtowytsch, is not satisfactory, since other important documents from Damasus' pontificate which do survive, such as his *Tomus fidei* (ed. Turner, EOMIA 1.281ff.) or the *Explanatio fidei* (ed. ibid., 155ff.) are widely distributed, cf. Maassen, *Geschichte* § 274.2 and 5. The fact

a series of questions on the rebaptism of Arian converts (c.1), the times of baptism (c.2), penance, the morals of clerics and the qualifications for spiritual office (c.6–15), which Himerius had sent to Pope Damasus, who had died in December 384. The Spaniard, no doubt, had expected the opinion of a legal expert, which is what he received from Damasus' successor Siricius. Apparently the decretal tradition reaches back further than Siricius' letter to Himerius, perhaps to Pope Damasus or to the pontificate of his predecessor Liberius (352–366). Siricius cited the 'generalia decreta' of Liberius when he rejected the rebaptism of Arians returning to the Church in chapter 1 of JK 255, though it is highly unlikely that he had in mind a decretal of the same sort as his own letter to Himerius.[33]

a. Definition of a Decretal

What distinguishes the decretals from those letters the Roman bishops had long written to their fellow believers, and of which so few are preserved before the end of the fourth century?[34] If one looks in modern handbooks and dictionaries under the relevant entries, one is at once struck by the general sparseness of information and, even more, by the fact that the early Church's developments in this area are usually mentioned only in passing, and now and then totally passed over. Naturally the stress is on the decretals and decretal collections after Gratian.[35]

---

that decretals are only extant from the pontificate of Siricius (384–399) might reflect the altered position of the papacy, as well as the perception that 'the twenty canons of Nicaea were not sufficient to form a system of law' as Turner, 'Organisation' 178ff., citation p. 180 so well described the situation.

33. PL 13.1133A. Probably reference was being made to Liberius' letter to the Northern Italian bishops, JK 223, ed. A. Feder (CSEL 65; Vienna 1916) 156ff., cf. Caspar, *Papsttum* 1.591, who cites P. Hinschius, *System des katholischen Kirchenrechts* (Berlin 1883) 3.684 n. 1.

34. See A. von Harnack, *Die Briefsammlung des Apostels Paulus und die anderen vorkonstantinischen christlichen Briefsammlungen* (Leipzig 1926), P. Nautin, *Lettres et écrivains chrétiens du IIe et IIIe siècles* (Patristica 2; Paris 1961) and E. Dassmann, *Kirchengeschichte, 1: Ausbreitung, Leben und Lehre der Kirche in den ersten drei Jahrhunderten* (Studienbücher Theologie 10; Stuttgart 1991) 175ff.

35. Cf. Van Hove, *Prolegomena* §§ 134–136, p. 138ff., Stickler, *Historia* 18–19. The article of H. Leclercq, 'Décrétales', *Dictionnaire d'archéologie chrétienne et de liturgie* 4.1 (1920) 364ff. is basically a French translation of the introduction of Maassen to his chapter on papal letters, p. 226ff. and a paraphrase of L. Duchesne, 'La première collection romaine des décrétales', *Atti del II° Congresso Internazionale di archeologia cristiana Roma 1900* (Rome 1902) 159ff. G. Mollat, 'Lettres pontificales', DDC 6 (1957) 408ff. deals with late-medieval decretals and their editions. Cf. also R. Naz, 'Décrétales (lettres)', DDC 4 (1949)1064–1065; A. M. Stickler, 'Dekretalen', LThK² 3 (1959) 205; G. Fransen, *Les décrétales et les collections de décrétales* (Typologie des sources du Moyen Age occidental 2; Turnhout 1972) 12; S. Chodorow, 'Decretals', DMA 4 (1984) 122ff. and 'Dekretalensammlungen', LMA 3 (1986) 656, dealing only with decretal collections beginning in the 1160s, and H. Van De Wouw, 'Dekretalen', LMA 3 (1986) 655–656, who also skips the early development.

Charles Duggan gives a good definition of papal decretals, going back to their origins, in his article in the *New Catholic Encyclopedia:*[36]

> The term decretal, *epistola decretalis* or *littera decretalis,* is used very generally to describe a letter containing a papal ruling, more specifically one relating to matters of canonical discipline, and most precisely a papal rescript in response to an appeal. The decretal is distinguished from the solemn *privilegia,* confirming rights or jurisdiction, and from other *litterae* touching on matters of political or nonjuristic interest. . . . The earliest decretals were *litterae praeceptoriae,* issued with emphatic and conscious mandatory force and modeled on the judicial formulae of Roman law. . . . Their use is clear from Siricius' pontificate, in the incorporating of such authoritative phrases as *volumus et mandamus;* and in the following centuries they were widely used in matters of canonical discipline. . . . The legal force of decretals was discussed by popes from the time of their earliest known use: on specific points by Siricius (385), Innocent I (405) and Zosimus (418); and as a general principle by Leo I in 443. Gregory I, Nicholas I, and Gregory VII are among the later popes known to have repeated and defined this principle, in demanding obedience to apostolic precepts expressed in decretal letters.[37]

b. Earlier Models for Papal Decretals

The most obvious element of a papal decretal is the 'responsa' of the Roman bishop explaining and, if necessary, creating the law in reply to a bishop's 'relatio'.[38] The contents of the 'responsa' focused on disciplinary problems and institutional questions more than on dogmatic issues. The decretals are characterized by juristic, and often authoritative, language.[39] Beyond these details of content and style, their internal structure is very

36. NCE 4.707–708.

37. The decretals reviewed in this article are Siricius, JK 255, Innocent I, JK 293, Zosimus, JK 339, and Leo I, JK 402. The phrase 'volumus et mandamus' does not appear in the oldest decretals; the term coming closest in these letters is in Siricius, JK 255 c.13(17): 'optamus et volumus' (PL 13.1144A). Naturally 'volumus' and 'mandamus' often appear separately, and the paired expression 'volumus et iubemus' appears beginning with Nicholas I, Ep. 6 (JE 2698), MGH Epp. 6.272.17, and is often found in the last books of Gregory VII's Register: Reg. 7.11, MGH Epp. selectae 2.474.20–21; 7.13, 478.19; 8.20, 543.8–9.; 9.28, 612.3; 9.30, 616.30–31.

38. This is how all the requests and reports directed to Rome are described, cf., for example, Siricius, JK 255, PL 13.1132B, Innocent I, JK 303, PL 20.527B, Zosimus, JK 332, ed. W. Gundlach (MGH Epp. 3) 9.17, Boniface, JK 348, EOMIA 1.565.6, Celestine I, JK 369 c.3(5), PL 50.433B, Leo I, JK 410, PL 54.653C and 656A. On relationships with the imperial chancery, cf. J. Gaudemet, *La formation du droit séculier et du droit de l'Église aux IVe et Ve siècles* (Paris 1957) 150.

39. Besides Getzeny's investigation, *Stil und Form,* and Caspar's penetrating interpretation of the decretals, *Papsttum,* particularly 1.215ff., 1.261ff., 1.298ff., Pietri, *Roma christiana,* 673ff. Gaudemet, *Formation* 148ff., and idem, *L'Église* 220ff., idem *Sources* 57ff., idem, *Église et Cité* 46ff.; P. A. McShane, *La Romanitas et le Pape Léon le Grand: L'apport culturel des institutions impériales à la formation des structures ecclésiastiques* (recherches 24; Tournai-Montréal 1979) 333ff., Wojtowytsch, *Papsttum und Konzile* 142ff., Ullmann, *Gelasius* 23ff., Mordek, 'Primat'

similar to the charters and documents written in the form of letters by the Roman emperors and imperial officials: 'intitulatio', the body of the letter ('arenga', 'narratio', 'dispositio', and 'sanctio'), with a greeting and date at the end. Beginning in the first century of the Christian era, these imperial documents show a cultivated style of elegant letter writing and speech that was becoming the fashion.[40] Out of the brief matter-of-fact legal explanations for individual actions that distinguishes the documents of the Roman Republic, there developed long-winded, rhetorically florid, and often moralizing explanations about the foundations of government or about individual situations. These were found, for the most part, at the beginning of a letter. In accordance with the rules of epistolary style, only after generalities did one come, gradually, to the point.[41] Naturally the 'royal We' is a feature of this style and the custom of opening the 'dispositio' section with commanding expressions like 'statuimus', 'iubemus', etc. These often stilted formulations ought not to be dismissed as simply eccentric pomposity but should be considered as an expression of contemporary taste.[42]

c. Arenga

The arenga is a characteristic section of the early papal decretals in the opening passages, filled with rich programmatic declarations of papal ideology. These long, florid passages in papal decretals were common from Siricius to Leo the Great.[43] We have already discussed Siricius' definitions of papal authority that became classical statements during the course of papal history. Pope Innocent I (401–417) made Siricius' well-known phrase that the apostolate and the episcopacy originated in Peter (JK 258) famous

---

544ff., P. Landau, 'Kanonisches Recht und römische Form: Rechtsprinzipien im ältesten römischen Kirchenrecht', *Der Staat* 32 (1993) 555ff.

40. See the thorough treatment by P. Classen, *Kaiserreskript und Königsurkunde: Diplomatische Studien zum Problem der Kontinuität zwischen Altertum und Mittelalter* (Byzantina Keimena kai meletai 15; Thessaloniki 1977) 60ff., Wenger, *Quellen* 473, F. Millar, *The Emperor in the Roman World (31 BC–AD 337)* (London 1977) 551ff., McShane, *Romanitas* 337ff., T. Honoré, *Emperors and Lawyers* (London 1981) 115ff., W. Selb, 'Quellen und Rechtsbildung', *Römisches Recht,* ed. H. Honsell, T. Mayer-Maly, and W. Selb (Enzyklopädie der Rechts-und Staatswissenschaft, 4th ed. Berlin-Heidelberg 1987) 16ff. with extensive bibliography, and D. Liebs, 'Recht und Rechtsliteratur', *Restauration und Erneuerung: Die lateinische Literatur von 284 bis 374 n. Chr.* (Handbuch der lateinischen Literatur der Antike 5; Munich 1989) 55ff.

41. Cf. Classen, *Kaiserreskript* 80.

42. See E. Norden, *Die antike Kunstprosa vom VI. Jahrhundert v.Chr. bis in die Zeit der Renaissance* (5th ed. Darmstadt 1958) 2.650ff.

43. See Caspar, *Papsttum* 1. References to individual papal letters can be found in his index, p. 629ff. See also M. Kopczynski, *Die Arengen der Papsturkunden nach ihrer Bedeutung und Verwendung bis zu Gregor VII.* (Bottrop 1936) 3ff., Pietri, *Roma christiana* 1466ff., Ullmann, *Gelasius* 23ff., Maccarrone, '"Sedes Apostolica"' 287ff. and Landau, 'Römische Form' 559ff.

in his decretal to Victricius of Rouen (JK 286 of February 15, 404). Innocent went further and drew broad conclusions, e.g., that ecclesiastical discipline could best be ensured when one strictly obeyed the 'forma quam tenet ecclesia Romana'. He reiterated the rule, until that time unheeded, that after a bishop had passed judgment, all important matters ('causae maiores') must be brought to the apostolic see ('ad sedem apostolicam . . . referantur').[44] Thus Innocent could describe his letter, which commented on a broad spectrum of disciplinary, marital, and hierarchical questions, as a 'liber regularum quasi didascalicus atque monitor'.[45] The 'prefatio' of a later decretal to Bishop Decentius of Gubbio (JK 311 of March 19, 416) had a similar aim. Here, in order to support his demand for 'Roman uniformity in all questions of discipline',[46] Innocent held that all the churches founded by bishops in the Western half of the Empire had been established by Peter or his successors. Innocent's successors Zosimus (417–418) and Boniface (418–422) liked to describe papal decrees as 'auctoritas apostolicae sedis' and introduced this phrase into the decretals and general papal vocabulary. This concept of 'auctoritas' was used to express the general power and authority of law more than the issuance of a single directive.[47] Also, at this time the emphasis shifted from the expression of the personal will of a single pope to the traditions of the Roman Church that were enforced by the incumbents of the see.[48] There are several other phrases besides 'auctoritas apostolicae sedis' which the popes used in order to refer obliquely to the legal force of their decretals. The 'liber regularum' to Bishop Victricius of Rouen (JK 286) has already been mentioned, and this phrase appears in the letters of Pope Sixtus III in the *Collectio Thessalonicensis* when he re-emphasized the phrase 'regularum et canonum observantia'.[49] We have also referred to the phrase 'decretalium norma constitutorum',[50] and Innocent characterized papal sanctioned law as 'Romanae ecclesiae norma atque auctoritas'.[51] Usually

44. Cf. Caspar, *Papsttum* 1.306–307, who refers on p. 307 n. 1, to the biblical origin of the concept of 'causae maiores' from Exodus 18:22 and refers to its broad interpretation, cf. further Wojtowytsch, *Papsttum und Konzile* 207ff. and Landau, 'Römische Form' 561.

45. PL 20.470A.

46. Edited by R. Cabié, *La lettre du pape Innocent Ier à Décentius de Gubbio (19 mars 416)* (Bibliothèque de la RHE 58; Louvain 1973) 18.12ff., the citation comes from Caspar, *Papsttum* 1.302; cf. also V. Monachino, 'La lettera decretale di Innocenzo I a Decenzio vescovo di Gubbio', *Ricerche sull'Umbria tardoantico e preromanica: Atti del II Convegno di studi Umbri Gubbio 24–28 maggio 1964* (Perugia 1965) 217–218.

47. See Classen, *Kaiserreskript* 57–58, for Roman law, with many examples.

48. Cf. Caspar, *Papsttum* 1.265.

49. JK 395 Silva-Tarouca, *Collectio Thessalonicensis* 39.5, JK 396, 41.23, 42.45; cf. on this Landau, 'Römische Form' 561.

50. Celestine I, JK 371, PL 50.436A.

51. Innocent I, JK 286, PL 20.469B.

decretal law was called 'statuta ('decreta') sedis apostolicae'[52] and the phrase 'decretalia constituta' is not frequently seen in the papal letters of the fourth and fifth centuries.[53] The phrase 'epistolae decretales', first encountered in one of the oldest decretal collections, *Epistolae decretales* (see below), from the first half of the fifth century, was used frequently in the legal compilations of the fifth and sixth centuries. Until the end of the eleventh century, the most frequent use of this phrase occurs in the writings of Pope Nicholas I (858–867).[54]

d. Decretals and Councils

'Auctoritas', 'regula', 'norma', and 'statuta' are concepts that were used in Roman law to refer to imperial laws and directives,[55] and in this sense the decretals resemble the imperial decrees. However, the concepts can also be used to describe conciliar canons, as in the *Corpus canonum Africano-Romanum* of c. 430, which called the decisions of the Council of Nicaea (325), the African canons, and the canons of Sardica, 'regulae'.[56] Apparently the popes claimed that decretals had a binding force equal to that of conciliar canons. In the first decretal, Siricius reminded Bishop Himerius of Tarragona of this principle, saying that no priest was permitted to ignore the 'statuta sedis apostolicae vel canonum venerabilia definita'. This precept was frequently repeated and found its classic expression in Pope Celestine's command to the bishops of Apulia and Calabria:

52. Cf. Siricius, JK 255 c.15(20), PL 13.1146B; Zosimus, JK 328, ed. Gundlach (MGH Epp. 3) 6.6, repeated in JK 331, ibid., 8.32; JK 337, Maassen, *Geschichte* 955; JK 339, PL 20.670B; Celestine, JK 369, PL 50.434A; JK 381, PL 50.528B. In JK 410, PL 54.652B Leo I rendered a decision 'non praeiudicantes apostolicae sedis statutis, nec beatorum patrum regulas resolventes', certainly meaning papal decretals and conciliar canons. The original, shorter version of this letter preserved by Pseudo-Isidore and most other collections gives a different text at this place: 'non praeiudicantes apostolicae sedis statutis nec praecessorum nostrorum nostrisque decretis', PL 54.661C.

53. Siricius, JK 255 c.15(20), PL 13.1146A; Celestine I, JK 371, PL 50.436A and 437A; Leo I, JK 402, ed. H. Wurm, 'Decretales selectae ex antiquissimis Romanorum pontificum epistulis decretalibus', *Apollinaris* 12 (1939) 92.8–9.

54. Cf. the data in Maassen, *Geschichte* 228 n. 4 and Nicholas I, Ep. 71, MGH Epp. 6.394.23, 395, also Ep. 57, 357.25; Ep. 88, 468.7 and Ep. 91, 518.13. Just as frequently he uses 'decretalia statuta' ('constituta') or only 'decretalia', cf. the pope's synodal sermon at Christmas, 864 A.D. Ep. 66a, 380.25 (the passage is repeated in Ep. 71, 393.25). Also to be noted Ep. 71, 393.30, 394.11, 395; Ep. 90, 496.36; Ep. 92, 538.11.

55. Cf. L. Wenger, *Canon in den römischen Rechtsquellen und in den Papyri* (SB Wien 220 Abh. 2; Vienna 1942) 62ff.

56. Cf. Turner, EOMIA 1.179 the version of Isidore, the 'Praefatio longa' of the council of Nicaea, ibid., 156.14ff. and the treatise on the African and Sardican canons, ibid., 540.1ff., cf. Mordek, 'Primat', 539 and idem, 'Rom' 362–363.

> Nulli sacerdotum suos licet canones ignorare. . . . Quae enim a nobis res digna servabitur, si decretalium norma constitutorum pro aliquorum libito . . . frangatur?[57]

During the fifth and sixth centuries papal decretals achieved an authority equal to that of conciliar canons. In his letter (JK 312) of June 2, 416, Innocent I criticized Aurelius of Carthage for consecrating bishops without due deliberation and ordered that his letter be read in all of the African churches. The Byzachene Council of Suffetula (416–417) incorprorated Innocent's words into a canon, later included in the *Breviatio canonum* of the Carthaginian deacon Ferrandus.[58] Another famous example is Siricius' decretal (JK 258) in which the pope conveyed the decisions of the Roman Synod of 386 to the African bishops. We know that this letter was read again at the Byzachene Council of Telepte (418) and adopted into the council's canon because, in his *Breviatio,* Ferrandus labeled Siricius' instructions conciliar decisions, and consequently this decretal is found under the heading 'Concilium Thelense'.[59] Similar examples are known for Gallican and Spanish synods. The Synod of Tours (461) referred to Siricius JK 255 c.1 or to Innocent I JK 286 c.9. The Council of Agde (506) supported its resolution on the sexual abstinence of priests and deacons with a long excerpt from Innocent I's decretal to Exsuperius of Toulouse (JK 293).[60] The First Council of Braga (563) and the Third Council of Toledo (589) c.1 stressed the equality of conciliar and papal decisions,[61] as did the author of the *Hispana,* who justified the inclusion of papal letters in his

<hr>

57. Siricius, JK 255 c.15 (20), PL 13.1146B and Celestine, JK 371, PL 50.436A. A half-century later, Pope Hilarus was able to decree at the Roman synod of 465, 'nulli fas sit sine status sui periculo vel divinas constitutiones vel apostolicae sedis decreta temerare', Thiel, *Epistolae* 161, cf. Gaudemet, *L'Église,* 223 and Ullmann, *Gelasius* 113–114.

58. Ferrandus, *Breviatio* c.2, ed. Munier, *Concilia Africae* 287, cf. Maassen, *Geschichte* 185, and K. Zechiel-Eckes, *Die Concordia canonum des Cresconius: Studien und Edition* (Freiburger Beiträge zur mittelalterlichen Geschichte 5; Frankfurt am Main–Berlin 1992) 1.179ff. who notes that the Codex Vercelli CLXV (second quarter of the ninth century) of the *Breviatio* of Ferrandus includes the letter of Innocent, JK 312, under the inscription, 'Incipit concilium Sufetulensem'.

59. Cf. Maassen, *Geschichte* § 153 p.167ff., the decretal of Siricius, JK 258, has been edited by Munier, *Concilia Africae* 59ff.; where the council met cannot be determined.

60. C. Munier, *Concilia Galliae* A. 314–A. 506 (CCL 148; Turnhout 1963) 143–144 (Tours 461 c.l), 196.84ff. (Agde 506 c.9). Canon 11 of the Council of Orléans, 549, cites from Celestine's decretal, JK 369, the chapter on canonical election, and canon 21 (20) of the Second Council of Tours (567) cites his ruling on virgins who do not keep their oath, from Innocent's decretal to Victricius von Rouen cc. 12–13, ed. Maassen (MGH Concilia 1; Hannover 1893) 104.3 and 128.23ff.

61. Cf. PL 84.561C–D on the First Council of Braga and G. Martínez Díez and F. Rodríguez, *La Colección canónica Hispana* (Monumenta Hispaniae Sacra 5; Madrid 1992) 5.109.730ff. on the Third Council of Toledo (589) cf. Maassen, *Geschichte* 227 n. 2.

collections by saying that in them 'pro culmine sedis apostolicae non impar conciliorum extat auctoritas'.[62] As early as the beginning of the sixth century, Dionysius Exiguus thought it necessary to collect all papal decretals. He was concerned that nothing touching matters of ecclesiastical discipline be omitted.[63]

e. The 'Corpus' of a Papal Decretal

In the 'dispositio' section, decretals were also different in style, form, and content from the letters of the Roman bishops of the first four centuries. As is generally found in early Christian letters, the oldest papal letters are characterized by a 'brotherly pastoral style'.[64] The letters did not contain rules and commands. These early Christian writers preferred persuasion, instruction, and pastoral admonitions to affirm their common faith. The letters were basically substitutes for preaching and oral teaching.[65] This style continued, without exception, until the time of Pope Damasus (366–384). Only in rare cases, in which problems of jurisdiction and discipline were being decided (especially the condemnation of heretics and schismatics), did the bishops of Rome use expressions taken from the vocabulary of Roman law, as the synods commonly did at that time.[66] The synods were the only legislative bodies in the Church, and they naturally employed the legislative language of Roman law.

In early decretals, questions of church order and discipline provided the most frequent theme.[67] There was also the urgent problem of how to

62. Martínez Díez and Rodríguez, *Colección* 3.45.47–48; see also Mordek, 'Primat' 553–554.

63. Ed. F. Glorie (CCL 85; Turnhout 1972) 45.3ff.

64. See Getzeny, *Stil und Form* 4ff., for a discussion of style, not in an esthetic sense (such as vulgar or classical Latin), but rather in the typological sense. Getzeny did, however, categorize individual styles schematically into a somewhat artificial system. See also Caspar, *Papsttum* 1.599, who points out that it is in fact 'the mixture of old and new which is characteristic'. On early Christian letters and their style, cf. further J. Schneider, 'Brief', *Reallexikon für Antike und Christentum* 2 (1954) 582ff. with extensive literature, C. Andresen, 'Zum Formular früchristlicher Gemeindebriefe', *Zeitschrift für die neutestamentliche Wissenschaft* 56 (1965) 233ff. and Classen, *Kaiserreskript* 99ff.

65. Cf. Getzeny, *Stil und Form* 5 and Eusebius, *Historia Ecclesiastica* 4.23.11: 'Today we celebrate the Holy Day of the Lord, and we have read out your letter (JK *58), which we shall always read for our edification as we did the earlier letter, sent to us by Clement' (= The First Epistle of Clement), cf. on this Nautin, *Lettres* 26ff.

66. Cf. the examples collected by Getzeny, *Stil und Form* 12ff., 20ff. which Classen, *Kaiserreskript* 99, has expanded.

67. The most frequent topics were the election and consecration of bishops and the ordination of other clerics. Of special concern was the catalogue of impediments to ordination, in order to ensure that the best possible men were chosen for the priestly office. The other most common topics of these letters were the discipline, morals, and education of clerics, monks, and nuns, as well as questions of marriage law and penitential practices, cf. McShane, *Romanitas* 334–335.

effect reconciliation with schismatics.[68] The widely distributed decretal of Innocent I to Bishop Decentius of Gubbio is a memorable example of the liturgical uncertainties that from time to time needed to be resolved.[69] By the time of Innocent, papal letters created and interpreted ecclesiastical norms and laid down disciplinary rules, but were no longer written in the pastoral style of earlier Christian letters. Rather they appeared in the form of a 'responsum', objective and purely factual information modelled on Roman imperial decrees and official documents.[70] In place of an endeavor to persuade and win over, there was now a command. 'Praecipimus', 'decernimus', ('decrevimus'),'iubemus' and 'iussimus', 'mandamus' and 'volumus' are the favorite expressions of the decretals, as is the aloof, almost arrogant way of beginning a sentence with 'Miramur'.[71] These expressions clarify the distance between the one posing the question and the one providing the answer. 'The tone in these letters was that of a superior: measured, unapproachable and occasionally of cutting courtesy'.[72]

f. Literary Sources

The most important sources for the decretals were biblical texts that were the foundation of the papal decrees, the canons of the Council of Nicaea (325) and, infrequently, the decisions of the pope's predecessors.[73]

68. For example, Siricius, JK 255 c.1(2), PL 13.1133–1134, and JK 258 c.8, Munier, *Concilia Africae* 61.69f. The issue was taken up again by Innocent I, JK 286 c.8(11), PL 20.475B, JK 303 c.3(7), PL 20.530Bf., JK 310 c.3 (4), PL 20.550A, cf. A. Schebler, *Die Reordinationen in der 'altkatholischen' Kirche unter besonderer Berücksichtigung der Anschauungen Rudolph Sohms* (Kanonistische Studien und Texte 10; Bonn 1936) 81ff.

69. Edited by Cabié, *Lettre* 18ff.; among others, the themes are confirmation, Saturday fasting, the creation of communion hosts, and annointing the sick, cf. the commentary Cabié, *Lettre* 36ff.

70. Classen, *Kaiserreskript* 100–101; Gaudemet, *Formation* 205, and idem, *L'Église* 225; Ullmann, *Gelasius* 23; Landau, 'Römische Form' 559–560.

71. Cf. Innocent I, JK 308, PL 20.544B; JK 315, PL 20.605C; Zosimus, JK 339, PL 20.670B; Leo I, JK 417, PL 54.709B; JK 420, PL 54.731B etc., and Caspar, *Papsttum* 1.304, who sees Innocent as the pope who introduced this form of expression into the linguistic repertoire.

72. Caspar, *Papsttum* 1.304.

73. Coustant's edition, whose margins are crammed with biblical citations, demonstrates the pope's reliance on Scripture. On the reception of Nicaean canons in papal writing, cf. Maassen, *Geschichte* § 39, pp. 35–36. Besides the citations given in Innocent I's letter to Victricius of Rouen (JK 286), the pope refers to Nicaea in the following letters: JK 288, PL 20.495A, JK 292, PL 20.489A and C, 492A, JK 294, PL 20.505A, JK 303, PL 20.532A, JK 310, PL 20.547B and 549A, JK 316, PL 20.606B. Among citations of predecessors should be mentioned: Innocent, JK 293 c.1 (2 and 4) Wurm, *Apollinaris* 12 (1939) 60.5f., 63.41, 64.47; Leo I, JK 404, Silva-Tarouca, *Collectio Thessalonicensis* 54.23 and John II, JK 888, ed. Gundlach (MGH Epp. 3) 48.7, are based on Siricius' decretal JK 255. Gelasius, in his treatise *De duabus naturis Christi* (JK 670), and Vigilius in his long letter against the 'Three Chapters' (JK 937), ed. Schwartz, *Publizistische Sammlungen* 104.33ff. and ACO 4.2 (Strasbourg, 1914) 167.3ff., refer to the *Tomus fidei* of Damasus.

These sources demonstrate clearly that the popes were not under the illusion that they were creating something new with their decretals. They were convinced that through their decrees they were only reminding Christians of the propositions and rules that had always existed under divine law.[74]

g. Distribution

We have considered the beginnings of the papal decretal letters, so expressive of the ideology of the emerging papacy, their claims to high authority, and the new organization of the 'corpus' of the letter. The last characteristic of a decretal is the pope's order for its distribution to the widest possible audience.[75] Frequently the popes expressly charge the recipient, usually the leader of an ecclesiastical province, to make the letter known to his fellow bishops and throughout the province,[76] or to bring it to the attention of the next provincial council, when it would usually be entered into the acts of the synod. From time to time the decretals were, from the outset, directed to a number of bishops as 'litterae generales'; this was true especially of the letters addressed to the bishops 'per diversas provincias' or to those of a specific region.[77] The instructions of Pope

74. Cf. Caspar, *Papsttum* 1.262; the novelty was not the competition with conciliar law, nor was it the coexistence of synodal law and papal law, but rather their seamless intermingling, just as the basic stylistic elements of the decretals and a pastoral style binds them irrevocably together. An absolute separation between decretal and papal letter is not possible. One has the impression that the style changed over time. By the ninth century every papal letter could be classed as an 'epistola decretalis'. For a good example of this change, see the debate between Peitz and Posner over the meaning of Excerpt R from Gregory I's register. John the Deacon summarized 684 of Gregory's letters as 'quaedam epistolae decretales per singulas indictiones excerptae' (*Vita* 4.71, PL 75.225B). W. M. Peitz, *Das Register Gregors I.: Beiträge zur Kenntnis des päpstlichen Kanzlei-und Registerwesens bis auf Gregor VII.* (Ergänzungshefte zu den Stimmen der Zeit, Zweite Reihe: Forschungen, 2. Heft; Freiburg 1917) 16ff. and 28ff. and E. Posner, 'Das Register Gregors I.' NA 43 (1922) 294ff. See also S. Chodorow, 'Decretals', DMA 4 (1984) 122, with the statement, 'Decretals are papal letters, but exactly what type of letters is hard to define'.

75. On this cf. Silva-Tarouca, 'Beiträge' 682ff., idem, 'Nuovi studi' 94ff. for the letters and decretals of Leo the Great. E. Schwartz, ACO 2.4 p. xxxx sees their claim to publication and circulation to be the essential difference between a decretal and a letter: 'decretales constituta sunt publico usui destinata, sicut imperatorum constitutiones et rescripta; longe aliter epistulae: paucae multis scribuntur, pleraeque singulis neque eo consilio ut publice edantur'.

76. Innocent I, JK 292, PL 20.489A: 'Sed haec generaliter de unitatis reformatione omnes, tamquam singulis scripta sint, accipiant sacerdotes'. Further, Siricius, JK 255, Innocent I in JK 286, 303, 304, 310, 312, Zosimus in JK 339, Leo I in JK 402, 525, 526, 543, etc. Besides the works of Silva-Tarouca in the previous note, see Turner, 'Organisation' 182, Wurm, *Studien* 110–111 and Gaudemet, *Formation* 153–154.

77. Cf. JK 263, PL 13.1164A and Caspar, *Papsttum* 1.262 and n. 3, or the regional letters of Leo I, JK 402, 405, 410, 414. The regional distribution of papal letters is very significant. Besides to their own synodal district, popes sent their decretals to all the regions of the West-

Siricius at the end of his decretal to Himerius of Tarragona offer an example:[78]

> Nunc fraternitatis tuae animum ad servandos canones et tenenda decretalia constituta magis ac magis incitamus, ut haec quae ad tua rescripsimus consulta, in omnium coepiscoporum nostrorum perferri facias notionem, et non solum eorum qui in tua sunt dioecesi constituti, sed etiam ad universos Carthaginenses ac Baeticos, Lusitanos atque Gallicios vel eos qui vicinis tibi collimitant, hinc inde provinciis, haec quae a nobis sunt salubri ordinatione disposita, sub litterarum tuarum prosecutione mittantur.

Not only is all of Spain supposed to be informed of the 'statuta apostolicae sedis'; Siricius intended it for the whole Church:[79]

> . . . ea quae ad te speciali nomine generaliter scripta sunt, per unanimitatis tuae sollicitudinem in universorum fratrum nostrorum notitiam perferantur.

Beginning with these presuppositions one can assume that after a short while a series of decretals and other important papal letters were available in the archives of many churches. They were probably assembled into small collections and eventually found their way into larger canonical works. Through this means they finally came to the attention of the general public.[80] Thus, in his letter to the bishops of Campania, Picenum, and Tuscia (JK 402 of 443), Pope Leo I could order, under pain of deposition:[81]

---

ern Empire as well as to Illyricum, with the exception of Northern Italy and the Imperial residences of Milan and Ravenna, and to the strictly organized and self-conscious African Church, cf. Turner, 'Organisation' 182.

78. PL 13.1146Af.; cf. on this Mordek, 'Primat' 545 n. 89. Silva-Tarouca, 'Beiträge' 689, points out linguistic parallels to the imperial chancery's orders for promulgation of letters.

79. PL 13.1146B; cf. Silva-Tarouca, 'Beiträge' 684. A different example of the distribution of important texts is given by the collection of Leo the Great's letters. In May, 450, the pope instructed Bishop Ravennius of Arles to make his *Tomus* to Flavian of Constantinople (JK 423) and the *Epistola dogmatica* of Cyril of Alexandria († 444) more widely known (JK 451 ed. W. Gundlach, MGH Epp. 3.22). Ravennius' task is known from a letter by the Bishops Ceretius of Grenoble, Salonius of Geneva and Veranus of Vence to Pope Leo. They requested that their copy of the *Tomus* be compared to the original in the papal archives and quickly returned to them . They wished to distribute these letters as soon as possible (Ep. Leonis 68 c.2, PL 54.889). A copy of the *Tomus* passed from Ceretius of Grenoble to Bishop Eusebius of Milan, who read it to eighteen bishops at the Synod of Milan (451) (Ep. Leonis 97 c.2, PL 54.946). In the same year Ravennius of Arles and forty-three bishops reported to Leo that they had carried out the pope's instructions (Ep. Leonis 99 c.2, PL 54.966f.). The *Tomus Leonis* was also sent from Gaul to Spain (Idacius, *Chronica,* ed. T. Mommsen, MGH Auctores Antiquissimi 11.25.145); cf. Silva-Tarouca, 'Nuovi studi' 101ff.

80. This is the conclusion of Silva-Tarouca, 'Beiträge' 677, 689, which was accepted by Wurm, *Studien* 111–112. In doing so they accept the view of C. H. Turner, 'A Group of MSS of Canons at Toulouse, Albi, and Paris', JTS 2 (1901) 272ff. and Steinacker, 'Deusdedithandschrift' 133ff., on the origins of Gallican canonical collections, who corrected Maassen, *Geschichte* 186–187, who held that early Gallican collections derived from chronologically ordered legal works, cf. also Mordek, *Kirchenrecht und Reform* 3 with n. 7.

81. Edited by Wurm, *Apollinaris* 12 (1939) 92.8ff. Cf. also Duchesne, 'La première col-

> . . . omnia decretalia constituta tam beatae recordationis Innocenti quam omnium decessorum nostrorum, quae de ecclesiasticis ordinibus et canonum promulgata sunt disciplinis, ita a vestra dilectione custodiri debere mandamus, ut si quis in illa commiserit, veniam sibi deinceps noverit denegari.

And in chapter 4.3.3 of the *Decretum Gelasianum de libris recipiendis et non recipiendis* (JK † 700), which was written at the beginning of the sixth century in Southern Gaul and transmitted in countless manuscripts, the papal decretals and the *Tomus Leonis* (JK 423) were included among the writings that were to be held in great respect:[82]

> Item decretales epistulas, quas beatissimi papae diversis temporibus ab urbe Roma pro diversorum patrum consultatione dederunt, venerabiliter suscipiendas esse.

2.2. The Earliest Decretal Collections

Eight decretals are always found in the oldest Italian and Gallican canonical collections of the fifth and sixth centuries:[83] Siricius to Bishop Himerius of Tarragona (JK 255); Innocent I to Bishop Victricius of Rouen (JK 286), to Exsuperius of Toulouse (JK 293), to the bishops of Macedonia and Dacia (JK 303) and to Bishop Decentius of Gubbio (JK 311); Zosimus to Bishop Hesychius of Salona (JK 339); and Celestine to the bishops of Vienne and Narbonne (JK 369) and to the bishops of Apulia and Calabria (JK 371). An obvious conclusion could be that the reference of Leo I (JK 402) to papal decretals mentioned above could refer to a collection of decretals that provided something like a compendium of Rome's disciplinary instructions.[84] Louis Duchesne began from the as-

---

lection' 159; C. H. Turner, 'From Pope Innocent's Epistle to Exsuperius of Toulouse (A.D. 405)', JTS 13 (1911–1912) 79, Silva-Tarouca, 'Beiträge' 681, Wurm, *Studien* 108, and Mordek, 'Primat' 547–548.

82. *Das Decretum Gelasianum de libris recipiendis et non recipiendis,* ed. E. von Dobschütz (Texte und Untersuchungen 38.4; Leipzig 1912) 39.201ff. The extensive literature on the difficult textual history of the pseudo-Gelasian letter is given by H. Mordek, 'Decretum Gelasianum', LMA 3 (1986) 625, and by W. Pohlkamp, *Francia* 19.1 (1992) 126ff. In general, chapters 4 and 5 are taken to have originated in southern Gaul at the start of the sixth century; chapters 1 to 3 rely upon texts of Pope Damasus, which its composer presented under the false colors of a papal decree in order to increase its authority. Gaudemet, *Sources* 62 n. 15, conjectured a Roman origin for the *Decretum,* as does E. Wirbelauer, *Zwei Päpste in Rom* (Quellen und Forschungen zur antiken Welt 16; Munich 1993) 133 n. 92, who supposes a 'direct connection with the conflicts between Symmachus and Laurentius'.

83. These include the Italian collections found in the manuscripts of Freising, Weingarten, the *Quesnelliana,* the manuscript of Chieti, the manuscript of Sankt Blasien *(Collectio Italica),* the Vatican manuscript and of the *Dionysiana* as well as the Gallic *Collectiones Corbeiensis, Coloniensis, Albigensis, Laureshamensis, Remensis, Pithouensis* and *Sancti Mauri.*

84. Cf. Innocent's designation of JK 286 as 'liber regularis', as well as the citations in McShane, *Romanitas* 334–335; Silva-Tarouca, 'Beiträge' 680–681; Caspar, *Papsttum* 1.297 and Mordek, 'Primat' 548–549.

sumption that there was a decretal collection produced in Rome. Its earliest form, produced during the pontificate of Innocent I, would have included his four decretals (JK 286, 293, 303, 311) and would gradually have grown into a collection of eight decretals which would have come to Gaul after 429, the date when Celestine wrote the last decretal of the collection (JK 371). Represented in its purest form by the *Collectio Quesnelliana*, which appeared about 495, this basic collection would have been received more or less completely into individual Italian and Gallican collections of ecclesiastical law under various titles.[85] Since the investigations of Harold Steinacker, Karl Silva-Tarouca, and Hubert Wurm, whose research refuted the importance Duchesne attached to the *Quesnelliana*, this tempting reconstruction can no longer be supported.[86] Their explanation of the Gallican collections of the fifth and sixth centuries is that they grew out of small collections, synodal canons, and individual items which were, for the most part, arbitrarily grouped together. This development was closely connected to the increasing frequency of synods in that area. The new explanation provides no support for the theory of a single collection as the point of departure for the compilations of decretals found in the individual canonical collections. In the last stage of the process of making these collections, the compilers integrated a number of small letter collections in circulation at that time into their collections and preserved the formats of the individual pieces. Three collections have been reconstructed which contain five or six decretals from Innocent I (JK 286, 293, 303), Zosimus (JK 339) and Celestine I (JK 369, 371).

a. Canones urbicani

The first of these collections is called *Canones urbicani*.[87] In the oldest manuscript of this collection, preserved in a sixth-century manuscript from Cologne, Innocent's decretal JK 293 is introduced with the title: 'Incipiunt canones urbicani. Innocentius Exoperio episcopo Tolosano. Consolenti tibi . . .'[88] The letters of Innocent I (JK 303), Zosimus (JK 339) and

85. Duchesne, 'La première collection' 160ff. and R. Massigli, 'La plus ancienne collection de décrétales', *Revue d'histoire et de littérature religieuses* 5 (1914) 416ff. G. Morin, 'Les Statuta ecclesiae antiqua sont-ils de S. Césaire d'Arles?' RB 30 (1913) 334ff. and C. H. Turner, 'Arles and Rome: The First Developements of Canon Law in Gaul', JTS 17 (1916) 236ff., are inclined to this opinion, cf. for a contrary view, Wurm, *Studien* 137–138 n. 68 and p. 32f. below.

86. Steinacker, 'Deusdedithandschrift' 120ff., Silva-Tarouca, 'Beiträge' 682 n. 1; Wurm, *Studien* 104ff., 143ff. and Mordek, *Kirchenrecht und Reform* 74–75 particularly n. 49.

87. Cf. Duchesne, 'La première collection' 161; Silva-Tarouca, 'Beiträge' 678ff., Wurm, *Studien* 116ff., for the older literature reaching back to Maassen, *Geschichte* 579–580; for later literature, see Gaudemet, *Formation* 158–159; idem, *Sources* 89–90 and Mordek, 'Primat' 546–547.

88. Maassen, *Geschichte* 579 under no. xxiii and Wurm, *Studien* 277 no. 23.

Celestine I (JK 369 and 371) that follow have been placed in the collection each without its own individual incipit. For this reason the heading 'canones urbicani' has been written on the relevant folios (69–76) of the Cologne collection.[89] This collection can also be recognized by the abridgement of Celestine's decretal JK 369 and the insertion of the remaining sections c.3–6 (no. 4–8) in JK 371. After the collection of the *Canones urbicani* comes Siricius' letter to Himerius of Tarragona (JK 255) with its own 'incipit', and Innocent I's decretal to Victricius of Rouen (JK 286).[90] The same collection contains, although only in fragments, the *Collectio Albigensis* and the *Collectio Laureshamensis* under the more complete rubric 'Incipiunt auctoritates vel canones urbicani'. The collection of the Lorsch manuscript begins all the other papal letters with the word 'auctoritas' followed by the pope's name. The *Collectio Remensis* preserved a muddled remnant of the collection when it included Innocent I's decretals JK 293 and 303 under 'Incipiunt canonis urbetani'; the *Remensis* may have obtained the decretals of Zosimus and Celestine from another source.[91] We can not say with any certainty where the *Canones urbicani*, found only in Gallican collections, were gathered together. The use of the rare word 'urbicanus' in the title, a word that otherwise is found only in the testament of Caesarius of Arles, suggests that the collection originated in Gaul. Or perhaps the material came from Rome and was later collected in Gaul.[92] It can not have been pure chance in the transmission of the *Canones urbicani* that all reproach against the customs of the monastery of Lérins (JK 369 c.1 and 2, no. 2–3) is deleted from the text. Further changes were the removal of the text recounting measures taken against the Pseudo-Bishop Daniel and Bishop Proculus of Marseille (c.6 no. 9–10) from Celestine's letter to the bishops of the provinces of Vienne and Narbonne (JK 369), and the insertion of the remaining chapters (3–6

89. Only the 'praefatio' and cc.1 and 2 (nos. 2–6) of JK 303 were adopted under the title 'Item alia auctoritas Innocentii papae', cf. Wurm, *Studien* 277 nn. 24–25.

90. The incipits of both decretals are in Wurm, *Studien* 277 nos. 27 and 28.

91. The protocol of the decretal of Innocent is edited in Wurm, *Studien* 288 no. 4; the decretal of Zosimus and the two letters of Celestine do not appear together, and they are also separated from the letters of Innocent, JK 293 and 303, since the compiler of the *Remensis* was concerned to place his sources in chronological order. Further, JK 369 and 371 of Celestine are preserved complete, in contrast with others, contained in the *Canones urbicani*, cf. Wurm, *Studien* 116.

92. Cf. Massigli, 'La plus ancienne collection' 415 n. 1 and Silva-Tarouca, 'Beiträge' 681–682. The authenticity of the testament of Caesarius is defended by Morin, 'Statuta ecclesiae antiqua' 97ff. against B. Krusch (MGH Scriptores rerum Merovingicarum 3; Hannover 1896) 450, and his opinion is accepted generally, cf. R. J. H. Collins, 'Cäsarius von Arles', TRE 7 (1981) 534. Mordek, 'Primat' 546, pleads instead for a Roman origin, citing Wurm, *Studien* 117–118, who however clearly says on 118: 'their (the *Canones urbicani*) compilation certainly took place in Gaul'.

no. 4–8) of this letter, which concerns episcopal and priestly ordinations, into Celestine's decretal to the bishops of Apulia and Calabria (JK 371). These changes must have been made while the conditions and incidents denounced by the pope were still vividly remembered.[93] The most likely time of origin is the years between 429 (JK 371) and 440, the beginning of the pontificate of Pope Leo the Great. The complete lack of the widely distributed decretals of Leo I could not be otherwise explained if the collection were given a much later date.

b. Epistolae decretales

The *Epistolae decretales* is definitely Italian.[94] This collection contains the decretals of the *Canones urbicani* to Innocent I's letter to Victricius of Rouen (JK 286). In the *Collectio Frisingensis* the *Epistolae decretales* begin with Innocent's letter (JK 286) under the heading: 'Incipiunt epistole decretalis diversorum episcoporum urbis Romae per diversas provincias misse'.[95] The decretals JK 293, 303, 339, 369, and 371 follow, without individual 'incipit'. Since the collection in the Freising manuscript is in roughly chronological order, the Acts of the Council of Carthage in 419 have been inserted between Zosimus JK 339 of 418 and Celestine's letter to the bishops of Vienne and Narbonne (JK 369 of 428).[96] The independence of the *Epistolae decretales* from the *Canones urbicani* can be seen both from the inclusion of an additional decretal of Innocent I (JK 286) and by the fact that Celestine's letter (JK 369) has been transmitted in its entirety in this collection.[97] A fragment of the *Epistolae decretales* is also found in the *Collectio Coloniensis* in which the introduction to Innocent's decretal (JK 286) resembles that in the *Frisingensis* with: 'Incipiunt epistolae decretalis universorum episcoporum urbis Romae per diversas provincias missae'.[98] Either the *Collectio Frisingensis* and the *Collectio Coloniensis* both derive from the same source[99] or, more probably, the author of the *Collectio Coloniensis* compared the *Epistolae decretales* with the *Canones urbicani* already in his manuscript and decided to supply Innocent's missing letter from the *Epistolae decretales*.[100]

93. Cf. Duchesne, 'La première collection' 162; Caspar, *Papsttum* 1.384–385; Wurm, *Studien* 141.

94. Cf. Duchesne, 'La première collection' 161; Silva-Tarouca, 'Beiträge' 680–681; Wurm, *Studien* 118–119 and Mordek, 'Primat' 547.

95. The protocol is edited by Wurm, *Studien* 237.

96. Cf. Maassen, *Geschichte* 483–484 and Wurm, *Studien* 237–238.

97. See above, p. 24.

98. Edited by Wurm, *Studien* 277–278.

99. Thus Maassen, *Geschichte* 580, in no. xxviii.

100. Thus Silva-Tarouca, 'Beiträge' 680; Wurm, *Studien* 118–119 and Mordek, 'Primat' 547.

c. Common Source of the Collectio Corbeiensis *and the* Collectio Pithouensis

A third *decretal* collection can be reconstructed from a series of letters common to the *Collectio Corbeiensis* and the collection of the Pithou manuscript, both from sixth-century Gaul.[101] The compilers of these two collections both used the same manuscript that included Innocent's letters JK 286, 293, 303, and both of Celestine's decretals (JK 369 and 371), all without individual headings, except for JK 286. Pope Zosimus' letter (JK 339) can be recognized as a later addition, as it also has its own 'incipit'.[102] On the same grounds used for dating the *Canones urbicani,* one can assume that these last two letter collections originated sometime in the 430s.

Leo the Great's admonition to abide by the regulations of Pope Innocent and all of his predecessors could have referred to any of the three collections just discussed. The *Epistolae decretales* is the most likely because there is a striking resemblance between the title of the collection and the address of Leo's decretal in which he made this demand.[103] Hubert Mordek does not want to exclude the possibility that Leo I himself initiated the compilation of a decretal collection like the *Epistolae decretales,* because this body of letters forms 'an internally consistent group of papal decrees concerning priestly ordination and the disciplinary regulations of the clerical state'.[104] The lack of reliable editions makes it impossible to state more exactly whether there are significant textual filiations among the three small decretal collections. In Wurm's critical edition of Innocent's decretal (JK 293) there are slight indications that the text of the *Canones urbicani,* the *Epistolae decretales,* and that of Dionysius Exiguus concur with one another more often than usually occurs in the process of text transmission.[105]

---

101. Cf. Wurm, *Studien* 119–120.

102. Cf. the protocol in Wurm, *Studien* 272–273 *(Corbeiensis)* and 284 *(Pithouensis).* The close connections of the two collections are shown by the common manuscript readings of the decretals of Innocent I, JK 293, and of Leo I, JK 402, edited by Wurm, *Apollinaris* 12 (1939) 51–52, 81 with notes, the list of recipients in JK 303 (Wurm, *Studien* 135 with n. 65), and the additional passage for c.15 of the decretal of Siricius JK 255 preserved in both collections, added by a hand of the eighth century in the *Corbeiensis* from an exemplar of the *Collection of Pithou,* cf. Mordek, *Kirchenrecht und Reform* 90–91, with an illustration of the note in the *Collectio Corbeiensis* (plate I) following p. 88.

103. Mordek, 'Primat' 548 calls attention to this; other scholars such as Wurm, *Studien* 112 connected the passage of the *Decretum Gelasianum* to the epigraph of the *Epistolae decretales.*

104. Cf. Mordek, 'Primat' 548–549; the citation derives from Silva-Tarouca, 'Beiträge' 681.

105. Cf. Wurm, 'Decretales selectae' 51–52 though his analyses of the protocols of JK 303, 339, and 371 (idem, *Studien* 134ff., 138f., 142) contradicts the impression given by JK 293.

d. Individual Items

Apparently Siricius' decretal to Himerius of Tarragona (JK 255) and the equally broadly distributed decretal from Innocent I to Bishop Decentius of Gubbio did not belong to these early collections.[106] They circulated as individual works before they were incorporated into the canonical collections where we find them today. This observation is proven by the totally different placement of these decretals in various collections. In the manuscripts these letters are usually separated from the earliest decretal collections just discussed, and they usually have their own 'incipit'.[107] The independent circulation of Siricius' decretal is obvious: in his February 405 letter to Exsuperius of Toulouse (JK 293), Pope Innocent took for granted that the twenty-year-old letter of Siricius was generally known and reiterated its message.[108] Since JK 293 appears in the *Canones urbicani*, the *Epistole decretales* and the model for the *Collectio Corbeiensis* and the *Collectio Pithouensis*, some Gallican compiler of canons must have made the effort to incorporate this important papal letter into his collection.

Pope Innocent I's decretal to Decentius of Gubbio (JK 311) circulated independently. The decretal appears in different places in different collections and always under its own heading. The *Collectio Frisingensis* introduces the letter immediately before the series of the *Epistolae decretales*, with 'Incipit epistola decretalis sancti papae Innocenti de celebritate mysteriorum'.[109] The author of the *Frisingensis*, who otherwise tried to arrange his sequence of letters chronologically, here placed JK 311 from 416 before Innocent's letter to Victricius of Rouen from 404 (JK 286). Dionysius repeated this error in his series of twenty-one of Innocent's letters, which opens with JK 311 and the heading 'Incipit epistola regularis papae Innocenti' (the only heading he gives these letters), and, just as in the *Frisingensis*, Dionysius then placed the decretal to Victricius (JK 286) after it.[110] Dionysius' motive is not clear. He probably did not take this arrangement from the Freising collection, but it is possible that he used another

106. JK 255, PL 13.1131ff.; JK 311 has been edited and commented upon by Cabié, *Lettre.*

107. On their position in the collections, cf. Wurm, *Studien* 120ff. and 124ff., as well as the protocol he edited from the *Collectiones Frisingensis* 236 no. 3–4 (JK 255, 311), *Corbeiensis* 272 no. 4 (JK 311), 276 no. 47 (JK 255), *Coloniensis* 277 no. 27 (JK 255), *Albigensis* 279 no. 18 (JK 311), 280 no. 30 (JK 255), *Pithouensis* 286 no. 88 (JK 255) and *Remensis* 288 no. a (JK 255). Unlike the *Canones urbicani*, the *Collectio Remensis* agrees with the collection of the manuscript of Chieti and the collection of Pithou in the text of the decretal of Siricius, while the collections in the manuscripts of Cologne, Albi and Lorsch and the manuscript from Corbie are based on a common source for JK 255: this version of Siricius' decretal begins at c.6; cf. Maassen, *Geschichte* 240–241 and Wurm, *Studien* 122.

108. Edited by Wurm, 'Decretales selectae' 59.4ff., McShane, *Romanitas* 336–337.

109. Wurm, *Studien* 237 n. 4.

110. See the protocol, Wurm, *Studien* 63ff.

unknown source.[111] It is also possible that matters of content, e.g. the stress on the validity of papal directives and the primacy of the Bishop of Rome, played a role in Dionysius' organizational scheme.[112] In the collection of the Corbie manuscript JK 311 stands with its own 'incipit' before the previously mentioned decretal collection which is also used by the *Collectio Pithouensis*.[113] The collection in the manuscript from Albi placed JK 311 unexpectedly between the canons of Neocaesarea (314) and Arles (314).[114] If Bishop Patroclus of Arles, who stayed in Rome in 417 and consecrated Innocent's successor Zosimus, brought the decretal JK 311 back to Gaul,[115] that would easily explain why it was received into the Gallican 'libri canonum' separately from the decretal collection.

Appendix I

The *Canones synodi Romanorum ad Gallos episcopos*— The Earliest Papal Decretal?

In our discussion of early papal decretals we now must consider earlier scholarly debates about the origins of these texts. A debate arose in the early twentieth century over the *Canones synodi Romanorum ad Gallos episcopos* (JK after 285). They are, as their title says, a Roman synod's answer to Gallican bishops' questions about church discipline and church administration problems. The *Canones'* first editors, Jacques Sirmond and Pierre Coustant, ascribed them to either Pope Innocent I or Pope Siricius. Charles E. Babut, relying mostly on their content but also on their textual tradition, tried to prove that Pope Damasus (366–384) had written them. Babut's theory has not remained unchallenged, so that today those in favor of ascription to Damasus balance those against.[116]

Until a short while ago the *Canones* were known only through the

111. The parallels between the *Collectio Frisingensis* and *Dionysiana* in the sequence of the letters of Innocent are striking, but the texts are not similar enough that one can say that the *Dionysiana* derives from the *Frisingensis,* or vice versa, or that they derive from a common source, cf. Wurm, *Studien* 119 and 137.

112. Thus Cabié, *Lettre* in the introduction to his edition, 15.

113. It is completely lacking in the *Pithouensis,* and in the *Collectio Corbeiensis* it is separated by Zosimus' decretal JK 339 from the decretal collection it shares with the Pithou manuscript, cf. Wurm, *Studien* 272 nn. 4–6.

114. Cf. Maassen, *Geschichte* 595, who refers to the relationship with the *Collectio Corbeiensis,* which has a list in chapters 1–4 that is similar to the one found in the *Collectio Albigensis* (cf. 557–558).

115. Wurm, *Studien* 127 assumes this, but Duchesne, 'La première collection' 160 saw the reason for its limited distribution in Gallican collections in the decretal's criticism of Gallican customs.

116. J. Sirmond, *Concilia antiqua Galliae* 1 (Paris 1629) 585ff. and n. 623; Coustant, *Epistolae* 685ff. and introduction 681ff. and E. Ch. Babut, *La plus ancienne décrétale* (Paris 1904) 69ff. A new edition of the *Canones* is being prepared by G. L. Thompson entitled *The Earliest Papal Correspondence.* After the doubts expressed by Silva-Tarouca, 'Beiträge' 692, Getzeny, *Stil und Form* 94ff. refutes Babut's thesis by repeating Coustant's argument. His followers are:

codices of the manuscript collection of St. Maur. The 'Capitulatio' of this collection, older than the collection itself, seemed to support the idea that Damasus was the author.[117] Thirteen times between the African Council of Telepte (418) and the Synod of Agde (506) it notes 'Canones Romanorum. Item de spiritu sancto'. This phrase could refer to the synodal letter and the *Tomus fidei* of Pope Damasus from the Roman Synod of 378. However, in the actual text of the manuscript, the *Canones* are placed after the African Synod of 418, nowhere near Damasus' *Tomus,* which begins the collection of the St. Maur manuscript.[118] In addition, there are two canonical collections from the Rhaetian Alps, as yet only recently analyzed, which are of equal importance with the *Collection of St. Maur.*[119] They may well go back to Italian, perhaps Roman, material and may have

---

Caspar, *Papsttum* 1.216 and 594; Haller, *Papsttum* 1.510; Feine, *Rechtsgeschichte* 94 note 11. Agreeing with Babut's position are: L. Duchesne, 'Le concile de Turin', *Revue historique* 87 (1905) 278f.; P. Batiffol, *Le siège apostolique (359–451)* (Paris 1924) 198ff.; Schwartz, 'Kanonessammlung' 63 n. 2 (*Gesammelte Schriften* 4.223f. n. 1); K. Baus, *Handbuch der Kirchengeschichte* 2.1 (Freiburg 1973) 262; and Maccarrone 'Sedes apostolica' 285. The latest detailed and well-founded description of Damasus can be found in Pietri, *Roma christiana* 764ff., who especially examined the biblical quotations he used. Also, R. Gryson, 'Dix ans de recherches sur les origines du célibat ecclésiastique: Réflexions sur les publications des années 1970–1979', *Revue théologique de Louvain* 11 (1980) 165ff.; idem, 'Les élections épiscopales en Occident au IVe siècle', RHE 75 (1980) 265ff. On stylistic grounds, Gryson excludes the possibility that the canons are either the product of the papal chancery or the work of Pope Damasus. Gaudemet, *Sources* 61, leaves the question of authorship undecided as had his predecessors: Van Hove, *Prolegomena* 139; J. Speigl, 'Das entstehende Papsttum, die Kanones von Nizää und die Bischofseinsetzungen in Gallien', *Konzil und Papst: Festgabe für H. Tüchle,* ed. G. Schwaiger (Munich-Paderborn 1975) 48; Wojtowytsch, *Papsttum und Konzile* 431. Cf. with more details, D. Jasper, 'Die Canones synodi Romanorum ad Gallos episcopos—die älteste Dekretale?', ZKG 107 (1996) 319ff.

117. All of the editions made to date have not taken into account the oldest manuscript of the collection, 's-Gravenhage (The Hague), Museum Meermanno-Westreenianum, 10.B.4 (previously 9), a French manuscript of the second half of the eighth century. Cf. W. Levison, NA 38 (1913) 513ff. and C. H. Turner, 'The Collection named after the MS of St Maur (F), Paris Lat. 1451', JTS 32 (1931) 1ff. Partly dependent on the aforementioned manuscript are the manuscripts of the collection at Paris, B.N. lat. 1451 and Vat. Reg. lat. 1127, both French, from the first half of the ninth century; cf. Mordek, *Kirchenrecht und Reform* 55 n. 81. On the 'Capitulatio' of the collection, see Maassen, *Geschichte* § 688 p. 622f. and Turner, 'St Maur' 4.

118. According to Schwartz, 'Kanonessammlung' 63 n. 2 (*Gesammelte Schriften* 4, 223 n. 1), the arrangement had previously been decided, although the author confused the *Tomus Damasi* with the resolutions of the Roman synod of 382. Pietri, *Roma christiana* 765f. agrees with Schwartz. Concerning the separation of the *Tomus Damasi* and the *Canones* see Maassen, *Geschichte* § 687 p. 616 and Turner, 'St Maur' 9f. The *Canones synodi Romanorum* have this position in all the manuscripts of the *Collectio Sancti Mauri* and also in the lost manuscripts.

119. Concerning the remnants of a canonical collection removed from the binding of a canonical-theological manuscript that was in Taufers in the fifteenth century and is now in Munich and the long well-known *Collectio Weingartensis,* see the analysis by R. Schieffer, 'Spätantikes Kirchenrecht in einer rätischen Sammlung des 8. Jahrhunderts,' ZRG Kan. Abt. 66 (1980) 164ff., especially 180ff. and H. Mordek, 'Spätantikes Kirchenrecht in Rätien: Zur Verwandtschaft von Tuberiensis und Weingartensis als Tradenten des ältesten lateini-

originated in the sixth century. They provide 'a Freising-Würzburg compilation organized like the St. Maur material'.[120]

The most noticeable difference between the *Canones synodi Romanorum ad Gallos episcopos* found in the collection of the St. Maur manuscript and those found in the Rhaetian manuscripts lies in the way they have been divided into sections: the Gallican collection put a list of six chapters in front of the synodal letters; the Taufers and Weingarten collections divide the decree into sixteen sections whose 'Capitulatio' has been preserved by the Weingarten manuscript.[121] The *Collectio Tuberiensis* continues with the synodal decree 'ad Gallos' after-African conciliar canons (no. 191–200) in the curious arrangement of the St. Maur manuscripts.[122] Next follows an unidentified chapter (no. 217), and then Siricius' decretal to Himerius of Tarragona (JK 255), then next, probably, Innocent I's letters to Victricius of Rouen (JK 286) and to Exsuperius of Toulouse (JK 293) and finally, the canons of Sardica.[123] In the *Weingartensis* the *Canones* are described as *Exempla sinodi Romani* and are placed after these Sirician and Innocentian decretals and the canons of Chalcedon and Sardica. It is as though the compiler put what did not particularly please him at the end of the collection and he stopped abruptly in the middle of a sentence on folio 81r.[124] Folio 82r, on a new quire[125] has the *Tomus Damasi* of 378 after the introduction:[126]

---

schen Corpus canonum,' ZRG Kan. Abt. 79 (1993) 16ff., especially 24ff., who suggests the name *Collectio Tuberiensis* for the fragment. The *Collectio Weingartensis* is described in detail and analyzed by: J. F. von Schulte, *Vier Weingartner jetzt Stuttgarter Handschriften* (SB Wien 117 Heft 11; Vienna 1889) 1ff.; J. Autenrieth, *Die Handschriften der Württembergischen Landesbibliothek Stuttgart* (Second Series 3; Wiesbaden 1963) 113ff.; J. Van der Speeten, 'Quelques remarques sur la collection canonique de Weingarten', *Sacris Erudiri* 29 (1986) 25ff.; and Mordek, 'Spätantikes Kirchenrecht' 20ff. By careful comparison it is possible to reconstruct the probable appearance of the collection from Taufers, and also the text of the canons shows that the Weingarten collection is a derived version when compared with the *Collectio Tuberiensis*. Cf. Mordek, 'Spätantikes Kirchenrecht' 27f.

120. Cf. Mordek, 'Spätantikes Kirchenrecht' 20.

121. In the collection from Taufers the canons contain chapters 201 to 216, as one can gather or reconstruct from the chapter numbering of the fragments; cf. Schieffer, 'Rätische Sammlung' 179, 182, and Mordek, 'Spätantikes Kirchenrecht' 33. Van der Speeten, 'Quelques remarques' 91 has edited the 'Capitulatio' of the Weingarten manuscript.

122. Ed. Munier, CCL 149. 312f.; also see Schieffer, 'Rätische Sammlung' 178ff. and Van der Speeten, 'Quelques remarques' 58ff.

123. See the reconstruction by Schieffer, 'Rätische Sammlung' 185f. and Mordek, 'Spätantikes Kirchenrecht' 31ff.

124. Cf. the reproduction of fol. 81r in Mordek, 'Spätantikes Kirchenrecht' after 32. That the author of the *Weingartensis* wanted to cancel his entry of the *Canones* here is also supported by the fact that the 'Capitulatio' and the first line of the text were crossed out (see Mordek 26f.).

125. Fol. 81v remained empty. In the twelfth or thirteenth century a Marian hymn was written on the blank page. See Schulte, *Weingartner Handschriften* 4 and Autenrieth, *Handschriften* 114.

126. Cited in Van der Speeten, 'Quelques remarques' 99. In the collection of the St. Maur manuscript the heading is missing; cf. Turner, EOMIA 1.284.28ff.

Item post synodum Nicenam hoc concilium quod in urbe Roma congregatum est a catholicis episcopis addiderunt de spiritu sancto.

In the Weingarten collection we find the same arrangement as in the 'Capitulatio' in the *Collection of St. Maur.* Since the 'Capitulatio' is older than the *Collection of St. Maur,* the relationship between the two cannot be a coincidence, because there are further indications for the relationship between the St. Maur 'Capitulatio' and the Rhaetian collections. The canons of Sardica follow the canons of Chalcedon in both collections.[127] Further, a peculiarity of the Weingarten collection, that the *Tomus* of Pope Damasus begins with 'item', is also found in the 'Capitulatio' of the collection of the St. Maur manuscript.[128] The direct connection of the *Canones synodi Romanorum ad Gallos episcopos* with the *Tomus* of Pope Damasus may have been a coincidence in the Weingarten collection. The different ordering of the *Canones* in both Rhaetian collections betrays uncertainty in regard to the text.[129]

In summary: if 'you cannot tell much from linguistic similarities and parallels' in the decretals, then the evidence for Damasus' authorship is weak: the use of vocabulary common only decades after Damasus,[130] the uncultivated language and the lack of any references to him, all argue

---

127. For St. Maur see Maassen, *Geschichte* § 686 p. 615; for the *Collectio Weingartensis,* Van der Speeten, 'Quelques remarques' 76ff. and Mordek, 'Spätantikes Kirchenrecht' 32f.

128. See Van der Speeten, 'Quelques remarques' 105; Turner, EOMIA 1.284.28ff.; and Maassen *Geschichte* § 686 p. 615.

129. See the comparison of *Tuberiensis* and *Weingartensis* in Mordek, 'Spätantikes Kirchenrecht' 32f.

130. For the vocabulary of the papal letters of the beginning of the fifth century see Ullmann, *Gelasius* 35ff. and Landau, 'Römische Form' 562f. The phrase: 'Si ergo una fides est, manere debet et una traditio. Si una traditio est, una debet disciplina per omnes ecclesias custodiri' (*Canones* c.9 Babut 78f.) resembles Siricius' phrase in JK 263 c.3(5): 'Praedico, ut unam fidem habentes, unum etiam in traditione sentire debeamus' (PL 13.1166B). The term 'apostolica disciplina' (*Canones* c.9 Babut 78) first appears either in Leo I, JK 407 c.3 (PL 54.631A) or in Gelasius, JK 621 c.9 (Thiel 334); Siricius used 'evangelica disciplina' (c.13 p. 82) in JK 263 c.1 (PL 13.1165A). The most frequently used term is 'ecclesiastica disciplina', see, for example: Zosimus, JK 342 (Günther, CSEL 35.115.11); Bonifatius I, JK 364 and 365 (Silva-Tarouca, *Collectio Thessalonicensis* no. 10 and 8, 34.6; 28.33); Celestine I, JK 369 (PL 50.431B); Sixtus III, JK 396 (Silva-Tarouca, *Collectio Thessalonicensis* no. 14, 41.22); Leo I, JK 410 (PL 54. 651 B). 'Sedis apostolicae auctoritas' (c.2 Babut p. 71), a favorite phrase of Pope Zosimus, is found in Damasus' correspondence only in the section forged under his name: JK † 243 (Hinschius 507.14): 'si quis episcopum absque sedis apostolice auctoritate condempnat' and JK † 244 (Hinschius 510.7): '. . . ut apostolice sedis auctoritate fulti, in nullo ab eius devietis regulis'. 'Homines coinquinati' (c. 6 Babut p. 77) occurs in early papal letters only when Titus 1:15 is cited: Siricius, JK 258 (Munier, CC 149.62.81ff); Innocent I, JK 286 (PL 20.476B) and 293 (PL 20.497B); Vigilius, JK 907 (PL 69.17A); and Gregory I, Reg. II. 56a (MGH Epp. 2.340.14f.) Except for its use in the *Canones* c.8 p. 78, the term 'antichristus' is first evident in the letters of Pope Leo the Great, e.g. in JK 423 (ACO 2.2 p. 31.2) 457 (ACO 2.4 p. 33.20 and 23), 486 (ACO 2.4 p. 137.23), 532 (ACO 2.4 p.102.19). The citation is from Schwartz, 'Kanonessammlungen' 63 n. 2 (*Gesammelte Schriften* 4.223 n. 1)

against his being the author of the *Canones synodi Romanorum*. And, consequently, Siricius' long letter to Bishop Himerius of Tarragona (JK 255) must be 'the oldest papal decretal'.

Appendix II

A Canonistic School at Arles?

If we ask the question where the earliest Gallican collections were compiled, we must turn to the studies of Louis Duchesne. In general French scholarship has connected the origin of the main part of the earliest Gallican canonical collections with the church in Arles in the fifth and sixth centuries, especially in the time of Metropolitan Caesarius of Arles (503–543).[131] In Arles, the political metropolis of southern Gaul and the center of the traffic between Rome and the Gallican Church, there may have been four basic collections of church law, derived from material preserved in the Arles church archives:

1. a collection of Greek and African councils and papal letters that today is best represented by the *Quesnelliana;*

2. an early form of the *Liber privilegiorum ecclesiae Arelatensis*, principally papal letters sent to Gaul;[132]

3. a collection of Gallican councils, similar to that transmitted by the collection of the manuscript of Lyon, Beauvais, and St. Amand; and

4. a compilation of imperial decrees that could have been a precursor of the *Constitutiones Sirmondianae.*

Using this arsenal to a greater or lesser degree, sixth-century compilers produced the *collectiones: Corbeiensis, Coloniensis, Albigensis, Laureshamensis, Pithouensis, Remensis,* and *Sancti Mauri.* From these later collections, one could reconstruct the outlines of the Arles models. The last stage of this tradition and its crowning achievement is the *Hispana* which, according to Jean Tarré, can be regarded as the most mature product of the canonistic school of Arles.[133]

The reaction of German scholarship to these hypotheses varies from skepticism to downright rejection. Harold Steinacker and Hubert Wurm have established in detail that there is no support in the canonical sources for the idea that Arles was the sole point of origin and distribution of

---

131. Cf. L. Duchesne, 'La primatie d'Arles', *Mémoires de la Société Nationale des Antiquaires de France* 52 (1893) 235ff., idem, 'La première collection' 159ff. and idem, *Fastes épiscopaux de l'ancienne Gaule* (2nd ed. Paris 1907) 1.142ff. Morin, 'Statuta ecclesiae antiqua' 334ff., Massigli, 'La plus ancienne collection' 416ff., Turner, 'Arles' 236ff., J. Tarré, 'Sur les origines arlésiennes de la collection canonique, dite Hispana', *Mélanges P. Fournier* (Paris 1929) 713ff.

132. Edited by W. Gundlach, MGH Epp. 3 p. 1ff.

133. Tarré, 'Origines arlésiennes' 720ff.

canon law and canonical collections in Gaul.[134] Neither textually, nor from fragments incorporated into the collections, is it possible to make the *Quesnelliana,* the *Liber privilegium* of the Church of Arles, or one of the conciliar collections like the *Collectio Lugdunensis,* into a plausible model for the Gallican canonical collections.[135] Further, the attempt to make the *Hispana* into an example of a school of Arles was not credible.[136] This observation does not dispute the importance of Arles for the life of the Church and for the development of ecclesiastical law in Southern Gaul. In the time of Caesarius of Arles there was a strictly organized Church in Gaul, bustling with synodal activity, and this was an important forum for the construction, comparison, and amplification of canonical texts and collections.[137] Because of its close relationship with Rome, Arles was certainly a frequent pathway into Gaul for the pronouncements of the Roman Church.[138] Beginning in the middle of the sixth century, the importance of Arles in church politics waned; the leadership role in the Gallican Church slowly passed to Lyon under its energetic metropolitans Nicetius (557–573) and Priscus (573–586). The synodal activity of this decade is a clear expression of this change. While the council of 554 was the last to assemble in Arles for a long time, in the period between 567 and 585 alone there were six provincial councils in Lyon.[139]

134. Steinacker, 'Deusdedithandschrift' 122ff., Wurm, *Studien* 144–145. Even before the thesis of a canonical school of Arles was developed, B. Bretholz, 'Die Unterschriften in den gallischen Concilien des 6. und 7. Jahrhunderts', NA 18 (1893) 531ff., noted that the variety of signatories' lists in Merovingian councils found in the collections arose from the various transcripts of the original protocol of the synods and could not have derived from a single exemplar. The position found in Fournier-Le Bras, *Histoire* 1.28–29 is a compromise.

135. Cf. Steinacker, 'Deusdedithandschrift' 128–129, 131ff. and Wurm, *Studien* 138–139, 144–145.

136. Cf. Wurm, *Studien* 148–149, Schwartz, ACO 2.4 p.viiii, G. Martínez Díez, *La Colección canónica Hispana* (Monumenta Hispaniae Sacra 1; Madrid 1966) 1.100.

137. Cf. Wurm, *Studien* 103ff., 146; on synods, O. Pontal, *Die Synoden im Merowingerreich* (Konziliengeschichte A: Darstellungen; Paderborn 1986) 49ff.

138. Cf. the process of distribution of the *Tomus Leonis* portrayed in n. 79 above, as well as Turner, 'Arles' 242ff. One sign of a close connection with Rome is the authentification notes found with the Nicaean canons in many Gallican collections, declaring they were transcribed 'de exemplaribus sancti episcopi Innocenti', cf. Mordek, 'Primat' 554ff., where these notes are cited. They could easily be interpreted to mean that Gallican materials had been compared with Roman manuscripts and augmented, thus receiving a sort of papal 'imprimatur', cf. C. H. Turner, 'The Genuineness of the Sardician Canons', JTS 3 (1902) 377–378 n. 3. According to Wurm, *Studien* 147–148, the canonical collection of Dionysius included in the *Collectio Lugdunensis* also came from Arles; the first use of both parts of the *Dionysiana* by a pope was found in the letter of John II to Caesarius of Arles (JK 888 from 534). There is some likelihood that either the pope sent a copy of the collection he was citing along with the letter or Caesarius tried to obtain a copy of the collection.

139. Cf. Mordek, *Kirchenrecht und Reform* 74–75. On the synods of Arles (554), Lyon (567–570), Chalon-sur-Sâone (579), Lyon (581), Mâcon (581–583), Lyon (583) and Mâcon (585), cf. Pontal, *Synoden* 108ff., 137ff., 156ff.

3. Other Surviving Papal Letters from Siricius to Sixtus III and Their Reception into the Canon

3.1. Siricius (384–399)

Besides the widely distributed decretal JK 255 to Himerius of Tarragona, which reached most of the old Italian and Gallican collections independently, a few other letters and decretals of Pope Siricius should be discussed briefly. The letter JK 258, which Siricius wrote in the name of the Roman Synod to communicate its decisions to the Church in Africa, can be found mainly in Gallican 'libri canonum'.[140] It survives only in the acts of the Byzachene 'Concilium Thelense' of 418, where the papal letter was read and incorporated into the official record of the synod. The letter was included in the more or less chronologically ordered collections and is generally found among the African or Gallican and Merovingian synods, but not among Siricius' letters.[141] This decretal was not forgotten in Rome, either. Siricius' successor Innocent used large sections in his decretal to Victricius of Rouen (JK 286 of February 404).[142]

Siricius' letter 'ad diversos episcopos' (probably of the province of Milan), which explains the sentence of excommunication passed by the Roman Synod on the monk Jovinian and his companions (JK 260 of 393), is usually combined with the response from Ambrose and his Milanese Synod (393) approving these measures.[143] JK 260 is found only in the *Hispana* (without Ambrose's letter) and six Italian collections. The oldest of these collections, the *Collectio Frisingensis*, offers the best version of the letter, textually speaking. JK 260 is derived from it as found in the collection of the Vatican manuscript and in the *Dionysiana aucta*, with, however, some

140. Edited by Munier, *Concilia Africae* 59ff.; see Maassen, *Geschichte* § 153 p. 167ff.

141. Cf. Maassen, *Geschichte* 499 (*Quesnelliana* LXII, from which it was taken into the collection of the Colbert manuscript, ibid., 541), 559 (*Collectio Corbeiensis* XIIII), 598 (*Collectio Albigensis*), 606 (*Collectio Pithouensis* L), 620 (*Collectio Sancti Mauri*): in these collections, the 'Concilium Thelense' is placed among African materials. In the Spanish Epitome XL (Maassen, *Geschichte* 656), in the collection of the manuscript of Beauvais (ibid., 779) and in the collection of the manuscript of Saint-Amand (ibid., 781) it is included among Gallican and Spanish synods. In the *Breviatio canonum* of Deacon Ferrandus there is often a double attribution of origin: 'Concilio Zelensi, ex epistola papae Siricii' (c.4, ed. Munier, *Concilia Africae* 287), cf. the further survey in Maassen, *Geschichte* 168–169.

142. Cf. indications in JK 286, on this letter see Caspar, *Papsttum* 1.304ff., Pietri, *Roma christiana* 984ff. and Wojtowytsch, *Papsttum und Konzile* 205ff.

143. Edited by M. Zelzer (CSEL 82.3; Vienna 1982) 296ff., the answer of Ambrose, ibid., 302ff. JK 261, condemning the teachings of Bonosus of Niš, should be removed from the letters of Siricius and be attributed to Ambrose and the Milan synod of 393, cf. the edition of Zelzer, Ep. 71 (CSEL 82.3) 7ff., and justification of this attribution, xxx–xxxi; on this cf. Caspar, *Papsttum* 1.284 and K. Schäferdiek, 'Bonosus von Naissus, Bonosus von Serdika und die Bonosianer', ZKG 96 (1985) 162ff., 174ff.

deterioration of the text. The archetype of the manuscript that provided the concluding portion of the *Epistulae extra collectionem* of Ambrose's letters is based on the *Dionysiana aucta*.[144]

Only the *Hispana* contained the decretal JK 263 to the bishops of the Roman metropolitan province concerning the ordination of priests and bishops.[145] This decretal found a place in the Pseudo-Isidorian Decretals and, probably because of its contents, was often cited in pre-Gratian collections. Pseudo-Isidore incorporated Siricius' three decretal letters, JK 255, 260, and 263, into the long version A1 and A/B as they are found in the Gallican *Hispana*. Later, the C-version of the False Decretals, of which we can first find textual evidence during the eleventh century,[146] expanded this core by adding Ambrose's response concerning the judgment of Jovinian and the decretal to the African bishops (JK 258) preserved in the acts of the 'Concilium Thelense'.

3.2 Innocent I (401–417)

Remarkably, the pre-Gratian canonical collections included excerpts from more than twenty of Pope Innocent I's letters. Texts from his major decretals occur most frequently, providing the largest portion of the decretal material in the *Canones urbicani*, the *Epistolae decretales*, and the common exemplar for the *Collectio Corbeiensis* and the *Collectio Pithouensis* (JK 286, 293, 303).[147] The textual history of Innocent's letters is partly explained by their transmission, probably going back to the decretal collection of Dionysius, who had collected the widely dispersed decretals JK 311, 286, and 293 and seventeen additional letters. Innocent's letters are brought to a close with JK 303, written to the Macedonian bishops.[148]

These seventeen letters give the impression of having been inserted into a pre-existing decretal collection.[149] They are contained only in

144. Cf. Zelzer (CSEL 82.3) cxli ff., who gives a number of examples. The tradition represented in the *Quesnelliana* and the *Hispana* may be seen as having a value approximately equal to that of the *Frisingensis*. The text of codex Cologne, Dombibl. 213 of the collection in the manuscript of Sankt Blasien *(Collectio Italica)* is certainly very old, but also exceptionally faulty.

145. PL 84.637ff. (PL 13.1164ff. Coustant's edition) and Maassen, *Geschichte* § 275.6, cf. Caspar, *Papsttum* 1.262ff. and G. Martínez Díez, *El Epítome Hispánico* (Comillas 1961) 64 and idem, *Hispana* 1.301–302.

146. Cf. Fuhrmann, *Einfluß und Verbreitung* 1.172 and D. Jasper, 'Romanorum pontificum decreta vel gesta: Die pseudoisidorischen Dekretalen in der Papstgeschichte des Pseudo-Liudprand', AHP 13 (1975) 107ff.

147. See p. 23ff. above; in addition, the decretal to Decentius of Gubbio, JK 311, entered the oldest collections after circulating independently.

148. Cf. Maassen, *Geschichte* § 276 nos. 18, 2, 4, and 10 pp. 242ff. on the tradition; on the protocol and the relationships of the texts, cf. Wurm, *Studien* 124ff.

149. The same sequence of JK 311, 286, 293, and 303 is shown in the *Collectio Frisingensis,*

Dionysius; full of inconsistencies in the formats of their protocols, they deal with a wide variety of subject matter. The first six letters (JK 314–316, 304, 317, and 313) discuss church discipline and are actual decretals. The next three letters (JK 297, 302, and 301) are private letters. The next six letters (JK 305–310) are dedicated to the settlement of the dispute about John Chrysostom and the restoration of communion between the ecclesiastical provinces. The last two letters (JK 318 and 299) are thematically linked to the first letters of the group.[150] There is no obvious reason why Dionysius included these letters in his collection. He probably did not use the Roman archival copies of these letters: the irregularities in the protocol formats and the absence of dates are clear indications that they were known to him from other sources.[151]

The twenty-one letters of the *Dionysiana* were taken up entirely by the *Collectio Hispana*, and the group was expanded to include JK 312.[152] At the end, an abbreviated decretal from Innocent to the participants in the Council of Toledo of 400 (JK 292 of 404) was added. The complete letter from the earliest Gallican collections was included under the attribution 'Tolosana synodus', altered from 'Toletana synodus', and consequently placed among the Gallican synods. Similarly, Siricius' decretal JK 258 was placed among the conciliar texts.[153] The *Hispana*, in the form of the *Hispana Gallica Augustodunensis* (Vat. lat. 1341), made up the basic core of Innocent's letters in the False Decretals, with a supplement of seven texts, four of which (Innocent's letters JK 321–324) were from an anti-Pelagian

---

the collection of the manuscript of Sankt Blasien *(Collectio Italica)* (JK 286, 293, 303), the *Collectio Corbeiensis* (JK 286, 293, 303; 311 is separate). The *Dionysiana*, the *Collectio Frisingensis* and the *Canones urbicani* have the same readings for JK 293 in contrast to other versions of the text (Wurm, *Apollinaris* 12, 51 n. 44); Wurm, *Studien* 135ff., also concluded that JK 303 in *Dionysiana* and *Canones urbicani* does not agree with the *Frisingensis* due to the reading 'Machedonibus et diaconis' in the address ('Machedoniae et daciis'). Perhaps both of the decretals of *Dionysiana* were taken from different exemplars, as Wurm, *Studien* 226–227 n. 59, believes. More precise statements will be possible only when critical editions are available.

150. Cf. Wurm, *Studien* 65ff., and concerning the usage of the Roman archives, 225ff.

151. Wurm, *Studien* 223ff., deals with this in detail and demonstrates that Dionysius refers to the use of the papal archives 'expressis verbis' (p. 230).

152. JK 312 to Aurelius of Carthage is placed between JK 301, also addressed to Aurelius of Carthage, and JK 302. The author of the *Hispana* knew the letter from the Spanish Epitome, see Martínez Díez, *Hispana* 1.298.

153. Cf. Maassen, *Geschichte* § 276 no. 3 and Wurm, *Studien* 128. The *Collectiones Corbeiensis* (Maassen, *Geschichte* 565), *Coloniensis* (p. 578), *Albigensis* (p. 598), *Pithouensis* (p. 607) treat the decretal as a conciliar document. The *Collectio Remensis* and the *Collectio Sancti Mauri* place it among the letters of Innocent I (cf. Wurm, *Studien* 288 no. 3 and 293 no. 6). The short version from the Spanish Epitome and the *Hispana* passed through the Gallican *Hispana* to Pseudo-Isidore.

dossier that had been included in the *Quesnelliana*.[154] Thus, with twenty-seven of Innocent's letters, the Pseudo-Isidorian Decretals provide the largest collection of his correspondence. The misplaced letters of Innocent I and Leo I in the decretal section of the Gallican *Hispana* (Wien, Österreichische Nationalbibliothek 411), which occurred through the transposition of a few quires, occurs also in the Pseudo-Isidorian Decretals.[155] Beginning with the earliest manuscripts, all of which served as exemplars for later generations of manuscripts, the redactors have tried to eliminate errors, with varying degrees of success. The oldest manuscript, Vat. Ottoboniani lat. 93, from Northern France circa 860, detached the six letters presumed to be those of Pope Leo I from Innocent's letters; however, the seamless connection between Innocent's decretal to Felix of Nocera (JK 314) and Leo I's letter to Anatolius of Constantinople (JK 483) c.2–6[156] remained. This combination became a marker for the manuscript family of the long version A1 of Pseudo-Isidore. Only one subgroup, found in a dozen manuscripts written from the ninth to the fifteenth centuries and labelled by scholars the Cluny version, did not repeat this error. The base manuscript of this recension is the New Haven, Yale University Beinecke Library 442 and comes from the third quarter of the ninth century in Northern France.[157] The scribe obviously recognized the confusion and marked the end of JK 314 on folio 115vb with the phrase: 'Finit

154. On the *Hispana Gallica* and the *Hispana Gallica* of Autun as the model for Pseudo-Isidore, cf. Fuhrmann, *Einfluß und Verbreitung* 1.151ff. as well as J. Richter, 'Stufen pseudoisidorischer Verfälschung: Untersuchungen zum Konzilsteil der pseudoisidorischen Dekretalen', ZRG Kan. Abt. 64 (1978) 5ff. On the anti-Pelagian dossier of the *Quesnelliana* cf. Maassen, *Geschichte 496*, and O. Wermelinger, *Rom und Pelagius: Die theologische Position der römischen Bischöfe im pelagianischen Streit in den Jahren 411–432* (Päpste und Papsttum 7; Stuttgart 1975) 165–166.

155. The confusion in the *Hispana Gallica* is described by Maassen, *Geschichte 713ff.*, and idem, 'Pseudoisidor-Studien, 2: Die Hispana der Handschrift von Autun und ihre Beziehungen zum Pseudoisidor', (SB Wien 109; Vienna 1885) 817ff. See also O. Mazal, *Wiener Hispana-Handschrift* (Codices selecti phototypice impressi 41; Graz 1974) 61ff. The compiler of the *Hispana Gallica Augustodunensis* made corrections to the texts; for example, the end of decretal JK 314 addressed to Felix of Nocera missing in the *Hispana Gallica* is supplied, cf. Maassen, 'Pseudoisidor-Studien' 819 (no. 14a).

156. On Ottobonianus lat. 93 cf. S. Williams, *Codices Pseudo-Isidoriani: A Paleographico-Historical Study* (MIC Series C: Subsidia 3; New York 1971) 60 no. 64 with earlier literature, Richter, 'Stufen pseudoisidorischer Verfälschung' 42ff., 46ff., investigating the relationship of the *Hispana Gallica* and the *Hispana Gallica Augustodunensis* to that codex. See also the references in Hinschius, *Decretales* xxv n. 102 and 533 n. 3.

157. Cf. K.-G. Schon, 'Eine Redaktion der pseudoisidorischen Dekretalen aus der Zeit der Fälschung', DA 34 (1978) 500ff. and B. A. Shailor, *Catalogue of Medieval and Renaissance Manuscripts in the Beinecke Rare Book and Manuscript Library Yale University*, 2: *MSS 251–500* (Medieval and Renaissance Texts and Studies 48; Binghamton, NY 1987) 381–395 gives a precise description of the manuscript and bibliography.

epistola Felici episcopo directa'. He then left the rest of the column, folio 116r, and the top third of 116va blank, and continued with 'Epistola concilii Carthaginensis ad sanctum Innocentium papam urbis Romae'. Then he added Innocent's six letters of the *Quesnelliana,* followed by his nineteen remaining letters of the *Hispana Gallica Augustodunensis.*[158] The third codex that must be discussed here, Vat. lat. 630 from Corbie, also from the third quarter of the ninth century, breaks off after the twenty-three letters of Innocent in the *Hispana* and the Carthaginian synodal letter from the *Quesnelliana* in the middle of the pope's answer to the *Epistola concilii Carthaginensis* (JK 321) and continues on, without any transition, with the papal letters from Pope Zosimus (417–418) to Sixtus III (432–440). Immediately following, before Leo's letters, are Innocent I's letter to the Carthaginian synod and the remaining five letters of Innocent's correspondence in the anti-Pelagian dossier of the *Quesnelliana.*[159] From this tradition may have developed the order of the later, fully developed manuscript classes B and C of Pseudo-Isidore, in which the letters of the *Quesnelliana* follow the letters that come from the *Hispana.*[160]

3.3. Celestine I (422–432)

Scholars have determined that Celestine I's most widely circulated decretals—to the bishops of Vienne and Narbonne (JK 369) and to the bishops of Calabria and Apulia (JK 371)—were included in the oldest decretal collections that they have been able to reconstruct. They are also present in many of the oldest extant canonical collections. In addition, Pope Celestine's letters to the Council of Ephesus may be the oldest existing collection of papal letters. Transmitted by the *Collectio Frisingensis* (Clm 6243, fol. 90v–115v) together with JK 369 and JK 371, there are twelve more papal letters (JK 372–375, 377–380, 385–388) under the heading: 'Incipiunt epistulae sancti Celestini papae ad orientales episcopos de causa damnationis Nestorii Constantinopolitani'.[161] The last four letters (JK

158. The scribe probably compared this text to an unfalsified exemplar of the letters of Innocent, analogous to the series of letters of Leo in the manuscript, where it is possible to detect corrections, additions and regroupings. In later manuscripts of this Cluny version, the empty space is eliminated: the *Epistola concilii Carthaginensis* follows JK 314 without interruption.

159. On Vat. lat. 630 see Williams, *Codices Pseudo-Isidoriani* 63–65 no. 67 and Richter, 'Stufen pseudoisidorischer Verfälschung' 46ff.

160. See Hinschius, *Decretales* lix n. 3 and lxviii n. 4.

161. Cf. Maassen, *Geschichte* 484–485 and Schwartz, ACO 1.2 VIII ff., who studied this tradition in his edition of the *Collectio Veronensis.* The letters passed into the collection of the Diessen manuscript (Clm 5508), cf. A. Scharnagl, 'Die kanonistische Sammlung der Handschrift von Freising', *Wissenschaftliche Festgabe zum zwölfhundertjährigen Jubiläum des Heiligen Korbinian,* ed. J. Schlecht (Munich 1924) 136, 138–139 and Schwartz, ACO 1.2.viiii.

385–388), of 15 March 432, were written a few months before Pope Celestine's death, leading Eduard Schwartz to suspect that Celestine's archdeacon, later Pope Leo I, was the compiler of the collection that was taken from the papal archives.[162]

Another version of Celestine's letters, different from the source used by the *Frisingensis,* was gathered during the time of the Three Chapters Controversy and is now called the *Collectio Veronensis* (Verona, Biblioteca Capitolare LVII [55]).[163] This collection in three parts includes materials from the Synod of Ephesus (431) and contains in part one: eight of Celestine's letters and two letters written to Celestine by Patriarch Nestorius of Constantinople († post 439); in part two: the *Gesta,* which tells of the judgment of the patriarch; and in the last part: the reconciliation between Cyril of Alexandria († 444) and John of Antioch († 441), the four last letters of Celestine (JK 385–388), from March 432, as well as two letters of Pope Sixtus III concerning the reconciliation (JK 391 and 392). These Sistine letters have not been preserved elsewhere.[164] The compiler's most important source was the original form of the *Collectio Turonensis* that included the proceedings of the Council of Ephesus.[165] A third small collection connected with the Council of Ephesus and containing three of Celestine's letters (JK 379, 374, 375), is preserved in the collection of the Vatican manuscript and in the manuscript Novara, Biblioteca Capitolare XXX (66).[166] This small collection had been taken from the *Vaticana* into the *Dionysiana aucta* and with these changes was collated with a codex of the *Collectio Turonensis* in Rusticus' version.[167]

When one considers the reception of the letters and decretals of the popes from Siricius through Sixtus III into the pre-Gratian canonical col-

162. Schwartz, ACO 2.4 p. xxxx. It had continued impact in the *Dionysiana* of Bobbio, where the decretals JK 369 and 371 are followed by the first two letters of Celestine in the *Collectio Frisingensis;* in any case a manuscript other than Clm 6243 was used, cf. Schwartz, ACO 1.2.x.

163. Edited by Schwartz, ACO 1.2, cf. his introduction, i ff. and Maassen, *Geschichte* 727ff.

164. Cf. Schwartz, ACO 1.2.v–vi; the letters of Celestine received into the first part are JK 372, 374, 375, 373, 379, 378, 380, 377.

165. Cf. on this Schwartz, ACO 1.3.viiii ff.; the version of the collection in the manuscripts Montecassino 2 and Vat. lat. 1319, reworked by the cousin of Pope Vigilius (537–555), has been edited by Schwartz, ACO 1.3 and 4 and described in the introduction. The collection influenced the *Collectio Salisburgensis,* where the *Veronensis* and *Turonensis* were combined, cf. Maassen, *Geschichte* 732–733 and Schwartz, ACO 1.2, iiii–v, x.

166. On folios 97–102 of the manuscript Novara, Bibl. Cap. XXX, the letters of Celestine are found, cf. E. Wirbelauer, *Zwei Päpste in Rom* 189–190, where other literature on the manuscript is mentioned.

167. Cf. Schwartz, ACO 1.2.x–xi.

lections, one realizes that those papal decretals that had been included in the *Dionysiana,* the *Hispana,* and Pseudo-Isidore had the best chance for having a wide circulation. Thus Siricius' decretal to Himerius of Tarragona (JK 255) was present in almost all of the systematic collections. But the decretal JK 258, contained in the 'Concilium Thelense', was not a part of the standard version of the *Dionysiana* and the *Hispana,* although it was in a number of Gallican collections and appeared in the C-version of the False Decretals. Further, there are no excerpts from JK 258.[168]

The situation is totally different for Pope Innocent's letters, more than twenty of which have been transmitted by the three definitive collections. Excerpts from his most important decretals predominate, although the excerpts are limited to certain themes. However, twenty-one of Innocent's decretals are included in the canonical collections.

The letters of Innocent's successors, Zosimus and Boniface, had only minor importance. Pope Zosimus' decretal to Hesychius of Salona (JK 339), which has been a stock item in collections of papal correspondence since the middle of the fifth century, is seldom found in them. Zosimus' letter to the bishops of Gaul (JK 328), found in a few Gallican collections and in the *Liber auctoritatum* of the Church of Arles, is almost as rare as JK 339.[169] The canonists ignored Zosimus' six other letters (JK 331–334, 340, 341). Pope Boniface's situation is similar: his letters (JK 350, 351, 363–365) in the *Collectio Thessalonicensis* were either quite unknown to the canonists or were ignored. In the canonistic literature, Boniface appears most frequently in letters forged in his name.[170]

Pope Celestine appears in canonical collections in excerpts from the decretals JK 369, 371, and 381 only because they were contained in the *Dionysiana, Hispana,* and Pseudo-Isidore. There are also two forgeries as-

168. On the preeminent position of JK 255 among the letters of Siricius, see, for example, the survey of the sources of Burchard of Worms in Hoffmann and Pokorny, *Burchard von Worms* 272 or that of Gratian in Friedberg, *Corpus iuris canonici* 1.xxvi–xxvii. The *Collectio Tripartita* took all eleven of its Siricius chapters in 1.36 from JK 255. In contrast, JK 263 is cited only four times in the canon collections referred to (see above, n. 9) (*Polycarpus* 1.5.3, 2.1.34 and 35, 2.31.35, cf. Horst, *Polycarpus* 224) and JK 260 was cited only by Deusdedit 2.47.

169. JK 339 was cited in the *Collectio Anselmo dedicata* 4.13.14 and 6.12, Anselm of Lucca, 6.24, 7.41; *Collectio Tripartita* 1.39.1, Ivo, *Decretum* 5.102, Gratian D.36 c.2, D.59 c.1, c.2 and D.77 c.2. JK 328 was cited in the *Collectio Tripartita* 1.39.2 and Ivo, *Decretum* 4.226 as well as in the *Collectio Britannica,* Varia I B 6.1.2.

170. Thus Burchard of Worms used texts ascribed to Boniface from Julian's *Epitome:* Burchard, *Decretum* 1.57, 168, 184, 202, which found reception in Gratian's *Decretum:* C.6 q.4 c.3, C.11 q.1 c.8 and D.86 c.25, cf. M. Conrat (Cohn), *Geschichte der Quellen und Literatur des römischen Rechts im früheren Mittelalter* (Leipzig 1891) 1.261–262, P. Fournier, 'Études critiques sur le Décret de Burchard de Worms', RHD (1910) 90 n. 2 (repr. *Mélanges* 1.296 n.2); M. Kerner, *Studien zum Dekret des Bischofs Burchard von Worms* (Diss. phil. Aachen 1969 typescript.) 1.130–131; 2.102–103.

cribed to him that first appear in Bonizo of Sutri 10.46.47 and *Polycarpus* 4.41.19–20, both of which found their way into Gratian's *Decretum* C.30 q.1 c.9 and 10.[171] The canonists showed no interest in Celestine's anti-Nestorian letters, although they were in many collections: the *Collectio Frisingensis*, the *Dionysiana* of Bobbio, the *Collectio Turonensis*, the *Collectio Veronensis*, the *Collectio Salisburgensis*, the collection of the Vatican manuscript, and the *Dionysiana aucta*.[172]

II. The Letters and Decretals of Pope Leo I (440–461)

1. The Earliest Traditions

No pope of the fifth or sixth century left behind a more extensive correspondence than Pope Leo I.[173] This achievement could be due, in part, to his long pontificate, but it is primarily due to the renewed struggle over Christological dogma. This struggle, known as the Eutychian controversy, claimed the pope's full attention. The issue was debated in the councils of Constantinople (448), Ephesus (449) and Chalcedon (451), and Leo the Great had a substantial influence on the resolution finally issued by the Council of Chalcedon.[174] Thus, most of his letters were directed to re-

171. Cf. Horst, *Polycarpus* 162.

172. Perhaps they were unknown to them as well. It should also be mentioned that the Cluny version of the Pseudo-Isidorian Decretals, which was probably undertaken in the second half of the eleventh century, included the *Collectio Turonensis* of the council of Ephesus, cf. Schon, 'Redaktion' 506, and on the manuscript Grenoble 473, P. Fournier, 'Une forme particulière des Fausses Décrétales d'après un manuscrits de la Grande Chartreuse', BEC 49 (1888) 330ff.

173. The letters of Leo the Great are listed in JK no. 398 through JK † 551 and vol. 2.692 (Addenda et Corrigenda) and 735–736 (Supplementum regestorum); their tradition in the legal collections in Maassen, *Geschichte* § 281 p. 256ff. The edition of the Ballerini brothers, reprinted in PL 54, is still standard for most of the decretals of Leo I; in what follows, the letter numbers of this edition will be given in addition to the JK numbers. The *Epistulae de fide* of Leo I have been edited twice on the basis of different sources: Schwartz, ACO 2.4 used the *Collectio Grimanica* (Paris, Bibl. Mazarine 1645, ninth century) as the basis of his edition, C. Silva-Tarouca, *Textus et documenta: Series theologica* 9, 15, and 20 (Rome 1932, 1934 and 1935) made the *Collectio Ratisbonensis* (Clm 14540, eighth-ninth centuries) his principal manuscript. These and other editions of particular letters are listed in Clavis 1656, p. 533ff. Additional mention must be made of the edition of JK 412 (Ep. 15) to Turibius of Astorga by B. Vollmann, *Studien zum Priszillianismus: Die Forschung, die Quellen, der fünfzehnte Brief Papst Leos des Großen* (Kirchengeschichtliche Quellen und Studien 7; St. Ottilien 1965) 122ff., with extensive research on stemmata. On the editions, see J. Jiménez Delgado, 'Hacia una nueva edición crítica del epistolario leonino', *Helmantica* 13 (1962) 236ff., B. Studer, *Initiations* 4.750ff., 756ff., 760ff. and his survey in TRE 20 (1990) 737ff., Pentini and Spadoni Cerroni, *Epistolari cristiani* 121ff. and H. R. Drobner, *Lehrbuch der Patrologie* (Freiburg 1994) 384ff.

174. The most important documents have been edited by E. Schwartz, *Der Prozeß des Eutyches* (SB München Heft 5; Munich 1929), and thoroughly discussed by Caspar, *Papsttum* 1.462ff. and T. G. Jalland, *The Life and Times of St Leo the Great* (London 1941); also cf. Wojtowytsch, *Papsttum und Konzile* 304ff., the survey by L. R. Wickham, 'Eutyches, Eutychia-

cipients in the Eastern half of the Empire, explaining his Christology in detail, as in the dogmatic letters to Flavian of Constantinople of June 13, 449 (JK 423 Ep. 28) and to Emperor Leo of August 17, 458 (JK 542 Ep. 165).[175] Of the 143 letters of Leo edited by the Ballerini brothers in their *Opera Leonis* (Venice 1753), 115 are addressed to the East and 112 categorized as 'Leo I's dogmatic letters'.[176] In contrast to the numerous dogmatic letters, there are only seventeen decretals of Leo that were sent to the bishops, primarily to his own metropolitan province. A few were sent to Gaul, Spain, and Illyricum, one to the bishops of Mauritania (JK 410 Ep. 12), and one to Dioscoros of Alexandria (JK 406 Ep. 9).[177] These letters are mostly

nischer Streit', TRE 10 (1982) 558ff. and A. Grillmeier, *Jesus der Christus im Glauben der Kirche,* 2.1: *Das Konzil von Chalkedon (451): Rezeption und Widerspruch (451–518)* (2nd ed. Freiburg 1991) 125ff.

175. Both doctrinal works have been edited by C. Silva-Tarouca, *S. Leonis Magni Tomus ad Flavianum episc. Constantinopolitanum (ep. 28) additis testimoniis patrum et eiusdem S. Leonis epistula ad Leonem imp. (ep. 165)* (Textus et documenta 9; Rome 1932) and by E. Schwartz, ACO 2.2.1 no. 5, p. 24ff. (Ep. 28); ACO 2.4 no. 104, p. 113ff. (Ep. 165) and p. 119ff. the witnesses. On the transmission see E. Schwartz, *Codex Vaticanus gr. 1431 eine antichalkedonische Sammlung aus der Zeit Kaiser Zenos* (Abh. München 32, Heft 6; Munich 1927) 137ff. C. Silva-Tarouca, 'Originale o Registro ? La tradizione manoscritta del Tomus Leonis', *Studi dedicata alla memoria di Paolo Ubaldi* (Milan 1937) 151ff. has thoroughly studied the transmission of Ep. 28. U. Dominguez-Del Val, 'S. León y el Tomus ad Flavianum', *Helmantica* 13 (1962) 193ff., Grillmeier, *Jesus der Christus im Glauben der Kirche* 137ff. and Drobner, *Patrologie* 389ff. examine the theological content. For the textual problems, see H. Arens, *Die christologische Sprache Leos des Großen: Analyse des Tomus an den Patriarchen Flavian* (Freiburger theologische Studien 122; Freiburg 1986).

176. Thus the title of a fundamental study by C. H. Turner, 'The Collection of the Dogmatic Letters of St Leo', *Miscellanea Ceriani* (Milan 1910) which provides, 692ff., a review of this correspondence and its appearance in the *Collectiones Grimanica* and *Ratisbonensis,* the most extensive collections of the letters of Leo I. It is supplemented and newly published with the letters arranged in chronological order by C. Silva-Tarouca, 'Die Quellen der Briefsammlungen Papst Leos des Großen', *Papsttum und Kaisertum: Forschungen zur politischen Geschichte und Geisteskultur des Mittelalters: P. Kehr zum 65. Geburtstag dargebracht* (Munich 1926) 44ff. The latest part of these *Epistulae de fide* is the instructional letter of Pope Leo to the Emperor Leo on 17 August 458 (JK 542). Only three decretals, JK 543–545 Epp. 166–168, are preserved from the last three years of Leo's pontificate, and five letters from 17 June and 18 August 460 (JK 546–550 Epp. 169–173) are preserved only in the *Collectio Avellana.* This led Schwartz, ACO 2.4 p. xxxxi. to the conclusion 'that no collection prior to the middle of the sixth century extended beyond the second tomus of Pope Leo'.

177. The appearance of the letters in the earliest legal collections are listed in Silva-Tarouca, 'Beiträge' 690 and Wurm, *Studien* 168. Five encyclicals were sent to bishops of the Roman metropolitan province: to all Italian bishops (JK 402 Ep. 4, JK 405 Ep. 7), to Sicilian bishops (JK 414 and 415 Epp. 16 and 17), and to bishops of Campania (JK 545 Ep. 168). Six decretals were sent to individual bishops: to various bishops of Aquileia (JK 398, 416, 536 Epp. 1, 18, 159); to the bishop of Altinum (JK 399 Ep. 2); to Dorus of Benevento (JK 417 Ep. 19); to Neo of Ravenna (JK 543 Ep. 166). See Caspar, *Papsttum* 1.439 with n. 1. Leo wrote to bishops in Gaul: to Bishop Theodore of Fréjus (JK 485 Ep. 108); and to Rusticus of Narbonne (JK 544 Ep. 167). Leo's judgment on Priscillianism is directed to the Spanish Bishop Turibius of Astorga and to Rusticus of Narbonne (JK 412 Ep. 15). For details see Vollmann, *Priszillianismus* 142ff.

replies to questions ('ad tua consulta': Epistolae 15, 18, 159, 166, 167, 168), reports ('relationes': Epistolae 4, 16, 19), or answers to appeals to the Roman See (Epistolae 10, 14, 17). They deal with questions of church discipline, clerical office, marriage law, baptismal practices, the hierarchical order, and problems arising out of conflicts with heretical movements.[178]

That the 'dogmatic letters' of Leo I have been preserved in such numbers may be due to an historical coincidence. A hundred years after the Eutychian controversy, decisions of the Council of Chalcedon, which had been regarded as untouchable in the West, were called into question in the Three Chapters Controversy. This conflict ended with the condemnation of three theologians, Theodore of Mopsuestia, Theodoret of Cyrrhus, and Ibas of Edessa, by the Second Council of Constantinople (553). Ecclesiastical rulers in Northern Italy had long opposed Eastern theologians' linking of Chalcedon to Nestorianism. These Italians gathered together anything that would show Pope Leo and Chalcedonian orthodoxy in the proper light. A number of manuscripts that preserve their efforts may have come from Verona, where some of them are still found today.[179] These Northern bishops probably produced and disseminated the most comprehensive collection of Leo the Great's letters, the *Collectio Grimanica* (Paris, Bibl. Mazarine 1645, ninth century).[180]

Given all that we know about the distribution of Leo I's letters, especially his *Tomus* addressed to Flavian,[181] we can assume that various collections of Leo's letters and decretals were in circulation even during his lifetime.[182] There are frequent allusions to them in the letters of Pope

178. Cf. the survey of McShane, *Romanitas* 334–335.

179. This consists of Vat. lat. 1322 with the 'versio antiqua correcta' of the acts of the Council of Chalcedon and the manuscripts Verona, Biblioteca Capitolare XXII (20) with the acts and letters of the Acacian schism (484–519), Verona, Biblioteca Capitolare LIII (51) with works of Facundus of Hermiane and Verona, Biblioteca Capitolare LIX (57) with excerpts from the acts of the Council of Chalcedon, derived from the 'versio correcta' of Rusticus. All of the manuscripts date to the sixth century, and even if Verona is not compelling as their place of origin, all of them were located in the Verona library in the middle of the ninth century, as is shown by the notes by Archdeacon Pacificus († 846). Cf. Turner, EOMIA 2.1.viii–ix, Schwartz, ACO 2.4 p. xxiiii and in more detail R. Schieffer, 'Zur Beurteilung des norditalischen Dreikapitel-Schismas: Eine überlieferungsgeschichtliche Studie', ZKG 87 (1976) 176ff., who refers to other fragments.

180. Thus Turner, 'Dogmatic Letters' 727–728 and Schwartz, ACO 2.4 p. xxiiii–xxv. B. Bischoff, 'Panorama der Handschriftenüberlieferung', *Karl der Große, 2: Das geistige Leben* (Düsseldorf 1965) 252 n. 144 considers Verona to be the home library; cf. also Schieffer, 'Dreikapitel-Schisma' 181.

181. See above, p. 21 n. 79.

182. Novara, Bibl. Cap. XXX (66) (second half of the ninth century) preserves the dossier of materials that were presented to the Roman synod of October 449, fol. 34r–69, in the middle of which stands *Tomus Leonis* Ep. 28, surrounded by the most important letters for condemning Eutyches. Their origin in the papal archives is shown by the conclud-

Simplicius (468–483), Pope Vigilius (537–555), and Pope Pelagius II (579–590), and in other sources like the *Epitome Feliciana,* which was part of the first redaction of the *Liber Pontificalis* (c.530). They are mentioned, with precise numerical references, in later recensions of the *Liber Pontificalis.*[183] All of these collections are lost, although they were partly preserved in the earliest canonical collections, in collections concerning the Council of Chalcedon, and in special collections of Leo's letters. However, scholars have not been able to unravel this tangled web of evidence and to reconstruct the original appearance of these early collections of Leo's correspondence.[184]

The oldest collection of Leo's letters that has been discovered is a group of seven letters and a few other documents from the Eutychian controversy in an appendix to the *Collectio Corbeiensis* (Paris, B.N. lat.

---

ing formula of the *Tomus Leonis* in this manuscript: 'Et alia manu: Tiburtius notarius iussu domini mei venerabilis papae Leonis edidi' (ACO 2.2.1 p. 33.3). The pope had used these works when he 'et sancta synodus, quae in urbe Roma convenit' on 13 and 15 October taking a position on the 'Robbers' Synod of Ephesus in letters to Theodosius II, Pulcheria, and to the residents and archimandrites of Constantinople (JK 438, 439, 443, and 444 Epp. 44, 45, 50, and 51), cf. Silva-Tarouca, 'Nuovi studi' 105ff., and Schwartz, ACO 4.2.xiiii ff. and ACO 2.2.1 p. v ff., who thoroughly examined the translation of most of the documents from Greek, which the pope deemed necessary; the collection of Novara also is edited in this volume. Cf. further Arens, *Christologische Sprache* 57ff. and on the manuscript, E. Cau, 'Scrittura e cultura a Novara (secoli VIII–X)', *Ricerche medievali V–IX in onore di B. Pagnin* (Pavia 1971–1974) 44ff. and 77ff. It is also possible that the collection of letters of Leo in Montecassino, Bibl. dell' Abbazia 2 goes back to the pontificate of Leo the Great, since it alone contains another translation from Greek of the *Libelli appellationis* of Eutyches, which differs from that in the manuscript of Novara, and the Montecassino manuscript also contains a thorough refutation of the theology of the archimandrite, a problem that would have arisen only in 449 or shortly thereafter, cf. Schwartz, *Prozeß des Eutyches* 4ff. and ACO 2.4 p. xiii and the edition of the text, ibid., 145ff.

183. Simplicius to Emperor Zeno, JK 573 of 476 (*Collectio Avellana* Ep. 56 Günther, CSEL 35.1 p. 127.1ff.) and to Acacius, JK 572 (*Collectio Avellana* Ep. 58, 132.3ff.); Vigilius to Emperor Justinian, JK 910 of 540 (*Collectio Avellana* Ep. 92, 352.26ff.) and Pelagius II to the bishops of Istria, JK 1055 and 1056 of 586 (Schwartz, ACO 4.2 p. 109.6ff.17ff. and 114.5ff.). Turner, 'Dogmatic Letters' 702ff., has collected the texts and extensively commented on them, also Silva-Tarouca, 'Quellen' 30ff., idem, 'Nuovi studi' 127ff. and Schwartz, ACO 2.4 p. xii–xiii, xxvi ff. Papal statements have always played a role in research on the letters of Leo because scholars have perennially attempted to identify the collections used in Rome with existing large-scale collections such as the *Collectio Grimanica* or the *Collectio Ratisbonensis.* Among Leo's dogmatic letters, the *Epitome Feliciana* gave special emphasis to the *Tomus* ('Hic fecit epistolas multas exponens fidem catholicam rectam quae hodie arcivo ecclesiae Romanae tenentur, et decretalem, quem per universum mundum spargens seminavit', *Liber Pontificalis* 1.90.24ff.), while the later version refers only to the dogmatic letters: 'Hic firmavit frequenter suis epistolis synodum Calcedonensem: ad Marcianum epistulas XII, ad Leonem Augustum epistulas XIII, ad Flavianum episcopum epistulas VIIII, episcopis per Orientem epistulas XVIII, quas fidei confirmavit synodi' (*Liber Pontificalis* 1.238.15ff.); cf. Duchesne, *Liber Pontificalis* cxxxii and Turner, 'Dogmatic Letters' 705.

184. Cf. Schwartz, ACO 2.4 p. xxxxi and Wurm, *Studien,* who after a precise examination of the protocols of individual decretals was able to identify a series of small collections that were incorporated into existing legal collections.

12097, after 524). This bundle of letters probably was given its final form in Gaul and was copied into the *Collectio Coloniensis* (Köln, Dombibl. 212, mid-sixth century) and the *Collectio Pithouensis* (Paris, B.N. lat. 1564, late sixth century), which are two more-recent collections using the same sources.[185] In the *Collectio Corbeiensis* and in the *Collectio Pithouensis*, this small group of Leo's letters is expanded to include a second small collection containing decretals and letters written to Gallican and Spanish bishops concerning the date of Easter (JK 512 Ep. 138); to Bishop Theodore of Fréjus (JK 485 Ep. 108) concerning penitential practices; and to Turibius of Astorga (JK 412 Ep. 15) concerning contact with the Priscillianists, supplemented only here by a *Breviarium adversus haereticos*.[186]

185. The protocol is printed by Silva-Tarouca, 'Quellen' 40, idem, 'Nuovi studi' 121–122 and ACO 2.4 p. 155. Actio VII of the Council of Constantinople, 448, and the letter of Flavian of Constantinople to Pope Leo (Maassen, *Geschichte* § 119 and § 418.1, both edited ACO 2.2.1 p. 12.38ff.) are placed before the seven letters of Leo, JK 423, 480, 425, 429, 514, 447, 542 (Epp. 28, 103, 31, 35, 139, 59, 165). It was probably the goal of this collection to provide a theological compendium for the struggle of Pope Leo against the errors of Eutyches, thus Schwartz, ACO 2.4 p. xiii. The beginning and the end of the collection can be seen from their common incipit and the notation of 'finit' after JK 542 Ep. 165 in all three collections, thus Wurm, *Studien* 171 n. 16, who corrected Maassen, *Geschichte* § 665 p. 569. The collection is found in an appendix that barely postdates the *Collectio Corbeiensis*; thus it was probably written in the middle of the sixth century, cf. C. H. Turner, 'The Corbie MS (C) now Paris. lat. 12097', JTS 30 (1929) 232; on the textual classification of Ep. 28, cf. Silva-Tarouca, 'La tradizione' 163ff., on the connections between the collections of Corbie and of Pithou, see Mordek, *Kirchenrecht und Reform* 90–91. The reception of this collection of letters of Leo appears to have been widespread. Under the title 'Papae Leonis epistolae missae ad Orientem de heresi Euthichiana numero V', the letters JK 514, 429, 425, 542, and 447 (Epp. 139, 35, 31, 165, 59) are found together with Prosper of Aquitaine's *De vocatione omnium gentium* in the manuscript Laon, Bibl. Municipale 122, which was written during the pontificate of Theodulf (788–821) in Orléans. Transcripts are contained in the codices Wolfenbüttel, Herzog-August-Bibliothek 179 Gud. (ninth-tenth century from Corvey), Vat. Reg. lat. 293, fol. 163ff. (eleventh century from Troyes), Paris, B.N. lat. 2156, fol. 36ff. (eleventh century, in the fifteenth century the manuscript belonged to the collegiate church of the Saints-Innocents in Paris) and Paris, B.N. lat. 2193, fol. 150ff. (fifteenth century from Montpellier), cf. Schwartz, ACO 2.4 xiii–xiiii, J. J. Contreni, *The Cathedral School of Laon from 850 to 930: Its Manuscripts and Masters* (Münchener Beiträge zur Mediävistik und Renaissance-Forschung 29; Munich 1978) 44 (on Laon 122), B. Bischoff, 'Die Schriftheimat der Münchner Heliand-Handschrift', *Beiträge zur Geschichte der deutschen Sprache und Literatur* 101 (1979) 167ff. (on Wolfenbüttel, Herzog-August-Bibliothek 179 Gud.), A. Wilmart, *Codices Reginenses Latini* (Vatican City 1945) 2.122ff. (on Vat. Reg. lat. 293) and P. Lauer, *Bibliothèque Nationale Catalogue général des Manuscrits latins* (Paris 1940) 2.345 and 360 (on the two Paris manuscripts).

186. The autonomy and unity are indicated by the peculiar protocol of these letters, cf. Wurm, *Studien* 275 and 286. Due to the presence of its own incipit and explicit, the adjoining anti-heretical tract might not have been associated with the letter collection from the beginning. Maassen *Geschichte* § 665 p. 569, was incorrect in seeing this collection also as the source of the *Collectio Coloniensis* that, however, lacks all four pieces, cf. Wurm, *Studien* 171 n. 16. The decretal JK 412 (Ep. 15) appears twice in the *Corbeiensis*, which is why the scribe breaks off in mid-text; the compiler of the *Collectio Pithouensis* completely omitted it at this point. Differences between the two versions of JK 412 in the *Corbeiensis* are so great that they must have come from different exemplars, cf. Vollmann, *Priszillianismus* 93 94, 110ff.

A few chapters of the *Quesnelliana* may have come from a related but older Roman tradition.[187] The collection in the Vatican manuscript (Vat. lat. 1342 et al.) and in the *Dionysiana aucta* (Rome, Biblioteca Vallicelliana A.5 et al.) used a different but equally old collection of Leo's letters.[188] The compilers of these two collections used a dossier of anti-Eutychian material, also used by the author of the *Hispana* at the beginning of his series of Leo's letters,[189] and a decretal collection of unknown origin for which no related collections have been found.[190] A third collection of Leo's letters consists of three letters from Pope Leo to the patriarchs of Jerusalem, Antioch, and Constantinople (JK 514, 495, 460 Epistolae 139, 119, 80) and two letters to Emperor Leo I (JK 521 and 542 Epistolae 145 and 165 with the witnesses). These letters warn readers of the importance of remaining orthodox. Scholars have dated the collection to the time of the Acacian Schism (484–519) and have also connected it to the Symmachian forgeries.[191] Any influence on other collections of canon law has not been demonstrated.

The collections of Pope Leo I's letters in the *Quesnelliana* and the *Collectio Grimanica* are the most extensive of Leo's correspondence. These collections are particularly important for the reception of his letters into the canonistic literature. Both of these collections influenced the reception of Leo's letters in the Pseudo-Isidorian Decretals: the *Quesnelliana* was already in existence when the forgeries were done; the *Grimanica*, from the late eleventh century on, influenced the later and most comprehensive form (Version C) of the False Decretals.[192]

The compiler of the *Quesnelliana* seems to have been especially interested in Pope Leo's writings. He gathered the letters that were available and put them at the end of his collection as numbers LXVII to XCVIII, although without any recognizable order or organization. He interrupted the series of 'epistulae de fide' twice with a group of Leo I's decretals (LXX–LXXVIII; LXXXII–LXXXIV). The decretal to Bishop Dorus of Ben-

187. Cf. Wurm, *Studien* 212 and 216, who discusses chapters 67–71, 79, 80, 88 of the *Quesnelliana* (JK 542, 514, 423, 485, 412, 425, 447, 429, Epp. 165, 139, 28, 108, 15, 31, 59, 35). *Quesnelliana* chapter 42 should be added, which preserves Actio VII of the Synod of Constantinople in 448, with which the anti-Eutyches collection in the *Collectio Corbeiensis* begins.

188. Cf. A. Chavasse, 'Les lettres de Saint Léon le Grand dans le supplément de la Dionysiana, et de l'Hadriana et dans la Collection du manuscrit du Vatican', *Revue des Sciences religieuses* 38 (1964) 169ff.

189. Cf. Martínez Díez, *Hispana* 1.296, 298ff. and Chavasse, 'Supplément de la Dionysiana' 170. This collection might have been influenced by the *Collectio de re Eutychis* of the codex Novara, Bibl. Cap. XXX, see Schwartz, ACO 2.4 p. iiii.

190. Cf. Chavasse, 'Supplément de la Dionysiana' 168–169.

191. Ibid. 172–173, 175–176.

192. See p. 55f. and 166 below.

evento (JK 417 Ep. 19), added as a postscript, is the last letter of the collection.[193] In all probability, the compiler of the *Quesnelliana* found most of the letters that he used in small letter collections. In his haste to complete his work, and maybe through the carelessness of scribes, the material was mixed up so that elements that actually belong together are widely separated in the *Quesnelliana*. The compiler's main goal seems to have been to maximize the number of Leonine letters in the collection and consequently he placed less stress on order or on the literary shape of his material.[194]

The *Collectio Grimanica,* so named after its most famous former owner, Domenico Cardinal Grimani, Patriarch of Aquileia († 1523), exists only in one ninth-century manuscript. It contains 104 of Leo the Great's letters in chronological order.[195] Its value is questionable, especially when it is compared to the next-largest collection of Pope Leo's letters in Clm 14540 (eighth century) that came from Saint Emmeram in Regensburg *(Collectio Ratisbonensis).*[196] This collection contains seventy-two of Leo's letters,

193. The 'capitulatio' of the letters of Leo preceding the collection and the 'incipit' of the letters in the collection are edited by Schwartz, ACO 2.4 p. iff., Wurm, *Studien* 251ff., published the protocol. Also cf. Maassen, *Geschichte* § 623 p. 499–500; Turner, 'Dogmatic Letters' 715–716; Silva-Tarouca, 'Nuovi studi' 141ff. Concerning the possible origin of the collection in Rome rather than in Gaul (Arles), see Wurm, *Studien* 85–86, cf. also Mordek, *Kirchenrecht und Reform* 238. A. Chavasse, *Sancti Leonis Magni Romani Pontificis Tractatus septem et nonaginta* (CCL 138; Turnhout 1973) xxviii, has analyzed the collection of the letters of Leo in the *Quesnelliana*, Oxford, Oriel College 42 (twelfth century from Malmesbury), which Turner, 'Dogmatic Letters' 715–716, could not classify. In this collection, the letters and decretals were completely separated and were supplemented by ten letters from Pseudo-Isidorian Decretals and organized according to recipients and subject.

194. This is the convincing conclusion of Wurm, *Studien* 210ff., opposing the view of Schwartz, ACO 2.4 p. iii–iv, that the author of the *Quesnelliana* simply added the collection of the letters of Leo I to his collection as a whole.

195. Paris, Bibliothèque Mazarine 1645. The manuscript was written at the end of the ninth century in Friuli. At the start of the sixteenth century the notary Antonio Belloni from Udine gave the codex to Cardinal Grimani, from whom it passed through several stations until it arrived in Paris, where it became an important source for Pasquier Quesnel's edition of the letters of Leo (Lyon 1675, 2nd ed. Lyon 1700). After the French Revolution it passed to the Bibliothèque Mazarine and fell into oblivion until Turner, 'Dogmatic Letters' 721ff., reintroduced it to scholarship in 1910. Also cf. Silva-Tarouca, 'Quellen' 32ff., idem, 'Nuovi studi' 147ff., Schwartz, ACO 2.4 p. xxiiii ff., further literature on the manuscript in Schieffer, ACO 4.3.1 p. 34. A transcription in Vat. Reg. lat. 1116 was made for the Carmelite Pietro Tommaso Cacciari for his edition of the letters of Leo, which appeared in 1755 shortly after the edition of the Ballerinis, cf. Silva-Tarouca, 'Nuovi studi' 14 and G. Pignatelli, 'Cacciari', DBI 16 (1973) 8ff.

196. See R. von Nostitz-Rieneck, 'Die Briefe Papst Leos I. im Codex Monacensis 14540', *Historisches Jahrbuch* 18 (1897) 117ff., Turner, 'Dogmatic Letters' 728ff., Silva-Tarouca, 'Quellen' 25ff. and 'Nuovi studi' 131ff., Schwartz, ACO 2.4 p. xxv ff., p. 135ff. with the 'capitulatio' of the manuscript. The paleographic description is in B. Bischoff, *Die südostdeutschen Schreibschulen und Bibliotheken in der Karolingerzeit* (Leipzig 1940) 1.185f. and *Codices Latini Antiquiores* (Oxford 1959) vol. 9 no. 1305. Silva Tarouca, *Textus et documenta* 9, 15, 20,

compiled hierarchically according to their recipients, and frequently according to their date of dispatch, thus betraying an editor's orderly hand.[197] Turner traces the origin of the *Collectio Grimanica* back to the sixth century and that of the Regensburg collection to the early years of Pope Vigilius' pontificate (537–555). Karl Silva-Tarouca describes it as a mixture of the *Quesnelliana,* the *Collectio Ratisbonensis,* Rusticus' collection, and the *Hispana,* loaded with forgeries utterly soaked in Pseudo-Isidorian thought, which could only have originated in the second half of the ninth century.[198] This view has not gained acceptance. Most likely, one should value both manuscripts as evidence of letter collections whose archetype arose in sixth-century Northern Italy in the circle of those who defended the Three Chapters.[199] The *Collectio Grimanica* was excerpted in

used this manuscript as the foundation of his edition of the letters of Leo I. There is a transcription of the twelfth century in codex Vienna, Österreichische Nationalbibliothek 829, to which Silva-Tarouca, 'Quellen' 26–27, refers; it is thoroughly described by M. Denis, *Codices manuscripti theologici Bibliothecae Palatinae Vindobonensis* (Vienna 1793) 1.899ff.

197. Thus Turner, 'Dogmatic Letters' 721 and 734 and Schwartz, ACO 2.4 xxvii–xviii. Also cf. Silva-Tarouca, 'Quellen' 26–27 and his survey, 44ff. The collection is divided into two parts. In the middle, after letter 36, there is the notice: 'Expliciunt capitula epistularum quae sanctae Calchedonensi synodo sunt praemissae. Incipiunt capitula epistularum quae post synodum missae sunt' (ACO 2.4, 136.10ff.).

198. Turner, 'Dogmatic Letters' 727–728, justifies his dating of the archetype of the *Collectio Grimanica* to the sixth century with the provenance of the codex, its orthographic peculiarities, and the false chronological ordering of JK 429 and 455 (Epp. 35 and 72) found here and in the collection of Rusticus. Concerning the origin of the Regensburg collection, he rejects the opinion of the Ballerini brothers that it had been used by Pope Pelagius II in his conflict with the Istrian adherents of the Three Chapters (JK 1056). Turner thinks that it was the Istrian bishops rather than the pope who made use of the collection. Later Pope Vigilius mentioned the collection in his letter to Justinian on 17 September 540 (JK 910): 'tamen ut cuncta pietatem vestram informent, . . . beatae . . . papae Leonis quae diversis ad Orientem sunt directa temporibus constituta, quanta de plurimis in praesenti necessaria credidimus superadiecimus' (*Collectio Avellana* Ep. 92, Günther, CSEL 35.352.26ff.). Turner's argument was adopted by Silva-Tarouca, 'Quellen' 30–31, *Textus et documenta* 15 ix ff. and 'Nuovi studi' 135, where the *Collectio Ratisbonensis* is characterized as 'a direct edition of the papal chancery'. This evaluation was contradicted by Schwartz, ACO 2.4 p. xxvi ff., whose argument that Pope Pelagius used the collection is not entirely convincing, cf. the remarks of P. P., *Analecta Bollandiana* 50 (1932) 171f. and V. Grumel, *Byzantinische Zeitschrift* 35 (1935) 420. Rather, it originated from two distinct collections that sought to document the policies of Pope Leo the Great in the East (p. xxviii). Consequently, the collection should not be dated earlier than the end of the sixth century. On the *Grimanica,* cf. Silva-Tarouca, 'Quellen' 32ff. and for more detail, idem, 'Nuovi studi' 147ff., with broad conclusions for the letters of Leo in the collection. He holds that Epp. 43, 74, 111–113, 118, 120, 137, and 141 are forgeries, Epp. 27, 36, 39, 47–49, 154, 157, and 158 have been falsified and Epp. 160 and 161 are dubious; cf. doubts expressed by H. Zatschek, MIÖG 47 (1933) 319ff. There has been no serious dispute with Silva-Tarouca's theses; Schwartz ignored them, and others such as B. Altaner, *Patrologie* (7th ed. Freiburg 1966) 357 adopted them ('Among the 173 entries in the Leonine epistolary collection, there are about 20 forgeries'.); cf. also Arens, *Christologische Sprache* 43ff., who agrees with Silva-Tarouca.

199. Thus Schwartz, ACO 2.4 p. xxiiii and xxviii and Schieffer, 'Dreikapitel-Schisma' 181.

the late ninth century, as we know from the fragmentary transmission of the Milan, Biblioteca Ambrosiana C.238 inf. Also, in the eleventh or twelfth century, one manuscript of this abbreviated collection provided an important source for a revision of the False Decretals.[200]

2. The Decretals of Pope Leo I

Apart from collections devoted exclusively to conciliar material, almost all of the chronologically ordered books of canonical materials from the sixth and seventh centuries included the decretals of Pope Leo the Great. With seventeen letters that qualify as decretals, Leo's *oeuvre* surpasses that of his predecessors and his successors by a wide margin.[201] The location of these decretals in the individual collections varies widely. When the compilers were not concerned about chronological order, as Dionysius and the authors of the *Collectio Frisingensis* and the *Collectio Remensis*, Leo's decretals were placed a little before the decretals of Leo's predecessors (as in the collections of the manuscripts of Chieti and St. Maur), or a little after the decretals of earlier popes (as in the *Collectio Sanblasiana*, the *Collectio Corbeiensis* and the *Collectio Pithouensis*), or between the decretals of these other popes (as in the *Collectio Albigensis*).[202]

It is, however, striking that Leo's decretals rarely appear as individual items. Instead, they were gathered very early into small collections and from here found their way into the canonical collections. Furthermore, in contrast to the similar partial collections of the decretals of Innocent I, Zosimus, and Celestine I, there is no uniform textual tradition for Pope Leo I's decretals. Precise collation of the 'incipit' and 'explicit' phrases makes it possible, however, to detect a few small collections of Pope Leo's decretals that served as models for the Italian collections of the Gelasian

200. In its first part, the Milan manuscript contains the register of Gregory the Great, which was bound with Leo's letters from another manuscript, cf. Ewald, 'Studien' 459 and D. Norberg, *In Registrum Gregorii Magni studia critica* (Uppsala Universitets Årsskrift 7; Uppsala 1939) 2.62–63. The collection of the letters of Leo was included in Schwartz' description of the manuscript tradition, see ACO 2.4 p. v–vi. Corrections in Vollmann, *Priszillianismus* 98 and 106ff., who shows that Milan, Bibl. Ambrosiana C.238 inf. and Paris, Mazarine lat. 1645 rely on a common model. Florence, Bibl. Laurenziana, Fiesole 46 (fifteenth century), which Schwartz regarded as a transcription of the Milan manuscript, was not copied directly from it. The Florence manuscript is extensively described by A. M. Bandini, *Bibliotheca Leopoldina Laurenziana: Supplementum* (Florence 1792) 2.741ff. According to Bandini, it contained the contents of the Milan manuscript, the *Tomus* (Ep. 28) and the decretals Epp. 108, 168, 2 and 1; see also Chavasse, *Sancti Leonis Magni Tractatus* cxxxvi.

201. Cf. the survey of the decretals and their appearance in the oldest law collections in Silva-Tarouca, 'Beiträge' 690 and Wurm, *Studien* 168.

202. Cf. Wurm, *Studien* 211 and the protocol of the individual collections p. 258–259 (*Teatina*), 263–264 (*Sanblasiana*), 273, 275–276 (*Corbeiensis*), 281 (*Albigensis*), 285–286 (*Pithouensis*).

Renaissance and the Gallican and Spanish canonical works of the sixth and seventh centuries, although from time to time the models were subject to rearrangement, expansion, or abbreviation.[203] But the conclusions must often remain hypothetical and vague, because a scholarly edition of Leo's decretals, which is a prerequisite for such investigations, has not yet been made.[204]

The *Quesnelliana*, the *Collectio Frisingensis*, and the *Dionysiana* must have used such a source. As reproduced in the *Quesnelliana*, Leo's letters were supplemented by two series of decretals as follows: to the *Tomus Leonis* (JK 423 Ep. 28 Quesnelliana LXIX) were added, as numbers LXX through LXXVIII, the decretals JK 485, 412, 544, 411, 536, 416, 402, 405, 414 (Epistolae 108, 15, 167, 14, 159, 18, 4, 7, 16); to the somewhat later chapters LXXXII through LXXXIV were added decretals JK 398, 399, and 410 (Epistolae 1, 2, 12). Dionysius knew only seven of Leo the Great's decretals, and these he inserted into his collection: JK 402, 405, 414, 416, 544, 411, 536 (Epistolae 4, 7, 16, 18, 167, 14, 159).[205] These decretals occur together in one block in the *Quesnelliana*, but in different order. However, if one switches the position of the last three (JK 402, 405, and 414) and the first three decretals of the combined series (JK 544, 411, and 536), one obtains the order followed in the *Dionysiana*, and thus the correct chronological order for which Dionysius strove with nearly complete success.[206] The author of the *Quesnelliana* did not pursue chronological correctness but rather incorporated his sources unchanged, so that his collection reflects the original order of the source.[207] Like the *Dionysiana*, the *Collectio Frisingensis*

203. Cf. Silva-Tarouca, 'Beiträge' 689ff. and Wurm, *Studien* 166ff. The expression 'Renaissance gélasienne' was introduced to scholarship by G. Le Bras, 'Un moment décisif dans l'histoire de l'Église et du droit canon: La Renaissance gélasienne', RHD 9 (1930) 506ff.; concerning the problems with this concept, see H. Mordek, 'Il diritto canonico fra tardo antico e alto medioevo', *La cultura in Italia fra tardo antico e alto medioevo: Atti Roma 1979* (Rome 1981) 1.160–161.

204. Exceptions are the editions by Wurm, 'Decretales selectae' 79ff. of JK 402 (Ep. 4) and of JK 412 (Ep. 15) by Vollmann, *Priszillianismus* 122ff.

205. That is expressed in the preface to the decretal section: 'Sanctitatis tuae sedulis excitatus officiis, quibus nihil prorsus eorum, quae ad ecclesiasticam disciplinam pertinent, omittit inquirere, praeteritorum sedis apostolicae praesulum constituta, qua valui cura diligentiaque collegi, et in quendam redigens ordinem, titulis distinxi compositis' (CCL 85, 45.3ff.).

206. JK 411 and 544 (Epp. 14 and 167) are chronologically in the wrong order, though they are preserved in all collections undated, cf. Wurm, *Studien* 74–75, 177ff. and the protocol on p. 239 no. 35 (*Frisingensis*), 252–253, no. 72–73 (*Quesnelliana*), 258 no. 2 (*Teatina*), 263 no. 10 (*Sanblasiana*), 266 and 270 nos. 28 and 55 (*Vaticana*), 276 nos. 45–46 (*Corbeiensis*). *Dionysiana* and *Quesnelliana* both end the addresses of JK 402 and 405 (Epp. 4 and 7) with the formula 'in Domino salutem', cf. Wurm, *Studien* 73–74, 254.

207. Cf. Steinacker, 'Registerwesen' 33ff. An indication of the successive stages of growth of the *Quesnelliana* is the double transcription of the witness lists to JK 542 (Ep. 165) in c.41 and 67, cf. Maassen, *Geschichte* § 623 p. 497ff. and Schwartz, ACO 2.4 p. i.

also contains seven decretals from Leo the Great, but the two collections have only JK 402, 411, and 536 (Epistolae 4, 14, 159) in common. Judging from the text of the protocol, we can determine that the *Quesnelliana* and the *Collectio Frisingensis* agree mutually but often differ from the text of the *Dionysiana*.[208]

The decretals JK 398, 399, and 410 (Epistolae 1, 2, 12), which were inserted later into the *Quesnelliana*, all came from another small decretal collection. All three letters have identical protocols and all exhibit the scribal note 'Contuli' after Ep. 12.[209]

A third model of the *Quesnelliana* that can be reconstructed involves the *Tomus Leonis* to Flavian (JK 423 Ep. 28). Joined to the decretals JK 485 and 412 (Epistolae 108 and 15), it begins the sequence of Pope Leo's decretals in the collection.[210] The same source was used for Boniface's manuscript in Fulda, Dommuseum 2 (eighth century), which is derived from Roman material, as can be determined from the recension of Leo's instructional letter and Ep. 108.[211]

There was probably a common source for the collection of the Chieti manuscript (Vat. Reg. lat. 1997), perhaps fashioned in Rome at the beginning of the sixth century, and the Gallican *Collectio Remensis* (Berlin,

208. Cf. Wurm's edition of JK 402 (Ep. 4), 'Decretales selectae' 81 n. 68, in which the most important variants between the Freising and *Quesnelliana* collections and the *Dionysiana, Corbeiensis, Albigensis,* and *Pithouensis* are listed; for JK 411 and 536 (Epp. 14 and 159), cf. Wurm, *Studien* 178ff. This example demonstrates clearly how little basic knowledge there is about the relationships between the various collections even today. So we read in Wurm, p. 173: 'D (= the *Dionysiana*) and Q (= the *Quesnelliana*) have here used the same source (for the decretals appearing in both collections)', only to learn on p. 180: 'an analysis of the tradition of the individual decretals in both the collections (*Dionysiana* and *Quesnelliana*) speaks against accepting an old collection as the source for D and Q'. Wurm's resolution: Epp. 4, 14, and 159 entered the *Frisingensis* and *Quesnelliana* as separate pieces but from the same source. This source was several steps further removed from the *Dionysiana*; for the remaining letters 7, 16, 18, 167 one may assume an exemplar for *Dionysiana* which was closely related to that used by the *Quesnelliana*. Wurm's analysis is not thoroughly convincing.

209. Cf. the protocol in Wurm, *Studien* 255 nos. 82–84 and p. 170, 217 on these chapters. On p. 219ff. is explained the significance of the word 'contuli', which often is appended to the end of the texts in the *Quesnelliana* and *Dionysiana*. 'Contuli' indicates that the text in question had been compared with or corrected from its source, although the word does not mean that papal registers or archives were consulted, cf. the doubts of Schwartz, ACO 2.4 p. iii as well as Silva-Tarouca, 'Quellen' 38 and idem, 'Nuovi studi' 132 n. 2.

210. Cf. Wurm, *Studien* 215–216 and 252, the protocol of the *Quesnelliana*.

211. Cf. Silva-Tarouca, 'La tradizione' 160ff. and Wurm, *Studien* 185–186. On the Fulda codex Bonifatianus 2, cf. R. Hausmann, *Die theologischen Handschriften der Hessischen Landesbibliothek Fulda bis zum Jahr 1600* (Wiesbaden 1992) 7ff. and C. Jakobi-Mirwald, *Die illuminierten Handschriften der Hessischen Landesbibliothek Fulda, 1: Handschriften des 6. bis 13. Jahrhunderts* (Stuttgart 1993) 18ff. It is unclear whether and to what degree this source is related to the model used by the *Collectiones Corbeiensis, Coloniensis,* and *Pithouensis* for the collections of Leo's letters and decretals; cf. the opposing views of Wurm, *Studien* 185–186 and 216.

Staatsbibliothek, Phill. 1743), made a few decades later, in the second half of the sixth century.[212] This source, containing the decretals JK 410, 423 (the *Tomus* to Flavian), 412, 414, 536 (Epistolae 12, 28, 15, 16, 159), and, separately, JK 398 and 399 (Epistolae 1 and 2), was expanded in both collections by the addition of Leo's long letter to Rusticus of Narbonne (JK 544 Ep. 167).[213] The Gallican collection of the Diessen manuscript (Clm 5508) from the early seventh century was also based on this source, as can be seen not only by the identical ordering of the series of letters from JK 412 (Ep. 15) to JK 399 (Ep. 2) but also by the presence of the same protocol as the other collections.[214] Whether, and if so, how, the papal decretals in the collection of the St. Blasien manuscript (St. Paul im Lavanttal 7/1 et al.)— which strongly influenced the *Collectio Diessensis* and the collection of the Vatican manuscript (Vat. lat. 1342 et al.)—were linked to the common source of the three above-mentioned canonical collections can be answered only when a critical edition of Leo's decretals is available.[215]

A last small decretal collection containing Pope Leo's letter to the bish-

212. Silva-Tarouca, 'Beiträge' 690–691 and Wurm, *Studien* 167ff. The *Collectio Teatina* was transcribed c.800 from a manuscript of Metz. The *Teatina* originated in Italy, was carried to Gaul and then brought back to Italy, cf. Mordek, *Kirchenrecht und Reform* 10–11 with n. 41, idem, 'Primat' 525–526 with n. 6 (with the older literature); a thorough description of the manuscript in Wirbelauer, *Zwei Päpste in Rom* 114ff., 211ff. On the *Collectio Remensis* cf. Mordek, *Kirchenrecht und Reform* 10 n. 38 with literature.

213. JK 398 and 399 (Epp. 1 and 2) are divided from the other decretals in the collection of Chieti, cf. Maassen, *Geschichte* § 639 p. 529–530 and the protocol in Wurm, *Studien* 258ff. nos. 2–7 and 21 and 22, while the *Remensis*, whose author tried to arrange his texts in chronological order, joined it with the other letters of Leo, cf. Wurm, *Studien* 289f. nos. 12–20. That JK 544 (Ep. 167) entered this collection after circulating independently can be seen from the extensive 'explicit' found in both collections: 'Incipit epistola sancti Leonis episcopi' and 'Explicit epystula sancti Leonis ad Rusticum episcopum' in the *Collectio Teatina. Remensis* reads: 'Haec epistola pape Lionis ad Rustico episcopo Narbonense directa' and 'Explicit epistula pape Leonis ad Rusticium episcopum Narbonensem', cf. Wurm, *Studien* 178, 258 no. 2 and 290 no. 20.

214. Cf. Maassen, *Geschichte* § 693 p. 627 nos. XXXIIII and XXXVIIII and p. 631 as well as Wurm, *Studien* 169. On the collection, cf. Mordek, *Kirchenrecht und Reform* 9 n. 32, B. Bischoff, *Die südostdeutschen Schreibschulen und Bibliotheken in der Karolingerzeit, 2: Die vorwiegend österreichischen Diözesen* (Wiesbaden 1980) 87ff. and Wirbelauer, *Zwei Päpste in Rom* 119, 122–123, and 186–187 with further literature.

215. The *Collectio Sanblasiana (Collectio Italica)* contains JK 544, 410, 398, and 399 (Epp. 167, 12, 1, and 2), the *Vaticana* JK 411 (Ep. 14) and, widely separated, JK 544, 414, 398, 410, 536, 412, 406 (Epp. 167, 16, 1, 12, 159, 15, 9), cf. Wurm, *Studien* 263–264, 266, and 270–271. On the *Sanblasiana* and its influence, cf. Mordek, *Kirchenrecht und Reform* 240–241 and Wirbelauer, *Zwei Päpste in Rom* 122ff., who would like to rename it and its derivatives in the Diessen manuscript (Clm 5508) and in the Colbert manuscript (Paris, B.N. lat. 1455) the *Collectio Italica*. On the decretals of the *Vaticana*, see Chavasse, 'Supplément de la Dionysiana', 168. The letters of Pope Leo in the *Collectio Bobbiensis* (Milan, Bibl. Ambrosiana C.238 inf.) correspond to a surprising degree with the Chieti manuscript. The order of decretals in *Bobbiensis*, JK 410, 544, 414, 536, and 412 (Epp. 12, 167, 16, 159, 15), is taken from the *Collectio Grimanica* and comes before the dogmatic correspondence, cf. Schwartz, ACO 2.4 p. v.

ops of Campania (JK 402 Ep. 4), his letter to the bishops of Italy (JK 405 Ep. 7), and his answer to Bishop Turibius of Astorga's *Libellus* concerning the Priscillianists (JK 412 Ep. 15) can be shown to be the source of the collections in the Corbie manuscript (Paris, B.N. lat. 12097), the Albi manuscript (Toulouse, Bibl. municipale 364) and the Pithou manuscript (Paris, B.N. lat. 1564), all from Southern and Western Gaul in the sixth century.[216] Each introduces the three decretals with the heading 'Incipiunt decreta papae Leonis', and each begins both JK 405 and JK 412 with 'Incipit eiusdem papae Leonis de Manichaeis'.[217] It is striking that Dionysius Exiguus began his Leonine decretals with the same two encyclical letters, JK 402 and 405, and with the same heading: 'Incipiunt decreta papae Leonis'.[218]

The *Hispana* contains many more of Leo the Great's letters, including not only the basic core found in the *Dionysiana*, but also the decretals found in the Spanish Epitome.[219] Before these disciplinary letters, there is a chronologically ordered collection of twenty-six letters of the dogmatic correspondence that must have originated at the end of the sixth century or early in the seventh century in Spain. It contains mostly letters addressed to the Emperor Marcian and Empress Pulcheria, defenders of the orthodox Faith.[220] Their importance for the history of the transmission of canonical materials lies in the fact that an *Hispana* in its Gallican form transmitted the basic core of papal letters that the compiler of the Pseudo-Isidorian decretals drew upon. Pseudo-Isidore was, in turn, an important source for the compilers of pre-Gratian systematic canonical collections.

3. Pope Leo I's Letters and Decretals in Pseudo-Isidore

The Pseudo-Isidorian Decretals provided the most extensive collection of Pope Leo I's writings; the number of his letters and the number

216. Cf. Maassen, *Geschichte* § 668 p. 573, § 677 p. 599–600, § 682 p. 610, Silva-Tarouca, 'Beiträge' 690–691, Turner, 'The Corbie MS' 235 with n. 1, and Wurm, *Studien* 170–171. On the origin and age of the collections, cf. Mordek, *Kirchenrecht und Reform* 15 n. 63 *(Corbeiensis)*, 39–40 nn. 13 and 14 *(Albigensis)* and 56 n. 82 *(Pithouensis)*.

217. Cf. the protocol in Wurm, *Studien* 273 nos. 10–12 *(Corbeiensis)*, 281 nos. 34–35 *(Albigensis)* and 284–85 nos. 58–60 *(Pithouensis)*.

218. Cf. Wurm, *Studien* 171, 176 and his edition of JK 402 (Ep. 4), 'Decretales selectae' 83.

219. Cf. Maassen, *Geschichte* § 716 p. 693ff., Turner, 'Dogmatic Letters' 716, Schwartz, ACO 2.4 p. vi ff. and Martínez Díez, *Hispana* 1.296ff.

220. Cf. the protocol in Schwartz, ACO 2.4 p. vii ff., who edited the letters using the *Collectio Grimanica* and the most important manuscripts of the *Hispana*; see also Martínez Díez, *Hispana* 1.300ff. In contrast to Dionysius Exiguus, who only wished to use papal decretals, the interests of the author of the *Hispana* were more comprehensive: 'Sedis apostolice presulum constituta que ad fidei regulam vel ad ecclesiasticam pertinent disciplinam in hoc libro diligenti cura collecta sunt . . .' The text is the same as Dionysius, except for the 'constituta que ad fidei regulam pertinent', which are lacking, cf. Martínez Díez, *Hispana* 1.277.

of manuscripts exceed that of any other collection.[221] The compiler of Pseudo-Isidore edited and reordered Leo's letters in three French manuscripts, only little younger than the forgeries themselves. They served as starting points for the various strands of the Pseudo-Isidorian tradition. The earliest of these codices, Vat. Ottoboniani lat. 93, took its letters from the confused decretal section of the *Hispana Gallica* (Vienna, Österreichische Nationalbibliothek 411), where the strict separation of letters from decretals was only slightly disturbed, but the textual quality of individual decretals is considerably diminished by the combination of several letters into one.[222] Fifteen more of Leo's letters from the *Quesnelliana* are placed before these letters from the *Hispana Gallica*.[223] It is not certain whether or not Leo's forged letter to Theodoret of Cyrrhus (JK 496), which starts the series of Leo's letters in Vat. Ottoboniani lat. 93, comes from this collection. This letter is found there only in combination with the forged *Damnatio Vigilii* (JK † 899) as an appendix to two related *Quesnelliana* manuscripts of lesser quality (Paris, B.N. lat. 1454 and 3842A). More likely, both Pseudo-Isidore and the *Quesnelliana* manuscripts came from a common source that is now lost.[224] A different story emerges in Vat. lat. 630 (third quarter of the ninth century). Here only Leo's letters found in the Gallican *Hispana* were included. They were gathered together and corrected with a polished text of the *Hispana Gallica Augustodunensis* (Vat. lat. 1341) so that the worst textual confusions were repaired, al-

221. See Fuhrmann, p. 158f., 166f. below. On the letters of Leo, A. Chavasse, 'Les lettres du pape Léon le Grand (440–461), dans l'Hispana et la collection dite des Fausses Décrétales', RDC 25 (1975) 28–39.

222. On Vat. Ottobon. lat. 93 cf. Williams, *Codices Pseudo-Isidoriani* 60–61 no. 64 with the older literature, and Richter, 'Stufen pseudoisidorischer Verfälschung' 42ff., 46ff., who examines the relationship of the *Hispana Gallica* and the *Hispana Gallica Augustodunensis* (Vat. lat. 1341) to the codex. The confusion in the *Hispana Gallica* is described by Maassen, *Geschichte* § 729 p. 713ff. On the letters of Leo see Hinschius, *Decretales* xxvi–xxvii no. 107 and Chavasse, 'Les lettres du pape Léon' 29 and 31.

223. Cf. Schwartz, ACO 2.4 p. xxx–xxxi and Chavasse, 'Les lettres du pape Léon' 30ff. Actually sixteen letters were taken from the *Quesnelliana*, because the decretal to Bishop Dorus of Benevento (JK 417) is inserted between chapters 3 and 4 of Leo's decretal to the bishops of Sicily and supplemented by the probably pre–Pseudo-Isidorian forgeries concerning the 'chorepiscopi' (JK † 551) and the *Damnatio Vigilii* circulating under the name of Pope Silverius (JK † 899).

224. See Schwartz's contrary opinion (completely genuine, ACO 2.4 p. xxxi; edition from the *Collectio Grimanica* and Pseudo-Isidore 78ff.) and Silva-Tarouca (completely false, *Textus et Documenta* 20 xxxiv ff.; edition from the two *Quesnelliana* codices, the *Collectio Grimanica* and Pseudo-Isidore 169ff.); cf. H. M. Klinkenberg, *Papst Leo der Grosse: Römischer Primat und Reichskirchenrecht* (Diss. phil. Cologne 1950) 146ff. and R. Schieffer, 'Der Brief Papst Leos d. Gr. an Theodoret von Kyros (CPG 9053)', *ANTIDORON: Hulde aan Dr. Maurits Geerard bij de voltooiing van de Clavis Patrum Graecorum* (Wetteren 1984) 1.81ff., who assumes that the forgery of JK 496 was made during the Controversy of the Three Chapters.

though other errors found in the source remained.[225] The third manuscript of the False Decretals to be mentioned here, New Haven, Yale University, Beinecke Library 442, which is as old as Vat. lat. 630, is the base manuscript for what is known as the Cluny version, which comprises a dozen manuscripts of the long version (A1) of the Pseudo-Isidorian Collection. The letters from the *Quesnelliana* and the *Hispana Gallica* that are found in two blocks in Vat. Ottoboniani lat. 93 are found in the Yale manuscript, melded together into a single body of texts.[226] The letters of the *Hispana Gallica* form the core of the manuscript, into which the letters from the *Quesnelliana* have been inserted according to no discernable criteria. They have been corrected and expanded with genuine, unforged texts.[227] Apart from the False Decretals, this collection of Leo's letters had a wide distribution in the twelfth century, both on its own and bound together with his sermons.[228]

Outside this collection of fifty-six letters, either written by or sent to Pope Leo I, the body of Leo's letters was doubled (to 102 items) in the most extensive redaction of the False Decretals (C-version). Manuscripts of this version come from the middle of the twelfth century, but the basic form of the C-version must have been in circulation, at the latest, by the end of the eleventh century.[229] Thirty-nine of Leo's letters taken from the *Hispana* make up the first cluster, which is similar to that found in the Vat. lat. 630.[230] Then follow sixty-two letters and decretals in which the se-

---

225. The collection is described by the Ballerinis as no. 10, PL 54.559–560. On Vat. lat. 630 cf. Williams, *Codices Pseudo-Isidoriani* 63–64 no. 67, Richter, 'Stufen pseudoisidorischer Verfälschung' 46ff. and Chavasse, 'Les lettres du pape Léon' 35. The connection between JK 405 and the rescript of Bishop Flavian of Constantinople (Ballerini, Ep. 22) was not corrected.

226. Cf. Schon, 'Redaktion' 50ff. and Shailor, *Catalogue Yale* 2.385ff. with a precise description of the manuscript from New Haven. The Ballerinis described the letter collection represented by this recension as collection 21 (PL 54.573–574); cf. further Chavasse, 'Les lettres du pape Léon' 32–33, who could not judge the importance of New Haven 442 because it was not available for examination before 1970.

227. The most important changes in this collection of Pope Leo's letters were: The combination of JK 405 (Ep. 7) with Flavian of Constantinople's rescript (Ep. 22) was eliminated. The letter of Leo I to the Palestinian bishops (JK 500 Ep. 124), of which the *Quesnelliana* had only the first two chapters, was completed with the addition of chapters 3–9 (cf. Hinschius, *Decretales* xxvi no. 107. 8 and p. 574 n. 2). The interpolated passage in JK 410 (Ep. 12) that was taken from Leo I's decretal to Dioscoros of Alexandria (JK 406 Ep. 9), as it appeared in the *Hispana Gallica,* was eliminated (cf. Schon, 'Redaktion' 50f.); and the *Damnatio Vigilii* (JK † 899) was attributed to Pope Silverius.

228. Chavasse, *Sancti Leonis Magni Tractatus* cvi and cxxvi ff.

229. Collection 12 of the Ballerinis, whose description was based on Vat. lat. 1340 (PL 54.561ff.); see also Schwartz, ACO 2.4 p. xxxii ff. and Chavasse, 'Les lettres du pape Léon' 37ff.

230. It is supplemented by the letter of Leo I to Emperor Theodosius II (JK 421) from

quential order of their various sources has been preserved. Here the editor used, in addition to the items already in the Vat. Ottoboniani lat. 93 and other texts from the *Quesnelliana,* mainly from the codices of the *Collectio Grimanica* and its derivative, the *Collectio Bobbiensis* (Milan, Bibl. Ambrosiana C.238 inf.).[231]

Another different collection of Leo the Great's letters, which lies between the Cluny version and the C-version of the Pseudo-Isidorian material, has been preserved by a manuscript in Grenoble, Bibl. municipale 473 (twelfth century), which came from Grande-Chartreuse.[232] This codex, representative of a Cluny version edited in the eleventh century, contains seventy-three letters, written by Leo or sent to him, and five chapters concerning the anti-Pelagian struggle.[233] The letters and decretals in this version that are not among the fifty-six letters of the Cluny manuscript occur again, mostly in the same sequence, in the manuscripts of Class C.[234] The compiler tried, with reasonable success, to order his letters according to recipients or (in the case of the decretals) according to the region to which they were sent. The additional letters were inserted into the core of fifty-six letters, in small groups of two or three, without removing the distinction between regular letters and decretals. The collection had a great impact. In the twelfth century this collection, like the collection of Leonine letters in the Cluny version, was added to many manuscripts of Leo the Great's sermons, especially those originating in Cistercian houses. Jakob Merlin included it in his first edition of Pseudo-Isidore in 1524.[235]

---

the *Collectio Grimanica* or the *Collectio Bobbiensis* which derives from it. The combination of JK 405 (Ep. 7) and the rescript of Flavian (Ep. 22) occurs, while letter 22 appears in its uninterpolated form.

231. A manuscript similar to the *Collectio Bobbiensis* was used for the letters of Leo nos. 41–43 and 59–68 of the C-version; from letter 80 through 102 the compilation is exclusively reliant on the *Collectio Grimanica.* In addition, the use of some Gallican collections similar to the *Collectio Corbeiensis* or the Pithou collection is probable, cf. Schwartz, ACO 2.4 p. xxxv.

232. Cf. P. Fournier, 'Une forme particulière des Fausses Décrétales d'après un manuscrit de la Grande-Chartreuse', BEC 49 (1888) 325ff., especially 339ff. and Williams, *Codices Pseudo-Isidoriani* 23 no. 20.

233. Cf. the survey in Chavasse, 'Les lettres du pape Léon' 34 who omits two letters: (1) the letter of Peter of Ravenna to Eutyches (no. 6 in the manuscript), in the shortened version found in the *Hispana* (ACO 2.3.1 p. 6); (2) between nos. 47 and 48 the synodal letter of the Council of Milan (451) is inserted (Ep. 97). A statement in the description of the collection needs to be corrected (p. 35–36): c.9–13 from JK 410, which are missing in the *Hispana,* have been added to JK † 551 on the 'chorepiscopi', which is characteristic of the Pseudo-Isidorian class C.

234. It is remarkable that the last portion of the letter collection of Leo I in the C manuscripts (nos. 80–102) has not left a trace in the collection of the Grenoble manuscript. Probably the compiler did not know about it.

235. Cf. the descriptions of Chavasse, *Sancti Leonis Magni Tractatus* ciii ff. Paris, Bibl. de

4. The Reception of Pope Leo I's Letters

The reception of Pope Leo I's letters and decretals into the pre-Gratian canonical collections has yet to be examined. Consequently, we shall give only a rough, provisional and somewhat statistical analysis, which is based on the examination of collections that have already been used to evaluate the later impact of Pope Leo's predecessors' letters.[236] From the more than one hundred letters written by Pope Leo in response to the Eutychian controversy, excerpts from merely sixteen letters were included in canonical collections, where they were usually completely isolated, or at most, had a limited influence.[237]

Leo's seventeen decretals had a much broader appeal. Except for JK 399 and 405 (Epistolae 2 and 7) they were all excerpted to varying extents in the canonical collections, but without exception the decretals were used more frequently than Leo's letters about dogmatic conflicts.[238] The long decretal to Rusticus of Narbonne (JK 544 Ep. 167) was the most frequently excerpted, appearing in the discussion of sixteen topics (in the *Hispana*, seventeen). This decretal was a series of questions and papal answers concerning problems of church discipline and morals, beginning with the famous canon on 'electio canonica' ('Nulla sinit ratio') and end-

---

l'Assemblée Nationale 27, which Merlin presumably used for his edition, represents a perfect C-version for the letters of Leo, so that the assertion made by Hinschius, *Decretales* lxxii–lxxiii does not apply to this part of the False Decretals.

236. They are: the *Collectio Anselmo dedicata*, Regino of Prüm's *De synodalibus causis*, Burchard's *Decretum*, the *Collection of 74 Titles*, the Collections of Anselm of Lucca and Deusdedit, Bonizo of Sutri's *Liber de vita christiana*, the *Collection of Santa Maria Novella*, the *Collectio Tripartita A*, Ivo of Chartres' *Decretum* and *Panormia*, the *Polycarpus* of Gregory of San Grisogono, and Gratian's *Decretum*.

237. The most frequently used was JK 483 (Ep. 106) addressed to Anatolius of Constantinople with five excerpts, of which two appear only in Ivo's *Decretum* 4.112 and 113 (which form only one chapter in Paris, B.N. lat. 14315) (Ep. 106 c.2 and 4, PL 54.1003B and 1005B) and another only in *Collection of 74 Titles* 116 (Ep. 106 c.6 1006A). The two final chapters passed into Gratian's *Decretum* D.47 c.6 and C.25 q.1 c.3 via the *74 Titles*, Anselm and *Polycarpus*. Secondly, a citation from the conclusion of a letter (whose genuineness is disputed) of Leo I to Theodoret of Cyrrhus JK 496 (Ep. 120), which was preserved in two distinct versions in the canonical collections: 'De his vero quae in—scientiae nomine glorietur' (PL 54.1054B = ACO 2.4 p. 81.19–25): Burchard 2.158, Ivo *Decretum* 6.249, *Polycarpus* 4.35.3, Gratian C.16 q.1 c.19 and 'Specialiter statuentes iubemus ut preter—scientiae nomine glorietur' (PL 54.1054B = ACO 2.4 p. 81.23–25): *74 Titles* 242, Anselm 7.122, Bonizo of Sutri 5.19 and *Polycarpus* 3.22.1. One excerpt stands quite isolated, drawn from JK 473 (Ep. 93), a letter of Leo to the Council of Chalcedon, in Deusdedit 1.116 and the famous letter Ep. 28 from Leo to Flavian is represented in the canonical collections only by one brief citation in Gratian C.24 q.3 c.30.

238. JK 399 was preserved by a series of earlier collections such as the *Quesnelliana* and the enlarged *Dionysiana* (cf. Maassen § 281.2), but it entered the False Decretals only at the end of the eleventh century (class C). JK 405, with its theme 'de Manichaeis', might have been too specialized.

ing with the question concerning how baptized children who had been reared among pagans should be reintegrated into the Christian community.[239] After JK 544, Leo's letter to the Mauritanian bishops (JK 410 Ep. 12) that dealt in detail with the ordination of bishops and other clergy[240] and the decretal to Metropolitan Anastasius of Thessalonika (JK 411 Ep. 14) whose central questions were the church hierarchy and the administration of dioceses and which contains the famous phrase about the papal-episcopal relationship, 'in partem sis vocatus sollicitudinis, non in plenitudinem potestatis', appear most frequently in the collections.[241]

The main sources from which the compilers of the canonical collections drew must have been the *Dionysio-Hadriana* and Pseudo-Isidore, and thus, indirectly, the *Hispana* and the *Quesnelliana*. But only a meticulous examination of the texts of each excerpt could provide evidence whether they were taken from these collections or whether another canonical collection was consulted. Burchard of Worms, for example, used the *Collectio Anselmo dedicata* or Regino of Prüm's *Libri duo de synodalibus causis* when he gathered together his numerous letters of Leo.[242] Ivo of Chartres and Gratian used more of Leo's letters than any other canonist. Gratian included more than eighty excerpts.[243] One can trace his use of Leo's letters to fifty-one chapters in the *Collectio Tripartita*. After incorporating Leo's decretals based on Pseudo-Isidorean material (*Tripartita* 1.43.4–41) into his collection, Ivo of Chartres then added ten more decretal excerpts (*Tripartita* 1.43.42–51). In both of these series of Leo's letters, their order in the original collection can be clearly seen.[244]

239. They were preserved almost completely by the *Collectio Anselmo dedicata*, cf. Besse, *Histoire des Textes* 84. They were preserved to a great extent by Burchard, cf. Hoffmann and Pokorny, *Burchard von Worms* 268; the *Collectio Tripartia* 1.43.8–20 and 46–47; Ivo's *Decretum* 1.236.238; 5.65; 6.67.68.202; 7.19–21; 8.139; 11.62; 13.25; 14.60; 15.80.107.135; (weaker in the *Panormia* 1.91.94; 3.106.182; 5.118; 6.35) and Gratian cf. Friedberg xxvii and also in Italian collections such as Anselm 2.76; 6.65.185; 11.12.26.89.121.123.129; the *Collection of Santa Maria Novella*, cf. Motta, *Liber Canonum* 344 or the *Polycarpus*, cf. Horst, *Polycarpus* 221 nos. 1244–1256.

240. On the various states of the texts in the individual collections, which were altered yet again in the False Decretals, cf. Maassen, 'Pseudoisidor-Studien' 2.845ff.

241. Cf. A. Marchetto, 'In partem sollicitudinis . . . non in plenitudinem potestatis: Evoluzione di una formula di rapporto Primato-Episcopato', *Studia in honorem eminentissimi Cardinalis Alphonsi M. Stickler* (Studia et Textus Historiae Iuris Canonici 7; Rome 1992) 269ff., where the older literature is given in 281 n. 68, and also R. Benson, 'Plenitudo potestatis: Evolution of a formula from Gregory IV to Gratian', SG 14 (1968) 195ff. Zechiel-Eckes, *Cresconius* 101ff. has stressed the great importance of this decretal in the later phase of the Controversy of the Three Chapters.

242. Cf. the list of sources in Hoffmann and Pokorny, *Burchard von Worms* 173ff.

243. Gratian included 26 letters of Leo in the *Decretum*. Half of them are decretals, which constitute three-fourths of the chapters; see Friedberg xxvii.

244. The order of Leo's letters in the *Collectio Tripartita* 1.43.1–41 corresponds by and

III. From Simplicius to Gregory I (468–604):
Transmission and Reception

After the pontificate of Leo the Great, the transmission of papal letters changed considerably. The great age of the pontificates of Siricius, Celestine, Innocent I, and Leo I, which produced influential decretals and instructional letters with wide circulation, was over. During the next 150 years, which is the focus of this section, only Gelasius' *Generale decretum* of 494 can be compared to them.[245] One reason for this change may lie in the compilation of Italian, mostly Roman, canonical collections like the *Collectio Frisingensis* and the *Quesnelliana* at the end of the fifth century, and the *Collectio Vaticana*, the *Collectio Sanblasiana (Italica)*, and the *Collectio Ingilramni*, in the first third of the sixth century.[246] When the canonists ceased compiling collections, avenues for the transmission of papal directives and letters were closed. Special collections, which frequently came into being in the wake of the struggle to establish the validity of the Council of Chalcedon, moved in to fill their place. Their authors were more interested in answering dogmatic questions or in documenting the ecclesiastical politics of a specific pope than in assembling a collection of the sources to be consulted about church discipline or teachings. Their propagandistic interests were more important to them than was canonical norms.[247] The most important sources of the papal letters of the late fifth and sixth centuries were collections like the Verona manuscript

---

large to the sequence in Pseudo-Isidore, see Hinschius, *Decretales* xxvii nos. 45–55. *Collectio Tripartita* 1.43.34 and 35 is taken from JK 410 (Ep. 12) c.1–4; *Collectio Tripartita* 1.43.36 from the decretal of Leo I to Dioscoros of Alexandria, JK 406 (Ep. 9) c.1 and c.37 of the *Tripartita* is another excerpt from JK 410 c.9–10. The combination of the two letters of Leo is a characteristic of the long version of Pseudo-Isidore in some A 1 manuscripts, cf. Hinschius, *Decretales* xxvii–xxviii, no. 51 and cii–ciii, as well as the literature cited above in n. 155. The manuscript, Rouen, Bibl. Municipale E 27 (707), mentioned by Hinschius and Maassen, 'Pseudoisidor-Studien' 2.848 as a representative of this version should be removed from the list, since it does not have the insert from JK 406. Vat. lat. 630 presents the text in the form of the *Hispana*. In the oldest representative of the Cluny version, New Haven, Yale U., Beinecke Libr. 442, fol. 171r, the text from JK 406 is obliterated by JK 410. In the *Collectio Tripartita* 1.43.42–51 more excerpts are presented from JK 402, 414, 416, 544, 411, 410, 543, and 406 (Epp. 4, 16, 18, 167, 14, 12, 166, and 9).

245. See the survey in Maassen, *Geschichte* § 275ff. The decretal of Siricius, JK 255, is found in fifteen collections; JK 258 in eleven; JK 286 of Innocent I to Victricius of Rouen in sixteen, JK 293 to Exsuperius of Toulouse in fifteen, JK 303 to the bishops of Macedonia in fourteen, JK 311 to Decentius of Gubbio in eleven collections. Celestine's letters JK 369 and 371 or Leo's decretals JK 402, 405, 410–412, 414 also occur frequently in later collections. Maassen could find ten collections with the decretal of Gelasius JK 636 and nine with Symmachus' letter to Caesarius of Arles (JK 764) (Maassen, *Geschichte* § 285.12 and § 287.7).

246. On the name, *Collectio Italica*, see above n. 215.

247. Cf. Schwartz, *Publizistische Sammlungen* 262ff. and Silva-Tarouca, 'Beiträge' 691–692.

(Verona, Biblioteca Capitolare XXII [20]), the Berlin manuscript (Berlin, Staatsbibliothek 79 [Phill.1776]), the *Collectio Avellana*, which collected rare and unusual texts, and the *Liber auctoritatum* of the Church of Arles, which served a different purpose.[248]

Something else also contributed. The extensive decretal production of the popes from Siricius through Leo I had provided an 'official' position on essentially all areas of church life and discipline, and there was no reason for constant reformulation. Gelasius summarized the state of affairs at the end of the century in twenty-eight chapters in his above-mentioned decretal *Necessaria rerum dispositione* (JK 636). He began with a call for flexibility and a plea for adapting the laws to the contemporary circumstances (c.1 f.). He continued by treating ordinations and the duties of clerics (c.3 ff.), suitable dates for baptism, marital problems, virgins and widows, and church expenses (c.27). It is probably because of this legal compendium that the decretal became well known and was entered into a few collections under the title *Generale decretum*.[249]

One might think, that in comparison to the previous period in which papal decretals flourished, that this situation must have hindered the reception of these fifth- and sixth-century papal letters into canonical collections until the time of Gratian. The reception of papal letters did diminish, and, to use Burchard of Worms as an example, his choice of letters was then limited by his sources.

After Burchard, the picture totally changes. The collections of the Gregorian reform (74 *Titles*, Anselm of Lucca, Deusdedit, etc.), the works of Ivo of Chartres, and Gratian's *Decretum* included fifth- and six-century papal letters containing canonical materials. Texts that had formerly been ignored by the Church were made into useful instruments for canon law.[250] Excerpts from papal registers like those supplied by the *Collectio*

248. The collections in Verona, Bibl. Cap. XXII (20) and Berlin, Staatsbibl. 79 (Phill.1776) have been edited by Schwartz, *Publizistische Sammlungen* 1ff. and 59ff.; the editions of the other collections are mentioned above n. 11.

249. Thus in the *Dionysiana* and *Hadriana*, cf. Wurm, *Studien* 152ff., where the protocol and the chapter numbers varying between 21 *(Collectio Frisingensis)* and 30 *(Hispana)*—the *Dionysiana* has 28—are analyzed. According to the oldest version found in the *Frisingensis* and the *Quesnelliana*, JK 636 was issued by a synod of 67 bishops, where it is likely that other important writings of Leo the Great were read, cf. Wurm, *Studien* 214–215. Other interpretations of this important letter are given by J. Gaudemet, 'Histoire d'un texte. Les chapitres 4 et 27 de la décrétale du Pape Gélase du 11 mars 494', *Mélanges H.-C. Puech* (Paris 1974) 289ff. (repr. in his selected studies, *La société ecclésiastique dans l'Occident médiéval* [London 1980] no. XIV), who discusses the historical situation and the textual and canonical tradition of both chapters on the consecration of churches; see also Ullmann, *Gelasius* 228ff.

250. P. Landau has stressed this point in 'Wandel und Kontinuität im kanonischen Recht bei Gratian', *Sozialer Wandel im Mittelalter: Wahrnehmungsformen, Erklärungsmuster, Regelungsmechanismen*, ed. J. Miethke and K. Schreiner (Sigmaringen 1994) 221ff.

Britannica (London, British Library Add. 8873), or collections of papal letters arranged chronologically according to pontificates like those contained in Ivo of Chartre's *Collectio Tripartita A* and the collection of Vat. lat. 3829, became important sources of papal letters for canonistic literature at the end of the eleventh century and in the first half of the twelfth century. This is especially true for the letters of Pope Gelasius and Pope Pelagius I (556–561), but also for the writings of later popes like Leo IV (847–855) and Nicholas I (858–867), whose letters gained a permanent place in church law.[251] A look at the Friedberg source index of Gratian's *Decretum* suffices to explain to what extent the excerpts from the letters of Pope Gelasius and Pope Pelagius I were valued as normative legal texts.[252] The relationship of the transmission and reception of decretals that have been sketched here, will now be examined through the use of individual examples.

1. Simplicius (468–483), Felix III (483–492), Gelasius (492–496)

The most extensive compilation of the letters of Pope Simplicius and Pope Felix III is preserved in the ninth-century manuscript, Berlin, Staatsbibliothek 79 (Phill. 1776) from Verdun.[253] The collection includes a total of fifty-nine pieces, mostly concerned with the Monophysite controversies. Pope Simplicius' thirteen letters are numbered 6 through 18; all of these letters, except for the last letter JK 589 to Acacius of Constantinople (†489), are found in the *Avellana*.[254] The collection of the Berlin manuscript and the *Avellana* used the same source (today lost), as can be seen from a whole series of common errors; the Berlin manuscript preserved the original order of the source.[255] The author of the *Collectio Berolinensis* also used thirteen letters of Pope Felix III (no. 20–23, 25–31, 33, 34) taken from this

251. Cf. Perels, 'Die Briefe Papst Nikolaus' I.', NA 39 (1914) 73ff. and Landau, 'Wandel' 221, who regards this reception as one of the 'most important accomplishments of canonical jurisprudence between 1080 and 1140'.

252. Cf. Friedberg xxvii f. no. 46 Gelasius and no. 54 Pelagius I, to which no. 57 Pelagius II should be added, since the letters ascribed to him all belong to Pelagius I. The frequency of reception becomes clearer when compared to Burchard of Worms' sources for the *Decretum,* cf. Hoffman and Pokorny, *Burchard von Worms* 252–253, giving sixteen citations of JK 636 and 637, while Pelagius I was entirely unknown.

253. Cf. the description of V. Rose, *Die lateinischen Meerman Handschriften des Sir Thomas Phillipps in der Königlichen Bibliothek zu Berlin* (Berlin 1892) 149ff., Günther, *Avellana-Studien* 28ff., and Schwartz, *Publizistische Sammlungen* 280ff. Maassen, *Geschichte* 764–765 only alluded to the collection, since the manuscript was unknown to him.

254. JK 578–582, 584, 587, 586, 573, 575, 572, 574, correspond to letters 61–66, 68, 69, 56–59 of the *Avellana.*

255. Thus Schwartz, *Publizistiche Sammlungen* 283. Among the common errors, the letter of Anastasius, JK 746, is attributed to Pope Gelasius; Günther, *Collectio Avellana* lvi–lvii and *Avellana-Studien* 35ff. gives further examples of errors.

lost source.[256] Only the synodal letter from the Roman Council of 485 to the priests and archimandrites of Constantinople and Bithynia (JK 604a) was included in the *Avellana* which omitted the remaining letters of Felix in favor of the forged letters to Patriarch Petrus Fullo of Antioch († 488). These letters are found in the Berlin manuscript at the end of the collection, probably in agreement with its source.[257] The next two texts, nos. 35 and 36, Pope Gelasius' tract about the two natures of Christ and the *Tomus Leonis* to Flavian of Constantinople, separate the Simplicius' and Felix's letters from the series of Gelasius' letters. These letters, which this manuscript shares to a great extent with the *Avellana*, are mostly addressed to the bishops of Dardania. Next there are two letters from Pope Symmachus (JK 763) and Hormisdas (JK 800) also addressed to Dardania and the East.[258] Following these, the compiler of the Berlin manuscript placed supplementary material drawn from an expanded version of the *Collectio Veronensis* (Verona, Biblioteca Capitolare XXII [20]), which will be discussed below. From common corruptions one can identify the origins of Simplicius' letter JK 589 (no. 18 in the Berlin manuscript), Acacius' letter *Sollicitudinem omnium ecclesiarum* (no. 19), and Felix's letter JK 599 (no. 24) from the *Collectio Veronensis*. The same source can be assumed for Gelasius' *Tomus de anathematis vinculo* (JK 701, no. 42), for Tract 2 (no. 43) falsely ascribed to him, and for his letter to Patriarch Euphemius of Constantinople (JK 620, no. 45) because the *Avellana* offers no tradition for these texts. Probably they are missing in the source common to the *Berolinensis* and the *Avellana*, whose origin Eduard Schwartz places in the year 518 and which was a product of the realignment of papal oriental policy.[259]

A second, similarly structured but less extensive collection of eleven letters of the three popes is preserved in the *Collectio Veronensis* (Verona,

---

256. JK 591, 592, 595, 593, 617, 600, 604a, 602, 608, 614, 615, 601, and 612. In addition there are the so-called *Gesta de nomine Acacii* (Berlin, Staatsbibl. Phill. 1776, no. 32) from the time of Felix III in a form shortened from *Avellana* Nr. 99 ed. Günther, *Collectio Avellana* 440ff., cf. idem, *Avellana-Studien* 110ff. and H. Koch, *Gelasius im kirchenpolitischen Dienste seiner Vorgänger, der Päpste Simplicius (468–483) und Felix III. (483–492)* (SB München Heft 6; Munich 1935) 66–67. Nos. 18–24 of the *Berolinensis* reappear in the same sequence in the collection of the Vatican manuscript nos. 72–81 and the expanded *Dionysiana* nos. 126–132; cf. on that Chavasse, 'Supplément de la Dionysiana' 158, 167–168. The *Hispana* took the letter of Acacius *Sollicitudinem omnium ecclesiarum*, and JK 599 of Felix III from the *Vaticana*, cf. Maassen, *Geschichte* 521; both of them found a place in the Pseudo-Isidorian Decretals.

257. Cf. Schwartz, *Publizistische Sammlungen* 284–285.

258. Cf. the edition and survey by Schwartz, *Publizistische Sammlungen* 106ff. and the commentary 284ff. The letters of the *Avellana* 101, 79, 95, 104, 140 correspond to the letters of Gelasius, JK 638 (no. 38 of the Berlin manuscript), 623 (no. 39), 664 (no. 41), to the letter of Symmachus JK 763 (no. 47) and to the letter of Hormisdas JK 800 (no. 48).

259. Schwartz, *Publizistische Sammlungen* 286–287.

Biblioteca Capitolare XXII [20], fol. 83ff.).[260] The first part of this manuscript (fol. 1 ff.) contains the oldest fragment of the *Liber pontificalis*, the *Fragmentum Laurentianum*, and Jerome's *De viris illustribus* in Gennadius' revised version.[261] The papal letter collection of the *Collectio Veronensis* is also found in the *Collectio Frisingensis* no. XLIII–LIII and directly connected to Gelasius' decretal *Necessaria rerum* (JK 636) and in the *Quesnelliana* as no. XLII–LI.[262] The compiler of the *Collectio Veronensis* opposed making any concessions to settle the dogmatic struggle with the Eastern Church, disagreeing with the position of Pope Anastasius II (496–498), Gelasius' successor. The collection probably originated at about the time of his death, at about the same time as the *Frisingensis* and the *Quesnelliana*.[263] It must have been circulated to some extent since it appears in three canonical collections at about the same time. The original version of this material is in the *Quesnelliana*, the most extensive, in the *Collectio Veronensis*.[264]

The collections of the manuscript from Berlin and Verona must have had little, if any direct influence on the wider distribution of Simplicius' and Felix III's letters, and their reception into the canon.[265] The tradition

260. They are: Simplicius, JK 589, Felix III, JK 599, Gelasius, JK 701, 622, 632, 664, 665, 611, 620, 628, 624, as well as a shortened version of the *Gesta de nomine Acacii* under the misleading title of *Narrationis ordo de pravitate Dioscori Alexandrini*, cf. Maassen, *Geschichte* § 516 p. 397–398.

261. Following the *Vita* of Symmachus, his successors' names and dates of office through Vigilius (537–555) are entered. Since Vigilius' day and hour of death are given, it must have been written shortly after his death; on the manuscript, cf. the literature given by Schieffer, ACO 4.3.1, p. 67, on its historical context, idem, 'Dreikapitel-Schisma' 176ff. and n. 179 above. On the *Fragmentum Laurentianum* cf. Duchesne, *Liber Pontificalis* 1.xxx ff., the text 43ff. as well as Wirbelauer, *Zwei Päpste in Rom* 145ff.

262. Cf. Maassen, *Geschichte* 486 and 498, Scharnagl, 'Die kanonistische Sammlung der Handschrift von Freising' 140–141. The capitulatio XLIII–LI of the *Quesnelliana* has been edited by Schwartz, *Publizistische Sammlungen* 262–263.

263. Thus Schwartz, *Publizistische Sammlungen* 274.

264. The final four pieces of the *Veronensis*, Gelasius, JK 611, 620, 628, and 624, are missing in the *Quesnelliana*. The *Collectio Frisingensis* has Gelasius' letter to Euphemius (JK 620), which is also missing in the *Quesnelliana*. It also supplements the beginning of the collection with the letter of Pope Simplicius to Emperor Zeno (JK 588).

265. See n. 256 above, where the transmission of Simplicius JK 589 and of the letters of Felix III JK 591, 592, 595, 593, and 599 from the *Collectio Berolinensis* into the *Collectio Vaticana*, *Dionysiana aucta* and the *Hispana* is discussed. Most collections include the letters of Simplicius preserved in the *Dionysio-Hadriana* JK 570 and 583. Anselm of Lucca 4.11 includes the letter of the Pope Felix to the Emperor Zeno (JK 601) which is, according to Maassen, *Geschichte* § 284.7 and Schwartz, *Publizistische Sammlungen* 81, preserved only in the Berlin manuscript. This canon was transmitted from Anselm through *Polycarpus* 1.20.1 to Gratian D.10 c.3. An interesting example of how these texts developed can be seen from Simplicius' letters in the Pseudo-Isidorian Decretals. There the long versions A1, A/B and B have JK 590 and the letter of Acacius, *Sollicitudinem omnium ecclesiarum*, (Maassen, *Geschichte* § 449) from the *Hispana*. The Cluny version, New Haven, Yale U., Beinecke Libr. 442, added the two letters of Simplicius from the *Dionysio-Hadriana*, JK 570 and 583, and, to save room, the

of Gelasius' letters is totally different. Pseudo-Isidore took his letters from two collections. Together with the Pseudo-Gelasian *Decretum de libris recipiendis et non recipiendis* (JK † 700), the *Quesnelliana* provided JK 622, 632, 664, and 665. The *Hispana* provided the *Decretum generale* (JK 636) and Gelasius' letter to the Sicilian bishops (JK 637) to the forgers. In the same way Pseudo-Isidore enriched his group of Leonine letters from the *Hispana* with fifteen more of Leo's letters from the *Quesnelliana*.[266] In version C of the False Decretals the four letters of Gelasius from the *Quesnelliana* are preceded by his *Tomus de anathematis vinculo* (JK 701) and are followed by his letter to Patriarch Euphemius of Constantinople (JK 620). This order reproduces exactly the sequence of letters in the *Collectio Veronensis* as it appears in the *Collectio Frisingensis*. Whether this sequence has occurred by coincidence or is the result of the textual tradition remains unanswered.[267]

Until the end of the eleventh century, only some excerpts of JK 636 were included in the canonical tradition.[268] Anselm of Lucca (1081–1086), Deusdedit (1083–1087) and Ivo of Chartres (1091–1096) drew upon extensive collections of material of the type found in the *Collectio Britannica* (London, British Library Add. 8873, c.1090) for papal letters.[269] *Britannica*, fol. 9ff., contains important canonical texts from sixty-seven Gelasian letters taken from the papal registers, perhaps directly, although that is not certain.[270] One may see how later canonists used this collection of material for their own purposes in the fifty-eight excerpts from Gelasius' let-

---

letter of Acacius was moved to the margin. The later C-version of Pseudo-Isidore accepted this order of texts, together with the addition of the widely circulated letter of Simplicius to Acacius, JK 589. A similar reworking of the text, using the *Dionysio-Hadriana*, can be found in the synodal letter of Felix III (JK 604a) within the Cluny version, cf. Schon, 'Redaktion' 502.

266. Cf. Fuhrmann, *Einfluß und Verbreitung* 1.188 n. 15; von Dobschütz, *Decretum Gelasianum* 186–187 deals with the position of the *Decretum de libris recipiendis*.

267. The order of the letters of Gelasius up to the *Decretum Gelasianum* (JK † 700) in the papal history of Pseudo-Liudprand, written about 1084, is remarkable and an indication for the existence of an early form of version C of Pseudo-Isidore in the eleventh century; cf. on this Jasper, 'Decreta vel gesta' 94–95.

268. Cf. the index of sources for Burchard of Worms in Hoffmann and Pokorny, *Burchard von Worms* 252, where fourteen chapters are listed as excerpts from the *Decretum generale* and one from JK 637.

269. Cf. P. Fournier, 'Un tournant de l'histoire du droit 1060–1140', RHD 41 (1917) 143ff. (repr. *Mélanges* 2.387ff.) and Landau, 'Wandel' 221ff. The *Collectio Britannica* was thoroughly described and analyzed by P. Ewald, 'Die Papstbriefe' 277ff., 505ff., also cf. R. Somerville, 'The Letters of Pope Urban II in the *Collectio Britannica*', *Proceedings Cambridge* (MIC Subsidia 8; Vatican City 1988) 105ff., M. Brett, 'Urban II and the Collections attributed to Ivo of Chartres', *Proceedings San Diego* (MIC Subsidia 9; Vatican City 1992) 34ff. See now R. Somerville, *Pope Urban II, The Collectio Britannica, and the Council of Melfi (1089)*, with the collaboration of S. Kuttner (Oxford 1996) 3ff.

270. Cf. Hageneder, 'Papstregister' 325–326 with further literature.

ters in the *Collectio Tripartita* 1.46. The sequence of the first twenty excerpts shows that they came from Pseudo-Isidore,[271] while chapters 24 to 58 are taken selectively from the Gelasian excerpts of *Britannica* no. 15–65 preserving, however, the original order.[272] Through the *Tripartita*, either directly or through Ivo of Chartres' other legal works, a great number of Gelasian texts reached Gratian's *Decretum* where they were arranged correctly and systematically.[273]

The text that was the most frequently copied and the most widely circulated was the *Decretum de libris recipiendis et non recipiendis*, usually ascribed to Gelasius. This text was an Index of Permitted (chapter 4) and Forbidden (chapter 5) Books. The Pseudo-Gelasian Index was included in almost every canonical collection and appears frequently in patristic, liturgical, and literary-historical manuscripts. It is preserved in hundreds of manuscripts and attained normative status through its inclusion in Gratian's *Decretum* (D.15 c.3).[274]

2. Papal Letters of the Sixth Century: Transmission and Reception into the Canon

Fourteen popes preceded Pope Gregory the Great in the sixth century. Among these popes, Pelagius I's (556–561) correspondence was the most extensively received into the canonical tradition.[275] Pelagius was not a particularly exceptional personality but attained his prominent position in the history of canon law through an accident of the transmission. A considerable part of the register from the last years of Pelagius' reign was included in collections of canonical materials made in the second half of the eleventh century.[276] The compilers of Gregorian reform collections and Ivo of Chartres used these collections.[277] The *Collectio Britannica*, c.

271. *Collectio Tripartita* 1.46.1 = JK † 700; c.2 = JK 622; c.3 = JK 664; cc.4–10 = JK 636 (c.1, 2, 5, 10, 11, 16); c.11 = JK 637 c.2; cc.12–19 =JK 636 (c.2–3, 7, 12–14, 19, 20, 27); c.20 = JK 637 c.1; c.21 = JK 693 is a false attribution: it is c.10 of the Roman Council of 875 (cf. the edition by Maassen, SB Wien 91; Vienna 1878, 786), which was attributed to Gelasius since Burchard 11.47: *74 Titles* 323, Anselm 12.28, Deusdedit 4.391, *183 Titles* 88.13f., Polycarpus 7.1.5, *Collectio Tripartita* 1.46.21, Ivo, *Decretum* 14.111, Ivo, *Panormia* 5.136, Gratian C.11 q.3 c.37.

272. See the explanation in Ewald, 'Die Papstbriefe' 594.

273. Cf. Landau, 'Wandel' 223 and the survey of the Gelasius texts from the *Britannica* in the *Decretum* (loc. cit. 230–231).

274. See the literature in n. 82, above.

275. Cf. Caspar, *Papsttum* 2.286ff. and J. Richards, *The Popes and the Papacy in the Early Middle Ages 476–752* (London 1979) 156ff.

276. Cf. Caspar, *Papsttum* 2.303–304. The excerpts permit a glimpse into the daily business of papal government, which includes important political events and commonplaces such as an order to mow a meadow within a week so that weeds do not spread (JK 1034, Ep. 76 Gassó and Batlle, *Pelagii I epistulae* 191).

277. Cf. the introduction to the edition of the letters of Pelagius by Gassó and Batlle, op. cit. xxxix–xl, xlix ff.

1090, is such a collection. There, on folia 21–38, items numbered LXIIII–CXXXIII, are seventy-two excerpts from Pelagius' letters written between August 558 and April 559, mostly in the correct chronological order. They appear to have been dictated rather than copied: there are a few errors typical of mishearing a spoken text.[278] The *Collectio Tripartita* 1.54 is very close to the *Britannica* because its author retained the order of the letters in the *Britannica* in the selections he used.[279] Ivo of Chartres went back to both collections in his *Decretum* and incorporated a whole series of Pelagius' letters in his collection which could have come only from the *Britannica*.[280] These three collections and the *Collection in Ten Parts,* which is dependent on Ivo (Florence, Biblioteca Nazionale Centrale, Conventi soppressi D.2.1476 et al.),[281] represent the eleventh-century French transmission of Pelagius' letters.

The Italian collections are distinguished by the use of other letters of Pelagius not in the French collections and by many textual deviations in those letters shared with the French tradition. Deusdedit's canonical collection and the collection in Vat. lat. 3829, which is a combination of the *Liber Pontificalis* and papal letters, strongly influenced by Deusdedit, form a subgroup of this Italian tradition.[282] Anselm of Lucca's *Collectio canonum,* Bonizo of Sutri's *Liber de vita christiana,* and Gregory of San Grisogono's *Polycarpus* (post-IIII), to name the most well known, form another subgroup. The *Collectio Caesaraugustana* and the appendix to the *Collection in 74 Titles* in Vienna, Österreichische Nationalbibliothek 2153 (early twelfth century), fol. 49v–56r cannot be assigned to either of these subgroups.[283] Both branches of the tradition were used in Gratian's *De-*

278. See the literature on the collection mentioned in n. 269, above; on the letters of Pelagius, Ewald, 'Die Papstbriefe' 533ff. and Gassó and Batlle, op. cit. xxxiff. and lxxiv with n. 3.

279. Cf. the survey in Ewald, 'Die Papstbriefe' 594–595, P. Fournier, 'Les collections canoniques attribués à Yves de Chartres' 657 (repr. *Mélanges* 1.463) and Gassó and Batlle xli–xlii. The *Tripartita* used a version of the *Britannica* that was older than that presently found in London, B.L. Add. 8873, which also might have been missing the registers of Alexander II (1061–1073) and those of the first years of Urban II (1088–1089), cf. Brett, 'Urban II' 33ff. and Somerville, *Pope Urban II* 15–16.

280. Corresponding to Ivo, *Decretum* 7.125–126 = *Britannica,* Pelagius nos. 33 and 36 (in the enumeration of Ewald); 7.148 = no. 49; 8.55 = no.51; 8.67 = no. 59. Concerning the use of *Collectio Tripartita* A in Ivo's *Decretum,* cf. Fournier, 'Collections canoniques' 35ff. (repr. *Mélanges* 1.514ff.).

281. Cf. Fournier-Le Bras, *Histoire* 2.299ff.

282. According to Gassó and Batlle's painstaking examination (p. xxxix–xl), only the following excerpts from the letters of Pelagius are cited by Deusdedit: 3.123 = Ep. 88; 3.128–132 = Epp. 86, 89, 83, 12, 13; 3.135 = Ep. 62. On the collection of Vat. lat. 3829 cf. Fournier-Le Bras, *Histoire* 2.210ff. and H. Fuhrmann, 'Ein Papst Ideo (zu Collectio Lipsiensis, tit. 27,5)', *Études Le Bras* 1.90ff.

283. Cf. Gassó and Batlle, *Pelagii I epistulae* xlvi ff. and lxvi ff. The Viennese manuscript is described by Gilchrist, *74 Titles* lviii ff.

cretum; however, whether a particular text came from Anselm, from the *Polycarpus,* or from Ivo's *Panormia* cannot yet be determined.[284] The inclusion of Pelagius' letters in canonistic literature, which led to its inclusion in the polemical writing of the Investiture Conflict, took place in the fifty years between Anselm of Lucca's canonical collection (1081–1086) and Gratian's *Decretum* (1140). Pelagius' letters were totally unknown to compilers of canonical collections before the eleventh century. The Pseudo-Isidorian forgeries of Pelagius II (JK † 1049, † 1050, and † 1051) were noticed only during the reception of Pelagius' letters into the canonical collections, albeit without distinguishing between Pelagius I and Pelagius II.[285]

Besides these Pelagian letters taken from the papal archives, there was in the archives of the Church of Arles a collection of letters that the church had received. Eleven of Pelagius' letters were used in the *Liber auctoritatum Arelatensis ecclesiae,* compiled in the mid-sixth century.[286] This collection was used in the ninth century by Agobard of Lyon († 840), Florus of Lyon († c.860), and Hincmar of Reims († 882).[287] After that, Pelagius and his letters were practically forgotten until the end of the eleventh century, when they were rediscovered. The *Liber auctoritatum* was also an important avenue of transmission for other papal letters of the sixth century. Five of the ten surviving letters of Pope Symmachus (498–514) are found in this collection; similarly, nine letters of Pope Vi-

---

284. An analysis of the precise sources of Gratian's chapters can only be accomplished by a careful comparison of texts, for which there is often no adequate edition available (as with Ivo or *Polycarpus*). On Gratian's use of sources, cf. P. Landau, 'Neue Forschungen zu vorgratianischen Kanonessammlungen und den Quellen des gratianischen Dekrets', *Ius commune* 11 (1984) 15ff. and idem, 'Das Register Papst Gregors I. im Decretum Gratiani', *Mittelalterliche Texte: Überlieferung—Befunde—Deutungen,* ed. R. Schieffer (Schriften der MGH 42; Hannover 1996) 125ff.

285. On the use of the letters of Pelagius in the Investiture Controversy (Anselm of Lucca, Wido of Ferrara, Bernold of Constance, Deusdedit) see Gassó and Batlle, *Pelagii I epistulae* xxiii ff. On the reception of the Pseudo-Isidorian letters of Pelagius II, see the index of citations in Fuhrmann, *Einfluß und Verbreitung* 3.802ff. nos. 127, 171, 273, 369, and 437 on JK † 1049, no. 32 on JK † 1050, and nos. 259 and 352 on JK † 1051. An exception to this transmission from Pseudo-Isidore may be the letter attributed to Pelagius II to the bishops of Germany and Gaul, *Cum in Dei nomine* on 'praefationes' (JK † 1065), which first appears in Burchard 3.69 and then *Collectio Tripartita* 1.54.1, Ivo, *Decretum* 2.77, *Panormia* 1.57 to Gratian, De con. D.1 c.71, cf. Fuhrmann, *Einfluß und Verbreitung* 1.138 n. 6 and Hoffmann and Pokorny, *Burchard von Worms* 97–98.

286. JK 940–945, 948, 947, 946, 939, 938 (Gassó and Batlle, Epp. 1–6, 8–9, 7, 10–11); cf. the introduction to the edition, xxvii ff.

287. Cf. Agobard of Lyon, Ep. 16, ed. E. Dümmler (MGH Epp. 5) 226.36ff., Florus of Lyon, *De expositione missae* c.47, PL 119.46A/B, Hincmar of Reims, *De una et non trina deitate* 2, PL 125.516–517, and Ep. 30.15, PL 126.197. JK 948 (Ep. 8) is quoted by Nicholas I in his letter to Emperor Michael III of Constantinople almost 'in toto' (Ep. 88 Perels, [MGH Epp. 6] 465.17ff.). Some excerpts from the corpus of letters of Pelagius in the *Liber auctoritatum* were received into the Varia 1 B 16 19 of the *Britannica,* cf. Ewald, 'Die Papstbriefe' 574.

gilius (537–555) are in the *Liber*.[288] Another large collection is the *Collectio Avellana*, in whose second section (no. 105–244) over seventy of Pope Hormisdas' letters have been gathered, most of them having been preserved only in this collection.[289] The *Hispana* contains the letters that Hormisdas wrote to the Spanish bishops.[290]

Individual letters from these popes were circulated more widely in canonical literature than just the collections discussed here. This is especially true for Pope Symmachus' rescript to Caesarius of Arles of November 6, 513 (JK 764) in which the pope answered some of the bishop's questions about church property, clerical ordinations, the abduction of women, nuns, and widows.[291] Symmachus' rescript occurs in most of the Gallican collections, in the *Hispana*, the *Dionysio-Hadriana*, and Pseudo-Isidore. It has been suggested that the Acts of the Roman synods of 499, 501 and 502 were appended to the rescript. There is no direct evidence for this supposition, but the synodal acts and the rescript as found in the collection of the Reims and Diessen manuscripts, and in the Pithou collection, seem to have been derived from a common source.[292] JK 764 was cit-

288. Symmachus JK 753, 754, 764, 765, 769, and Vigilius JK 906, 912–915, 918, 919, 925: they were edited by Gundlach (MGH Epp. 3) 33ff. nos. 23–29, p. 57ff. nos. 38–45. The letters of Vigilius, which are preserved in the acts of the Fifth Ecumenical Council of Constantinople, 553 (JK 922; in Actio VII: JK 920, 921, 927, 924–926 in the 'Versio longa' of the council, Paris, B.N. lat. 16832 from the tenth century), have left no trace in the canonistic literature, cf. the edition by J. Straub, ACO 4.1, p. 11f., 187ff. The *Liber auctoritatum* is lacking the canonistically significant letter of Pope John II to Caesarius of Arles (JK 888 of 534) in which Bishop Contumelius of Riez was deposed and Caesarius was ordered to place him in lifelong house arrest in religious foundation. Appended to the letter are six canons 'de clericis criminosis' derived from the *Dionysiana*, the first evidence of the papacy's use of that collection, cf. Maassen, *Geschichte* § 291.4 and p. 437, Wurm, *Studien* 44; see also Caspar, *Papsttum* 2.203–204. John II's two other letters to the Gallican bishops (JK 886) and to the clergy of Riez (JK 887) about this matter are in the collection of Arles. JK 888, which Caesarius circulated in his own metropolitan district with his own appendix, was included in the *Collectiones Corbeiensis, Coloniensis,* and *Laureshamensis,* all three originating in southern Gaul.

289. They are edited by Günther, *Epistulae imperatorum pontificum* (CSEL 35.2).

290. JK 828, 786–788, 855, 856. In addition, Hormisdas' letter to Emperor Justin I (JK 857), Justin's answer, the confession of Patriarch John II of Constantinople (Maassen, *Geschichte* § 460), and the pope's letter to Patriarch Epiphanius of Constantinople (JK 861), which were also preserved in the *Avellana* and included in Pseudo-Isidore. Martínez Díez, *Hispana* 1.297, 301ff. sees the letters of Hormisdas as part of an older collection of decretals that was compiled during his pontificate, probably in Andalusia. This collection was later enlarged with additional material and became the source of the *Epitome Hispana* and the *Hispana*.

291. *Epistolae Arelatenses* 26 (MGH Epp. 3.37ff.); on its textual tradition see Maassen, *Geschichte* § 287.7, who omits the *Collectio Remensis* (Berlin, Staatsbibl. Phill. 1743). See Wurm, *Studien* 162 and Wirbelauer, *Zwei Päpste in Rom* 119–120.

292. Cf. L. Duchesne, *L'Église au VIème siècle* (Paris 1925) 113; Wurm, *Studien* 163–164 disagrees. Wirbelauer, *Zwei Päpste in Rom* 119–120 inclines to Duchesne's view.

ed in all of the important canonical collections from Regino to Gratian, as were the three Symmachian synods of 499 to 501, widely known through the *Dionysio-Hadriana* and Pseudo-Isidore. In contrast, only a rather modest number of genuine Pseudo-Isidorian texts from Symmachus' pontificate were included in canonical collections.[293]

Perhaps Pseudo-Isidore was the vehicle through which Pope Hormisdas' decretal to the Spanish bishops (JK 787) arrived in the canonical collections of the tenth and eleventh centuries.[294] This decretal was preserved only in the *Hispana* and in the collection of the Diessen manuscript. It deals with three central questions of church discipline: canonical election, simony, and the command to hold annual councils. Pseudo-Isidore's falsified letter of Pope Vigilius to Bishop Profuturus of Braga (JK 907) may have had a similar textual tradition.[295]

In the mere fourteen years between Pope Hormisdas' death (523) and the beginning of Vigilius' pontificate (537), six popes ruled in Rome, all of whom were later furnished with letters fabricated by the Pseudo-

293. Cf. Fuhrmann, *Einfluß und Verbreitung* 1.188–189, nn.16–19. The so-called Sixth Synod of Symmachus (Hinschius, *Decretales* 679ff.) is most frequently cited in canonical collections: cf. the list in Fuhrmann, *Einfluß und Verbreitung* 3, nos. 234, 348, 416.—The forgeries of Symmachus should be noted. They were written during the dispute between Symmachus and Laurentius (498–507) and were published by Coustant, *Epistolae*, Appendix 27ff. This edition was replaced by Wirbelauer, *Zwei Päpste in Rom* 228ff., who critically edited and translated the texts and reevaluated each one. The core of the work consisted of five forgeries: the *Constitutum Silvestri* (Maassen, *Geschichte* § 539.3), the *Gesta Liberii* (§ 557), the *Gesta de Xysti purgatione* (§ 558), the *Gesta de Polychronii accusatione* (§ 559), and the Synod of Sinuessa (§ 537). There were also additional texts: The view of Symmachus was preserved in a putative letter of the council fathers of Nicaea to Sylvester (Maassen § 538), the letter of Sylvester JK † 174, *Gaudeo promptam* (§ 539.1), and a reworking of the *Constitutum Silvestri*. The Laurentians responded with their own version of the council fathers of Nicaea's letter, Silvester's letter *Gloriosissimus*, JK † 175 (§ 539.2) and the Roman council of 275 bishops (§ 539.4). While Wirbelauer investigated the origin and history of the forgeries, S. Vacca, *Prima sedes a nemine iudicatur: Genesi e sviluppo storico dell'assioma fino al Decreto di Graziano* (Pontificia Universitas Gregoriana. Miscellanea Historiae Pontificiae 61; Rome 1993) dealt thoroughly with the reception of the forgeries; see the review of Wirbelauer in *Gnomon*. Also cf. P. Landau, 'Gefälschtes Recht in den Rechtssammlungen bis Gratian', *Fälschungen im Mittelalter* 2.16ff. and Mordek, 'Primat' 552–553 n. 125.

294. The text was received in Regino of Prüm 1.239, Burchard 1.23, *74 Titles* 124, Anselm of Lucca 6.19, *183 Titles* 18.3 and 7, 27.3, 97.8, Ivo, *Decretum* 5.77, *Polycarpus* 2.1.11, 2.37.5, 3.19.1, and Gratian D.61 c.2 and 3. The seven remaining decretals of Hormisdas in the *Hispana* that were included in Pseudo-Isidore have not received any attention. As with those of Simplicius and Felix III, the Hormisdas' letters were included in the Cluny version (A1) of Pseudo-Isidore, with the addition of the letter of Emperor Justin I to the pope *(Quo fuimus semper)* and the *Exemplar precum* of the people of Jerusalem and Antioch to the emperor, both from the *Dionysio-Hadriana*. In this respect the Cluny version shows the same text as the version C of Pseudo-Isidore, see Hinschius, *Decretales* lxx and Schon, 'Redaktion' 502.

295. Cf. Fuhrmann, *Einfluß und Verbreitung* 1.189 n. 21, on the reception, cf. the list of citations, ibid., 3, nos. 70 and 245.

Isidorian forgers.[296] These letters were without exception received into the pre-Gratian canonical collections. With increasing frequency, the canonists—Anselm of Lucca, Ivo of Chartres *(Decretum),* and finally Gratian—placed them in their collections.[297]

In addition, the later popes John III (560–573) and Pelagius II (578–590) appear only in the Pseudo-Isidorian Forgeries. The forged story that Peter selected Linus and Cletus as his 'adiutores' and not as his 'successores' attributed to John III was frequently quoted even in historical works. Pelagius II also can be found only in three forged letters that are mixed with the letters of Pelagius I.[298]

3. Gregory I (590–604)

We have today more than 850 letters from Gregory the Great, far more than from any of his predecessors or from any successors before the end of the eleventh century. With few exceptions, they are from the pope's register of letters,[299] which was first mentioned as 'registrum' by Ildefonsus of Toledo († 667) in his *De viris illustribus.*[300] The original register has been lost but was still extant at the end of the ninth century. Between 873 and 875 John the Deacon wrote a *Vita* of Pope Gregory I, based

296. John I (523–526) JK † 872 and † 873, Felix IV (526–530) JK † 878 and † 879, Boniface II (530–532) JK † 883, John II (533–535) JK † 889, Agapetus I (535–536) JK † 895, and Silverius (536–537) JK † 899 and † 901.

297. On JK † 872 cf. the index of citations in Fuhrmann, *Einfluß und Verbreitung* 3, no. 281; on JK † 873 no. 95; on JK † 878 no. 191 and 364; on JK † 883 nos. 14 and 265; on JK † 899 no. 141; on JK † 901 nos. 357 and 453.

298. JK † 1042, cf. Fuhrmann, *Einfluß und Verbreitung* 3, index of citations no. 389. An example of Peter's choice is given in the history of Pseudo-Liudprand, PL 129.1152A ff. cf. M. Tangl, 'Forschungen zu Karolinger Diplomen', *Archiv für Urkundenforschung* 2 (1909) 314–315 (repr. *Das Mittelalter in Quellenkunde und Diplomatk* [Berlin 1966] 1.464–465). On Pelagius II, JK † 1049 cf. Fuhrmann, no. 127, 171, 273, 369, and 437; on JK † 1050 no. 32 and for JK † 1051 nos. 259 and 352. See also n. 285, above.

299. Edited by Ewald and Hartmann, MGH Epp. 1 and 2 and by Norberg, CCL 140. For a critical evaluation of the editions, see Pitz, *Papstreskripte* 37f., who complained rightly that the edition of Norberg did not have historical notes as did the edition of the MGH. Norberg's edition is better philologically. The edition of the MGH will be cited; the numbers of the letters in Norberg will be placed in parentheses when they differ from MGH. The following letters were not in Gregory's register: 1.14a (Append.2), 1.24a, 1.39a (Append.1), 4.17a, 5.53a, 5.57a, 6.50a (6.53), 11.56a, 12.16a; for the most part these texts contain the prefaces of Gregory's works.

300. Ed. G. von Działowski, *Isidor und Ildefons als Litterarhistoriker: Eine quellenkritische Untersuchung der Schriften 'De viris illustribus' des Isidor von Sevilla und des Ildefons von Toledo* (Kirchengeschichtliche Studien 4.2; Münster 1898) 132: 'Extant et ipsius ad diversos epistolae plurimae, limato quidem et claro stilo digestae . . . Has itaque uno volumine arctans in libris duodecim distinxit, Registrum nominandum esse decrevit'. This witness enabled the editors of twenty-four editions produced before the Maurist edition of 1705 to divide the fourteen indictions of his pontificate into twelve books, see Ewald, NA 3 (1878) 512ff. and Działowski, op. cit. 133f. n. 7.

largely on the pope's letters. He has given us a clear picture of the register's appearance. He tells us that at the end of his life, Gregory I gave up writing books:

> . . . ab exponendis tamen epistolis, quamdiu vivere potuit, numquam omnino cessavit, quarum videlicet tot libros in scrinio dereliquit, quot annos advixit. Unde quartum-decimum epistolarum librum septimae indictionis imperfectum reliquit, quoniam ad eiusdem indictionis terminum non pertingit. Ex quarum multitudine primi Hadriani papae temporibus quaedem epistolae decretales per singulas indictiones exerptae sunt et in duobus voluminibus, sicut modo cernitur, congregatae.[301]

It is not clear why the fourteen volumes of Gregory the Great's papal register were excerpted during Hadrian I's pontificate. Perhaps it was part of a campaign to preserve the contents of the original that may have deteriorated. Another example of early medieval preservation efforts was Charlemagne's concern to have the *Codex Carolinus* compiled.[302]

Hadrian's selection of 684 letters from Gregory I's original register is known to modern editors as R. It was preserved in a great number of manuscripts from the ninth to the fifteenth centuries, either in one volume or, according to John the Deacon's *Vita,* in two volumes, of which the first part (symbol 'r' in the editions) records Gregory's reign from 590 to August 597 (indictions IX to XV) with 391 letters, and the second (symbol 'ρ', Ewald-Hartmann, symbol 'e', Norberg), September 597 to March 604 (indictions I to VII) with 293 letters.[303] The R collection circulated in West Francia in the ninth century and was quoted in the synods of Meaux-Paris (845–846) and Verberie (853).[304]

---

301. *Vita Gregorii* 4.71, PL 75.223A–B and similarly in the preface, in which the reader was directed to the papal archives for proof of the facts of the *Vita*. There he would turn the pages of 'tot charticios libros epistolarum eiusdem patris (Gregory I) quot annos probatur vixisse' (col. 62C). Peitz also interpreted the passage, *Register Gregors I.* 16ff., Posner, 'Register' 246, Norberg, *Studia critica* 29f. and Pitz, *Papstreskripte* 33f., who understood 'epistolae exponere' not as the writing of letters, but as 'auswählendes Komponieren von Briefen zu einem Corpus'. B. Pferschy-Maleczek, MIÖG 99 (1991) 512 argued that Pitz was perhaps mistaken.

302. See Posner, 'Register' 298.

303. See Ewald, NA 3 (1878) 440ff. with a description of the manuscripts; and the introduction by Hartmann, MGH Epp. 2.viii ff. Also Peitz, *Register Gregors I.* 5ff. and the overview of the collection R, p. 178ff. Peitz' attempt to prove that R was the original Lateran register has been completely rejected by M. Tangl, 'Gregor-Register und Liber Diurnus: Eine Kritik', NA 41 (1919) 741ff., reprinted in his selected studies *Das Mittelalter in Quellenkunde und Diplomatik* (Forschungen zur mittelalterlichen Geschichte 12.2; Berlin 1966) 2.709ff. and Posner, 'Register' 281ff., and adopted by Norberg, *Studia critica* 32f., Lohrmann, *Register Johannes' VIII.* 158 und J. Modesto, *Gregor der Große: Nachfolge Petri und Universalprimat* (Studien zu Theologie und Geschichte 1; St. Ottilien 1989) 90 n. 9.

304. See W. Hartmann, MGH Concilia 3, 97.21, 119.3.5 and 304.25ff. and Tangl, 'Gregor-

There are also two earlier collections of excerpts from the Gregorian register. Scholars have placed their composition in the first half of the eighth century, and the oldest manuscripts come from the end of that century.[305] The C collection contains 200 chronologically ordered letters from the years 598–599 (indiction II, Reg. 9) and is the only source for 146 of Gregory's letters. C occurs only in connection with another collection, P, which, with fifty-four of the pope's letters, is the smallest of the three letter collections. P unites two originally separate collections of Gregory's letters (no. 1–37, no. 38–51, and three additional items), and the oldest P manuscript has preserved the letter that Paul the Deacon sent with the collection from Friuli to Abbot Adalard of Corbie, sometime between 782 and 786.[306] Out of these three manuscript classes Paul Ewald reconstructed the probable appearance of Gregory's register. By and large, his conclusions are still accepted today.

At the beginning of the eighth century the Venerable Bede had the priest Nothelm, later Archbishop of Canterbury († 741), make copies of Gregory I's letters from the papal archives. Bede then included these letters in his *Historia ecclesiastica* 1.27–32. Among these letters one finds Gregory's famous *Libellus responsionum* to Augustine of Canterbury[307] that was frequently included in canonistic materials. This letter was not entered into any of the manuscripts of the register and presumably was never included in it.[308] This important letter for missionary work inspired St.

Register' 745f. (repr. *Das Mittelalter* 712f.), Posner, 'Register' 297, and Lohrmann, *Register Johannes' VIII*. 97.

305. Norberg, *Studia critica* 31.

306. For the collections and manuscripts, see Ewald, NA 3 (1878) 464ff. (to C), 472ff. (to P) and Peitz, *Register Gregors I*. 29ff. to P and 51ff. to C, as well as a general overview of both collections, p. 205ff. Peitz concluded that the original form of P was excerpted from the registers at the order of Pope Hadrian I and that C was a formulary from the chancery compiled ca. 600; his conclusions were rejected by Tangl, 'Gregor-Register' and Posner, 'Register'. The Dedicatory Letter of Paul the Deacon is edited in MGH Epp. 4.508f., cf. H. Löwe in Wattenbach-Levison-Löwe, *Deutschlands Geschichtsquellen im Mittelalter* (Weimar 1953) 2.219 n. 171.

307. JK 1843; printed Reg. 11.56a, MGH Epp. 2.331 ff.

308. Bede, *Ecclesiastical History*, Praefatio and 1.27ff., ed. B. Colgrave and R. A. B. Mynors (Oxford Medieval Texts; Oxford 1969) 4 and 78ff. as well as the commentary by J. M. Wallace-Hadrill, *Bede's Ecclesiastical History of the English People* (Oxford 1988) 37f. Fundamental is T. Mommsen, 'Die Papstbriefe bei Beda', NA 17 (1892) 387ff., who corrected Ewald's mistake that Gregory's letters in Bede originated from the recipients' letters. The authenticity of JK 1843 has been disputed and this discussion has produced abundant literature, which J. Machielsen, *Clavis patristica pseudepigraphorum medii aevi* 2 (CCL 2A; Turnhout 1994) no. 795 p. 221f. lists. To the textual tradition of this letter, see Mordek, *Kirchenrecht und Reform* 223 n. 38. Its absence in the register has produced many explanations; the most likely is Posner's suggestion 'Register' 285ff. that the text deals with problems of ecclesiastical law and is not a letter; therefore it is not in the register. Norberg, *Studia critica* 30 n. 3 accepts Posner's thesis.

Boniface († 754) to obtain other letters from Gregory's register. Despite the unwillingness of the Cardinal Deacon Gemmulus to grant his request, Boniface's stubbornness and lavish gifts effected success several years later. In 746/47 Boniface was in a position to send Gregory's letters from the Roman archives to Archbishop Ecbert of York with the offer to send more if required: 'quia multas (epistolas) inde (de scrinio Romane ecclesiae) excepi'.[309] Thus Boniface had a collection of letters from the Gregorian register that had been compiled according to his own criteria, which, however, was not similar to either the P collection or the C collection. It seems not to have survived.[310]

The reception of Gregory I's letters into canonical collections remained modest until the end of the ninth century, despite the large number of letters that circulated and a considerable manuscript distribution.[311] This slow reception was because the important canonical collections of late antiquity were already complete. When, for example, the *Dionysiana* was expanded to become the *Hadriana,* the P and C collections of Gregory's letters were already in circulation but not used. On the other hand, the *Hispana* added four of Gregory's letters to its collection: three written to Leander of Seville (Reg. 1.41, 5.53, 9.227 [228], JE 1111, 1369, 1756) and one to the Visigothic King Reccared (Reg. 9.228/29 [229], JE 1757). These letters all occur in the register manuscripts of the R and C-classes. Nonetheless, the complete 'superscriptio' and 'subscriptio' suggest that the compiler of the *Hispana* took them from collections preserved by recipients of the letters. A Spanish collection of papal letters probably served as a source for the *Hispana*.[312] Often the decisions of the Roman Synod of 595, frequently described as 'Decretum Gregorii papae', were simply added to the older collections.[313] This text and Gregory's *Libellus responsionum,* well known through Bede's *Historia ecclesiastica,* were incorporated into a few

309. *Epistolae Bonifatii* nos. 33, 54, and 75, ed. Tangl, MGH Epp. selectae 1 p. 57.15ff., p. 96.21ff., p. 158.13ff.; see Posner, 'Register' 251ff. and Norberg, *Studia critica* 32.

310. Peitz, *Register Gregors I.* 47f. conjectured that Boniface's collection was the original form of P. Modesto, *Gregor der Große* 90 thought that C was an excerpt by Boniface. Posner, 'Register' 253, however, rejects Peitz' views in light of the collections' contents.

311. Ewald, NA 3 (1878) 552ff. and the overview by Maassen, *Geschichte* § 296 p. 301ff., who lists fourteen letters and the protocol of the Roman synod of 595. However, Gregory's letters were frequently used as models for letter writing by the eighth century.

312. Martínez Díez, *Hispana* 1.301f. Ewald and Norberg proposed the thesis that the recipients were the source of Gregory's letters in the *Hispana*: Ewald, NA 3 (1878) 553 and Norberg, *Studia critica* 50. In some manuscripts of the *Hispana* and the *Hispana systematica* Gregory's four letters were supplemented by two other texts: a letter to the subdeacon Petrus (Reg. 1. 39a [Append. 1], JE 1102) and the canons of the Roman synod of 595 (Reg. 5. 57a), see Martínez Díez, op. cit. 116, 120, 303 n. 6, who found these two texts in Paris, B.N. lat. 10741 (second half of the ninth century) appended to the *Dacheriana*.

313. Maassen, *Geschichte* § 296.4, p. 302.

Gallican manuscripts of the eighth and ninth centuries, such as the collection of the Saint-Amand manuscript or the collection of the manuscript from Fécamp.[314] However, the *Libellus responionum,* together with the synodal canons from 595, was probably distributed more widely by their inclusion into an appendix of the *Collectio Vetus Gallica* in the mid-eighth century. The appendix of the *Vetus Gallica* also included Gregory's letter to Bishop Etherius of Lyon[315] and his letter to Queen Brunhilde[316] in a version preserved in the manuscripts Bern, Burgerbibl. 611 (c.727) and Chartres, Bibl. municipale 41 (late eighth century), and the Roman Synod of Gregory II of 721. The compiler of the *Collectio Herovalliana* (Titles LXXII–LXXVI) took these texts from the *Vetus Gallica* in the second half of the eighth century, and by this route these letters of Gregory began to be circulated widely.[317]

The Pseudo-Isidorian Decretals provided a vehicle for an even broader reception of Gregory I's letters. Besides the pope's three letters from the *Hispana Gallica Augustodunensis*[318] to Leander of Seville and King Reccared, Pseudo-Isidore included the *Libellus responsionum,* the synodal acts of 595, both readily available in Gaul, and a forged version of the letter to the Recluse (Inclusus) Secundinus from the P collection of Gregorian letters.[319] A later version of Pseudo-Isidore (the C-version) incorporated an alleged exchange of letters between Gregory and Bishop Felix of Messina concerning questions about marriage. Gregory's letter to Theoctista, Basileus Mauricios' sister, appears for the first time in a canonical collection as a part of Pseudo-Isidore,[320] and its exceptionally frequent use in the conflict between Hincmar of Reims († 882) and Hincmar of Laon († 879) may not have been a coincidence.[321]

These seven letters and conciliar canons are in all the manuscript class-

---

314. See the edition, MGH Epp. 2.331f. and the list of manuscripts in P. Meyvaert, 'Les "Responsiones" de S. Grégoire à S. Augustin de Cantorbéry', RHE 54 (1959) 881, who listed fourteen manuscripts with canonical material from the eighth and ninth centuries.

315. Reg. 9.218 (219), JE 1747.

316. Reg. 9.213 (214), JE 1743.

317. See Mordek, *Kirchenrecht und Reform* 217ff. On p. 87–88 n. 112 Mordek deals with JE 1743 and 1747 in the manuscript Bern, Burgerbibl. 611, perhaps written in Corbie, and in Chartres, Bibl. mun. 41, which burned in 1944. On p. 114ff. he examines the relationship between *Vetus Gallica* and *Herovalliana.*

318. JE 1111, 1756, 1757.

319. Reg. 9.147 (148), JE 1673.

320. Reg. 11.27, JE 1817.

321. Fuhrmann, *Einfluß und Verbreitung* 1.189f. examines Gregory's letters in Pseudo-Isidore. On JE 1817 see P. McKeon, 'A Note on Gregory I and the Pseudo-Isidore', RB 89 (1979) 305ff.

es of the long version of Pseudo-Isidore (A1, A/B, B and C).[322] The twelve codices of the so-called Cluny version, which form a subclass of manuscript class A1, and which go back to the time of the forgeries, provide another arrangement and a further selection of Gregory's letters.[323] They begin with the signed synodal decretal of Gregory the Great (Reg. 5.57a), followed by the *Libellus,* which, contrary to the usual Pseudo-Isidorian tradition, is introduced by the original foreword to the *Libellus,* and an address that has not been transmitted elsewhere.[324] In the manuscripts of the Cluny version there are even more Gregorian letters appended to the three letters from the *Hispana Gallica Augustodunensis;* they do not occur elsewhere in the Pseudo-Isidorian collections. They begin with Gregory's letters to Etherius of Lyon and to Queen Brunhilde (JE 1747 and 1743) in the same version that was used by the *Vetus Gallica* and its derivatives. Consequently, both collections must have gone back to similar compilations of Gregory's letters.[325] The subsequent letters to Theoctista (JE 1817) and to the Inclusus Secundinus (JE 1673) conclude the additional Gregorian letters. The letter to Secundinus, as in all the Pseudo-Isidorian manuscripts, has the interpolated text, and it breaks off shortly before the end in the middle of a sentence.

The compiler of the Cluny version, of which New Haven, Yale University, Beinecke Library 442 is the oldest and most important, added a *florilegium* of forty-six excerpts from Gregory's letters. Under the rubric 'Quae secuntur ex epistolis predicti Gregorii papae per diversa loca sunt excerpta ac primum ex epistola eiusdem Secundino servo Dei secluso directa', it begins with a long quotation from the closing section of the genuine decretal JE 1673.[326] The bulk of the excerpts come from Book Nine of the register; some are taken from Book Five and from Book Eleven. It is

322. There is an important textual variation that defines the C-class of manuscripts of Pseudo-Isidore. In the C-class Gregory II's letter to Boniface (Ep. Bon. 26, JE 2174, ed. Tangl MGH Epp. selectae 1.44ff.) in its short form is placed before Gregory I's *Libellus responsionum.* This combination is first found in the Collection of Saint-Amand and is much older than Pseudo-Isidore. In all the manuscripts, JE 2174 lacks an address and is appended to JE 1843 with either an initial or a blank line. It is noteworthy that all the manuscripts of the Collection of Saint-Amand and the short form of Gregory's letter JE 2174 come from Reims or the surrounding area.

323. Schon, 'Redaktion' 500ff.

324. MGH Epp. 2.332 and Meyvaert, 'Responsiones' 888ff.

325. See Mordek, *Kirchenrecht und Reform* 218 n. 29 and 226 n. 60.

326. On the *florilegium,* see M. Kerner, F. Kerff, R. Pokorny, K. G. Schon, H. Tills, 'Textidentifikation und Provenienzanalyse im Decretum Burchardi', SG 20 (1976) 36ff., where they list the excerpted texts in n. 79. The excerpt from JE 1673 can be found in MGH Epp. 2.147.13–148.24.

quite clear that the author of this *florilegium* used a register manuscript in which the P and C collections were combined.[327] The reception of this *florilegium* into canonistic literature has not yet been completely investigated. Burchard of Worms may have used it in his *Decretum*.[328] However, the most interesting thing about the *florilegium* is its large circulation in the Pseudo-Isidorian Decretals. Although the *florilegium* circulated in the Cluny version, it was not confined to it, being found also in Paris, B.N. lat. 1557, fol. 20v–24v, which was written somewhat later than the New Haven manuscript and forms the closing section of the famous Laon Pseudo-Isidorian codex written between 872 and 882, Paris, B.N. lat. 9629.[329] From there it must have been transmitted to the two A1 manuscripts from the eleventh century in northern France: Rouen, Bibl. municipale E.27 (702) and Vat. lat. 3791.[330]

Another collection of thirty-six Gregorian letters was connected with the False Decretals.[331] One cannot ascertain the criteria that the compiler of this letter collection used to choose items from his class R copy of the register. The collection was added to a group of five manuscripts from the ninth to the fifteenth centuries and to two modern copies of the short version of the Pseudo-Isidorian material. This collection of thirty-six letters of these manuscripts, closely related to one another, were the textual basis for the canonical collection of Pseudo-Remedius of Chur from the last third of the ninth century, originating in northern Italy, possibly Vercelli.[332] The author of Pseudo-Remedius probably owed his three ex-

327. Providing to each excerpt the numbers of the letters in C and P, demonstrates that the compiler first took from Collection C texts from epp. 29, 8, 23, 29, 48, 67, 77 through 198 and then from Collection P the series epp. 3, 8, 10, 15 through 53. At the end he added other texts from P and C.

328. SG 20 (1976) 35 and Hoffmann and Pokorny, *Burchard von Worms* 190f.

329. J. J. Contreni, 'Codices Pseudo-Isidoriani: The Provenance and Date of Paris, B.N. MS lat. 9629', *Viator* 13 (1982) 1ff. (repr. *Carolingian Learning, Masters and Manuscripts* [Aldershot 1992] no. XVI). It is worth mentioning that Vat. lat. 1344 (twelfth century), which contains the Cluny version of Pseudo-Isidore, also contains the *florilegium* and that this Cluny version probably originated in the time of Hincmar of Laon, see Schon, 'Redaktion' 510f.

330. Williams, *Codices Pseudo-Isidoriani* no. 58 p. 54f. and no. 72 p. 68, as well as SG 20 (1976) 38 n. 88.

331. Hinschius, *Decretales* xlvi, MGH Epp.2.X and Norberg, *Studia critica* 64.

332. See the detailed analysis of H. John, *Collectio canonum Remedio Curiensi episcopo perperam ascripta* (MIC Series B, 2; Vatican City 1976) 63ff. and Fuhrmann, *Einfluß und Verbreitung* 2.415ff. The text is found in Sankt Gallen, Stiftsbibl. 670 (ninth century), Stuttgart, Landesbibl. HB VI.105 (ninth or tenth century), Köln, Dombibl. 114 (eleventh century), Mantova, Bibl. Com. 205 and Vat. lat. 3788, both dated to the eleventh or twelfth century. John 64 n. 22, concluded that Gregory's letters were formerly in Vat. lat. 3788. They are also contained in the copies from the sixteenth and seventeenth centuries, Madrid, Bibl. Nac. Ff. 8 (lost) and Vat. lat. 4873. Additionally Merseburg, Dombibliothek B I 104 (ninth or tenth century from Northern Italy or Southern France), which on fol. 98ff. contains a part of Gregory's letters, John, op. cit. 91.

tensive excerpts from Gregory the Great's letters in chapters 75, 76, and 78 to this collection.[333] It is not clear whether this collection of Gregorian letters influenced later canonical collections. The reception of Gregory's letters in pre-Gratian collections has not yet received a thorough examination.[334]

The author of the *Collectio Anselmo dedicata* made more use of Gregory the Great's register than any other canonist. This work from the end of the ninth century included approximately 300 Gregorian letters and excerpts. The author divided each of the twelve books of his collection into three parts: councils, papal letters, and patristic writings; Gregory's letters; and Roman law.[335] As a source he used a two-volume exemplar of the R manuscript class, although in the wrong order: indictions I to VII (598–604) came first, and the beginning of Gregory I's pontificate, indictions IX to XV (590–597), were in the second volume. In general, the exemplar's numbering scheme for the letters was retained.[336] Burchard of Worms depended on the *Collectio Anselmo dedicata* and, to a lesser extent, on Regino of Prüm's handbook for the Gregorian letters he put in his *Decretum*.[337] The compiler of the *Collection in 74 Titles* included forty-nine chapters attributed to Gregory in his work and did not always differentiate between Gregory I, Gregory II, and Gregory IV. Often we cannot de-

333. Edition by John, op. cit. 66ff., 88ff. and H. Fuhrmann, 'Die sogenannte Kanonessammlung des Remedius von Chur', DA 18 (1962) 233f. C. G. Mor, 'Una piccola collezione di testi gregoriani del secolo VIII', *Études Le Bras* 1.284ff., analyzes 44 excerpts in Paris, B.N. lat. 12448 (ninth or tenth century), and connected them to a smaller collection of excerpts in Milano, Bibl. Ambrosiana G.58 sup. (tenth century from Bobbio) and the same version of the excerpts in a Pseudo-Isidore manuscript from Livorno, Bibl. Com. Labronica, sine numero (earlier 10) (eleventh or twelfth century, from Brescia). Mor conjectured that the collection originated at the end of the seventh century, see Fuhrmann, *Einfluß und Verbreitung* 2.425f. n. 7.

334. P. Fournier's studies still provide the basic information about *Collectio Anselmo dedicata*, Anselm of Lucca, Deusdedit, Bonizo and for Ivo of Chartres' collections. They are all published in his collected studies *Mélanges de droit canoniques*. See also J. Gaudemet, 'L'héritage de Grégoire le Grand chez les canonistes médiévaux', *Gregorio Magno e il suo tempo: XIX Incontro di studiosi dell'antichità cristiana in collaborazione con l'École française de Rome, Roma, 9–12 maggio 1990* (Studia Ephemeridis *Augustinianum* 34; Rome 1991) 199ff., who mentions Gregory's letters in passing.

335. For the manuscript tradition of the collection, see H. Fuhrmann, 'Fragmente der Collectio Anselmo dedicata', DA 44 (1988) 539ff.

336. P. Fournier, 'L'origine de la collection "Anselmo dedicata"', *Mélanges P. F. Girard* (Paris 1912) 1.488f. n. 2 (repr. *Mélanges* 2.202f. n. 2), who noted that some texts are only in Collection P (*Anselmo dedicata* 7.6 and 12 = Reg. 11.43 and 2.34; JE 1833, 1189; and 10.17 = Reg. 9.147, JE 1673, which is the forged conclusion of the letter to the Inclusus Secundinus and is edited in a very different version in MGH Epp. 2.147.37ff.). Mor, 'Piccola collezione' 285ff. noted a small collection of excerpts in Paris, B.N. lat. 12448, but it did not influence *Anselmo dedicata*.

337. See the overview on the sources in Hoffmann and Pokorny, *Burchard von Worms* 254f.

termine whether a Gregorian letter comes from the Pseudo-Isidore, from John the Deacons's *Vita*, from the register, or from another intermediate source.[338]

There has been no detailed examination of the approximately 140 excerpts from Gregory I's letters in Anselm of Lucca's canonical collection (1083/86). A great number of these letters occur in Book Six, which deals with canonical elections, and in Book Seven, which concerns the *vita communis*. These chapters were taken partly from the *Collection in 74 Titles* and partly from a two-volume version of the register.[339]

Deusdedit included in his canonical collection (1083–1087) compact blocks of excerpts in all four books, 148 excerpts in all, which are frequently provided with an attribution of provenance, 'ex registro'.[340] At times he adopted a numbering scheme for the letters that agrees with that of R[341], and this evidence suggests that, for the most part, the excerpts must have come from an exemplar of the R version of the register.

In the *Collection of Santa Maria Novella* (c.1085), the 151 excerpts from Gregory's works indicate his popularity. This quantity is surpassed only by the number of Augustinian excerpts, and there are far fewer extracts from the works of the other Church Fathers.[342] For most of the letters, i.e. 129 of the 151 excerpts, the compiler probably worked from an exemplar of the R manuscript class.[343]

Bonizo of Sutri incorporated sixty texts from Gregory I's letters in his *Liber de vita christiana* (post-1090). We do not know whether he took them from Burchard, Anselm, Deusdedit, from a *florilegium* of Gregorian let-

338. See J. Gilchrist's Prolegomena to 74 *Titles*, xc n. 6 and xcii. Cc. 273–275, which are excerpts of Gregory I's letters, taken from Pseudo-Isidore and the *Vita* of John the Deacon, are followed by cc.276–289, which contain the decisions of the Roman synod of 721. The compiler did not understand that these texts were from Gregory II: 'Incipiunt quaedam capitula a beato Gregorio in generali synodo disposita'. Cc.13–16 are excerpts from the forged letter of Gregory IV (JE † 2579).

339. P. Fournier, 'Les collections canoniques romaines de l'époque de Grégoire VII', *Mémoires de l'Académie des inscriptions et belles-lettres* 41 (1920) 305f. (repr. *Mélanges* 2.459f.).

340. Deusdedit 1.142–144, 183–218, 230–234; 2.66–85; 3.67–106; 4.100–121, 340–348. In addition there are individual pieces in Deusdedit 2.58, 3.48.49, which are for the most part not taken from the register, such as the decisions of the Roman synod of 595; see the overview of Gregory's letters in Deusdedit in Peitz, *Register Gregors I*. 213ff., who lists the precise source of the chapters, and his comments on p. 48ff. See Fournier,' Collections canoniques romaines' 337f., 381f. (repr. *Mélanges* 2.491f., 535f.).

341. In Deusdedit 4.340. 341. 343, the numbers XLVI, LXXVII, and XCIII correspond to R's (r), in the Indictio X–XI, see Peitz, *Register Gregors I*. 49.

342. Motta, *Liber canonum* xxxviii f. and his count of the texts: 175 from Augustine, 60 from Leo the Great, 27 from Ambrose, 22 from Jerome, and 11 from Cyprian.

343. One can presume this if the numbering of the register of R was adopted by the compiler, e.g. *183 Titles* 47.3, 48.2.3, 49.1.2, Motta 84f.

ters, or from a register exemplar. We also do not know if Anselm, Deus-dedit, and Bonizo could have gone back to a common source for their ex-tracts from Gregorian letters, as they probably did for the letters of Pelag-ius I and Nicholas I. Bonizo had great respect for Gregory's register and declared that it was 'ad regendam ecclesiam satis utilis' [sic] (Bonizo 4.41). It is important to note the high number of forgeries attributed to Grego-ry on questions of marriage and church discipline in the *Liber de vita chris-tiana*.[344]

None of the large Gregorian collections exercised much influence on the arrangement of the 112 excerpts from Gregory I found in the *Collectio Tripartita* 1.55; among those excerpts are quite a number of pieces wrong-ly attributed, such as (1) Gregory II's letter to Boniface (JE 2174 c.9 and 29), (2) Gregory IV's alleged letter to Aldrich of Le Mans (JE † 2579 c.1.32 and 104), and (3) the forged letter from Gregory V to the French Queen Con-stantia (JL † 3890 c.110). There are also extracts from other authentic works of Gregory I.[345] The totally different form of the 'inscriptio' of in-dividual texts and their illogical arrangement occasioned Fournier's judg-ment that 'les fragments rassemblés par le compilateur . . . ont été rap-portés de toutes parts pour former une mosaïque assez incohérente'.[346]

Next to the Pseudo-Isidorian Decretals, Gregory's register formed the most important source of papal decretals that the cardinal priest Gregory of San Grisogono inserted into his collection, the *Polycarpus* (1104–1111).[347] He must have had a detailed knowledge of the register, because he filled

344. P. Fournier, 'Les sources canoniques du "Liber de vita christiana" de Bonizo de Sutri', BEC 78 (1917) 117ff. (repr. *Mélanges* 2.667ff.), Perels lists the sources and gives a con-cordance of the canons in his edition, p. xxix ff. and p. 365f. Cf. W. Berschin, *Bonizo von Sutri: Leben und Werk* (Beiträge zur Geschichte und Quellenkunde des Mittelalters 2; Berlin 1972) 67ff.

345. Other forgeries attributed to Gregory I in the collection are: c.18 (JE † 1366), c.39 (JE † 6613a), c.52 (JE † 1939), c.69 (JE † 1987), c.111 (JE † 1937). For a detailed discussion of Gregory's letters in the *Tripartita*, cf. Fournier, 'Collections canoniques' 662f. (repr. *Mélanges* 1.468f.).

346. Fournier, 'Collections canoniques 663 (repr. *Mélanges* 1.469). A striking parallel ex-ists between the beginning of Gregory's excerpts in the *Tripartita* and the French collection in the manuscript from Sémur (Madrid, Bibl. Nac. 428 and other manuscripts) from the third quarter of the eleventh century. The compiler of the *Tripartita* must have taken his texts, 1.55.2–16, from it, which correspond to *Collectio Sinemuriensis* 1.179–180, 183–185, 188–189, 204–206, 209–211, 213, and 217, cf. L. Fowler-Magerl, 'Vier französische und spani-sche vorgratianische Kanonessammlungen', *Aspekte europäischer Rechtsgeschichte: Festgabe für H. Coing zum 70. Geburtstag* (Ius commune Sonderheft 17; Frankfurt 1982) 124ff. The ex-tent of the relationship between the two collections must be explored.

347. P. Fournier, 'Les deux recensions de la collection canonique romaine dite le Poly-carpus', *Mélanges d'archéologie et d'histoire de l'École française de Rome* 37 (1918–1919) 70 (repr. *Mélanges* 2, 718) and Horst, *Polycarpus* 10 and 83, as well as the 180 excerpts in the list of sources, p. 209ff.

out incomplete 'inscriptiones' and corrected erroneous attributions from information he obtained from other canonical collections.[348]

There has been no thorough examination of the origin of most of the excerpts from Gregory I's letters in Gratian's *Decretum*. Jean Gaudemet dealt with this issue selectively, giving some evidence of the *Decretum's* strong relationship to Anselm of Lucca's collection and the *Collectio Tripartita*. More exact statements about these relationships can be made only after a detailed comparison of the texts, including collections like the *Polycarpus* and the *Collection in Three Books* that also were important sources for the *Decretum*.[349]

A survey of the reception of Gregorian letters into the canonical collections until the middle of the twelfth century shows a regular increase in the number of excerpts from Gregorian letters in the reform collections, triple the number in Burchard of Worms' *Decretum*.[350] On the other hand, the number of texts from Gregory's other works, like the *Dialogi* or the *Regula pastoralis*, is considerably smaller in the reform collections, where they constitute only a fraction of the Gregorian material. Burchard had, in contrast, incorporated Gregory's letters and other works in equal proportion.[351] The compilers of the reform collections may have used more of the letters because these excerpts are usually more concrete, many having been based on specific cases. Consequently, when they were removed from their immediate context, they could be easily reshaped to form a general juristic rule.[352]

A second phenomenon should be mentioned: beginning in the eleventh century, and especially in the reform collections, forgeries attributed to Gregory the Great show a remarkable increase. These are mostly concerned with questions about marriage law and the degrees of consanguinity.[353] However, at the turn of the twelfth century, forgeries con-

348. Horst, *Polycarpus* 83. The exemplar that Gregory of San Grisogono used must have been divided into books as in the modern editions, with the letters numbered consecutively.

349. J. Gaudemet, 'Patristique et Pastorale: La contribution de Grégoire le Grand au "Miroir de l'Evêque" dans le Décret de Gratien', *Études Le Bras* 1.138ff. (repr. *La société ecclésiastique dans l'Occident médiéval* [London 1980] no. XI). Idem, 'L'héritage' 210ff. and Landau, 'Register Gregors I.' 125ff. For Gratian's sources, see P. Landau, 'Gratian', TRE 14 (1985) 126f. with bibliography.

350. See the overview of sources in Hoffmann and Pokorny, *Burchard von Worms* 254f., who list 38 excerpts from the register. Anselm of Lucca included ca. 140 excerpts, Deusdedit 148, *Collectio Santa Maria Novella* 129, *Polycarpus* 180, and Gratian ca. 270.

351. 183 *Titles* took ten from the *Dialogi*, and four from *Moralia in Job*, see Motta, *Liber canonum* 339. Gregory of San Grisogono inserted into the *Polycarpus* fifteen texts from the *Dialogi*, ten from the *Moralia in Job*, and four from *Regula pastoralis*; cf. Horst, *Polycarpus* 209.

352. Gaudemet, 'Patristique et Pastorale' 136.

353. L. Machielsen, 'Les spurii de S. Grégoire le Grand en matière matrimoniale, dans les collections canoniques jusqu'au Décret de Gratien', *Sacris Erudiri* 14 (1963) 251ff. *Polycar-*

cerning the right of monks to exercise sacerdotal office, like JE † 1366, *Quam sit necessarium,* and JE † 1951, *Ex auctoritate huius decreti,* also enjoyed a very wide circulation.[354] Almost all of them made their way into Gratian's *Decretum* and from there became a part of the *ius commune.*

IV. Collections of Papal Letters

1. Collectio ecclesiae Thessalonicensis

The *Collectio ecclesiae Thessalonicensis* contains: twenty-four letters written by popes from Damasus (366–384) to Hilary (461–468); an exchange of letters between Emperors Honorius and Theodosius II (post-421); and two letters to Pope Leo I from Emperor Marcian (450) and Patriarch Anatolius of Constantinople (454).[355] The sole purpose of the collection was to establish proof of the popes' uninterrupted ecclesiastical and jurisdictional sovereignty over Eastern Illyricum from the end of the fourth century. This information comes from the introductory texts of the letter collection transmitted by the acts of the Roman synod of December 7 and December 9, 531. At this synod the complaint of Metropolitan Stephen of Larissa was brought before Pope Boniface II by Stephen's suffragan Theodore of Echinum. Stephen objected to his deposition, which had come about because of his uncanonical ordination by the Patriarch of Constantinople and the permanent synod (synodos endemousa). Stephen had refused to defend himself anywhere but in Rome; nevertheless he was condemned. His judges thought that his refusal to submit to the Church of Constantinople had caused severe damage to it.[356] To prove the correctness of his position, Theodore brought a collec-

---

pus 6.4 was most important for this development, see Horst, *Polycarpus* 74f. and Landau, 'Gefälschtes Recht' 43ff.

354. J. Gilchrist, 'The Influence of the Monastic Forgeries attributed to Pope Gregory I (JE † 1951) and Boniface IV (JE † 1996)', *Fälschungen im Mittelalter* 2.263ff., where JE † 1366 is also discussed, and G. Constable, 'The Treatise "Hortatur nos" and Accompanying Canonical Texts on the Performance of Pastoral Works by Monks', *Speculum Historiale: Festschrift für J. Spörl* (Munich 1965) 569ff.

355. For the collection, see Clavis no. 1623 p. 522; it was first critically edited on the basis of the only reliable manuscript in Vat. lat. 5751 by C. Silva-Tarouca, *Epistularum Romanorum pontificum ad vicarios per Illyricum aliosque episcopos Collectio Thessalonicensis* (Textus et documenta 23; Rome 1937). The inadequate first edition of 1662 was based on the papers of L. Holste and was entitled *Collectio Romana bipartita.* This edition was not based on any known manuscript. When the Ballerini brothers edited the letters of Leo I, they used the collection and named it *Collectio ecclesiae Thessalonicensis* (PL 54.566), which is not wholly appropriate. Vat. lat. 5751 disappeared from view for a long time, see n. 358, below.

356. This argument appears in the appeal of the three Thessalian suffragans of Stephen of Larissa, ed. Silva-Tarouca, *Collectio Thessalonicensis* no. 3 p. 14.22ff. For the synodal proceedings, see Caspar, *Papsttum* 2.207f. and E. Schwartz, 'Die sog. Sammlung der Kirche von Thessalonich', *Festschrift R. Reitzenstein* (Leipzig-Berlin 1931) 139f.

tion of papal letters to Rome. He read them to the synod, and they were incorporated in the synodal acts. Their authenticity was checked against the copies of the corresponding letters in the papal archives.[357] The collection has been transmitted only incompletely by Vat. lat. 5751, fol. 55r–75r (late ninth century).[358] The copy ends with 'Item recitata est', but the expected letters do not follow, and the final judgment of the synod on Stephen of Larissa's case has not been preserved. One suspects here that the confusion comes from an incomplete and mixed-up exemplar, because on fol. 75v–77r can be found homilies of Gregory the Great and Augustine.[359] The original appearance of the collection is clear from Pope Nicholas I's decretal to Emperor Michael III in which the pope requested the reinstatement of the vicariate of Thessaloniki, which had been abolished in 733:

> . . . quae antecessorum nostrorum temporibus, scilicet Damasi, Siricii, Innocentii, Bonefacii, Caelestini, Xysti, Leonis, Hilari, Simplicii, Felicis atque Hormisdae sanctorum pontificum sacris dispositionibus augebatur.[360]

The evidence of the popes after Leo I is missing in the *Collectio Thessalonicensis* as we have it today. Only the fragment of a letter from Pope Hilary (JK † 565) can be shown to come from a letter of this collection.[361] The fragment, long suspected to have been a forgery, was used in a compilation of 'auctoritates et exempla piaque documenta', which the deposed Archbishop Gunthar of Cologne submitted to the synod of Pavia (865). We have evidence in three other cases that the collection was used in the early Middle Ages: (1) the letter of Pope Hadrian I to the Spanish bishops (JE 2479 from 784/85), (2) the letter of Nicholas I from 860, and

---

357. Silva-Tarouca, *Collectio Thessalonicensis* 15.97ff. It is not a collection of legal rights for the Church of Thessaloniki, see Wurm, *Studien* 103.

358. For the manuscript see R. von Nostitz-Rieneck, 'Die päpstlichen Urkunden für Thessalonike und deren Kritik durch Prof. Friedrich', *Zeitschrift für katholische Theologie* 21 (1897) 4ff., Schwartz, 'Sammlung' 144ff. and idem, ACO 2.4 p. x, R. Schieffer, ACO 4.3.1, p. 59 with bibliography and R. Kottje, *Die Bußbücher Halitgars und des Hrabanus Maurus* (Beiträge zur Geschichte und Quellenkunde des Mittelalters 8; Berlin 1980) 73f. Bobbio was the first home of the manuscript; it was taken from there to the Vatican Library in 1618. It may have been written in Verona. A copy of the manuscript was made in the seventeenth century, Vat. lat. 6339, from which another copy was made during the same century, Vat. Barb. lat. 650. None of these manuscripts can be proved to be the basis of the first edition of 1662.

359. In the last letter of this collection (Silva-Tarouca no. 26–27 p. 62ff.) the first part of the text is a letter of Leo I from 446, to which is appended the end of a letter of Boniface I, JK 351. Schwartz, 'Sammlung' 151ff. discovered this combination of texts.

360. JE 2682, MGH Epp. 6.438.31ff.

361. H. Fuhrmann, 'Ein Bruchstück der Collectio ecclesiae Thessalonicensis', *Traditio* 14 (1958) 371ff.

(3) the propagandistic writings of the deposed Archbishop of Cologne.[362] All of the letters in the collection were taken from the archives of recipients, most likely from those of the Church of Larissa or from other episcopal archives of Eastern Illyricum. In these archives, quickly compiled little collections of important documents and letters must have been made due to the complicated relationships among Rome, Thessalonika, and other bishoprics.[363]

2. Collectio Avellana

'A most remarkable collection, this *"Avellana"*,' is how Paul Ewald characterized the compilation of 243 papal and imperial letters dating from the time of the schism of Ursinus and Damasus (366/67) to the *Constitutum de tribus capitulis* of Pope Vigilius (JK 935 of 553).[364] It received its name from the Ballerini brothers (as did the *Collectio Thessalonicensis*), who in their treatment of the old canonical collections 2.12 (PL 56.179ff.) described in detail an example of the *Avellana,* Vat. lat. 4961, from the early eleventh century.[365] This manuscript is dependent on the very slightly

362. See H. Fuhrmann, 'Eine im Original erhaltene Propagandaschrift des Erzbischofs Gunthar von Köln (865)', *Archiv für Diplomatik* 4 (1958) 1ff. The text of JK 565 is edited by Fuhrmann, 'Bruchstück' *Traditio* 14 (1958) 374 from three manuscripts: Köln, Dombibl. 117 (ninth century), Berlin, Staatsbibl. Phill. 1764 (tenth century) and Salzburg, Sankt Peter a.IX 32 (eleventh century).

363. See Schwartz, 'Sammlung' 142 and Silva-Tarouca, *Collectio Thessalonicensis* x ff. The authenticity of the letters exchanged by the emperors Honorius and Theodosius II (*Collectio Thessalonicensis* nos. 15 and 16 p. 43ff.) is doubted. Presumably Theodosius' constitution of 421 (CTh. 16.2.45; Cod.1.2.6) that denied the authority of the Roman church in Illyricum was abrogated by these letters. The diplomatic, linguistic, and administrative terminology all argue against the authenticity of Theodosius' rescript (*Collectio* no. 16 p.44f.), as E. Chrysos, 'Zur Echtheit des "Rescriptum Theodosii ad Honorium" in der "Collectio Thessalonicensis",' *Kleronomia* 4 (1972) 240ff. demonstrates; he places the forgery of the rescript after the appearance of Justinian's *Codex* (534).

364. See Clavis nos. 1570–1622 p. 516ff. The collection was edited by O. Günther, CSEL 35 (1895–1898), who gave a detailed description in his *Avellana-Studien* and in the introduction to his edition, p. i–lxxxix. Cf. also Schwartz, *Publizistische Sanmmlungen* 283ff. H. Steinacker, 'Registerwesen' 5ff. as well as Peitz, *Register Gregors I.* 110ff. examined the collection with the purpose of understanding the writing and making of the papal registers. The last part of the collection is an incomplete Latin translation of the work of Epiphanius of Salamis († 403) about the precious stones on the pectoral of the high priest. This section has not been considered a part of the original collection. The citation by Ewald is from *Historische Zeitschrift* 40 (1878) 154.

365. See the description in Günther, CSEL 35.xvii ff. The note on fol. 109 was not written by a fourteenth-century hand as Günther (p. xvii) thought but rather in the eleventh: 'Iste liber est monasterii sancte crucis fontis Avellane Eughubin. dioc.' and fol. 157v and 161v: 'Hunc librum adquisivit Domnus Damianus sanctae Cruci'. This 'Domnus Damianus' is probably not Peter Damian († 1072), and it is also doubtful that he is Damian's cousin Peter, the prior of Avellana, abbot of Nonantola, and cardinal. See G. Mercati, 'Il Codice dell'Avellana e "Domnus Damianus",' *Opere minori* (Studi e testi 77; Vatican City 1937) 245ff.

older codex, Vat. lat. 3787, and the remaining nine exemplars from the fifteenth to the seventeenth centuries go back to both of these eleventh-century manuscripts.[366]

The compiler of the *Avellana* was a seeker of curiosities: more than 200 of the 243 texts of the collection have been handed down only here. However, he did not systematically search for rare texts, but rather put together in one volume various existing collections of ecclesiastical political and dogmatic problems, for which some of the sources can be deduced.[367] Numbers 1 to 40—chiefly documents about the double elections of 366/67 (Damasus and Ursinus) and of 418/19 (Boniface I and Eulalius)—come largely from the archives of the prefecture of the city of Rome; according to the latest scholarship, they must have been gathered together shortly before 500 by the supporters of Anti-pope Laurentius.[368] The letters of the next group, numbers 41 to 50, were also used, in part, by the *Quesnelliana*. They include four of Innocent I's letters (JK 323, 325–327) and two letters from Pope Zosimus (JK 329, 330), and because of the exclusive reference to Africa, were probably gathered from sources in the archives of the Church of Carthage.[369] Next comes a small group comprising the last five remaining letters of Pope Leo I, dated June 17 and August 18, 460 (JK 546–550); these have been transmitted only through the *Avellana*.[370] Following these is a larger group concerned with the Acacian schism; it includes papal letters and tracts from Simplicius, Felix III, Anastasius II, and Gelasius (no. 56–81 and 94–103). This is, to a large extent, also preserved in the so-called *Collectio Berolinensis*, which arose in ninth-century Verdun.[371] Both go back to a common model whose appearance has been better preserved by the Verdun collection than by the *Avellana*.[372] A dossier of letters containing the writings of Pope John II, Pope Agapetus, and Pope Vigilius (533–540, 553), has been awkwardly inserted into the col-

---

and G. Picasso, 'Le tradizione libraria di Fonte Avellana', *Fonte Avellana nella società dei secoli XI et XII: Atti del II Convegno del Centro di studi Avellaniti* (Fonte Avellana 1979) 355ff. Probably the manuscript was written in Nonantola, see M. Palma, 'Da Nonantola a Fonte Avellana: A proposito di dodici manoscritti e di un Domnus Damianus', *Scrittura e civiltà* 2 (1978) 221ff.

366. Cf. Günther, CSEL 35.iiii ff. and xviii ff. with examples of the manuscripts' filiation.

367. Günther, *Avellana-Studien* 2ff. and Schwartz, *Publizistische Sammlungen* 283ff.

368. Günther, *Avellana-Studien* 3ff. and on the *Collectio Avellana* Epp. 1 and 2, M. R. Green, 'The Supporters of the Antipope Ursinus', JTS N.S. 22 (1971) 531ff. Cf. also Wirbelauer, *Zwei Päpste in Rom* 136ff. on the time of composition.

369. Günther, *Avellana-Studien* 19ff.

370. Schwartz, ACO 2.4 p. xiiii and xxxx.

371. On the collection and the manuscript, see p. 61ff., above.

372. With much detail, Günther, *Avellana-Studien* 27ff. and Schwartz, *Publizistische Sammlungen* 283ff.

lection. One cannot really blame the redactor of the *Avellana* for this poorly arranged material, as he must have found the inserted letters in his archtype.[373] The collection ends with 138 items from the papal register (no. 105–243), the correspondence of Pope Hormisdas during the years 515/521, and one assumes that the *Collectio Avellana* was assembled directly after this date.[374]

The *Avellana* seems to have had no greater influence on pre-Gratian works than did other collections of the same sort, like the *Collectio Britannica*. The Italian *Collection in Two Books*, which was compiled in the 1080s (Vat. lat. 3832), may have used the *Avellana* for some Gelasian excerpts, but whether directly or through intermediate collections is not clear. In Book 2 chapters 371 to 373 are found a long excerpt from the acts of the Roman synod from March 13, 495, the complete text of Gelasius' justification of Acasius' anathematization (JK 664), and an excerpt from JK 638. The synodal acts and JK 638 occur only in the *Avellana* and in the *Collectio Berolinensis*. The complete version of the decretal JK 664, which was actually included in countless canonical collections, but always without the end of the letter (cf. Maassen, *Geschichte* § 285.16 [p. 282–83]), quite likely came from the *Avellana* and the *Collectio Berolinensis*.[375] Presumably the *Collection in Two Books* was the source for these texts in Anselm's canonical collection, which put them in various places.[376] The excerpt from JK 638 passed through *Polycarpus* 7.1.8 or 31 to reach Gratian's *Decretum* C.24 q.2 c.4, as did a short passage from the synodal acts that is found in C.22 q.2 c.5.

3. *Liber auctoritatum ecclesiae Arelatensis*

A third historically significant collection which has remained relatively unimportant for legal history is the *Liber auctoritatum ecclesiae Arelaten-*

373. Steinacker, 'Registerwesen' 9ff. conjectured that the Lateran Register was the source of the letters; cf. also Günther, *Avellana-Studien* 46f., Schwartz, *Publizistische Sammlungen* 285, and Wirbelauer, *Zwei Päpste in Rom* 136.

374. On the letters of Hormisdas, see Günther, *Avellana-Studien* 48ff., Steinacker, 'Registerwesen' 29f., and Wirbelauer, *Zwei Päpste in Rom* 136ff.

375. The *Collection in Two Books* in Vat. lat. 3832 is analyzed and partly edited by J. Bernhard, *La collection en deux livres (Cod. Vat. lat. 3832)*, RDC 12 (1962), who, p. 534ff. prints excerpts from the acts of the synod (c.371= *Avellana* ep. 103, p. 483.2–484.3, 485.3–19) and from JK 638 (c.373 = *Avellana* ep. 101, p. 467.6–20). The full text of JK 664 (= c.372) is printed as Ep. 95 of the *Avellana* (369ff.). The short form of the text was edited by Günther in Appendix I of his edition (774ff.). It is possible that Pope Hadrian I had used the *Avellana* when he cited JK 638 in his letter to his legate in Spain, Bishop Egila (JE 2445).

376. Anselm of Lucca 11.30 (= *Two Books* 2.373; JK 638), 11.69 (= *Two Books* 2.372; JK 664), 13.22 (= *Two Books* 2.371; synodal acts of 495). On its reception, see Günther, CSEL 35. p. lxxiv and *Avellana-Studien* 102ff.

sis.[377] It is found in four manuscripts from the ninth, eleventh, and twelfth centuries, of which Paris, B.N. lat. 5537 (eleventh/twelfth century) has transmitted the most complete version, comprising fifty-five letters from popes Zosimus (JK 328 A.D. 417) to Pelagius I (JK 938 from 557/58). Preceding the letters is a decree (418) of Emperors Honorius and Theodosius II of 418, by which Arles was made the premier city of the *Septem Provinciae.*[378] Closely related to this manuscript is the manuscript Paris, B.N. lat. 3880, fol. 70–91v (twelfth century), which is missing Pelagius' letters.[379] The best transmission of the *Liber auctoritatum* is in Paris, B.N. lat. 3849, which was written in the ninth century in eastern Gaul; since one quire has been lost, it contains only forty-five letters of the Arles collection.[380] Similar to this exemplar is Paris, B.N. lat. 2777, fol. 20–42v, probably written in the monastery of Lérins in the first half of the ninth century. It contains Rusticus' collection of Leo's letters, 'ante gesta Chalcedonensia', followed by the *Liber auctoritatem,* which through lost leaves has been reduced to thirty-eight papal letters.[381] This transmission of the *Liber auctoritatum* stands out due to the fact that there are short content summaries and scribal commentaries written in the margins. This may be relevant to the issue of whether both manuscripts go back to a common source (as Gundlach thought) or if, for 2777, an additional copy should be assumed to have been the model, on which Paris, B.N. lat. 5537 is also dependent (as per Gassó-Batlle).

The collection is considerably older than the ninth-century manuscripts would lead one to suspect. The post-524 collection of the manuscript from Cologne (Köln 212), which arose in southern Gaul, and the *Collectio Albigensis* (Toulouse 364 et al.), which was probably written in Ar-

377. Clavis no. 1625 p. 523. Now as before, the research of W. Gundlach, 'Der Streit der Bisthümer Arles und Vienne um den Primatus Galliarum', NA 14 (1889) 251ff., 15 (1890) 11ff., 235ff., is fundamental. An enlarged edition of his work appeared as a book and will be subsequently cited (Hannover 1890). Gundlach edited the collection in MGH Epp. 3 (Berlin 1892) 1ff. as *Epistulae Arelatenses genuinae.*

378. Maassen, 'Bibliotheca' 259ff., Gundlach, *Streit* 27ff., Gassó-Batlle, *Pelagii I epistulae* xxviii. Two modern copies were made from the manuscript in the sixteenth and seventeenth centuries but are of no editorial value: Roma, Bibl. Vallicelliana G.99, written for Cesare Baronio (cf. Maassen, 'Bibliotheca' 409) and Carpentras, Bibl. municipale 1856 (Peiresc 74.1), fol. 50–96, cf. M. Liabastres, *Catalogue général* 36 (Paris 1902) 173ff.

379. Maassen, 'Bibliotheca' 254f. and Gundlach, *Streit* 34ff. and 43ff., where the common lacunae and errors of the manuscripts are listed.

380. See Maassen, 'Bibliotheca' 243ff., idem, *Geschichte* § 787ff. p. 768ff., Gundlach, *Streit* 38ff. with a note on the missing quires; Gassó-Batlle, *Pelagii I epistulae* xxviii.

381. See *Bibliothèque Nationale: Catalogue général des manuscrits latins* 3 (Paris 1952) 76f. and Gassó-Batlle, *Pelagii I epistulae* xxviii. The appended formulary collection from St. Denis on fol. 43rff. was part of another manuscript. On the missing quires, see Gundlach, *Streit* 40f.

les in the mid-sixth century, were both influenced by the *Liber auctoritatum ecclesiae Arelatensis,* from which they took blocks of respectively four and nine letters.[382] The *Liber auctoritatum,* which grew and shaped itself only gradually, is probably about as old as its latest portion, Pope Pelagius I's confession of faith (JK 938) from April 557 or early 558. This was also the time when the once-glorious metropolitan see of Arles relinquished its leadership role in the Gallic Church in favor of the up-and-coming metropolitan see of Lyon.[383]

Whether the *Liber auctoritatum ecclesiae Arelatensis* was used by later authors and canonical collections has not been investigated in detail. Pope Pelagius I's only known letters, the eleven transmitted in this collection (JK 938–948), were consulted at Lyon and by Hincmar of Reims in the ninth century. It was not until the second half of the eleventh century that shortened excerpts from Pelagius I's letters from copies of the Pelagian register were added to the reform collections and the polemic of the Investiture Controversy.[384] The *Liber auctoritatum* is encountered a last time in the Varia I of the *Collectio Britannica.* There, in section B, which contains excerpts from genuine and forged papal letters from Clement (JK † 10) through Gregory VII (JL 5290), numbers 6 through 19 have been taken from the Arles collection numbers 2, 4, 7f., 11, 13, 15, 19, 24, 27, 51, 53–55.[385] The *Liber auctoritatum* seems to have remained unknown, on the other hand, to the authors and redactors of the pre-Gratian collections.[386]

---

382. See Wurm, *Studien* 278 nos. 40–43 (*Collectio Coloniensis*) and 282f. nos. 61–69 (*Collectio Albigensis*): these texts correspond to cc.2, 3, 5–7, 10, 26–28 of the *Liber auctoritatum* in Paris, B.N. lat. 5537 and the texts from the *Collectio Coloniensis* are cc.2, 7, 26, and 28. Additionally the *Collectio Coloniensis* took the imperial constitution of Honorius and Theodosius *Saluberrima magnificentiae tuae suggestione* (*Liber auctoritatum* no. 1), which, because of the remark 'accepta Arelate X Kalendas Iunias', can only have been taken from the *Collectio Arelatensis,* cf. Gundlach, *Streit* 57ff.

383. See above, p. 33.

384. Gassó-Batlle, *Pelagii I epistulae* xxi ff.

385. Ewald, NA 5 (1890) 573f. and Gundlach, *Streit* 60f. n. 4.

386. This conclusion is based on an examination of the collections with the help of incipit and source lists, as well as concordances of canons and texts.

PART II

Papal Letters of the Merovingian and Carolingian Periods

I. Papal Letters of the Seventh Century

The century between the death of Gregory the Great (604) and the death of Pope Constantine I (715) is characterized by frequent changes of pope.[1] The *Liber Pontificalis* lists twenty-four pontificates, mostly very short; only Popes Honorius I (625–638), Vitalian (657–672), and Sergius I (687–701) had pontificates of more than ten years.[2] In contrast to the large number of popes, though perhaps also conditioned by it, the number of papal letters and charters in this period is modest. Pietro Conte has arrived at a total of 71 fully or partially surviving genuine documents, 80 'deperdita' and 76 forged or suspicious texts.[3] The problems dealt with in these texts were partly dogmatic in nature, resulting from the Monothelite dispute—a constant preoccupation of the papacy throughout the century—and from the after-effects of the Three Chapters dispute in North-

---

1. Cf., from an extensive writings on this topic, Caspar, *Papsttum* 2.515ff., with detailed discussion of the papal letters of this century, and J. Richards, *The Popes and the Papacy in the Early Middle Ages, 476–752* (London 1979) 137ff.

2. Cf. *Liber Pontificalis* 1.315–395, and, for more intensive textual criticism, the edition of T. Mommsen, *Gesta pontificum Romanorum* (Berlin 1898); there is an English translation, with a good introduction and up-to-date bibliography, by R. Davis, *The Book of Pontiffs (Liber Pontificalis)* (Translated Texts for Historians 5; Liverpool 1989) 62ff.

3. P. Conte, *Chiesa e primato nelle lettere dei papi del secolo VII* (Pubblicazioni dell' Università Cattolica del S. Cuore. Saggi e ricerche, serie 3, Scienze storiche 4; Milan 1971) 35f. In his appendix is a helpful calendar of papal letters, although its critical discussions of individual documents are not always free of error. H. H. Anton analyses the roughly 20 forged monastic privileges issued in the names of popes of this period in his *Studien zu den Klosterprivilegien der Päpste im frühen Mittelalter* (Beiträge zur Geschichte und Quellenkunde des Mittelalters 4; Berlin 1975) 49ff. Further items not listed in Jaffé's *Regesta* (1885) are listed in Kehr's *Regesta pontificum Romanorum*; see R. Hiestand, *Initienverzeichnis und chronologisches Verzeichnis zu den Archivberichten und Vorarbeiten der Regesta pontificum Romanorum* (MGH Hilfsmittel 7; Munich 1983) 106ff., and L. Santifaller, *Saggio di un Elenco dei funzionari, impiegati e scrittori della Cancelleria Pontificia dall'inizio all'anno 1099*, BISM 56 (1940) 22ff., 235ff.

ern Italy, which came to an end only at the Synod of Pavia of 698–699.[4] Later churchmen had only limited interest in these doctrinal questions fought over at Pavia and elsewhere, and to a large extent understanding of these problems was lost. Consequently, the relevant texts were seldom included in the later canonistic tradition. This fact largely explains the limited reception of seventh-century papal letters.

A few letters from Honorius I's register occur in Deusdedit's collection (JE 2010, 2011, 2013, 2015, 2031*–2036*), and reached the Varia Two of the *Collectio Britannica* (JE 2012, 2025–2029). These letters reflected no particularly complex legal cases but were examples of papal administration. Thus Deusdedit's chapters 3.138, 139, 208–213 (JE 2011, 2013, 2031*–2036*) 'ex registro Honorii papae' contained leases of Roman and Sicilian patrimonial estates, the refusal of the pallium to the Metropolitan of Nicopolis (JE 2010; 1.235), and a dispute about papal jurisdiction in Sardinia (JE 2015; 1.236). From the *Britannica* we learn something about the prosecution of a runaway monk (JE 2026), of an adulterer (JE 2025), of a murderer in Salerno (JE 2027), and about the disciplining of the Bishop of Syracuse because of his dissolute life (JE 2029).[5]

Four letters of Pope Leo II and one of his successor, Benedict II, to Spain from the years 683–684 are preserved only in one canonical collection, the *Hispana Vulgata,* datable to between 694 and 702.[6] These letters

4. Cf. H. Fuhrmann, 'Studien zur Geschichte mittelalterlicher Patriarchate, II. Teil', ZRG Kan. Abt. 40 (1954) 43ff. and Schieffer, 'Zur Beurteilung des norditalischen Dreikapitel-Schismas' 167ff., who examines, p. 176ff., the formation of various council and decretal collections, such as the Verona, Bibl. Cap. XXII (20), LIII (51), LIX (57), Vat. lat. 1322 and the forerunner of the famous *Collectio Grimanica* of the letters of Leo the Great, compiled in the course of this theological dispute. On the origins of monotheletism, cf. Caspar, *Papsttum* 2.530ff., Richards, *The Popes* 181ff., and G. Kreuzer, *Die Honoriusfrage im Mittelalter und in der Neuzeit* (Päpste und Papsttum 8; Stuttgart 1975). The Byzantine point of view is expounded by J. L. van Dieten, *Geschichte der Patriarchen von Sergios I. bis Johannes VI. (610–715)* (Geschichte der griechischen Patriarchen von Konstantinopel 4 = Enzyklopädie der Byzantinistik 24; Amsterdam 1972).

5. Cf. Caspar, *Papsttum* 2.524 n.1; Conte, *Chiesa* 407ff. nos. 39ff.; and A. Thanner, *Papst Honorius I. (625–638)* (Studien zur Theologie und Geschichte 4; St. Ottilien 1989) who on 196ff. translates into German the few texts of Honorius, genuine and alleged. On the whole complex in Deusdedit 3.184–289 and the fluctuation in the citation of sources between 'tomus' and 'registrum', cf. R. Schieffer, 'Tomus Gregorii papae: Bemerkungen zur Diskussion um das Register Gregors VII', *Archiv für Diplomatik* 17 (1971) 172ff. Ivo of Chartres incorporated most of the chapters from the *Collectio Britannica* Varia 2.1–6 in his *Decretum* (they are completely lacking in *Collectio Tripartita,* the *Panormia,* and in Gratian): *Collectio Britannica* Varia 2.1 = Ivo, *Decretum* 7.132 (JE 2025); Varia 2.3 = *Decretum* 10.187 (JE 2027); Varia 2.5 = *Decretum* 12.25 (JE 2012), and Varia 2.6 = *Decretum* 8.309 (JE 2029).

6. *La Colección canónica Hispana,* ed. G. Martínez Díez and F. Rodríguez (Monumenta Hispaniae Sacra, Serie canónica 3; Madrid 1982) 3.190ff. On the letters see Conte, *Chiesa* 484f.

were addressed to the whole episcopate (JE 2119), to the Metropolitan Quiricus of Toledo (JE 2122), to Count Simplicius (JE 2121), and to the Visigothic King Erwig (JE 2120). A few pieces were added as an appendix from the proceedings of the Sixth Ecumenical Council in Constantinople (680). The papal letters contained translations of pieces from the conciliar acts: the confession of faith, the oath of allegiance to the emperor, and the final edict of the emperor that the Spanish bishops were ordered to approve with their signatures. Before this mandate was carried out, Leo II died 3 July 683, and his successor, Benedict II, renewed Leo's order to the papal legate, Peter (JE 2125), to collect the episcopal signatures.[7]

The Fourteenth Council of Toledo (684) concerned itself with the papal requests; it approved the 'definitio fidei' of the Sixth Ecumenical Council in the form mandated by Leo II, and in canons six and seven it laid down that this definition should be entered into the *Hispana* after the canons of the Council of Chalcedon.[8] This command was not carried out exactly: the confession of faith and the five papal letters occur in the Vulgate recension of the *Hispana* under the title 'Item canones Constantinopolitani concilii CLXIII episcoporum'. These canons followed those of the Second Ecumenical Council of Constantinople (381) and thus became the Second Council of Constantinople in the *Hispana*.[9]

The letters did not bear further fruit, although they contained important elements for the development and reformulation of the theory of papal primacy. In Leo II's letter to the Spanish bishops (JE 2119) the phrase 'Haec sancta ecclesiarum omnium mater' is limited exclusively to Rome, and the emperor is not referred to generally as 'Filius ecclesiae', but is apostrophized as 'clementissimus noster, immo beati Petri apostoli filius'. These sharply formulated phrases created a link between the language used by the ancient Church and that used by the medieval Church, and they have been part of the common stock of ecclesiastical vocabulary since Pseudo-Isidore.[10]

---

nos. 250–253 and Caspar, *Papsttum* 2.613f. on the Vulgate recension of the *Hispana*, see *La Colección canónica Hispana, 1: Estudio*, ed. G. Martínez Díez (Monumenta Hispaniae Sacra, Serie canónica 1; Madrid 1966) 238ff., 327.

7. Edited in *Colección Hispana* 3.199ff.; on the 'regionarius' notary Peter, see Santifaller, *Saggio* 24.

8. Toledo 14, cc.6 and 7, ed. J. Vives, *Concilios visigóticos e hispano-romanos* (España Cristiana, Textos 1; Barcelona and Madrid 1963) 444f. On this cf. Maassen, *Geschichte* 704f., and Silva-Tarouca, 'Nuovi studi' 54f.

9. Edited in *Colección Hispana* 3.57 and 181.

10. Cf. Caspar, *Papsttum* 2.592f. and among the notes 781f. with further references, especially in disagreement with H. Koch, *Cathedra Petri* (Beihefte zur Zeitschrift für die neutestamentliche Wissenschaft 11; Gießen 1930) 71ff. The use of terms such as 'sedes apostolica', 'mater omnium ecclesiarum', etc., and the invocation of Peter in the older period

We know of four letters of Pope Vitalian from the year 668 through a similar textual tradition in a single canonical collection, namely the Pseudo-Isidore.[11] These letters dealt with the unlawful deposition from office of the Cretan Bishop John of Lappa by his metropolitan, Paul of Gortyn. The pope ordered his restoration after John, having escaped from prison, had lodged an appeal to Rome and a papal synod had cancelled the sentence against him as illegal.[12]

The first people who were interested in these letters seem to have been Bishop Hincmar of Laon (858–871) and his followers. Hincmar incorporated them into his first collection of excerpts concerning the rights of a bishop, which he compiled from texts in Pseudo-Isidore. This work survives in Berlin, Staatsbibliothek Phill. 1764.[13] At almost the same time the Vitalian letters were preserved in a manuscript of the False Decretals (Rome, Biblioteca Vallicelliana D. 38), which had been written in the Reims area and which linked the letters with materials concerning the case of Bishop Rothad of Soissons against his metropolitan, Hincmar of Reims. These letters were preserved sporadically in the French Pseudo-Isidore manuscripts, Paris, B.N. lat. 3854 and Vat. lat. 1344, both of the twelfth century,[14] and in the last manuscript group, the C-class, of the Pseudo-Isidorian Decretals. The C-class, fully complete from the middle of the twelfth century, spread outwards from Reims. The four letters of Vitalian were placed between the Roman Synod of Gregory II of 721 and the letter of Pope Martin I to Amandus of Tongeren (JE 2059).[15] Bishop Rothad of Soissons may have brought them to France. He went to Rome in 864 to conduct his claim against Hincmar of Reims personally. There, we may assume, the Vitalian letters, which have features of the papal reg-

---

are dealt with in detail by Wojtowytsch, with attention to the secondary material, which is still difficult to survey, *Papsttum und Konzile;* a short summary is provided by G. Haendler, 'Zur Frage nach dem Petrusamt in der alten Kirche', *Studia Theologica* (Oslo) 30 (1976) 89ff. (repr. *Die Rolle des Papsttums in der Kirchengeschichte bis 1200* [Göttingen 1993] 69ff.).

11. JE 2090–2093; Conte, *Chiesa* 460f. nos. 191–194. The letters are critically edited, with detailed commentary, by R. Schieffer, 'Kreta, Rom und Laon', *Papsttum, Kirche und Recht im Mittelalter: Festschrift für H. Fuhrmann zum 65. Geburtstag* (Tübingen 1991) 15ff.

12. On the proceedings see Caspar, *Papsttum* 2.585f. and Schieffer, 'Kreta' 20ff., who examines the credibility of the reports.

13. Cf. Fuhrmann, *Einfluß und Verbreitung* 3.678f.

14. Cf. Schieffer, 'Kreta' 16. Schon, 'Redaktion' 508ff. proves Vat. lat. 1344 to be an unusual form of the Cluny version of the Forged Decretals, whose oldest witness is the manuscript New Haven, Yale University, Beinecke Library 442, from the third quarter of the ninth century. Vat. 1344 may make it likely that Hincmar of Laon referred to a codex of this type for his works (510f.).

15. An exception to this is Reims Bibl. mun. 672 fol. 216f. which gives the chronologically correct order: Martin I, Vitalian, Gregory II; cf. Schieffer, 'Kreta' 16ff. on the editions of the letters in the council collections.

isters and may have been taken from them,[16] offered such an interesting parallel to his own case that he took them with him to France, where Hincmar of Laon and the Pseudo-Isidorian forgers used them.[17]

More influential was a dictum of Agatho (678–681) about the papal office. This excerpt of a letter purports to be from one that Agatho sent to all bishops (JE 2108). However, its authencity cannot be confirmed. Probably it is an echo of statements at the Sixth Ecumenical Council, in which it was established that Saint Peter had spoken through Agatho.[18] The text first appears in the *Collection of Seventy-Four Titles*, c.183, and from there found its way by means of the most important collections of canons into Gratian's *Decretum*, D.19 c.2.[19] It is one of the most widely distributed decrees of any seventh-century pope in canon law and is surpassed only by two forgeries attributed to Boniface IV (608–615) and Deusdedit (615–618). The text attributed to Boniface (JE † 1996) claims to be a council decision which allegedly agrees that monks should be allowed to exercise pastoral care.[20] Appearing only in the last third of the eleventh century, it is transmitted most often together with a forged decretal of Pope Gregory I on the same topic (JE † 1951).[21] The canonists of the eleventh and twelfth centuries seem to have been sceptical about the text, since

16. Cf. Fuhrmann, *Einfluß und Verbreitung* 3.679 n. 162 and Schieffer, 'Kreta' 24.

17. This also explains the variations in the extent to which the letters were incorporated into the long (A1) and the short (A2) versions of the Pseudo-Isidorian Decretals, and the full attention paid to them in the C-version, which was only completed later: cf. Schieffer, 'Kreta' 24. E. Wirbelauer, 'Zum Umgang mit kanonistischer Tradition im frühen Mittelalter', *Schriftlichkeit im frühen Mittelalter*, ed. U. Schäfer (Tübingen 1993) 216f. assumes that there was a similarly separate transmission of JE 2136, an excerpt concerning baptism as a precondition for the priesthood, perhaps taken from a decretal of Sergius I (Maassen, *Geschichte* 971f.).

18. Cf. Caspar, *Papsttum* 2.604 n. 5; A. Michel, *Die Sentenzen des Kardinals Humbert, das erste Rechtsbuch der päpstlichen Reform* (MGH Schriften 7; Leipzig 1943) 48; Fuhrmann, *Einfluß und Verbreitung* 3.708 n. 266; and S. Kuttner, 'Auctor noster beatus Petrus apostolus: Pope Agatho on the papal office', *Studia in honorem eminentissimi Cardinalis A. M. Stickler* (Studia et Textus Historiae Iuris Canonici 7; Rome 1992) 215ff.; p. 222f. for the listing of the false attribution of the Dictum to the Roman Synod of 680 and to the English synod of 679.

19. *74 Titles* c.183; Deusdedit 1.145 (= *Collectio Britannica* Varia 2.27); *Collectio Tripartita* 3.9.1; Ivo, *Decretum* 4.238 and *Panormia* 2.101; *Polycarpus* 1.19.6 and Gratian D.19 c.2; cf. Kuttner, 'Auctor noster' 219ff. who cites further collections.

20. Gratian C.16 q.1 c.25; Conte, *Chiesa* 400 no. † 9. An edition of the text based on Clm 27129 is provided by G. Constable, 'The Treatise "Hortatur nos" and Accompanying Canonical Texts on the Performance of Pastoral Work by Monks', *Speculum historiale: Geschichte im Spiegel von Geschichtsschreibung und Geschichtsdeutung*, ed. C. Bauer and others (Freiburg and Munich 1965) 569ff. 574ff. Cf. J. Gilchrist, 'The Influence of the Monastic Forgeries Attributed to Pope Gregory I (JE † 1951) and Boniface IV (JE † 1996)', *Fälschungen im Mittelalter* 2.263ff.

21. Gratian C.16 q.1 c.24; on the distribution, see Gilchrist, 'Influence'.

they did not include it in their collections. Scribes, however, added it to manuscripts of Burchard's *Decretum,* Anselm of Lucca, the *Collectio Lanfranci,* Ivo of Chartres' *Panormia,* and in a series of collections of canonistic and non-canonistic materials. Judging by the spread of manuscripts the place of origin of JE † 1996 was probably France.[22] The forged letter of Pope Deusdedit to the Spanish Bishop Gordianus (JE † 2003) is older. It treats the problem of spiritual kinship after marriage.[23] The letter purports to be based on research in the papal archives and on the decisions of Popes Julius, Innocent I, and Celestine I.[24] Consequently, the text claimed to be authoritative and authentic. Forged entirely in the style of Pseudo-Isidore, the letter occurs first in Burchard, *Decretum* 17.44 and was later incorporated into other canonical collections. It also circulated as a separate text.[25]

Just as Boniface IV and Deusdedit have to thank forgeries for the extent to which they are known in canonistic literature, the influence of Pope Martin I is based on the fact that he is very often named as the author of the 84 *Capitula* of Bishop Martin of Braga.[26] The *Capitula Martini,*

22. The finding of Gilchrist, 'Influence' 285ff.

23. Cf. J. Freisen, *Geschichte des kanonischen Eherechts bis zum Verfall der Glossenliteratur* (2nd ed. Paderborn 1893) 550 and P. Landau, 'Gefälschtes Recht in den Rechtssammlungen bis Gratian', *Fälschungen im Mittelalter* 2.28f. n. 72.

24. JE † 2003: 'Invenimus autem in archivo huius apostolicae sedis' . . . and 'Beatae memoriae sanctissimi patres Iulius, Innocentius et Celestinus cum episcoporum plurimorum et sacerdotum conventu' could have been used to answer the question (Burchard, 17.44, PL 140.928B–C); cf. Fuhrmann, *Einfluß und Verbreitung* 2.263 and n. 67. Gratian cites in C.30 q.1 (whose first chapter is JE † 2003) two Pseudo-Celestine passages (JK † 382f.) in cc.9 and 10, and in C.30 q.4 c.3 he gives a forged Innocent excerpt whose provenance has not been discovered. These citations are also to be found in *Polycarpus* 4.41.19 and 20 and 6.6.1, and the two forged Celestine citations also occur in Bonizo 10.46 and 47, in *Caesaraugustana* 15.37f. and in the second recension of *Tarraconensis* 1.204; cf. also Freisen, *Eherecht* 508.

25. D. Blondel, *Pseudo-Isidorus et Turrianus vapulantes* (Geneva 1628) was the first to include this letter in his analyses of Pseudo-Isidore; cf. Fuhrmann, *Einfluß und Verbreitung* 1.138f. n. 6. In addition to Burchard 17.44, JE † 2003 occurs in Anselm 10.29, *Collectio Tripartita* 3.2.18, Ivo's *Decretum* 1.305 and his *Panormia* 6.127, *Polycarpus* 6.4.24, in the *Collection in 183 titles* 153.1 and 5, and Gratian C.30 q.1 c.1. However, the text is older than Burchard's *Decretum* and can be found in Italian manuscripts of the tenth century: Vercelli, Bibl. Cap. CXLIII (159), fol. 128v and Bamberg, Staatsbibl. Fragment IX A 13, fol. 1r. On this see G. Hägele, *Das Paenitentiale Vallicellianum I* (Quellen und Forschungen zum Recht im Mittelalter 3; Sigmaringen 1984) 29 and 41, and Hoffmann and Pokorny, *Burchard von Worms* 158. When copied as a single item, the letter occurs as an addition to the *74-Titles* of Engelberg, Stiftsbibl. 52, fol. 50v; cf. DA 31 (1975) 74 n. 251, or as an appendix of the eleventh or twelfth century in the Pseudo-Isidorian manuscript Pistoia, Bibl. Cap. 130 (102) of the ninth century. See L. Chiappelli, 'I manoscritti giuridici di Pistoia con testi e documenti inediti', *Archivio giuridico* 34 (1885) 241.

26. *Martini episcopi Bracarensis opera omnia,* ed. C. W. Barlow (Papers and monographs of the American Academy in Rome 12; New Haven 1950) 123ff. on which the critical com-

incorporated into all forms of the *Hispana* in various places with differing 'inscriptiones' and also incorporated into the Pseudo-Isidorian Decretals,[27] are cited often in the canonical collections from Regino of Prüm and later, sometimes with a completely false statement of their origin, sometimes with the falsified heading 'Ex decretis' or 'Ex concilio Martini papae'. The process is made uniform in the *Tripartita* 2.54: between the Second and Third Council of Braga the author of the collection placed the 84 *Capitula* under the inscription 'Ex concilio Martini papae'.[28] Under this inscription, around sixty chapters of the *Capitula Martini* were entered into Gratian's *Decretum*.[29] This large number of texts misattributed to Martin I is hardly counterbalanced by the two authentic excerpts in D.50 c.2 and c.12 taken from his letter to Amandus of Tongeren (JE 2059), which he sent to accompany the acts of the Lateran Synod of 649.[30] Gratian incorporated them from Alger of Liège's treatise *De misericordia et iustitia* 2.42, which relied on a C-class manuscript of the Pseudo-Isidorian Decretals as its source.[31] In all codices of the C-version, the papal letter JE

---

ments by S. Williams in his review, *Speculum* 29 (1954) 255f. should be noted. G. Martínez Díez, 'La colección canonica de la iglesia sueva los capitula martini', *Actas do Congresso de estudos da comemoração do XIII centenário da morte de S. Frutuoso* 1 (Bracara Augusta 21 [1967]) 224ff. analyses the collection; the literature is gathered together in J. Gaudemet, '"Traduttore, traditore"—Les Capitula Martini', *Fälschungen im Mittelalter* 2.51ff.

27. Cf. Martínez Díez, *Colección Hispana* 1.211, 233f. and Gaudemet, '"Traduttore"' 52f. n. 19; on Pseudo-Isidore cf. Fuhrmann, *Einfluß und Verbreitung* 1.185.

28. Cf. P. Fournier, 'Les collections canoniques attribuées à Yves de Chartres', BEC 57 (1896) 673 (repr. *Mélanges* 1.479) and P. Conte, *Il sinodo Lateranense dell'ottobre 649: La nuova edizione degli atti a cura di Rudolf Riedinger: Rassegna critica di fonti dei secoli VII–XII* (Collezione teologica 3; Vatican City 1989) 390ff. In Burchard we find the headings 'Ex concilio Bracarensi' (1.10; 3.179–181; 8.25; 9.20; 10.6, 13.19ff., 38) or 'Ex decretis Martini papae' (1.215; 2.135 = Regino 1.337; 10.15; 17.2 = Regino 2.196) but also 'Ex decretis Fabiani papae orientalibus missis' (2.10 = *Capitula Martini* 20) and 'Ex epistula Bonifatii papae' (1.73 = *Capitula Martini* 7).

29. Cf. the survey of the sources in Friedberg, xxii.

30. Ed. by R. Riedinger, ACO 2.1 (Berlin 1984) 422ff. and thoroughly interpreted by G. Scheibelreiter, 'Griechisches-lateinisches-fränkisches Christentum: Der Brief Papst Martins I. an den Bischof Amandus von Maastricht aus dem Jahre 649', MIÖG 100 (1992) 84ff. Silva-Tarouca, 'Nuovi studi' 51ff. examines their authenticity; further studies are cited by Conte, *Chiesa* 446 no. 145; Conte, *Sinodo Lateranense* in the index under the name Amando; G. Cremascoli, 'Le lettere di Martino I', *Martino I Papa (649–653) e il suo tempo: Atti del XXVIII Covegno storico internazionale Todi, 13–16 ottobre 1991* (Atti Tudertina N.S. 5; Spoleto 1992) 245ff. In addition, a text from Martin I's letter to Theodoros, a member of the fraternity of the Spudaioi (JE 2079) is included in Deusdedit 2.59, Bonizo 4.96 and in the collection Vat. lat. 3829, fol. 266v (from Deusdedit): here the pope expresses the fundamental rule that his exile did not justify the election of a successor. On the circumstances of the letter see Caspar, *Papst-tum* 2.566ff.

31. R. Kretzschmar, *Alger von Lüttichs Traktat 'De misericordia et iustitia': Ein kanonistischer Konkordanzversuch aus der Zeit des Investiturstreits: Untersuchung und Edition* (Quellen und Forschungen zum Recht im Mittelalter 2; Sigmaringen 1985) 288 on dict. and can. c and d, with commentary on them 103f.

2059 is added onto the anathemas of the Fifth Ecumenical Council, in the version of the Lateran Synod of 649. From the ninth century, these anathemas were placed in an appendix of a separate branch of the long version of Pseudo-Isidore (A 1).[32] JE 2059 owed its circulation in Northern France and also in Reims, the place of origin of the C-version, to Milo of St-Amand († 871–872). When he was expanding the *Life of St Amandus*, Milo had access to the original manuscript, on papyrus, of the acts of the council, which included this letter.[33] This combination is still observable in codices that were compiled roughly contemporaneously with Gratian's *Decretum* (ca. 1140). As examples we could cite the manuscripts Leipzig, Universitätsbibl. 836 and Göttweig, Stiftsbibl. 53 (56), two manuscripts of excerpts from a C-class Pseudo-Isidore.[34] Following an extract from Vitalian's letter JE 2092 to Archbishop Paul of Gortyn, the *Capitula Martini* are placed under the heading 'Martinus' (Leipzig 836, fol. 110v) or 'Martinus papa in his que ex orientalium patrum synodis collegit et ordinavit' (Göttweig 53, fol. 45v). They are followed by, respectively, the texts cited by Alger of Liège from JE 2059, marked in the Leipzig manuscript merely by an initial, and by those cited by Gratian from JE 2059, identified in the Göttweig codex with the heading: 'Martinus papa Amando episcopo in ea epistola cuius initium est: Confraternitatis tue studio'.[35]

II. The Papal Letters in the Correspondence of Boniface

The collection of Boniface's letters provides the source for most of the writings of Gregory II (715–731), Gregory III (731–741), and Zacharias (741–752), which found their way into canonical compilations.[36] This col-

32. Cf. Schon, 'Redaktion' 500ff.; see, in addition, R. Schieffer, 'Das V. Ökumenische Konzil in kanonistischer Überlieferung', ZRG Kan. Abt. 59 (1973) 20ff., and R. Riedinger, 'Griechische Konzilsakten auf dem Wege ins lateinische Mittelalter', AHC 9 (1977) 272ff., who edits the canons in ACO Ser. 2.1.225ff.

33. *Vita Amandi episcopi II auctore Milone*, ed. B. Krusch, (MGH Scriptores Rerum Merovingicarum 5; Hannover 1910) 452.8–18; on this see E. Caspar, 'Die Lateransynode von 649', ZKG 51 (1932) 76, Silva-Tarouca, 'Nuovi studi' 50, and Conte, *Sinodo Lateranense* 337ff.

34. On Leipzig, Universitätsbibl. 836 cf. Williams, *Codices Pseudo-Isidoriani* 88 Excerpta 30; on Göttweig, Stiftsbibl. 53 (56), cf. J. F. Schulte, 'Die Rechtshandschriften der Stiftsbibliotheken von Göttweig, Heiligenkreuz, Klosterneuburg, Melk, Schotten in Wien' (SB Wien 57; Vienna 1868) 560ff., M. Sdralek, *Die Streitschriften Altmanns von Passau und Wezilos von Mainz* (Paderborn 1890) 64ff., and M. Brett, 'The Collectio Lanfranci and Its Competitors', *Intellectual Life in the Middle Ages: Essays Presented to M. Gibson* (London 1992) 161.

35. The combination in the collection in Vat. lat. 3829 from the 1120s is quite similar. Under the heading 'Decreta Martini papae' are entered several capitula of Martin of Braga (fol. 256v, 265r), followed on fol. 266r by an excerpt, taken from Deusdedit, from JE 2059. On the collection cf. Fournier-Le Bras, *Histoire* 2.210ff. and 217, and H. Fuhrmann, 'Ein Papst Ideo (zu Collectio Lipsiensis, tit. 27, 5)', *Études Le Bras* 1.90ff.

36. *Die Briefe des heiligen Bonifatius und Lullus*, ed. M. Tangl (MGH Epp. selectae 1; Berlin

lection, put together shortly after the death of Boniface in 754, consists of two parts: Boniface's correspondence with the popes, entitled by Tangl the *Collectio pontificia,* in which, with only a few exceptions, only papal letters are preserved, and the correspondence with other people, Tangl's *Collectio communis.* The parts were probably joined together as one collection during the pontificate of Archbishop Hrabanus Maurus of Mainz (847–856) and enlarged with further Mainz material.[37] A sister manuscript of the Karlsruhe codex Rastatt 22 (referred to as manuscript 2 in the edition) reached France early, for Benedictus Levita made generous use of the letters of Boniface in his false capitularies, as did Pseudo-Isidore in his forged papal letters. Archbishop Hincmar of Reims (845–882) also knew the letters.[38]

The letter collection survives in six manuscripts or groups of manuscripts. Tangl considered groups 4, 5, and 6 to be the work of Otloh of St Emmeram († after 1067), compiled in connection with the composition of his *Vita Bonifatii* (1062–1066).[39] Reinhold Rau put forward serious arguments for separating group 4 (which for us is of particular interest) from Otloh's work.[40] Group 4 is a selection of 26 letters from the *Collectio pontificia* and two from the *Collectio communis* made with the aim of putting together items from Boniface's letters that are important for canon law. This collection occurs exclusively as an appendix to the C-class of the Pseudo-Isidorian Decretals. These manuscripts first appear in Northern France during the middle of the twelfth century, but they go back to earlier versions compiled in the eleventh century or before. They may already have been compiled in the ninth century.[41] Since Pseudo-Isidore

---

1916); on this see his extensive analysis: 'Studien zur Neuausgabe der Briefe des hl. Bonifatius und Lullus' Part 1, NA 40 (1916) 639–790; Part 2, NA 41 (1917) 23–101 (repr. *Das Mittelalter* 1.60–240). There is an English translation by E. Emerton, *The Letters of Saint Boniface* (Records of Civilisation, Sources and Studies 31; New York 1940) and a German translation of some of the letters by R. Rau, *Briefe des Bonifatius: Willibalds Leben des Bonifatius* (Freiherr vom Stein-Gedächtnisausgabe 4b; Darmstadt 1968). Since the classic work by T. Schieffer, *Winfried-Bonifatius und die christliche Grundlegung Europas* (Freiburg 1954; repr. with addenda; Darmstadt 1972), new surveys have been supplied by K.-U. Jäschke, 'Bonifatius (Winfrith)', TRE 7 (1981) 69–74, *The Greatest Englishman: Essays on St Boniface and the Church at Crediton,* ed. T. Reuter (Exeter 1980) and, with extensive bibliographical references, L. E. von Padberg, *Wynfreth-Bonifatius* (Wuppertal-Zürich 1989).

37. Cf. the summary by Tangl, 'Studien zur Neuausgabe' 1.686f. (repr. *Das Mittelalter* 96f.).

38. Cf. Tangl, 'Studien zur Neuausgabe', 2.71ff. (repr. *Das Mittelalter* 217ff.).

39. Tangl, 'Studien zur Neuausgabe', 1.687ff., esp. 709ff. (repr. *Das Mittelalter* 97ff., esp. 113ff.) and briefly in the introduction to his edition, xxix.

40. Rau, *Briefe* 16ff., and R. Rau, 'Ein unechter Brief des Papstes Gregor II. (Jaffé 2162)', ZKG 75 (1964) 337f.

41. Apart from the manuscripts considered by Tangl, Montpellier, Bibl. de la Faculté de

C-class was compiled in the Reims area and since Boniface's letters were used there in the second half of the ninth century, one can suppose that a collection like the one represented by group 4 of the manuscripts of the Boniface letters originated in Reims during the second half of the ninth century rather than as a work of Otloh.[42]

Because of a general lack of critical editions, it cannot be decisively shown whether this collection exercised influence on canonical collections before the time of Gratian. However, the collection may have had some influence. It contains the letters JE 2174 of Gregory II, JE 2239 of Gregory III, and JE 2264 of Zacharias, which provide more than half of the canons excerpted from papal letters in Boniface's correspondence.[43]

The letters' influence on Regino of Prüm and on Burchard of Worms' *Decretum* was practically nonexistent. Of the five chapters of Burchard that are taken from letters of the three popes, three come from Benedict

---

Médecine H.3 and H.13, Vat. lat. 1340 and Venice, Bibl. Naz. Marciana, Zanetti 169, there are also Paris, B.N. lat. 3857 (s.xiii), fol. 240v–251v, Prague, Národní České Republiky IV.B.12 (s.xv), fol. 160va–181ra, Paris, Bibl. de l'Assemblée Nationale 27 (s.xii), fol. 240rb–248ra. Leipzig, Universitätsbibl. 836 (s.xii) contains an excerpt from the fourth class of manuscripts on fol. 113v–115r. The oldest Pseudo-Isidore manuscript of the C-version, Reims, Bibl. mun. 672 (G 166) also contains Boniface letters of class 4 on fol. 217r–222v. Tangl's judgment ('Studien zur Neuausgabe', 1.790, repr. *Das Mittelalter* 177) that this was only an incomplete excerpt was faulty, for a loss of several leaves between fol. 218 and 219 containing eight papal letters has led to a mutilation of the transmission. The manuscript Paris, Assemblée Nationale 27 was the basis of the first edition of Pseudo-Isidore, by J. Merlin in 1524. Here the letters of the fourth manuscript class were printed for the first time (Tangl failed to notice this in his edition, xxxi). On the C-version of manuscripts of the Forged Decretals see the comments in Fuhrmann, *Einfluß und Verbreitung* 2.500f. n. 204; Schieffer, 'Kreta' 16f.; and Williams, *Codices Pseudo-Isidoriani* 35ff. nos. 34f., 40 no. 39, 50f. no. 53, 52 no. 55, 65f. no. 69, 70f. no. 75, on the manuscripts named above; on Paris, B.N. lat. 3857 cf. Fuhrmann, *Einfluß und Verbreitung* 1.169 n. 61.

42. Cf. Tangl, 'Studien zur Neuausgabe', 1.705ff. (repr. *Das Mittelalter* 111ff.) and Rau, *Briefe* 18ff., who assumes that Collection 4 was created in Mainz about 200 years before Otloh's time but does not say why he thought Mainz was the place of origin.

43. An evaluation of the collections of Regino, Burchard, the 74 *Titles*, Anselm, Deusdedit, and Bonizo of Sutri, the *Collectio Britannica*, and the *Collectio Tripartita*, Ivo's *Decretum* and *Panormia*, Polycarpus, and Gratian's *Decretum* shows the following: the reception in canonistic writings was based with only a few exceptions in the collection of the Boniface letters. Only two Gregory II excerpts and only three from Zacharias come from another source. Of the nine excerpts from letters of Gregory II, which are transmitted through Boniface's letters, seven come from JE 2174 (Ep. 26); of eleven canons from letters of Gregory III, eight are from JE 2239 (Ep. 28) and from 17 chapters from letters of Pope Zacharias five are from JE 2264 (Ep. 51); cf. Tangl's survey of their influence in canon law, NA 41 (1917) 71ff. (repr. *Das Mittelalter* 217ff.). JE 2174 is discussed in detail by W. Kelly, S.J., *Pope Gregory II on Divorce and Remarriage: A Canonical-Historical Investigation of the Letter Desiderabilem mihi, with special reference to the response Quod proposuisti* (Analecta Gregoriana 203 Sectio B 37; Rome 1976), who, however, does not examine the peculiarities of the textual transmission of the letter, but repeats Tangl's findings.

Levita and thus only indirectly from Boniface's correspondence.[44] Pope Zacharias' letter to the Frankish nobility, urging them to observe ecclesiastical instructions (JE 2288; Ep.83), is attributed to St. Augustine in Burchard 15.30.[45] A similarly small reception is evident among Italian canonical collections before Gratian. Deusdedit included two letters of Gregory II and Gregory III, which occur only in his collection, while Anselm incorporated only the three chapters of Gregory III and Zacharias that Gratian ultimately took from the *Polycarpus* and placed in his *Decretum*.[46]

By contrast, the compilers of the *Collectio Britannica* and the *Collectio Tripartita*, and also Ivo of Chartres, made extensive use of the papal letters in Boniface's correspondence. In the *Collectio Britannica*, excerpts from eighteen papal letters of Gregory II, Gregory III and Zacharias were entered *en bloc* (fol. 136v–142v).[47] The author's exemplar must have contained the *Collectio pontificia* and the *Collectio communis*. After placing excerpts from nine papal letters in his collection (Boniface, Epistolae 28, 17, 45, 59, 60, 80, 87, 51, 58, JE 2239, 2160, 2251, JE p. 265, 2274, 2286, 2291, 2264, 2271), then following with excerpts from four letters of Boniface and his episcopal oath (Epistolae 75, 33, 73, 78, 16), he turned his attention again to papal

44. The excerpts from Ep. 26 in Burchard 3.186 and 7.11 are taken from Benedictus Levita 3.281 and 2.80. The letter JE † 2187 on vows of permanent widowhood, which was attributed to Gregory II by Regino App. 1.48 (repeated App. 2.29) and by Burchard 8.45, is a falsification of Benedictus Levita Add. 4.88; cf. the concordance to the canons of Burchard in Hoffmann and Pokorny, *Burchard von Worms* 210.

45. The letter of Pope Zacharias on repeated baptisms in Bavaria included by Burchard 4.43 (Ep. 68, JE 2276) is from an unknown source. A section of the letter occurring in Gratian, De con. D.4 c.86 and Ivo, *Panormia* 1.65, is contained in Paris, B.N. lat. 14315 (Ivo's *Decretum*) as a supplement to the *Decretum*, 1.149; this source is omitted from the printed version of the *Decretum*.

46. Deusdedit 3.140 (Gregory II, JE 2173) and 1.237 (Gregory III, JE 2253); both are preceded by the heading 'Ex registro Gregorii iunioris'. Deusdedit, at 3.141, takes over Gregory II's letter of recommendation for Boniface (JE 2160, Ep. Bon. 17), which occurs in excerpt form also in the *Collectio Britannica*, Ep. Bon., no. 2, fol. 137r, in *Collectio Tripartita* 1.56.1 and in Ivo, *Decretum*, 6.116, without signs of textual relationship between them. The passages cited by Anselm at 7.97 (from JE 2251, Ep. Bon. 45) and 7.158 (from JE 2239, Ep. Bon. 28) made their way by means of *Polycarpus* 2.35.2 and 8.6.4 into Gratian, D.68 c.2 and C.13 q.2 c.21. Anselm 10.27 comes from the ban on contraction of marriage between spiritual kin, widely distributed in canon law collections, issued by Pope Zacharias (JE 2306, also in Bonizo, *De vita christiana* 9.75f.; Ivo, *Decretum* 1.307; Ivo, *Panormia* 6.128; *Polycarpus* 6.4.29; and Gratian C.30 q.3 c.2); on this cf. Freisen, *Eherecht* 511 and n. 12. The concluding chapter of Anselm 10.28, a forgery attributed to the popes Deusdedit and Zacharias (JE † 2004 and † 2303), deals with the same subject and was incorporated into Gratian's *Decretum* (C.30 q.3 c.3) by way of *Polycarpus* 6.4.37; cf. Landau, 'Gefälschtes Recht' 42f. JE † 2303, a forgery in the name of Zacharias, is old, if it is the case that Hrabanus Maurus appealed to it in his letter to Bishop Humbert of Würzburg († 842), as stated by E. Dümmler in his edition, MGH Epp. 5.445.12 n. 3.

47. Cf. Ewald, NA 5 (1880) 284ff.; and Tangl, NA 41 (1917) 91ff. (repr. *Das Mittelalter* 232ff.)

decretals with excerpts from Ep. 28 (Gregory III, JE 2239), Ep. 26 (Gregory II, JE 2174), and from the pair of letters Epistolae 86–87 (Zacharias, JE 2291).[48] One must presume that the *Britannica* kept the sequence of letters in its exemplar, and, judging by the order and by a few variant readings, this exemplar must have been a codex closely related to Clm 8112 (manuscript 1 of the edition).[49] Tangl supposed that this manuscript was available in Rome and might have been brought there by Fulda monks with other materials for a new recension of Willibald's *Life of Boniface*. The monks expected that Leo IX would revise the *Vita Bonafatii*. The manuscript would have remained in Rome when Leo died early in 1054. Tangl also thought that the author of the *Britannica* would then have used Boniface's letters and that Deusdedit would also have made use of this manuscript. This sequence of suppositions is unfortunately not supported by any source. The very short passage of Boniface's Ep. 17 (p. 31, lines 6–10) available for comparison between Deusdedit 3.141 and *Britannica* (fol. 137) does not support the conclusion that they used the same source.[50]

We reach firmer ground with the *Collectio Tripartita*. This contains, under title 1.56, eight excerpts from letters of Gregory II and Gregory III, of which two are false attributions. A citation from JE 2174 (Gregory II, Ep. 26) is among the excerpts taken from the register of Gregory the Great (1.55.9). Each of the subsequent titles, 1.57 and 1.58, contains two excerpts from letters of Boniface (Epistolae 73 and 86) and Pope Zacharias (Ep. 87, JE 2291). In most cases the source was the *Britannica*, though one must bear in mind that the copy used by the *Tripartita* was not the only surviving manuscript London, British Library Add. MS 8873, but a collection very similar to this manuscript. Since only two excerpts are given from letters of Alexander II and Urban II in the *Tripartita*, the copy of the *Britannica* used by the compiler probably still lacked the numerous excerpts from the registers of Alexander II (87 passages) and Urban II (47 passages) which are contained in Add. 8873 on fol. 38v ff. and 142v ff.[51] The two false attributions in title 56 occur in Varia 2.48 and 85 of the *Britanni-*

---

48. Cf. the list in Tangl, NA 41 (1917) 91f. (repr. *Das Mittelalter* 232f.). To be added is an excerpt from Ep. 73 on fol. 140v, 'Apud Grecos enim et Romanos . . . sit Deo' (148.37–149.9), which was incorporated by Ivo into the second part of 7.129 of his *Decretum* (the opening part consists of the preceding section of the *Britannica* from Ep. 73 p. 148.13–27).

49. In the *Britannica* Ep. 17 (JE 2160) comes after Ep. 28 (JE 2239) and Ep. 51 (JE 2264) after Ep. 87 (2291), reflecting features of the Munich manuscript; cf. Tangl, NA 41 (1917) 93f. (repr. *Das Mittelalter* 234). In Ep. 78 manuscript 1 and the *Collectio Britannica* (fol. 141r) show the same lacuna; cf. the edition, 164.1 variant n.

50. Cf. Tangl, NA 40 (1916) 695 and NA 41 (1917) 93f. (repr. *Das Mittelalter* 103, 234); M. Brett, 'Urban II and the Collections Attributed to Ivo of Chartres', *Proceedings San Diego* (MIC Subsidia 9; Vatican City 1992) 37 n. 33, is sceptical about Tangl's hypothesis.

51. Cf. Fournier, 'Collections canoniques' 665f., and BEC 58 (1897) 47 (repr. *Mélanges*, 1.471f. 526), and Fournier-Le Bras, *Histoire* 2.62. On the letters of Alexander II in the *Britan-*

ca, into which they were incorporated from Deusdedit's collection 1.200 and 2.144, though Deusdedit had rightly attributed the letters to Gregory I and Jerome.[52]

Ivo of Chartres took many more papal letters from Boniface's correspondence for his *Decretum:* nine canons come from letters of Gregory II, five from letters of Gregory III, and twelve from letters of Zacharias.[53] Several excerpts are attested only in the *Decretum,* so that Ivo, in addition to using the *Tripartita* and a collection similar to the *Britannica,* must also have had access to a manuscript of Boniface's letters, which, however, cannot be assigned to any of the manuscript groups.[54]

Gratian, with 22 chapters from letters of the three popes, among which are to be found four forgeries, offers a similarly large number of excerpts as those taken by Ivo for his *Decretum.*[55] However, Gratian obtained

---

nica see T. Schmidt, *Alexander II. und die römische Reformgruppe seiner Zeit* (Päpste und Papsttum 11; Stuttgart 1977) 224ff. On the letters of Urban II in the *Britannica,* see F. J. Gossman, *Pope Urban II and Canon Law* (The Catholic University of America, Canon Law Studies 403; Washington 1960) 49f., and his list on 103f.; R. Somerville, 'The letters of Pope Urban II in the Collectio Britannica', *Proceedings Cambridge* (MIC Subsidia 8; Vatican City 1988) 103ff.; Brett, 'Urban II' 38ff.; Brett, 'Collectio Lanfranci' 163ff.; and now Somerville, *Pope Urban II* 1ff., who edited Urban's letters 41ff.

52. Cf. Fournier, 'Collections canoniques' 658 (repr. *Mélanges* 1.464). The extract from JE † 2305 in *Tripartita* 1.58.2 has no parallels in *Britannica.* The forged decretal about the indissolubility of a marriage between a female slave and a free man, when contracted 'consensu amborum', which was also used by Gratian (C.29 q.2 c.2), is derived from the *Paenitentiale Theodori* 2.13.5 and *Benedictus Levita* 2.95, though these two did not claim Zacharias to be the author: cf. E. Seckel, 'Studien zu Benedictus Levita VII', NA 34 (1909) 349f., and on this issue also Freisen, *Eherecht* 285f.

53. Among these are also to be found forgeries like JE † 2187 in Ivo, *Decretum* 7.63 and *Panormia* 3.204 or JE † 2305 in *Collectio Tripartita* 1.58.2 and Ivo, *Decretum* 8.53: cf. the summary by Tangl in NA 41 (1917) 94ff. (repr. *Das Mittelalter* 235ff.). Ivo, *Decretum* 9.26 and Burchard 7.11, which Tangl 96ff. (repr. *Das Mittelalter* 236) cited to prove Ivo's closer relation than Burchard to the original source, are not comparable. The chapter in Ivo clearly comes from the forged letter of Gregory I to Felix of Messina (JE † 1334), while the Burchard chapter comes from Benedictus Levita 2.80 (= Add. 4.75). Burchard 7.11 was taken by Ivo, *Decretum* 9.46a (= *Panormia* 7.77); the chapter is omitted in the printed version. On the text see L. Machielsen, 'Les spurii de S. Grégoire le Grand en matière matrimoniale, dans les collections canoniques jusqu'au Décret de Gratien', *Sacris Erudiri* 14 (1963) 261ff. and n. 39.

54. Only in Ivo's *Decretum,* 1.127 and 8.78 are from Ep. 26 (JE 2174), 1.149 is from Ep. 45 (JE 2251), and 10.34 is from Ep. 61 (JE 2264); on Ivo's special material cf. Tangl, NA 41 (1917) 96 (repr. *Das Mittelalter* 236). Ivo used the *Britannica* as a source for his *Decretum* (in addition to 7.129, on which see above, n. 48), 1.150 (*Britannica,* Epp. Bon., no. 5, fol. 137v), 1.169 (*Britannica,* Epp. Bon., nos. 6a–c, fols.137v–138v), 11.7 (*Britannica,* Epp. Bon., no. 8d, fol. 139v), and 11.91 (*Britannica,* Epp. Bon., nos. 15 and 16, fol. 141v–142r), which are all the same length as in *Britannica.* On the type of exemplar, see Tangl, NA 41 (1917) 97ff. (repr. *Das Mittelalter* 237).

55. These are the forgeries attributed to Gregory II (JE † 2187 in C.27 q.1 c.2) and to Zacharias (JE † 2303–† 2305, cited in C.30 q.3 c.3, C.29 q.2 c.2, and C.35 q.5 c.3 and c.4). Cf. the survey by Tangl, NA 41 (1917) 98f. (repr. *Das Mittelalter* 238f.) for the vain attempt to identify more closely the exemplar which Gratian used for the Boniface letters.

these letters from other collections, such as the *Tripartita*, Ivo's *Panormia*, the *Britannica*, or Gregory of San Crisogono's *Polycarpus*.[56]

III. Papal Letters from the Mid-Eighth to the Mid-Ninth Century

If we discount forgeries and false attributions, the popes from the middle of the eighth to the middle of the ninth century, from Stephen II (752–757) to Gregory IV (827–844), were hardly represented in canonical collections before Gratian. There are three examples of forgeries or of misattributed texts to the popes of this period in the canonical collections. Hadrian I (772–795) had extensive influence on canon law through the *Capitula Angilramni*, which were ascribed to him. Gratian took the *Capitula* from Burchard, 74 *Titles*, and especially from Anselm of Lucca.[57] Thus they became an important part of the *ius commune*.

The *Epistola Widonis* was considered an important papal document. Although Guido of Arezzo wrote this letter around 1031, during the reign of Archbishop Aribert of Milan (1018–1045), as a critique of the simoniacal practices in Milan, it was often attributed to a certain Paschasius or Paschalis. From the 1070s it appears in numerous canonical collections and polemical writings of the Investiture Contest, and, in a fragmentary form, also in Gratian (C.1 q.3 c.7) as the decretum of Pope Paschasius or Pope Paschalis (Pope Paschal I, 817–824).[58]

A third example is a forged letter attributed to Gregory IV addressed to Bishop Aldrich of Le Mans, dated 833 (JE † 2579), which, because of its closeness to Pseudo-Isidorian formulations, was an important piece of ev-

56. Ivo's *Decretum* was obviously not used by Gratian: cf. P. Landau, 'Neue Forschungen zu vorgratianischen Kanonessammlungen und den Quellen des gratianischen Dekrets', *Ius Commune* 11 (1984) 25ff. On the passages common to both the *Collectio Britannica* and Gratian's *Decretum* see Landau, 'Wandel und Kontinuität' 232.

57. Cf. Fuhrmann, *Einfluß und Verbreitung* 3.1017f., sub verbo *Capitula Angilramni*, with the numbers from the list of citations given there. Anselm headed his extensive series of texts from *Capitula Angilramni* 28–51 and 1bis–20bis in 3.89 'Ex decretis Adriani papae'. On the *Capitula Angilramni*, see Fuhrmann, p. 149ff., below. On the special emphasis given to the Roman origins of the *Capitula Angilramni* and thus to their claim to authenticity and authority, see R. Schieffer, 'Redeamus ad fontem: Rom als Hort authentischer Überlieferung im frühen Mittelalter', *Roma—Caput et Fons* (Opladen 1989) 65.

58. Edited by F. Thaner, MGH Libelli de lite 1.5ff. J. Gilchrist edited and analyzed a longer version from the manuscript Florence, Bibl. Med. Laurenziana Conv. soppr. 91 (s.xii in.): 'Die Epistola Widonis oder Pseudo-Paschalis: Der erweiterte Text', DA 37 (1981) 576–604. Gilchrist was able to establish the short form in about twenty canonical collections, all differing from each other, from the eleventh and twelfth centuries. Similarly successful were the forgeries composed at the end of the eleventh century ascribed to Gregory I (JE † 1951) and Boniface IV (JE † 1996) concerning the priestly service of monks.

idence in earlier scholarly discussion about whether the Forged Decretals originated in Le Mans.[59] It was introduced into canonistic literature by the author of the *Collection in Seventy-Four Titles* under title 1, 'De primatu Romanae ecclesiae', with four subsections (cc.13–16), which were then all taken by Gratian from Anselm of Lucca and *Polycarpus*.[60]

A similar picture emerges with the conciliar decisions of this period. The acts of the Roman Synod of Pope Stephen III of 769 aroused the interest of Anselm, Deusdedit, *Polycarpus,* and Gratian because of their stipulations about papal elections, candidates being restricted to those who were priests and deacons of Roman titular churches and laymen being excluded from the electoral proceedings.[61] Burchard included the oath of purgation made by Leo III at the Roman Synod of 800 in his collection as did Ivo in the *Decretum* and *Panormia,* and Gratian, but the Italian reform canonists ignored it.[62] The authors of the pre-Gratian collections showed some interest in Pope Eugenius II's Roman reform synod of 826, the decisions of which were repeated by Leo IV in December 853. The author

59. Ed. by K. Hampe, MGH Epp. 5.72–81; in addition to Paris, B.N. lat. 1557 the Pseudo-Isidorian manuscript Reims, Bibl. mun. 672, fol. 206v–207v, should be reckoned as a further witness. P. Hinschius undertook a comprehensive analysis of the sources of the text in the introduction to his edition of Pseudo-Isidore, clxxxviiiff. W. Goffart tried to prove the authenticity of the letter: 'Gregory IV for Aldric of Le Mans (833): A genuine or spurious decretal?' *Mediaeval Studies* 28 (1966) 22ff.; against this, D. Lohrmann, QF 48 (1968) 403f. Further literature cited, and a discussion of the links of the Gregory letter to Pseudo-Isidore in Fuhrmann, *Einfluß und Verbreitung* 1.192ff. and 2.241f., n. 13.

60. Gratian D.12 c.2 (= 74 *Titles* 14); D.19 c.5 (= 74 *Titles* 15); C.2 q.6 c.11 (= 74 *Titles* 13); C.2 q.7 c.42 (= 74 *Titles* 16). In addition in D.45 c.4 there is a canon from *Collectio Tripartita* 1.55.107, which, like all the excerpts from JE † 2579 in the *Tripartita*, is attributed to the letters of Gregory the Great. The opening of JE † 2579 (= 74 *Titles* 13) adopted Leo I's famous formula about the connection between 'sollicitudo' and 'plenitudo potestatis' from JK 411 in an altered form, so that this theme occurs more often in Gratian's *Decretum;* cf. Benson, 'Plenitudo potestatis' 200ff., 214ff., and Marchetto, 'In partem sollicitudinis' 269ff., esp. 289ff.

61. On the transmission see the edition of A. Werminghoff, MGH Concilia 2.74ff., esp. 86–92, and Hartmann, *Synoden der Karolingerzeit* 25 and 84ff. on the council's sessions. In Anselm's collection four canons of the synod occur only in Recensions B and C, after 6.24 (= 6.23, C); cf. P. Landau, 'Die Rezension C der Sammlung des Anselm von Lucca', BMCL 16 (1986) 35. Hadrian I made frequent use of the synodal proceedings in his defence of the Second Nicaean Council (JE 2483/85); cf. K. Hampe, 'Hadrians I. Vertheidigung der zweiten nicänischen Synode gegen die Angriffe Karls des Großen', NA 21 (1896) 103ff., and L. Wallach, 'The Greek and Latin Version of II Nicaea, 787, and the Synodica of Hadrian I (JE 2448)', *Traditio* 22 (1966) 124f. (repr. *Diplomatic Studies in Latin and Greek Documents from the Carolingian Age* [Ithaca 1977] 25f.).

62. Cf. M. Kerner, 'Der Reinigungseid Leos III. vom Dezember 800: Die Frage nach seiner Echtheit und frühen kanonistischen Überlieferung', *Zeitschrift des Aachener Geschichtsvereins* 84/85 (1977/8) 147ff., disagreeing with L. Wallach, 'The Genuine and the Forged Oath of Pope Leo III', *Traditio* 11 (1955) 45ff. (repr. *Diplomatic Studies* 306ff.), who wrongly saw the text of the oath, preserved at Salzburg, as a forgery influenced by Pseudo-Isidore

of the *Collectio Anselmo dedicata* included more of these synodal canons. From Eugenius' letters, on the other hand, almost nothing survives.[63]

The *Codex Carolinus* preserves papal correspondence with Frankish rulers, including letters exchanged by popes from Gregory III (731–741) to Hadrian I (772–795). This *Codex* was compiled in 791 on the orders of Charlemagne in order to rescue papyrus copies threatened with decay. It contains 99 letters, almost exclusively papal, and survives today in Vienna, Österreichische Nationalbibliothek 449, in a copy probably made at Cologne during the pontificate of Archbishop Willibert (870–889).[64] The preface of the *Codex Carolinus* appears to refer to a second part that may have contained letters of Byzantine rulers, now lost, but it has not been established whether this section belonged to the letter collection.[65] Parallel copies of *Carolinus'* letters have not yet turned up. We must assume that the collection gathered dust in an archive and remained unknown in the high and the late Middle Ages, since there is no evidence that it was ever cited or used in later works.[66] The letters lack dates, and the copyists of the Viennese manuscript wholly failed to retain the correct chronological order. Consequently, the research on this unusual source—hitherto rather limited—has concentrated on chronological problems and on the diplomatic study of the letters as a guide to the character of papal registers.[67]

Modern scholars have studied these letters to determine which canon-

63. Cf. the edition of the 826 Roman Synod in MGH Concilia 2.552ff. and of the 853 Roman Synod, ibid. 3.308ff., with a summary of their influence on later canonical materials, ibid., 314ff. The texts from the Synod of 826 incorporated into *Anselmo dedicata* are listed by J.-C. Besse, *Histoire des Textes* 78, at no. 30. This collection was the source for Burchard 5.37 (c.17), 8.54 (c.29), 9.17 (c.37); cf. Hoffmann and Pokorny, *Burchard von Worms* 265.

64. MGH Epp. 3.476ff., ed. W. Gundlach. The edition met with severe criticism, because the manuscript was not recollated, nor was its sequence of the letters preserved: cf. P. Kehr, in *Anzeigen Göttingen* (1893) 876ff. Since then a facsimile edition has been published: *Codex Epistolaris Carolinus: Österreichische Nationalbibliothek Codex 449*, with introduction by F. Unterkircher (Codices selecti phototypice impressi 3; Graz 1962), which enables the investigation of points in dispute. On the state of research and further literature, see (in addition to Unterkircher, *Codex Carolinus* vii ff.) H. Förster, 'Codex epistolaris Carolinus', *Archivalische Zeitschrift* 59 (1963) 159ff., and M. Kerner, 'Codex Carolinus', LMA 2 (1981–1983) 2022f.

65. MGH Epp. 3.476 line 11. J. Haller, *Die Quellen zur Geschichte der Entstehung des Kirchenstaates* (Leipzig 1907) viii, connects the 'epistolae de imperio directae' with the letters of the Roman populace preserved in the manuscript.

66. The first dated mention of the *Codex Carolinus* was 1554 by the Imperial Hofrat Kaspar von Niedbruck; cf. Unterkircher, *Codex Carolinus* viii ff. on study of the manuscript.

67. Cf. W. Gundlach, 'Über den Codex Carolinus', NA 17 (1892) 548ff.; P. Kehr, 'Über die Chronologie der Briefe Papst Pauls I. im codex Carolinus', *Nachrichten Göttingen* (Göttingen 1896) 103ff.; and D. Bullough, 'The Dating of Codex Carolinus Nos. 95, 96, 97: Wilchar, and the Beginnings of the Archbishopric of Sens', DA 18 (1962) 223ff. Silva-Tarouca, 'Nuovi studi' 24ff., investigated the 'superscriptio' of the letters of the *Codex Carolinus* in his diplomatic studies on the papal registers.

ical sources the popes drew upon.[68] Probably the best example of this scholarship is the answer of Pope Zacharias, dated 747, to 27 questions posed by Pippin concerning ecclesiastical administration, law, and the disciplining of clerics, monks, and nuns (*Codex Carolinus* Ep.3, JE 2277). The pope answered but supported his opinions solely with the 'traditions' of the Holy Fathers, the authority of the holy canons, strengthened by his own authority.[69] In this letter he relied throughout on the *Dionysiana*, whose two parts he clearly distinguished from each other as the *Liber canonum* (the part relating to councils) and the *Liber decretorum* (the part containing decretals). One may conclude that these two canonical collections had not been fully merged into each other as they would be later in the *Dionysio-Hadriana*.[70] On the other side, Zacharias cited Carthaginian (c.3) and African canons (cc.11, 12) exactly as they would be in *Dionysio-Hadriana*. Quite clearly Pope Zacharias was using 'a *Collectio Dionysiana* with *Hadriana* features'.[71] Zacharias had lightly edited his texts: some of his abridgments and verbal changes of the texts do not alter their meanings, but in some passages intention of the original text is mitigated. For example, in c.14 on the question of how one should deal with priests who are guilty of crimes he altered the meaning of the text.[72]

The popes used the letters of Gregory the Great fairly frequently. Stephen II, for example, drew on them for help in formulating the introduction of his last letter (JE 2335; *Codex Carolinus* Ep. 11). He reformulated these letters but committed stylistic errors in the process. Hadrian I praised Gregory I highly. He used his letters for their linguistic style and even more for their content.[73]

68. H. Fuhrmann, 'Zu kirchenrechtlichen Vorlagen einiger Papstbriefe aus der Zeit Karls des Großen', DA 35 (1979) 357ff.; and, at greater length, H. Fuhrmann, 'Das Papsttum und das kirchliche Leben im Frankenreich', *Nascita dell'Europa ed Europa carolingia* (Settimane di studio del Centro italiano di studi sull'alto Medioevo 27; Spoleto 1981) 1.419ff.; H. Mordek, 'Kirchenrechtliche Autoritäten im Frühmittelalter', *Recht und Schrift im Mittelalter* (Vorträge und Forschungen 23; Sigmaringen 1977) 237ff.; Schieffer, 'Redeamus ad fontem' 45ff.

69. MGH Epp. 3.480.16ff. It is striking that the formulation, 'ius novas leges condendi', which became problematic at the time of the Investiture Contest, is mentioned in the letter; cf. L. F. J. Meulenberg, *Der Primat der römischen Kirche im Denken und Handeln Gregors VII.* (The Hague 1965) 102ff., and H. Fuhrmann, 'Das Reformpapsttum und die Rechtswissenschaft', *Investiturstreit und Reichsverfassung* (Vorträge und Forschungen 17; Sigmaringen 1973) 190ff., with further bibliographical information.

70. Cf. Maassen, *Geschichte* 437f. 445ff., and Wurm, *Studien* 44.

71. Fuhrmann, 'Das Papsttum' 433. Maassen, *Geschichte,* gives the variants of the *Dionysio-Hadriana* from the second recension of the *Dionysiana* in the numbering of the Council of Carthage (419) 447 no. 12, and emphasizes, on 449, that Zacharias in his letters used not only the numbering but also the description of the *Hadriana*.

72. MGH, Epp. 3.483.37f.; cf. Fuhrmann, 'Das Papsttum' 426.

73. Cf. Fuhrmann, 'Kirchenrechtliche Vorlagen' 358ff., who prints in parallel columns

Pope Hadrian not only borrowed from Gregory. He took long extracts from decretals of his predecessors, Boniface I (418–422; JK 364) and Gelasius I (492–496; JK 638), in two letters to the Spanish bishops and to Bishop Egila, the Frankish emissary in Spain, because he saw parallels between his juridical problems and those of his predecessors.[74] The letters of both Boniface I and Gelasius I were addressed to the bishops of Illyricum, an area, which, like Spain, was in constant danger of splitting away from Rome because of doctrinal or organizational differences. Both letters stress the primacy and the solicitude of the Roman Church. In his decretal Boniface gave Roman authority its classical expression by linking Roman primacy with c.6 of the Council of Nicaea and by employing the analogy of a head and its members for the first time.[75] Boniface's letter (JK 364) occurs only in the *Collectio Thessalonicensis,* and Gelasius' (JK 638) only in the *Collectio Avellana.* One may conclude that both collections must have been available to the papal chancery.[76] Hadrian I also used the *Collectio Dionysio-Hadriana,* the law book presented to Charlemagne in Rome in 774, whose dedicatory poem stresses the general authority of the collection.[77] In addition, Hadrian was still making use of the *Dionysiana;* that is proven by his use of JE 2431 of 781, in which canon eight of the Carthaginian Council of 419 is introduced with the words 'Simul et in Africano concilio capitulo octavo fertur';[78] only the *Dionysiana* gives this attribution to the text. The papal chancery also used other collections like Deacon Rusticus' for the Council of Chalcedon.[79] Although the papal cu-

---

Codex Carolinus Ep. 11 (JE 2335) with Gregory I, *Register* 9.228 (JE 1757), *Codex Carolinus* Ep. 51 (JE 2413) with Gregory I, *Register* 9.13 (JE 1537), and *Codex Carolinus* Ep. 93 (JE 2477) with Gregory I, *Register* 9.214 (JE 1754).

74. JE 2479, 2445; *Codex Carolinus* Epp. 95, 96.

75. JK 364, ed. Silva-Tarouca, *Collectio Thessalonicensis* 34f. no. 10. Cf. Caspar, *Papsttum* 1.120f.; on the historical background, see E. Caspar, 'Hadrian I. und Karl der Große', ZKG 54 (1935) 164ff.

76. Cf. Fuhrmann, 'Kirchenrechtliche Vorlagen' 363f. Wallach, 'Synodica' 122 (repr. *Diplomatic Studies* 23f.), assumes that the *Avellana* was the only possible source for the letter of Gelasius, JK 664, in the two Hadrian letters JE 2448 and 2491, although other collections, for example the *Quesnelliana,* are conceivable; cf. Maassen, *Geschichte* § 282.16.

77. MGH, Poetae 1.90f. On the interpretation cf. A. Hauck, *Kirchengeschichte Deutschlands* (3–4 ed. 1912 Leipzig) 2.239f.; Mordek, 'Autoritäten' 239f.; and Schieffer, 'Redeamus ad fontem' 45f. Fuhrmann, 'Kirchenrechtliche Vorlagen' 365, points to other examples of the use of *Dionysio-Hadriana* in *Codex Carolinus,* Epp. 77, 91, 94, 95.

78. MGH Epp. 3.596.23ff. The correction by Jaffé and Gundlach: 'immo Carthaginensis concilii cap. 8', shows that they did not understand the contents clearly.

79. It was perhaps referred to in JE 2434 (*Codex Carolinus* Ep. 70), in which there is a citation from Leo I's letter JK 443, which only occurs in Rusticus' collection; cf. Fuhrmann, 'Das Papsttum' 432f.; on Rusticus' collection cf. Maassen, *Geschichte* 745ff. and Schwartz, ACO 2.3 p. xi ff.

ria used canonical collections often during the eighth and ninth centuries, their use in Rome was not systematic.[80]

Hadrian I's letters treating the Second Nicaean Council (787)—to the Byzantine emperor (JE 2448), to the patriarch Tarasius (JE 2449), and to Charlemagne with his defense of the Council's decisions (JE 2483–2485)[81]—enjoyed a wider circulation than did the letters of the *Codex Carolinus*. The *Collectio Britannica* contained the most extensive extracts from all these letters while retaining the original order. Varia 1 C chapter 34 listed eight passages from JE 2448, c.35 to c.54 gave twenty excerpts from Hadrian's letter of defense, and in c.55 there were two excerpts from JE 2449. Ivo of Chartres included a few texts from JE 2483–2485 from the *Britannica* in his *Decretum*.[82] They all have the same text and the same inscriptions as those with which the *Britannica* began its series of excerpts in c.35: 'Responsiones Adriani papae contra obiectiones quorundam ad Karolum'. The *Britannica* Varia 1 C 34, 5.7.8 and Anselm 1.84 (= Deusdedit 4.11) cited the same text from Hadrian's letter to the Empress Irene and her son Constantine (JE 2448); however, it is not possible to say with certainty that the compilers of the three collections made use of the same source.[83]

80. Cf. Mordek, 'Autoritäten' 243ff.; Schieffer, 'Redeamus ad fontem' 58f.; and Fuhrmann, 'Kirchenrechtliche Vorlagen' 367, who concludes: 'Von einer außerordentlichen und andere Sammlungen verdrängenden Bevorzugung der Hadriana kann keine Rede sein'.

81. JE 2448 and 2449 are printed in Mansi 12.1055–1072 and 1078–1084; JE 2483/85 were critically edited by K. Hampe, MGH Epp. 5.5–57, and analyzed in his article 'Hadrians I. Vertheidigung' 83–113. L. Wallach's thesis, collected together in his *Diplomatic Studies*, that the *Synodica* JE 2448 were forged in the ninth century, was refuted by H. Ohme, 'Das Quinisextum auf dem VII. Ökumenischen Konzil', AHC 20 (1988) 337ff. and M. Maccarrone, 'Il Papa Adriano I e il Concilio di Nicea del 787', AHC 20 (1988) 71ff. (repr. *Romana ecclesia Cathedra Petri* [Italia Sacra 47; Rome 1991] 456ff.). On the historical background, see Caspar, 'Hadrian I.' 164ff.; D. S. Sefton, *The Pontificate of Hadrian I (772–795): Papal Theory and Political Reality in the Reign of Charlemagne* (Ph.D. Dissertation, Michigan State University 1975) 199ff.; and P. Classen, *Karl der Große, das Papsttum und Byzanz: Die Begründung des karolingischen Kaisertums*, ed. H. Fuhrmann and C. Märtl (Beiträge zur Geschichte und Quellenkunde des Mittelalters 9; Sigmaringen 1985) 34ff.

82. Ivo, *Decretum* 4.83 (= *Britannica* Varia 1 C 42); 4.126 (= *Britannica* Varia 1 C 46); 4.127 (= *Britannica* Varia 1 C 50); 4.128 (= *Britannica* Varia 1 C 54); 4.141 (= *Britannica* Varia 1 C 53); 4.225 (= *Britannica* Varia 1 C 43); 4.229 (= *Britannica* Varia 1 C 48); and 10.66 (= *Britannica* Varia 1 C 41).

83. This is contradicted by the varying length of the texts: Anselm 1.84, paragraph 2 (= Deusdedit, 4.11, paragraph 2) is longer than *Britannica* Varia 1 C 34.5; *Britannica* Varia 1. C 34.6 is lacking in Anselm and Deusdedit, while Anselm 1.84, section 3 (= Deusdedit, 4.11, section 3) is fuller than *Britannica* Varia 1 C 34.7 and 8; in addition there are numerous textual variations between the two collections.

IV. The Letters of Pope Leo IV (847–855)

Our knowledge of the letters of Leo IV (847–855) is based almost entirely on the texts entered into *Collectio Britannica*, fol. 160v–171r,[84] which contains excerpts from forty-five letters, although Ep. 25 and Ep. 43 in the *Britannica* are part of the same letter,[85] making the total forty-four. According to the inscription preceding Ep. 1 (*Collectio Britannica*, fol. 160v), they came from Leo IV's register, a statement disputed by scholars in the case of a few of the letters.[86] The distribution of Leo IV's letters became widespread at the end of the eleventh century through collections similar to *Britannica*. They were then included into the most important collections, the *Collectio Tripartita* and Ivo's collections of canons, and found their way into Gratian's *Decretum* with twenty-six excerpts.[87] No text from a letter of Leo IV occurs in Regino of Prüm, Burchard, or the 74 *Titles* or the less significant canonical collections of that time. The Italian reform canonists, such as Anselm, Deusdedit, and Gregory of San Crisogono, omitted almost all of Leo IV's letters. From a lengthy letter that Leo wrote in answer to the bishops of Brittany (JE 2599) they took one or two chapters.

This letter was, because of its useful and practical contents, the most frequently copied decretal of Leo IV.[88] In contrast to the Italian canonists,

---

84. Cf. Ewald, NA 5 (1880) 375–398; the texts of the *Britannica* are edited with reference to other canon collections (*Collectio XII Partium, Collectio Tripartita,* Ivo's *Decretum* and *Panormia*) by A. von Hirsch-Gereuth, MGH Epp. 5.585–614. In addition there exist a few privileges of Leo IV (JE 2535, 2603a, 2605, 2606, 2616, 2653, 2655) that have left no traces in canonical materials. See, with more details, K. Herbers, *Leo IV. und das Papsttum in der Mitte des 9. Jahrhunderts: Möglichkeiten und Grenzen päpstlicher Herschaft in der späten Karolingerzeit* (Päpste und Papsttum 27; Stuttgart 1996) 63ff. and 489ff.

85. In Ivo's *Decretum* 4.181 the second paragraph of Ep. 43 is joined together with Ep. 25 to make a single letter (JE 2638); cf. MGH Epp. 5.600 and 608 and n. 3.

86. See below, p. 109f.

87. Cf. the Tabula fontium in Friedberg xxx. The reference to C.33 q.2 c.13 should be enlarged: it incorporates JE 2640, which occurs in *Britannica* as the 26th letter of Leo, and also occurs in *Collectio Tripartita* 1.59.12 and 13; cf. the edition, 600 no. 26 and Herbers, *Leo IV.* 494.

88. Deusdedit 3.63, *Polycarpus* 3.11.10, and the *Collection in 183 Titles* 54.8 have the chapter on tithes (c.12); in addition *Polycarpus* 3.20.5 the chapter on canonical authorities (c.14) of JE 2599. Anselm and Bonizo incorporated no chapter from any of Leo IV's letters, so we have to assume that these were unknown to them. The canons of Leo IV's Roman Synod of December 853 were included by Anselm, Deusdedit, Gregory of San Crisogono and smaller Italian collections; cf. the list in MGH, Concilia 3.315f. On the transmission of JE 2599 cf. the details given in the edition, p. 593, which are not completely reliable. For example, it does not note that *Collectio Britannica* lacks c.4 of the text, and places c.7 at the end. The most important old copy, in the collection of the Beauvais manuscript (Vat. lat. 3827, fol. 76), which was the basis for the first edition by Carafa, and which breaks off with c.8 because of missing folios, were not used for the MGH edition. Cf. Herbers' edition in *Leo IV.* 458ff. and the table p. 495.

the *Collectio Tripartita* incorporated twenty-three excerpts of Leo's letters. Nine came from JE 2599. The other fourteen excerpts were taken from eleven letters in a collection very similar to the *Britannica*. Obviously the author of *Tripartita* copied from his source the first nineteen canons in order and added to this series four other canons from *Britannica* 19, 20 (JE 2613, 2600), and 40, 41 (JE 2625, 2646).[89]

It is not clear to what extent the *Tripartita* was the source of the twenty-three chapters taken from the letters of Leo IV in Ivo's *Decretum*. Ivo probably borrowed only four or five chapters from *Tripartita*. Fourteen excerpts in the *Decretum* are found only in the *Britannica,* and Ivo must have taken them from a source very similar to it.[90] Of these fourteen texts Ivo placed only four in the *Panormia,* from which Gratian took them for his *Decretum*. For the most part, Gratian drew the remaining twenty-two passages from Leo's letters from the *Tripartita*.[91]

Since Paul Ewald's study of the *Britannica,* scholars have critically examined the letters of Leo IV in it and have concluded that the collection was not as reliable as it was first thought. At the turn of the nineteenth and twentieth centuries, R. Parisot and J. Calmette judged letters 12 and 13 (JE 2607 and 2608), which granted Hincmar of Reims the right to wear the pallium daily, to be Reims' forgeries from the time of Flodoard († 966). They were not to be linked with the policy of Leo IV and the positions taken by Hincmar and Nicholas I (JE 2823) over the rights of metropolitans in 866. This thesis was countered by Emile Lesne with forceful arguments that have been widely accepted by French scholars.[92] Fifty years

---

89. *Collectio Tripartita* 1.59.2–10 corresponds to JE 2599 cc.2, 3, 5, 6, 11–14, 7. Cf. the list by Fournier, 'Collections canoniques' 659 (repr. *Mélanges* 1.465) and Herbers, *Leo IV.* 494. Fournier's statement that *Collectio Tripartita* 1.59.11 (Fournier wrongly has 1.59.13) is not in the *Britannica* needs correction, for the eleventh chapter corresponds to *Britannica,* Leo IV Ep. 21; cf. Brett, 'Urban II' 38 n. 37.

90. Ivo, *Decretum* 10.83–88 corresponds to *Britannica* Leo IV Epp. 1, 7, 8, 17, 28, 43; *Decretum* 10.87 is in *Collectio Tripartita* 1.59.15–17, though this cannot be the exemplar, since c.17 is shorter than the *Decretum* 10.87; cf. Brett, 'Urban II' 42f. In addition to these series of chapters in both collections, we should mention the following: Ivo, *Decretum* 4.176 (= *Britannica* Leo IV Ep. 29); 4.181 (= Epp. 25 and 43); 4.182 (= Ep. 44); 4.196 (= Ep. 45); 4.210 (= Ep. 35); 9.11 (= Ep. 16); 10.73 (= Ep. 42).

91. Cf. Ivo, *Panormia* 2.149 = Gratian D.10 c.9; 2.152 = D.10 c.13; 8.27 = C.23 q.8 c.7; 8.28 = C.23 q.8 c.8. Gratian took no chapters from Ivo's *Decretum* if they were not included in the *Panormia* or the *Tripartita;* on Gratian's use of Ivo's work see Landau, 'Neue Forschungen' 25ff. and idem, 'Wandel und Kontinuität' 233.

92. R. Parisot, *Le royaume de Lorraine sous les Carolingiens* (Paris 1899) 737ff.; J. Calmette, *La diplomatie Carolingienne* (Paris 1901) 187ff.; against them, E. Lesne, 'Hincmar et l'empereur Lothaire', *Revue des questions historiques* 78 (1905) 22ff., esp. 37ff., followed by L. Halphen and F. Lot, *La règne de Charles le Chauve (840–877)* (Paris 1909) 1.181 n. 3, and apparently by P. Fournier, who had agreed with Parisot (p.741f. n. 8) that the whole structure of the *Britannica* must be examined again and from different assumptions than Ewald's.

later, Walter Ullmann, on the grounds of their contents, argued against the authenticity of the letter fragments 19, 21, and 40 (JE 2613, 2615 and 2646), which expatiate on the installation of priests and on papal immunity; Ullmann declared them to be offshoots of the Investiture Contest. His main argument was that Ep. 19 and Ep. 40 are first cited in the treatise *De penitentia regum,* a work whose origin he linked with the penance at Canossa in 1077. Ullmann's last argument, however, is certainly incorrect in the light of the latest research.[93] Janet Nelson studied letter 31 (JE 2645), on the anointing of Alfred the Great. On the basis of content and language she considered it to be a forgery of the 1060s or 1070s, at a time when Alexander II and Gregory VII were trying to bind England more tightly to the papacy by feudal law.[94] The scholarly discussion on Leo's letters cannot be gone into any more deeply here, but it should now be clear that scholars should use the *Collectio Britannica* critically. A complete, detailed analysis of *Britannica*'s contents is still a scholarly need.[95]

V. The Letters of Pope Nicholas I (858–867)

It is not the least symptomatic feature of Nicholas's state of mind that the writings of his predecessors in the papal office come so readily to his pen: Leo I, Gelasius I, Gregory I, and a whole host of others whose official communications form the backbone of Nicholas's own products. In accepting the Eastern challenge to the *principatus* of the Roman Church, Nicholas I was given the opportunity of re-stating the papal-hierocratic theme and in so doing he

Fournier never followed his own criticism, even in the *Histoire.* Cf. also J. Devisse, *Hincmar: Archévêque de Reims* (Travaux d'histoire éthico-politique, 29; Geneva 1975) 1.38ff., and the summing-up by Brett, 'Urban II' 37 n. 32 and Herbers, *Leo IV.* 52ff. and 62f.

93. W. Ullmann, 'Nos si aliquid incompetenter . . . (Some observations on the Register Fragments of Leo IV in the Collectio Britannica)', *Ephemerides juris canonici* 9 (1951) 3ff. (repr. *The Church and the Law in the Earlier Middle Ages* [London 1975] no. VII.). On the treatise *De penitentia regum* (MGH Libelli de lite 3.609ff.) cf. C. Märtl, 'Ein angeblicher Text zum Bußgang von Canossa: "De penitentia regum",' DA 38 (1982) 555ff., who refutes a concrete political motivation for the compilation of the text.

94. J. Nelson, 'The Problem of King Alfred's Royal Anointing', JEH 18 (1967) 147ff. More doubts about the reliability of the texts preserved in the *Britannica* were noted by F. Dvornik, *The Photian Schism: History and Legend* (Cambridge 1948) 325ff., and S. Kuttner, 'Urban II and the Doctrine of Interpretation: A Turning Point?' SG 15 (1972) 74ff. (repr. *The History of Ideas and Doctrines of Canon Law in the Middle Ages* [London 1980] no. IV, with retractationes on 5ff., with the information that sentences from the prologue to Ivo's canonistic works were interpolated into Urban II's letter JL 5383). Cf. also Herbers, *Leo IV.* 54ff.

95. The view of W. Ullmann, *Gelasius* 227 n. 36. The widely circulated *Admonitio synodalis* is sometimes attributed to a Pope Leo as a sermo or epistola; C. Baronio proposed an identification with Leo IV: cf. R. Amiet, 'Une "Admonitio synodalis" de l'époque carolingienne: Étude critique et édition', *Mediaeval Studies* 26 (1964) 71ff. P. Brommer gives an overview of the manuscript circulation of the *Admonitio,* ZRG Kan. Abt. 60 (1974) 119f. n. 16, and lists further bibliography in *Capitula episcoporum: Die bischöflichen Kapitularien des 9. und 10. Jh.* (Typologie des sources 43; Turnhout 1985) 23 n. 37.

powerfully buttressed papal ideology. . . . Nevertheless, whilst the Eastern theatre of war provided, so to speak, only a theoretical battle ground, the transformation of Western society gave Nicholas the opportunity to assert the papal-hierocratic theme most forcefully.

With these words, Walter Ullmann perceptively described the contents of Pope Nicholas I's letters.[96] A keen sense of papal authority and power led Nicholas to write extensively about papal rights, and the canonical collections of the ecclesiastical reform of the eleventh and twelfth centuries made extensive use of his formulations of papal authority.[97] Gratian summed up Nicholas' influence by placing many of his letters in the *Decretum*: 116 excerpts taken from 47 of his letters. Only the number of texts from Gregory I's register surpasses Nicholas'.[98] Gelasius I is, according to my calculation, quoted in 93 canons, and there are about 80 texts in the *Decretum* from the letters of Leo the Great.

Nicholas' importance began in his own times. His pontificate was barely nine years long, yet even then his letters must have been thought significant. The wide distribution of his letters began during his ponficate, or shortly after his death, and continued unabated in later centuries. Copies were made not from his registers but from those of the recipients. Their transmission began in private collections by contemporaries such as Archbishop Ado of Vienne (860–875) in Vat. Reg. lat. 566[99] and Archbishop Hincmar of Reims (845–882).

Hincmar's collection was ordered according to subject in Laon, Bibl. municipale 407.[100] The letters of Nicholas brought together in this manu-

---

96. W. Ullmann, *The Growth of Papal Government in the Middle Ages: A Study in the Ideological Relation of Clerical to Lay Power* (3rd ed. London 1970) 190.

97. Cf. Fournier-Le Bras, *Histoire* 2, as well as Fournier, 'Collections canoniques' and his 'Les collections canoniques romaines' (both repr. *Mélanges* 1.456ff. and 2.425ff.). The investigations of E. Perels, 'Die Briefe Papst Nikolaus' I., A. Die Handschriften', NA 37 (1912) 537ff. and 'B. Die kanonistische Überlieferung', NA 39 (1914) 45ff., remain basic.

98. According to Perels, 'Briefe' NA 39 (1914) 45, whose data were checked with the *Wortkonkordanz zum Decretum Gratiani* 3 (MGH Hilfsmittel 10.3; Munich 1990) *sub verbo* 'Nicolaus'.

99. Probably a copy made in the tenth century; the letters are on fol. 51–65v, and an incomplete sister manuscript is to be found at La Rochelle, Bibl. mun. 387 (s.x); on this cf. Perels, NA 37 (1912) 564f. A complete description of the manuscript (which is made up of many fragments) is provided by L. Bethmann in *Archiv der Gesellschaft für ältere deutsche Geschichtskunde* 12 (1874) 292ff. The first part, fol. 1–32, comes from Fleury: cf. M. Mostert, *The Library of Fleury: A Provisional List of Manuscripts* (Hilversum 1989) 268. Perels (564f. n. 5) pointed out the remains of a collection of letters sent to Ado by laypeople, in Paris, B.N. lat. 1452.

100. On the manuscript see detailed account by Perels, NA 37 (1912) 557ff. He ascribed the marginal notes on Nicholas' letters to Hincmar of Reims; this has been put in doubt by modern research, cf. W. Hartmann, 'Fälschungsverdacht und Fälschungsnachweis im früheren Mittelalter', *Fälschungen im Mittelalter* 2.119, and also by J. Devisse, *Hincmar:*

script treat the case of those priests who were consecrated by Archbishop Ebo of Reims 840–841, then deposed by Hincmar in 853, and finally reinstated by Pope Nicholas I after the Synod of Soissons in 866 under the leadership of Wulfad, later Archbishop of Bourges.[101]

Another collection, perhaps actually made in Nicholas' lifetime and possibly connected with Bishop Rothad of Soissons († 869), contains only writings concerning Rothad's case against his metropolitan, Hincmar of Reims. This collection contains fifteen letters of Nicholas from the years 863 to 865 and the *Libellus proclamationis* of the Bishop of Soissons (864), as well as the conciliar address given by the Pope at the trial of Rothad at Christmas 864. This group of letters is always combined with the Pseudo-Isidorian Decretals in the manuscripts.[102] The oldest manuscript (Rome, Biblioteca Vallicelliana D. 38) was produced in the ecclesiastical province of Reims in the second half of the ninth century.[103] Closely related to it (as far as Nicholas' letters are concerned) are Vat. lat. 1343 (Italian, tenth or eleventh century) and Vat. lat. 1344 (French, twelfth century).[104] To this group also belongs the copy in Rome, Biblioteca Vallicelliana C. 15, fol. 137–167v, put together in the circle of the *Correctores Romani* in the sixteenth century. For Nicholas' letters the compilers relied on a 'codex antiquus' of Achilles Statius († 1581), the founder of the Vallicelliana. Ernst Perels justly suspected that the 'codex antiquus' was the Vallicelliana D. 38.[105]

A Pseudo-Isidorian manuscript, Paris, B.N. lat. 3854 (probably Rouen, twelfth century), is another important witness for Nicholas' letters for

---

Archévêque de Reims 845–882 (Travaux d'histoire éthico-politique 29, Geneva 1976) 2.942ff., though he took no notice of Perels' discussions. A comparable collection of materials that probably goes back to Hincmar is contained in the manuscript Brussels, Bibl. Royale 5413-22 (Van den Gheyn 2606), analysed in detail by H. Silvestre, *Sacris Erudiri* 5 (1953) 174ff.; cf. also Fuhrmann, *Einfluß und Verbreitung* 3.726f. n. 318.

101. The letters are, in the order given here, Epp. 75 (JE 2803), 74 (JE 2802), 77 (JE 2811), 59a (JE 2664), 59 (JE 2720), 78 (JE 2824), 79 (JE 2822), 80 (JE 2823), 81 (JE 2825), 101 (JE 2882), and 100 (JE 2879). The two last letters do not belong to the group in terms of their contents; Ep. 100 asks the pope for doctrinal support in the dispute with the Greeks and letter 101 to Charles the Bald urges him to support Hincmar's preparations for the council.

102. On the disagreement between Bishop Rothad of Soissons and Hincmar of Reims see Hartmann, *Synoden der Karolingerzeit* 313ff., with further bibliographical references.

103. Cf. Williams, *Codices Pseudo-Isidoriani* 53f. no. 57 with further references; also Fuhrmann, *Einfluß und Verbreitung* 2.269ff.

104. On these two manuscripts see *A Catalogue of Canon and Roman Law Manuscripts in the Vatican Library,* compiled under the direction of S. Kuttner and R. Elze (Studi e testi 322; Vatican City 1986) 1.86ff. on Vat. lat. 1343; 94ff. on Vat. lat. 1344, with further references. On the whole group of manuscripts see Perels, 'Briefe' NA 37 (1912) 547ff.

105. On the manuscript see Perels, NA 37 (1912) 550ff.; on its derivation from Vallicelliana D. 38 see E. Perels, 'Zur Wiederauffindung verschollener Handschriften der Bibliotheca Vallicelliana', NA 43 (1922) 607ff.

Rothad's trial. It represents a different textual tradition from Vallicelliana D. 38. However, some evidence indicates that both manuscripts had a common source. Although it dates to the twelfth century, the Paris manuscript was copied from a ninth- or tenth-century exemplar; this is made clear by its list of popes, which breaks off with Sergius III (904–911) and which supplies dates for pontificates only to Benedict III (855–858).[106]

The most important and compendious collection of Nicholas I's letters is found in Paris, B.N. lat. 1557.[107] Unlike the manuscripts just discussed, the contents were not assembled by concentrating on a particular problem; rather, the collection contained 45 letters with a geographical focus: all the letters were written to recipients in the Frankish kingdoms. In the manuscript, they are followed by 27 letters of Nicholas' successor, Hadrian II (867–872). This manuscript is the most important source of Hadrian's letters.[108] Until recently scholars dated the manuscript to the early tenth century.[109] John J. Contreni demonstrated from quire markings and marginal notes that Paris, B.N. lat. 1557 and the famous Pseudo-Isidorian manuscript Paris, B.N. lat. 9629 had originally formed a single codex. It was probably produced between 872 and 882 and most likely belonged to Laon cathedral.[110]

The same sequence of Nicholas' letters in Paris, B.N. lat. 1557 is provided by a copy in the above-mentioned manuscript, Vallicelliana C. 15 of

106. K. Hampe, 'Reise nach Frankreich und Belgien im Frühjahr 1897', NA 23 (1898) 631; Perels, 'Briefe' NA 37 (1912) 547, and Williams, *Codices Pseudo-Isidoriani*, 42 no. 42. Hampe concluded that the provenance of the manuscript was Rouen on the basis of a copy of Nicholas' letters made in the sixteenth century, Paris, B.N. lat. 1458, fol. 202–230, which has an entry on its provenance 'Ex Bibliotheca Rothomagensi'; cf. also P. Lauer, *Bibliothèque Nationale: Catalogue général des manuscrits latins* 2 (Paris 1940) 14.

107. Cf. the description in Perels, 'Briefe' NA 37 (1912) 566ff. and E. Perels, 'Papst Nikolaus I. im Streit zwischen Le Mans und St. Calais', *Papsttum und Kaisertum: Festschrift P. Kehr* (Munich 1926) 160f.; also Lauer, *Catalogue général* 2.65ff.

108. Hadrian's letters are followed by another two letters of Nicholas I: Epp. 101 (JE 2882) and 100 (JE 2879), which form a commonly joined pair, since they turn up in the same sequence in Laon, Bibl. mun. 407 and Brussels, Bibl. Royale 5413–22 that both belonged to the circle of Hincmar of Reims, as well as in Paris, B.N. lat. 2864 (s.ix–x) fol. 1f., from St-Denis, which contains, after the letters, the 'Liber adversus Graecos' of Aeneas of Paris; cf. Lauer, *Catalogue général* 3 (1952) 175.

109. Cf. the bibliography cited in n. 107 and K.-G. Schon, 'Exzerpte aus den Akten von Chalkedon bei Pseudoisidor und in der 74-Titel-Sammlung', DA 32 (1976) 549 n. 18.

110. Contreni, 'Codices Pseudo-Isidoriani' 1ff., esp. 9ff., expanding observations of B. Merlette, 'Ecoles et bibliothèques, à Laon, du déclin de l'Antiquité au développement de l'Université', *Actes du 95e Congrès national des sociétés savantes Reims 1970* (Paris 1975) 32 n. 61 and his own findings in his book *The Cathedral School of Laon from 850 to 930: Its Manuscripts and Masters* (Münchener Beiträge zur Mediävistik und Renaissance-Forschung 29; Munich 1978) 62 n. 81. It is probably no coincidence that the two manuscripts Paris, B.N. lat. 1557 and 9629, when they passed from the possession of Colbert into the Bibiothèque Royale, were numbered Regius 3887.8.B and 3887.8.A respectively.

the sixteenth century, fol. 168–256v, whose source is stated to be a now-lost 'codex antiquus S. Mariae supra Minervam qui fuerat Cardinalis de Turrecremata'.[111] The age of this 'codex antiquus' is unknown, although it was not copied directly from the Parisian manuscript. The reason is that in Vallicelliana C. 15, parts of Boniface's correspondence and also letters of Gregory IV and Benedict III are present but are not in Paris, some letters of Nicholas in Paris are omitted, but others are added, and Hadrian's letters that are in Paris are missing.[112]

Another ninth-century collection of letters, in Paris, B.N. lat. 1458, fol. 162ff., displays at times the same sequence of Nicholas' letters as Paris, B.N. lat. 1557.[113] Just as Paris, B.N. lat. 1557 should be ascribed to the circle around Hincmar of Laon, this manuscript fragment is likely to have been produced in France, possibly in Beauvais as Henri Omont supposed.[114]

A third textual tradition of Nicholas' letters reflects another theme of papal policy, namely the conflict with the Greek Church. The oldest representative of this group, from the third quarter of the ninth century, comes from Beauvais (Vat. lat. 3827).[115] The manuscript attaches sixteen letters of Nicholas I of 860–866 concerning the Photius dispute to a col-

111. Fol. 112, 168. Another manuscript derived from the 'codex antiquus' of Santa Maria is Paris, B.N. lat. 3859A (s.xvii): cf. Perels, 'Briefe' NA 37 (1912) 565ff.

112. The lost Codex S. Maria supra Minervam and its letters of Boniface have been dealt with in detail by A. Nürnberger, 'Verlorene Handschriften der Briefe des hl. Bonifatius', NA 7 (1882) 358ff., esp. 363ff.; Perels analyzed Nicholas' correspondence in 'Briefe' NA 37 (1912) 550ff.

113. For descriptions of this manuscript, which is made up of fragments of French manuscripts of the ninth to the sixteenth centuries, see V. Wolf von Glanvell, *Die Kanonessammlung des Kardinals Deusdedit* (Paderborn 1905) xxvff.; H. Quentin, 'Lettre de Nicolas I pour le concile de Soissons et formules ecclésiastiques de la province de Tours dans un manuscrit de Nicolas Le Fèvre', *Le Moyen Age* 17 (1902) 102ff.; and Lauer, *Catalogue général* 2.12ff. Three separate groups of letters can be established in Paris, B.N. lat. 1458 and 1557 and in Rome, Bibl. Vallicelliana C.15: (1): JE 2701, 2699, 2698, 2703, 2704, 2725 (Epp. 4–8, 10); (2): JE 2731, 2706, 2728, 2763, 2729 (Epp. 15, 108, 12, 28, 16); (3): JE 2727, 2732 (Epp. 61, 14). On this see Perels, NA 37 (1912) 571f.

114. H. Omont, 'Recherches sur la Bibliothèque de l'église cathédrale de Beauvais', *Mémoires de l'Académie des inscriptions et belles-lettres* 40 (1916) 74 and n. 1, who points to Beauvais as the provenance of fol. 64–87, the remains of a canonical collection from the beginning of the ninth century. Perels, 'Briefe' NA 37 (1912) 570, saw Paris, B.N. lat. 1458 as the 'wertvollste unter den Hss. mit Briefen Nikolaus' I.', a judgment which, in view of the new evaluation of the age and the provenance of Paris, B.N. lat. 1557, fits the latter better. Also his assumption that the collection of Nicholas' letters was put together in Rome, being taken either directly or indirectly from the register (followed also by D. Lohrmann, *Das Register Papst Johannes' VIII.* [BDHI 30; Tübingen 1968] 206) needs to be corrected. The heterogeneous contents point to a collection from recipients' copies, accessible by whatever means, and, if Laon is accepted as the provenance of Paris, B.N. lat. 1557, the interest in letters of Nicholas I and Hadrian II is obvious.

115. On the manuscript cf. P. Brommer, MGH Capitula episcoporum (Hannover 1984) 1.94f. and H. Mordek, *Biblioteca capitularium regum Francorum manuscripta* (MGH Hilfsmittel 15; Munich 1995) 858ff. with further references.

lection of Gallican and Frankish councils *(Collectio Bellovacensis)*, a few letters of Hadrian I and Leo IV, and the First Capitulary of Theodulf of Orléans. In this collection, the letter of Nicholas to Emperor Michael III (Ep. 88, JE 2796), cited extremely frequently by reform canonists because of its fundamental declarations concerning the privileges of the Apostolic See, is copied twice into the manuscript from different sources. The whole collection is rounded off with the letter of Nicholas I to the Bulgars (Ep. 99 JE 2812) that the reform canonists also often cited.[116] Not as old as the Beauvais manuscript and independent of it, Vat. lat. 3789 contains the same letters of Nicholas I dealing with the dispute with the Greeks, though without Ep. 99.[117]

Like the ninth-century papal letters, the oldest copies of the Eighth Ecumenical Council (869–870) in the translation made by Anastasius Bibliothecarius also belong to the late ninth century. These are to be found in Vat. lat. 4965 of 871 from Verona and in Vat. lat. 5749 of 871–880 from Bobbio. Five letters of Nicholas I and five of Hadrian II are inserted into the acts of the council.[118]

In addition to these oldest and most complete collections of Nicholas' letters, there are many old manuscripts that preserve single letters or collections of two or three. They are listed and analyzed by Ernst Perels.[119]

---

116. On fol. 127ff. are Epp. 88 (JE 2796) and 98 (JE 2821), to which the following letters are inserted or appended: Nos. 82–86 (JE 2682, 2683, 2690, 2692, 2691), no. 88 (JE 2796), and nos. 90–97 (JE 2813, 2819, 2814–2818, 2820), and also his letter to the Bulgars (Ep. 99 = JE 2812); there is a modern copy of Ep. 99 from another source preserved in Vat. lat. 3554, previously in the possession of Cardinal Carafa; cf. Perels, 'Briefe' NA 37 (1912) 541f., 545. A detailed examination of the contents and German translation of Ep. 99, though without any comment on the circulation of the letter, is provided by L. Heiser, *Die Responsa ad consulta Bulgarorum des Papstes Nikolaus I. (858–867): Ein Zeugnis päpstlicher Hirtensorge und ein Dokument unterschiedlicher Entwicklungen in der Kirche von Rom und Konstantinopel* (Trierer theologische Studien 36; Trier 1979). The passages on marriage law are analyzed by M. Sheehan, 'The Bishop of Rome to a Barbarian King on the Rituals of Marriage', *In Iure Veritas: Studies in Canon Law in Memory of Schafer Williams*, ed. S. Bowman and B. E. Cody (Cincinnati 1991) 187ff.; for further bibliography, see Sheehan, 'Bishop of Rome'. The legal sources of the letter are examined by B. Paradisi, '"Il Diritto Romano nell' alto medio evo, le epistole di Nicola I e un 'ipotesi del Conrat', *Collectanea S. Kuttner* (SG 11; Bologna 1967) 211ff. (repr. *Studi sul medioevo giuridico* 1 [Istituto Storico Italiano per il Medio Evo 163; Rome 1987] 225ff.).

117. Cf. F. Schneider, 'Reise nach Italien (October und November 1902)', NA 28 (1903) 722f. and Perels, 'Briefe' NA 37 (1912) 540f.

118. Nicholas I: Epp. 82, 83, 85, 86, 91 (JE 2682, 2683, 2692, 2691, 2819); Hadrian II: Epp. 37–41 (JE 2908, 2909, 2913, 2914, 2943). See C. Leonardi, 'Anastasio Bibliotecario e l'ottavo concilio ecumenico', *Studi Medievali* Series 3; 8 (1967) 68ff., 104ff., 146ff.; on the papal letters, 97ff. and D. Lohrmann, 'Eine Arbeitshandschrift des Anastasius Bibliothecarius und die Überlieferung der Akten des 8. ökumenischen Konzils', QF 50 (1971) 427ff.

119. Perels, 'Briefe' NA 37 (1912) 584ff. gives a list of manuscripts discussed, including modern copies and lost codices.

In contrast to the numerous surviving copies, often reaching back into the ninth century, Nicholas I's letters entered into canonical literature slowly.[120] Two hundred years after his pontificate, Anselm of Lucca, Deusdedit, Ivo of Chartres, and Gratian all enthusiastically included Nicholas' letters in their collections. The first citation of Nicholas's letters in synodal legislation occurred at the Council of Worms in 868.[121] Canons 3–5 and 8–19 repeat almost verbatim parts of Nicholas' letters to Archbishops Liutbert of Mainz and his predecessor Charles.[122] The Pope had answered their enquiries about disciplinary questions and rendered a judgment about the punishment appropriate to the offenses.[123] Extracts from two letters of Gregory II to Boniface appear in Worms.[124] To explain the Council's use of these letters, Emil Seckel postulated the use of a chronologically arranged Mainz collection of papal letters, including letters from Boniface's correspondence as well as the three letters of Nicholas to Liutbert and Charles.[125] It is noteworthy that the participants in the synod confirmed papal pronouncements. The adoption of contemporary papal letters into synodal legislation gives the impression that the papacy was enjoying growing respect as a decision-making authority, especially in the East Frankish kingdom.[126] Nonetheless, papal legislative authority was not yet universally accepted in this period.

A year later, in 869, Bishop Hincmar of Laon compiled a collection of excerpts from Pseudo-Isidorian decretals, known as *Pittaciolus,* and used several letters of Nicholas I extensively as a canonical justificaton, supported by the Roman tradition, for the correctness of his view of the relationship between a suffragan and his metropolitan.[127] In his *Opusculum*

120. Perels' studies are fundamental: NA 'Briefe' 39 (1914) 45ff.

121. Cf. W. Hartmann, *Das Konzil von Worms 868: Überlieferung und Bedeutung* (Abh. Göttingen 3rd Series 105; Göttingen 1977) 49ff. and Hartmann, *Synoden der Karolingerzeit* 301ff.

122. Liutbert: Ep. 169, JE 2869 for canons 3–5; Charles: Ep. 156A, JE 2709 for c.8–15 and Ep. 155, JE 2710 for c.16–19.

123. The letters JE 2709, 2710, and 2869 used to be regarded by scholars as forgeries because of the Worms canons; this view has been disproved by Hartmann, *Konzil von Worms* 56ff.

124. Epp. 18 and 26 of the Boniface letters, JE 2161 for cc.6–7 and JE 2174 for cc. 20 and 22.

125. E. Seckel, SB Berlin; Berlin 1920, 557, agreed to by P. Kehr, 'Emil Seckel: Ein Nachruf', NA 46 (1926) 177f.

126. Cf. Hartmann, *Synoden der Karolingerzeit* 304.

127. The texts from the letters 86, 88, and 90 (JE 2691, 2796, and 2813) are listed by Perels, 'Briefe' NA 39 (1914) 50 and in the edition of MGH Epp. 6. On the *Pittaciolus* of Hincmar of Laon see H. Fuhrmann, 'Zur Überlieferung des Pittaciolus Bischof Hinkmars von Laon', DA 27 (1971) 517ff.; idem, *Einfluß und Verbreitung* 1.221ff. and 3.712ff.; P. R. McKeon, *Hincmar of Laon and Carolingian Politics* (Urbana 1978) 71ff. and R. Schieffer, 'Der Pittaciolus Hinkmars von Laon in einer Salzburger Handschrift aus Köln', *Aus Archiven und Bibliotheken: Festschrift für R. Kottje zum 65. Geburtstag* (Freiburger Beiträge zur mittelalterlichen Geschichte: Studien und Texte 3; Zürich 1992) 137ff.

LV capitulorum, Hincmar of Reims energetically rejected the conclusions of his refractory nephew, Hincmar of Laon. These particular excerpts of Nicholas's letters did not leave any traces worth mentioning in later canonical writings.[128]

Turning from this polemical literature to the canonical collections, the author of *Collectio Anselmo dedicata* took no notice of Nicholas I's letters. This collection was chronologically nearest to Nicholas' pontificate; it was probably dedicated to Archbishop Anselm II of Milan, and it enjoyed a larger circulation than used to be believed.[129] Later, Regino of Prüm used several letters of Nicholas in his synodal handbook (c. 906), especially Ep. 48 (JE 2872) addressed to Charles the Bald on Lothar II's marriage case. Five of the seven excerpts attributed to Nicholas come from this letter. Regino probably knew of this letter and of Ep. 46 (2.108), both of which he quoted in his chronicle, from an old and now lost Trier collection of documents on Lothar II's divorce process. This collection may have origniated in the curia of Bishop Adventius of Metz (858–875); its original appearance can be deduced from the partial copy made in Trier by the Jesuit Christoph Brouwer († 1617) which is now Rome, Biblioteca Vallicelliana J. 76.[130]

Bishop Burchard of Worms incorporated all of Regino's letters from Nicholas I, with the exception of Reg. 2.113, an extract from Ep. 48, into his *Decretum* (1008/12, at the latest 1022).[131] He added a letter of Nicholas to Bishop Ratold of Strasbourg (Ep. 139, JE 2850) about the penance for matricide (6.46). Paul Fournier conjectured that this text could have been known to Burchard through the tenth-century manuscript Clm 27246, of a Freising provenance or one like it. Indeed, Burchard did take the deci-

---

128. Cf. nos. 59, 134, 140 (from Ep. 88), and 203 (from Ep. 86) in the concordance of canons in Perels, NA 'Briefe' 39 (1914) 140ff., which show different contents and can hardly derive from Hincmar of Laon. S. Kuttner studied the textual history of no. 59 (Ep. 88, 480.15–481.14) in 'Urban II and the Doctrine of Interpretation' 81ff.

129. Cf. the list of sources by Besse, *Collectio Anselm dedicata;* Fuhrmann, 'Fragmente der Collectio Anselmo dedicata' 539ff. examines the textual transmission.

130. On the manuscript see E. Dümmler, MGH Epp. 6.207f., who edited from it the *Epistolae ad divortium Lotharii II regis pertinentes;* also Perels, 'Briefe' NA 37 (1912) 563 and the detailed study by N. Staubach, *Das Herrscherbild Karls des Kahlen: Formen und Funktionen monarchischer Repräsentation im früheren Mittelalter* (Münster 1981) 155ff., who on 161ff. examines the use of the 'Adventius Collection' by Regino in his chronicle.

131. The extract from Ep. 157 (JE † 2711), which Burchard took from Regino 2.129, first was given the caption 'Ex epistola Nicolai ad Carolum Moguntinum episcopum missa' in Burchard's *Decretum* 9.28 and this attribution appears in the canonical collections up to Gratian C.32 q.7 c.25, whereas Regino still referred to (correctly for the first part of the text) 'Ex lege Romana' (= *Lex Romana Visigothorum: Pauli Sententiae* 2.20.4); cf. Perels, 'Briefe' NA 39 (1914) 61 and J. Müller, *Untersuchungen zur Collectio Duodecim Partium* (Münchener Universitätsschriften. Juristische Fakultät. Abh. zur rechtswissenschaftlichen Grundlagenforschung 73; Ebelsbach 1989) 164ff.

sions of the synods of Hohenaltheim (916), Koblenz (922), and Erfurt (932) from a manuscript similar to the one from Freising.[132]

The compiler or compilers of the *Collectio Duodecim Partium* made more general use of Nicholas' letters than Regino and Burchard did. The collection probably was compiled in Northern Italy or Southern Germany in the early eleventh century.[133] *Collectio Duodecim Partium* incorporated all the chapters of Nicholas that occur in Burchard. He also included five excerpts from Nicholas I's letter to Archbishop Charles of Mainz (Ep. 156, JE 2709), which had served as a source for the Worms Synod of 868, and four chapters from Nicholas' answer to questions of Bishop Salomo III of Constance (Ep. 138, JE 2849).[134] Both letters were preserved in four manuscripts of canonical materials dating to the ninth to eleventh centuries. The core of these collections was the decisions of the Synod of Tribur of 895 and the Pseudo-Isidorian collection of Pseudo-Remedius. The oldest manuscript, Clm 6245 (ninth and tenth centuries), from which the other three stem, was written in Freising. Five originally independent sections were bound together there in the tenth century.[135] The *Collectio Duodecim Partium* probably took its extracts from JE 2709 and 2849 out of this collection or one now lost of a similar type.[136]

Burchard of Worms' *Decretum* became the most influential legal work of the eleventh century. His work became authoritative in several geographical areas.[137] Few canonical collections were compiled in the mid-eleventh century, and it may be that Burchard's great importance and authority inhibited the compilation of new collections until the last quarter of the century. The Investiture Controversy raised many new questions about the structure of the Church and sparked the need for new collections. This need was met mainly by Italian canonists. At this time, too, Ivo of Chartres wrote his significant and influential works on ecclesiastical law.[138]

132. P. Fournier, *Études critiques sur le Décret de Burchard de Worms* RDH 34 (1910) 27 (repr. *Mélanges* 1.273). The manuscript was described in detail by H. Fuhrmann, MGH Concilia 6.1.6ff., and by Hoffmann and Pokorny, *Burchard von Worms* 81ff.

133. Müller, *Collectio Duodecim Partium* 350ff. believes that the collection originated in Freising.

134. On the reception of the Nicholas letters see Müller, *Collectio Duodecim Partium* 161ff., with table 19.

135. These are the collections in Munich, Clm 6245, Clm 6241, Vienna, Österreichische Nationalbibliothek 2198, and Bamberg, Staatsbibl. Can. 9, fol. 128ff., all from the tenth and early eleventh centuries. On this group of manuscripts, see H. John, *Collectio canonum Remedio Curiensi episcopo perperam ascripta* (MIC Series B, 2; Vatican City 1976) 29ff.; Hoffmann and Pokorny, *Burchard von Worms* 76ff.; and R. Pokorny, 'Die drei Versionen der Triburer Synodalakten von 895: Eine Neubewertung', DA 48 (1992) 433ff.

136. Müller, *Collectio Duodecim Partium* 166.

137. Cf. Fuhrmann, *Einfluß und Verbreitung* 2.460f.

138. Cf., from an abundant literature, P. Fournier, 'Yves de Chartres et le droit canon-

If we consider which features of Nicholas' letters were relevant to canon law up to the early eleventh century, we see that his opinions on penitential practice and ecclesiastical discipline were of primary importance. The participants at the Synod of Worms (868), the authors of the *Collectio Duodecim Partium*, Regino, and Burchard were all interested in problems of unchaste priests, sexual offenses, matrimonial cases, the murder of relatives or of priests, and other homicide cases.[139] These collections completely omit Nicholas' theological pronouncements contained in his letters on the Photius dispute, and also his opinions on the structure of the Church, such as the role of the metropolitan or the right of appeals. These issues were central in his correspondence with Hincmar of Reims and formed the core of Nicholas' letters in the oldest manuscripts.[140]

Collectio Duodecim Partium, Regino, and Burchard were compiled and circulated in the East Frankish, later German, kingdom. Consequently, Nicholas' letters on theological matters were probably unknown there. There must have been compilations in circulation containing the materials on Lothar II's divorce, an affair that led to the deposition of Archbishops Gunthar of Cologne and Thietgaud of Trier. Such collections would have resembled the Trier or Cologne letter collection, or collections of Nicholas' letters on specific legal cases, like the one from Mainz postulated by Seckel. In any case, these collections are now lost, but the canonists must have taken their material from them.[141] There is a late echo of these collections in the papal history of Pseudo-Liudprand, written in Osnabrück in the 1080s, a combination of papal lives from the *Liber Pontifi-*

---

ique', *Revue des questions historiques* 63 (1898) 384ff. and P. Fournier, 'Un tournant' 129ff. (both repr. *Mélanges* 1.727ff. and 2.373ff.). Fuhrmann, *Einfluß und Verbreitung* 2.339ff.and W. Hartmann, 'Autoritäten im Kirchenrecht und Autorität des Kirchenrechts in der Salierzeit', *Die Salier und das Reich, 3: Gesellschaftlicher und ideengeschichtlicher Wandel im Reich der Salier* (Sigmaringen 1991) 425ff. The concept of continuity between canon law of the reform period and of the previous epoch is emphasized by H. Mordek, 'Kanonistik und gregorianische Reform: Marginalien zu einem nicht-marginalen Thema', *Reich und Kirche vor dem Investiturstreit*, ed. K. Schmid (Sigmaringen 1985) 65ff.

139. Cf. Table 19 in Müller, *Collectio Duodecim Partium* 161f. Burchard 9.28 and 49–53, derived from Regino and also occurring in the *Collectio Duodecim Partium* (Müller nos. 6, 13–17), focus on problems of marriage law; for questions of sexual morality and the treatment of murder cases, Worms c.11f., 30, 33 and the *Collectio Duodecim Partium* made use of JE 2709 (cf. Müller nos. 1, 3, and 5).

140. See above, p. 111ff. and Y. M.-J. Congar, *L'ecclésiologie du haut moyen-age: De Saint Grégoire le Grand à la désunion entre Byzance et Rome* (Paris 1968) 207ff.

141. On the Mainz collection, whose contours can barely be discerned, see above, p. 116; on the Trier collection, see above, p. 117, and n. 130. The Cologne collection (Trier, Stadtbibl. 1081/29, fol. 47v ff., s.xi/xii) was described in detail by I. S. Robinson, 'Zur Entstehung des Privilegium Maius Leonis VIII papae', DA 38 (1982) 34ff.; on its compilation, not completely explained, see D. Lück, 'Miszellen zur Geschichte Annos II. von Köln und ihren Quellen', *Annalen des Historischen Vereins für den Niederrhein* 173 (1971) 182ff.

calis, Pseudo-Isidorian and genuine papal letters. The author pillaged an original and extensive collection that contained canonical materials and the letters of Nicholas I.[142] Similar exemplars were used in a Weingarten canonical collection dating to the end of the eleventh century from the circle around Bernold of Constance († 1100) (Stuttgart, Landesbibliothek HB VI 107) and in a Salzburg manuscript from the middle of the twelfth century, related to the Stuttgart text (Vienna, Österreichische National-bibliothek 354). Among extracts from Burchard's *Decretum,* both of these manuscripts contain, in the same order and to the same extent, a series of canons which the author of Pseudo-Liudprand and the participants at the Synod of Worms (868) had both found in their copies of the Mainz collection.[143]

The great collections of the Gregorian reform offer quite a different picture, both in respect to the number of chapters taken from Nicholas' letters and to the number of the topics held to be important. Anselm of Lucca included 46 excerpts from thirteen of Nicholas' letters in his canonical collection (1083–1086).[144] Only two chapters, about the indissolubility of marriage (10.21) and matricide (11.43), come from Burchard's *Decretum;*[145] the other 44 come from different manuscript traditions. Half the

142. See Perels, NA 39 (1914) 63ff.; W. Levison, 'Die Papstgeschichte des Pseudo-Liudprand und der Codex Farnesianus des Liber Pontificalis', NA 36 (1911) 427ff.; and D. Jasper, 'Die Papstgeschichte des Pseudo-Liudprand', DA 31 (1975) 17ff. A. Spicker-Wendt, *Die Querimonia Egilmari episcopi und die Responsio Stephani papae* (Studien und Vorarbeiten zur Germania Pontificia 8; Cologne 1980) 128f. n. 7, seems to favor a date around 900 for its composition, in an unidentifiable place, providing Pseudo-Isidorian research with a sensational result: the most recent version of the Pseudo-Isidorian Decretals (Hinschius' Class C) must already have been available in a completed form. The link between papal *Vitae* and decretals, which became ever more common in the eleventh and twelfth centuries, has been dealt with by Fuhrmann, 'Ein Papst Ideo' 90ff., and D. Jasper, 'Romanorum pontificum decreta vel gesta' 110ff.

143. On the Nicholas fragments in both collections see Perels, 'Briefe' NA 39 (1914) 68ff. The Stuttgart manuscript is described by J. Autenrieth, *Die Handschriften der ehemaligen Hofbibliothek Stuttgart,* 3: *Codices iuridici et politici* (Die Handschriften der Württembergischen Landesbibliothek Stuttgart 2.3; Frankfurt 1963) 100ff. and by J. Gilchrist, *Collectio in LXXIV titulos digesta* lv ff. with further bibliographical references. On the Vienna manuscript, see O. Mazal, 'Die Salzburger Domkapitelbibliothek vom 10. bis zum 12. Jahrhundert', *Paläographie 1981* (Münchener Beiträge zur Mediävistik und Renaissance-Forschung 32; Munich 1982) 79.

144. Cf. the list by Perels, 'Briefe' NA 39 (1914) 74. The 74 *Titles,* which was compiled earlier, has only an excerpt from JE 2879 (c.17 = MGH Epp. 6.606.19–21), though reordering the clauses, which makes the tone of the original more emphatic.

145. Anselm 10.21 takes Burchard 9.49 and Anselm 11.43 incorporates Burchard 6.46; cf. Fournier, 'Les collections canoniques romaines' 301f. (repr. *Mélanges* 2.455f.) on Anselm's use of Burchard. The fact that Burchard's other extracts from letters of Nicholas I on marriage law are omitted by Anselm because of the more rigorous conception of marriage by the reformers, for whom Burchard's position was too ambivalent and lax, cf. U. Lewald, *An der Schwelle der Scholastik: Bonizo und das Kirchenrecht seiner Tage* (Weimar 1938) 62ff.; G. Tel-

excerpts from thirteen of Nicholas' letters were provided by Epistle 88 to the Byzantine Emperor Michael III (JE 2796), a letter fundamental for the conception of Roman primacy. In Anselm 1.72, eighteen passages have been gathered together in the order of the original text under the rubric 'Quod sacerdotibus imperatores obedire debent non iubere'.[146] The dominant themes of Nicholas' letters in Anselm's collection were the unconditional submission to the judgments and privileges of the Apostolic See (1.21; 2.64, 66, 71; 5.39), the preservation of the hierarchical order (2.65, 67; 7.135), and an emphasis on the greater authority of ecclesiastical legislation over secular law (12.33). Anselm's collection marks a turning point in the subject matter of canonical collection. In contrast to the major themes of the older canonical collections, ecclesiastical discipline and criminal law recede completely into the background.[147]

Deusdedit also used Nicholas I's letters extensively in his canonical collection (ca. 1087). He excerpted fifteen of Nicholas' letters and other pronouncements, and divided them into 54 parts.[148] In 41 of the canons, he adopted the same wording as in Anselm. Perels showed through detailed collation of both texts that Anselm did not use Deusdedit's *Collectio Canonum* and that Deusdedit did not use Anselm, because his text agrees with the original form of Nicholas' letters, while Anselm deviates from it.[149] They must have used a single source for the letters of Nicholas. Both canonists could not have copied their texts from the letters of Nicholas independently, since the excerpts are mostly of the same length and sometimes follow the same order, and because of the large number of common deviations from the original letters.[150] This collection of canonical

---

lenbach, *Libertas: Kirche und Weltordnung im Zeitalter des Investiturstreits* (Forschungen zur Kirchen- und Geistesgeschichte 7; Stuttgart 1936) 158; and Horst, *Polycarpus* 29, with further bibliographical references.

146. Ed. F. Thaner, p. 39–48 = Deusdedit 4.159–173 = Bonizo, *Liber de vita christiana* 4.86a. The transmission of the letter in canonical collections has been discussed by Kuttner, 'Urban II' 81ff. Not quite a hundred years earlier, JE 2796 provided important arguments for the letter of protest written by Leo, abbot of San Bonifacio e Alessio, papal legate, to King Hugh Capet, to counter the attacks of the Synod of Saint-Bâle (991) on the papacy; cf. the parallel edition by Perels, 'Briefe' NA 39 (1912) 57ff. and H. Zimmermann, 'Abt Leo an König Hugo Capet: Ein Beitrag zur Kirchengeschichte des 10. Jahrhunderts', *Festschrift K. Pivec* (Innsbrucker Beiträge zur Kulturwissenschaft 12; Innsbruck 1966) 332ff., who failed to notice Perels' studies. Fuhrmann, *Einfluß und Verbreitung* 2.325f. and n. 77, considers the use of other letters of Nicholas, such as JE 2785 (Ep. 71), in the writings of Leo. This makes it clear that the papacy, even before the reform period, valued JE 2796 as an important document for papal conceptions of its office.

147. Cf. n. 145.

148. Cf. Perels, 'Briefe' NA 39 (1912) 75ff.

149. Perels, 'Briefe' NA 39 (1912) 82ff.

150. Cf. the examples in Perels, 'Briefe' NA 39 (1912) 84ff. The same order can be found

materials that they used, however, has not survived. One may only speculate about its form and contents.[151] The likeliest model would be collections of materials like the *Collectio Britannica* (London, British Library Add. 8873), completed around 1090, or the *Collectio Tripartita A*, written at the same time, both of which were exploited by Ivo of Chartres for his *Decretum*. Scholars believe that these putative collections would have been written in the last years of Pope Gregory VII's pontificate. Since the materials of these collections were generally merged into other collections, they have disappeared.[152]

Deusdedit's canonical collection provided the source for most of the forty extracts from thirteen letters of Nicholas contained in the *Collectio Britannica*. In contrast to the extracts from the registers of Popes Gelasius I, Pelagius I, Alexander II, John VIII, Urban II, Stephen V, and Leo IV, they

---

in Anselm 2.70, 71 = Deusdedit 1.163, 164 (excerpts from Epp. 71, 52), or Anselm 12.34, 35 = Deusdedit 4.175, 176 (excerpts from Epp. 51 and 46); these and other examples in Perels, NA 39 (1912) 80. Fournier, 'Les collections canoniques romaines' 365ff. (repr. *Mélanges* 2.519ff.), discussed the links between the collections of Anselm and Deusdedit.

151. On these often-discussed intermediate collections, see T. Sickel, *Das Privilegium Otto I. für die römische Kirche vom Jahre 962* (Innsbruck 1883) 67ff., who concluded that Anselm and Deusdedit used a collection of imperial privileges that had already been worked over. On the letters of Nicholas I, Perels, 'Briefe' NA 39 (1914) 85f., also concluded that both canonists had had recourse to a common exemplar, which, however, in contrast to Sickel, he pictured as being much more extensive: 'man (wird) sich darunter eine auf breiter Basis—wahrscheinlich vornehmlich auf Grund der päpstlichen Register—gefertigte grosse kanonistische Sammlung vorzustellen haben, bei deren Anlage das chronologische Prinzip vorgeherrscht haben dürfte'. This summary has been accepted by Fournier, 'Un tournant' 143ff. (repr. *Mélanges* 2.387ff.); by Fuhrmann, *Einfluß und Verbreitung* 2. 517ff., who established that both canonists must have used an intermediate collection for the Pseudo-Isidore chapters in their collections; and by Horst, *Polycarpus* 46ff.

152. Sickel, *Privilegium* 77ff.; agreed to by Perels, 'Briefe' NA 39 (1914) 85 n. 3, though on 79ff. he treated Sickel's proposal that Deusdedit was the author or inspirer of his 'privilege collection' with scepticism. It is possible that Bonizo of Sutri used a similar canonical exemplar in his *Liber de vita christiana*, cf. Perels in the introduction to his edition, xxx ff.; Fuhrmann, *Einfluß und Verbreitung* 2.538ff.; and Berschin, *Bonizo von Sutri* 56. It is, however, questionable whether he used such a collection for his excerpts from Nicholas' letters, since six of the nine canons come from Burchard's *Decretum*: Bonizo 6.58 = Burchard 8.47; Bonizo 8.37 = Burchard 9.28; and Bonizo 8.49–52 = Burchard 9.49–51, 53. Bonizo may not have valued the letters of Nicholas I in comparison with Anselm and Deusdedit. Bonizo neglected issues of church government and focused on the concept of a society divided into lay and clerical orders. Thus Letter 88 (JE 2796), important for the Roman primacy claims, did not belong to the original contents of the *Liber* (it occurs only in a later manuscript under 4.86a), and Ep. 71 (JE 2785), which deals with the same theme, is cited only once in 4.76. The *Polycarpus* of Gregory of San Grisogono, whose eleven chapters from Nicholas letters are to be found largely in Burchard and Anselm, uses the same source as Anselm in 1.22.1, an excerpt from Ep. 88 (JE 2796): cf. Horst, *Polycarpus* 61 n. 206. Perels, 'Briefe' NA 39 (1914) 118, assumed that the *Collection in 7 Books*, Vat. lat. 1346, served as the exemplar for *Polycarpus*, but this thesis was disproved by unpublished researches of Carl Erdmann: either *Polycarpus* was the source for Vat. lat. 1346 or both made use of the same exemplar, cf. Horst, *Polycarpus* 9 n. 32.

were placed in the last part of the manuscript, the Varia 2, in chapters 31ff., 113ff., and 130ff.[153] Chapters 17–127 are extracts from Deusdedit's collection, and the compiler of the *Britannica* retained the sequence of his exemplar fairly exactly, though from time to time shortening the length of the text.[154] It is not possible to say with certainty where he obtained the texts from Epistolae 71 (JE 2785), 144 (JE 2855), 138 (JE 2849), and 70 (JE 2784) in Varia 2.130–133. Letter 138 to Salomo of Constance was widely circulated in canonistic writings,[155] and Epistolae 70 and 71 were likely known in Italy and France, thanks to their inclusion in the letter collection on the 'causa Rothadi', which was always linked with Pseudo-Isidore manuscripts. Ep. 71 in *Britannica* Varia 2.130 must have come from a copy of the *Pittaciolus* of Hincmar of Laon, a work that now survives only in the manuscript Paris, B.N. lat. 5095 of Bishop Dido of Laon (882–891), for the compiler attached to the twelve excerpts of Nicholas' letters the commentary of the younger Hincmar.[156] Varia 2.131 was for Perels the only text of letter 144, but this letter originally circulated more widely. The collection of Vat. lat. 3829 (early twelfth century), a combination of *Liber Pontificalis*, historical reports, and papal letters up to and including Paschal II, which has not yet been examined in detail, has preserved a second, better text of the letter, from which it emerges that the instructions of Nicholas I were destined for Bishop Braidingus of Mâcon (853–862).[157]

Different from the *Collectio Britannica* and similar to the just-mentioned collection in Vat. lat. 3829, the *Collectio Trium Partium* (1091–1096) offers a compact series of 74 excerpts from 33 letters of Nicholas in the

153. Cf. the survey in Ewald, 'Papstbriefe' NA 5 (1880) 586ff., to which should be added an excerpt from Ep. 129 (JE 2852) in Varia 1 C 32 (fol. 98v) of the collection (MGH Epp. 6.650.16–36). We can only speculate as to why no register extracts were prepared of Nicholas' letters. Was there no exemplar of the register in the second half of the eleventh century or did people think that an extract was superfluous in view of the plentiful supply of copies? Cf. Ewald, NA 5 (1880) 593.

154. Cf. Ewald, 'Papstbriefe' NA 5 (1880) 582, and Perels, 'Briefe' NA 39 (1914) 88f., with a concordance for *Britannica* Varia 2. 31ff., 113ff. = Deusdedit 1.150ff. and 4.159ff.

155. Cf. the commentary in the edition, MGH Epp. 6.656f.

156. Texts from PL 124.1053B, 1056B–C, 1059A–B and D, and 1067 B–C were attached to the excerpts from JE 2785 (Ep. 71): cf. Perels, 'Briefe' NA 39 (1914) 89ff., who treated the commentary of Hincmar of Laon as a possible letter of Nicholas in the edition Ep. 160, p. 683f., but corrected his error on p. 811. This evidence, with extracts from the letters of Hadrian II to the synods of Troyes, Soissons and to Charles the Bald and texts from the *Annals of St-Bertin* and from Aimoin's *Gesta Francorum* in Varia 2.11–14 are clear pointers to a French variant of the *Britannica* in the form in which it survives in London, B.L. Add. 8873. Cf., with additional references, Brett, 'Urban II' 35ff.

157. The excerpts from Nicholas' letters in Vat. lat. 3829 come mostly from Deusdedit, cf. Fournier-Le Bras, *Histoire* 2.216. The address and closing sentence of *Britannica*, are provided by Fuhrmann, 'Ein Papst Ideo' 92 n. 14.

sixty-first title of its decretal section. In this collection only the 112 excerpts of Gregory the Great exceed the total of Nicholas' letters.[158] There is no evidence of a uniform exemplar or of an independent excerpt from Nicholas' register. In any case, a common exemplar is unlikely, given the chronological disorder and the inclusion of the interpolated letter 117 (JE 2765). The *Collectio Britannica* provided the text for the first 11 extracts in title 61 of the *Tripartita*. The compiler of the *Tripartita* searched through Varia 2 looking specifically for letters of Nicholas, which formed the kernel of his collection of texts.[159] The exemplar of *Tripartita* is probably to be sought in an eleventh-century collection of canons very similar to the *Britannica*, without the Alexander and Urban material. It is not possible to state with certainty which other sources were used for Nicholas' letters in *Tripartita*. In a few sections (1.61.19–24: Epistolae 115 and 156), the collection shows surprising parallels to the excerpts in the slightly later papal history of Pseudo-Liudprand and in the canonical collection of the manuscript Stuttgart, Landesbibliothek HB VI 107.[160]

Ivo of Chartres was responsible for yet another striking increase in extracts from letters of Nicholas in his *Decretum:* 111 excerpts from 44 letters. One of his most important sources was the *Collectio Tripartita*, whose texts Ivo sometimes incorporated at suitable places into his *Decretum* in the same sequence.[161] In addition he almost certainly used the *Britannica*, as shown by false inscriptions[162] or by remarkably similar length of the extracts.[163] The *Britannica* must have been in a form augmented with extracts from the registers of Alexander II and Urban II, since several of their letters occur in the *Decretum* and the *Panormia*.[164]

Ivo's third source that we can identify with certainty is Burchard's *Decretum*, which Ivo merged into his work almost completely. In a third of the excerpts we cannot know the source from which Ivo took them. Pos-

158. Cf. Fournier, 'Collections canoniques' 663f. (repr. *Mélanges* 1.469f.) and, with a few additions, Perels, 'Briefe' NA 39 (1914) 98ff. However, among the letters of Gregory I in the *Tripartita* are extracts from his *Moralia in Job,* and from letters of Gregory II, IV and V; cf. the demonstration by Fournier, 'Collections canoniques' 662f. (repr. *Mélanges* 1.468f.).

159. Cf. Fournier, 'Collections canoniques' 660 (repr. *Mélanges* 1.466), and Perels, 'Briefe' NA 39 (1914) 101f.

160. Cf. Perels, 'Briefe' NA 39 (1914) 101 n. 1.

161. Ivo, *Decretum* 5.17–19 = *Tripartita* 1.61.1, 2, 5; *Decretum* 6.119–122 = *Tripartita* 1.61.45, 48, 51, 55; further examples listed by Perels, NA 39 (1914) 106.

162. *Decretum* 5.35 = Varia 2.31 and probably also *Decretum* 4.188 = Varia 2.115h.

163. *Decretum* 14.70 = Varia 2.115b; cf. Perels, 'Briefe' NA 39 (1914) 107.

164. See the summary in Ewald, 'Papstbriefe' NA 5 (1880) 350 for Alexander II and 370ff. on Urban II. Brett, 'Urban II' 42ff. has shown the importance to Ivo of a collection similar to the *Britannica* and its use in the *Decretum* in addition to the *Britannica*. On the letters of Alexander and Urban in the *Collectio Britannica*, see the literature cited above n. 51, especially Somerville, *Pope Urban II* 14ff.

sibly he had access to letter collections like Vat. lat. 3827 from Beauvais, where, before becoming bishop, he had been provost of the collegiate church of St Quentin. This hypothesis of Perels might explain Ivo's generous use (19 excerpts) of the *Responsa ad consulta Bulgarorum* (Ep. 99, JE 2812), which is preserved only in this manuscript.[165]

Ivo's *Panormia* is more or less an abbreviation of his *Decretum*. Nevertheless, two letters of Nicholas are found in the *Panormia* that are not in the *Decretum*.[166]

Gratian's *Decretum* surpasses all earlier collections, with 116 extracts from 47 letters, but, apart from three forgeries, all of his texts can be traced to earlier collections.[167]

VI. The Letters of Hadrian II (867–872), John VIII (872–882), and Stephen V (885–891)

As with Nicholas I's letters, Paris, B.N. lat. 1557 provides the most important and the fullest transmission of the letters of his successor, Hadrian II. Twenty-seven papal letters to recipients in the Frankish kingdoms are entered on fol. 79–93v in the hand of the copyist of Nicholas's letters.[168] A leaf was cut out between fol. 83 and 84, so that of Hadrian II's letter to the participants at the Synod of Douzy in 871 (Ep. 34, JE 2945), in which he quashed the sentence passed by the synod on Hincmar of Laon, only the opening sentences and closing formula are present.[169] This exci-

165. Perels, 'Briefe' NA 39 (1914) 108f.

166. Perels, 'Briefe' NA 39 (1914) 111f. takes his evidence from three passages, from which the attribution in *Panormia* 2.155 to Nicholas I is proved to be the work of the editor, Vosmédian. The Munich *Panormia*-manuscripts, Clm 2593, fol. 46v and Clm 17000, fol. 187 both have the inscription 'Leo nonus Michaheli patriarchae Constantinopolitano', which also occurs in Ivo's *Decretum* 4.223. The printed version, PL 161.1119, has inserted the words 'consuetudines, si illis canonica non obstat auctoritas' into Leo's text from Nicholas' letter JE 2691 (MGH Epp. 6.451.2). The passage occurs in *Panormia* manuscripts of the thirteenth century but is lacking in earlier copies of the *Panormia*: compare Clm 4545, fol. 41v (s.xiii) with Clm 6354, fol. 33 (s.xii). On the rubrics and inscriptions of the *Panormia*, cf. P. Landau, 'Die Rubriken und Inskriptionen von Ivos Panormie', BMCL 12 (1982) 31ff. *Panormia* 4.10 may be taken from the *Collection in Four Books* 1.17 or from the *74 Titles* c.17: cf. Fournier, 'Une forme' BEC 58 (1897) 303f. (repr. *Mélanges* 1.567f.). *Panormia* 3.136 is taken from JE 2709 (ep. 156). As a source, Perels cites *Collectio Duodecim Partium*, 2.243, which, however, has the text of the 'forma uberior', whereas *Panormia* 3.136 uses the 'forma brevior'. Ivo's passage most closely resembles c.11 of the Synod of Worms 868.

167. Cf. Perels, 'Briefe' NA 39 (1914) 125ff.

168. On the manuscript see above, p. 113 nn. 107 and 110; the letters are edited by E. Perels, MGH Epp. 6.69ff., with the order of the letters in the manuscript given on p. 692. P. R. McKeon, 'Toward a Reestablishment of the Correspondence of Pope Hadrian II: The Letters Exchanged between Rome and the Kingdom of Charles the Bald regarding Hincmar of Laon', RB 81 (1971) 169ff., pays much attention to dating problems.

169. Ep. 34, 738 variant e, and at the end, 740 variant t.

sion is probably not a coincidence but purposefully made. The Pseudo-Isidorian manuscript Paris, B.N. lat. 9629, once a part of Paris, B.N. lat. 1557, lacks precisely the passage from Pseudo-Julius that guarantees a bishop an unhindered appeal to Rome.[170] Hincmar of Laon based his argument against his opponents on this point; they later destroyed the textual basis of his case.[171]

About two and a half centuries later, a canonist copied Hadrian's letters again on a quire of Reims, Bibl. municipale 672. Although eight of Hadrian's letters of the Parisian manuscript lat. 1557 are missing, the anonymous canonist enlarged the collection by adding the acts of the Synod of Ponthion (876) and three letters of Pope John VIII from the same year. The text is inserted as a quire in a Pseudo-Isidore of the C-version, after the famous forgery of Gregory IV (JE † 2579) and before Martin I's letter to Amandus of Tongeren-Maastricht (JE 2059).[172]

The Reims dossier possibly derives from an old exemplar. It preserves Letter 34 of Hadrian II (JE 2945), most of which Hincmar of Laon's opponents removed from Paris, B.N. lat. 1557. Thus it must have been copied before Hincmar's enemies removed the text. A further argument for a very early source is the cessation of entries after events of the year 876. Hadrian's letters in Laon, Bibl. municipale 407 are connected to the same textual tradition. The first five letters in Laon show the same sequence as the first letters in Paris, B.N. lat. 1557 and Reims, Bibl. municipale 672.[173] Other old textual witnesses are another five letters of Hadrian II, which are inserted into the acts of the Eighth Ecumenical Council.[174]

In spite of extensive copying, Hadrian II's letters have left almost no traces in canonistic materials. The *Collectio Britannica* included a few letters.[175] The source is obvious, for the Paris, Reims, and Laon manuscripts

170. See the edition of JK † 196 in Hinschius, *Decretales* 467 n. 24 and 469 n. 8.

171. Contreni, 'Codices Pseudo-Isidoriani' 7, 12 (repr. *Carolingian Learning* no. XVI), who concluded from the loss of folios that the codex got into the hands of enemies of Hincmar of Laon, perhaps in Reims, and was there mutilated.

172. On the manuscript see above, p. 97 with n. 41. The organization of the written material shows that there is an insertion in the manuscript. Fol. 207vb is empty for half a column after JE † 2579; on fol. 208ra begins the series of Hadrian letters, followed by parts of the acts of the Synod of Ponthion, 876 (nos. vii, iv, viii, i and ii according to Albert Werminghoff's list, NA 26 [1901] 648ff.) and letters JE 3041, 3039, and 3037 of Pope John VIII (MGH Epp. 7.326ff., 320ff., and 317f., which only repeat Sirmond's printed version). After the copy of JE 3037 fifteen lines are left free on fol. 215vb, and on fol. 216ra comes the letter of Martin I to Bishop Amandus, which always belongs to the contents of the Pseudo-Isidorian manuscripts of the C- class.

173. Cf. MGH Epp. 6.693.

174. JE 2908, 2909, 2913, 2914, 2943, ed. MGH Epp. 6.747ff., nos. 37–41. On the manuscripts see the references cited on p. 115 in n. 118; Perels lists single copies of letters of Pope Hadrian II on 693f.

175. In Varia 2.11–13 are four excerpts from Ep. 3 (2.11), 8 (2.12), and 7 (2.13a and b).

all begin their collections of Hadrian's letters with the texts in the same order.[176] Canon 22 of the Eighth Ecumenical Council occurs fairly often under Hadrian II's name, but other collections provide the correct attribution: 'Ex octava synodo'.[177]

The letters of Pope John VIII (872–882) have been preserved quite differently. The Abbey of Montecassino requested a copy of John's register for the period between September 876 and August 882 (Indictions X–XV). The resulting compilation contained 314 of his letters copied in the 1070s at Santa Maria in Pallaria, a dependent house of Montecassino.[178] This manuscript is the earliest volume of the series of registers in the Vatican archive (Reg. Vat. 1) today; the next item is the original register of Gregory VII (Reg. Vat. 2 and 3). According to Lohrmann, who made a careful examination, John VIII's original register must have consisted of two volumes, which were then copied by two Cassinese scribes, supervised and where necessary corrected by one corrector, probably John of Gaeta, later Pope Gelasius II (1118–1119). It should not be assumed that the copy offers only a selection from John VIII's registers.

From chronological evidence, we can draw some conclusions about John's original registers. The scribes worked continuously, but sometimes letters were not enregistered immediately. Periods of inactivity seem to have occurred when the Pope was not in Rome, such as the years 878–879 during his visit to France. The papal scribes worked from drafts, since the final copy of the letter had long since been sent off. They copied the drafts into the register immediately after the pope's return.[179]

176. Cf. Brett, 'Urban II' 36. The canon Varia 2. 11 from JE 2894 occurs elsewhere only in Ivo, *Decretum* 5.34.

177. Anselm 6.20, Bonizo 2.17, *Polycarpus* 2.1.33, the *Collection in 183 Titles* 4.18, and Gratian D.63 c.1 ascribe the famous canon concerning the election and consecration of bishops to Hadrian, whereas Deusdedit 4.18, Ivo, *Decretum* 5.122, *Panormia* 3.8, *Tripartita* 2.18.1, and Gratian D.63 c.2 mention the provenance only as 'ex octava synodo'.

178. The findings of Lohrmann, *Das Register Papst Johannes' VIII.* 102ff., accepted by O. Hageneder, reviewing Lohrmann in ZRG Kan. Abt. 56 (1970) 429. Doubts about this reconstruction were raised by H. Hoffmann, 'Studien zur Chronik von Montecassino', DA 29 (1973) 130 n. 37. H. Bloch, *Monte Cassino in the Middle Ages* (Rome 1986) 1.321 summarizes Lohrmann's conclusion. The letters were edited by E. Caspar, MGH Epp. 7, part 1 (1912), with commentary in his fundamental study, 'Studien zum Register Johanns VIII.', NA 36 (1911) 79ff., with addenda in Caspar's 'Studien zum Register Gregors VII.', NA 38 (1913) 218ff.; Caspar's work was largely confirmed by Lohrmann, *Das Register Papst Johannes' VIII.*

179. Cf. Caspar, 'Studien' NA 36 (1911) 102ff., accepted and confirmed by Lohrmann, *Das Register Papst Johannes' VIII.* 179ff. This copy of John's register has provided the material for the debate about early medieval papal registers for decades. The questions about how they were compiled (whether from drafts or originals), how they were written (whether continuously or in sudden bursts), whether the copy reproduces the exemplars faithfully and completely, or even what purpose the register served (did they assist the justification of papal policy, provide canonists with material, or were they only a formulary?) were central,

Excerpts from 62 letters of John survive from the earliest years of his pontificate, December 872 to August 875 (Indictions V–VIII). They too were taken from the register and were then transmitted exclusively through canonical collections. As is so often the case, the *Collectio Britannica* is here the most plentiful source. Fifty-five letters of John are copied into the *Britannica* on fol. 120r–136v. The compilers omitted all the formalities of the letters, such as protocols and eschatocols, and, apart from the names of the recipients, which they abbreviated radically, mostly excerpted the parts of the letters that were of legal importance.[180] Seven further letters of John VIII or parts of them from this period are known only through Deusdedit's collection of canons.[181]

The reception of John's letters into canon law and the copying of part of the register by monks of Montecassino between 1070 and 1080 occurred simultaneously. Before this, the letters of John VIII seem not to have been known to authors of canonical collections, because no excerpt from any of his letters is to be found in Regino, Burchard, or in the *74 Titles,* or even in the collections of the pre-Gregorian period that did not circulate widely.[182] After *Collectio Britannica,* Deusdedit and Ivo of Chartres

but no general agreement about them has been reached. In contrast to these often embittered disputes, mostly centered on questions of codicology and diplomatics, the questions of how the texts were copied and used by canonists have played (if at all) only a marginal role; cf. Caspar, 'Studien' NA 36 (1911) 105ff. and Lohrmann, *Das Register Papst Johannes' VIII.* 3, 114, and 156, who, pp. 157ff., summarizes research since the beginning of the twentieth century; Lohrmann grappled especially with thesis of F. Bock, 'Bemerkungen zu den ältesten Papstregistern' 15ff., that Reg. Vat. 1 was based on dossiers of drafts and that the Cassinese copy was not a real register volume but a compilation of historical documents in a high-quality manuscript (p. 19). Lohrmann rejects this (160ff.), as Löwe, *Deutschlands Geschichtsquellen im Mittelalter* 4.455 had done earlier. There is a brief survey of the making of papal registers to 1200 by Hageneder, 'Papstregister und Dekretalenrecht' 320ff.

180. On the letters of Pope John in the *Collectio Britannica,* see Ewald, 'Papstbriefe' NA 5 (1880) 295ff. They are edited, in the order given by the *Britannica,* by E. Caspar, with reference to the collections of Anselm, Deusdedit, and Ivo, in MGH Epp. 7.273ff. The references to register provenance were retained in the *Britannica* for JE 2986 and in Deusdedit 2.90 for JE 2995; cf. 290.38 and 294.37, as well as Lohrmann, *Das Register Papst Johannes' VIII.* 161.

181. Deusdedit 2.90 (Ep. 36; JE 2995), 3.142 and 4.181 (Ep. 62; JE 3028), 3.143 (Ep. 31; JE 2989), 3.144 (Ep. 24; JE 2980), 4.182 (Ep. 59; JE 3019), and 4.382 (Ep. 61; JE 3027). In the seventh letter, no. 60 (JE 3023), the edition lacks a reference to the text in Deusdedit 4.259, which is slightly different from, and longer than, Gratian C.23 q.8 c.1. Apart from the register texts, 27 privileges of John VIII, a few letters of the ninth indiction (876) (for which manuscript exemplars do not survive), and some synodal acts are preserved; cf. the edition of the letters in MGH Epp. 7.313ff., and Lohrmann, *Das Register Papst Johannes' VIII.* 3.

182. JE 3258, from the register (MGH Epp. 7.156, no. 195), is an exception. Burchard took over a number of canons of the Synod of Rome in 875 into his *Decretum,* but then attributed them to different popes, such as Damasus (Rome c.2; Burchard 1.25), Honorius (Rome cc.3 and 11; Burchard 1.211, 11.49), or Gelasius (Rome cc.9 and 10; Burchard 11.48 47); cf. the list of sources in Hoffmann and Pokorny, *Burchard von Worms,* for the passages in question.

in his *Decretum* introduced a large number of John's letters into their collections. The two collections hardly ever have identical texts,[183] so that one can assume that there were two geographically distinct areas of reception, Italy and France. Deusdedit's collection contains, in addition to many letter excerpts included by him alone, about a dozen canons that are also in Anselm of Lucca, Bonizo of Sutri's *Liber de vita christiana,* or the *Collectio Britannica.*[184] We cannot know which collections of his letters were used (for example, canonical collections of materials), since this question could be answered only by a careful textual comparison.[185]

Ivo of Chartres included 31 passages from letters of John in his *Decretum,* making him the most enthusiastic collector of John's letters among the canonists. His main source was a collection like the *Collectio Britannica.* A similar collection, though in a less developed form, provided material for the *Collectio Tripartita.*[186] The compiler of the *Tripartita* placed seven excerpts in his collection that were taken from the 55 letters of the *Britannica.* Ivo of Chartres used the *Tripartita* for a few chapters; for the remainder of John's letters he turned to a form of the *Britannica.*[187]

All the letters of John VIII appearing in canonical collections come

183. Only Deusdedit 4.180 and Ivo, *Decretum* 4.230 and 6.115 (longer than Deusdedit) from Ep. 52 agree with each other. Deusdedit 4.434 and Ivo in the *Prologue* included the same excerpt of a Latin retranslation of John's letter to the Byzantine emperor (JE 3271, August, 879), which had been translated into Greek, with passages interpolated by the supporters of Photius; on this see G. Hofmann, 'Ivo von Chartres über Photios', *Orientalia Christiana Periodica* 14 (1948) 118ff., and Dvornik, *Photian Schism* 302ff. The limited number of similarities between the two collections looks more impressive when one takes note of the fact that Ivo incorporated 31 texts from letters of John VIII and Deusdedit included only 18.

184. Deusdedit 1.239–243 corresponds to Bonizo 4.90–94, and Deusdedit 1.240, 1.243, and 4.182 to Anselm 4.46, 2.73, and 1.79. Deusdedit 1.239 (= Bonizo 4.90) shares one section from JE 2962 with the *Britannica,* although his version of the text is shorter, whereas Deusdedit 3.144 from JE 2980 included one chapter more than the *Britannica.*

185. Cf., in addition to the literature cited above on p. 122 in nn. 151f., P. Fournier, 'Les sources canoniques' 124ff. (repr. *Mélanges* 2.674ff.), with the corrections by Perels in his introduction to the Bonizo edition, xxix ff.

186. On this see Brett, 'Urban II' 37ff. and Somerville, *Pope Urban II* 15f. Ewald, 'Papstbriefe' NA 5 (1880) 595, had already pointed out the provenance of the John excerpts in *Tripartita* 1.62.2–8, from *Britannica* Epp. Joh. 13–16 and 48, 49; 1.62.1 is identical with *Britannica Varia* 2.38 (= Deusdedit 1.166) and quotes c.1 of the Council of Ravenna of 877. Cf. Fournier, 'Collections canoniques' 660 (repr. *Mélanges* 1.466).

187. *Tripartita* 1.62.6–8= *Decretum* 6.114–15. Ivo used the *Britannica* for *Decretum* 8.118f., 122f.= *Britannica* Epp. Joh. 51, 52, 16, and 18, and *Decretum* 10.68–71, in which Ivo copied *Britannica* Epp. Joh. 5, 11, 36, and 46; cf. Brett, 'Urban II' 43. The provenance of *Decretum* 6.114 and 115 from the *Tripartita* is proven by the insertion of a Pseudo-Isidorian text (Hinschius, *Decretales* 127.9–11) into *Tripartita* 1.62.8. This is repeated in *Decretum* 6.115, although it lacks Ep. 49 of the *Britannica;* cf. Fuhrmann, *Einfluß und Verbreitung* 2.551 n. 338. The parallels between the *Collectio Britannica* and Gratian's *Decretum* are listed by Landau, 'Wandel und Kontinuität' 232.

from the first years of his pontificate, 872 to 875. From the extant part of John's registers (Reg. Vat. 1) only his letter to Bishop Anselm of Limoges of 879 (JE 3258) found its way into canonical collections. It first appears in Book 9.128 of the *Collection in Nine Books* of Vat. lat. 1349, compiled in the early tenth century. During the next 150 years, Anselm 10.30, Bonizo 1.41, the *Collection of Santa Maria Novella* 153.2, and *Polycarpus* 6.4.15 placed the letter in their collections; finally, Gratian included it in his *Decretum*, C.30 q.1 c.7.[188] Consequently, John's register remained completely unknown to the canonists. Only thus can we explain the fact that Deusdedit 4.434 and Ivo, in the *Prologue* to his *Derectum*, used a Latin retranslation of John VIII's letter to the Byzantine emperor. This letter to Basilius I and his sons, written August 879 (JE 3271), was rendered into Greek by Photius, who, in the translation process, considerably falsified large parts of it.[189] This letter belonged to the Latin translation of the acts of the Council of Constantinople (879). Deusdedit and Ivo would not have been deceived by Photius' letter if they had had knowledge of the authentic copy in John's register.[190]

A simple coincidence may have prevented eleventh-century canonists from learning of the later part of the register. If we assume, as Lohrmann did, that the compilation of the collection of materials ordered by Pope Gregory VII from John VIII's and other registers occurred at the same time as the copying of Reg. Vat. 1 by the monks of Santa Maria in Pallaria, then the papal scribes and others would not have had access to the letters of John's later years. Consequently, only the letters recording John VIII's earliest years were available to the authors of the *Collectio Britannica*. And only these letters became a part of the canonical tradition.[191]

The transmission and limited reception of the letters of Stephen V (885–891) present a picture very similar to that of John VIII. Here too the

---

188. Cf. P. Fournier, 'Un groupe de recueils canoniques italiens du Xe et XIe siècles', *Mémoires de l'Académie des inscriptions et belles-lettres* 40 (1916) 157 n. 1 (repr. *Mélanges* 2.275 n. 1). In Ivo's *Decretum* the chapter occurs only in the printed version as 1.306, and is missing from the St-Victor manuscript (Paris, B.N. lat. 14315); cf. P. Landau, 'Das Dekret des Ivo von Chartres: Die handschriftliche Überlieferung im Vergleich zum Text in den Editionen des 16. und 17. Jahrhunderts', ZRG Kan. Abt. 70 (1984) 38, and Lohrmann, *Das Register Papst Johannes' VIII.* 156.

189. JE 3271; cf. the edition and the commentary of Caspar, MGH Epp. 7.166ff., who prints the text of the letter in the register parallel to the Greek falsified version; cf. also above, p. 129 n. 183.

190. Lohrmann, *Das Register Papst Johannes' VIII.* 113f.

191. Ibid. 114f. n. 91. Two centuries later, during the pontificate of Clement IV (1265–1268), the canonists rediscovered Reg. Vat. 1, and they marked texts of legal interest with 'Nota', as Lohrmann, *Das Register Papst Johannes' VIII.* 122ff., first noted.

older canonical collections did not adopt Stephen's letters, nor were canonists of the reform period, like Anselm or Deusdedit, particularly interested in them. The authors of the *Polycarpus* and the *Collection of Santa Maria Novella* omit them completely. Extracts from Stephen V's letters were entered into the *Britannica* on fol. 153–159v.[192] These were the only letters that had any influence; the few surviving copies made by recipients of Stephen's letters and privileges left no traces in canonistic writings.[193]

Fragments of registers provided the exemplars for the nine excerpts from letters of Stephen in the *Collectio Tripartita*, which, with the *Britannica*, was the source for the dozen canons taken from Stephen's letters by Ivo for his *Decretum*. Gratian probably took the bulk of Stephen's letters from the *Tripartita* and Ivo's *Panormia*.[194] Anselm and Deusdedit did not use *Britannica* but another collection. The following examples illustrate this point: Anselm 1.83 (= Deusdedit 4.183) occurs in *Britannica* only in *Varia* 2.117, an extract from Deusdedit, and Anselm 6.30 (= Deusdedit 1.244 and 245; Bonizo 4.78 and 79) is put together from two of Stephen's letters (JL 3450 and 3442). Of these, JL 3450 only occurs in *Varia* 2.50 in the *Britannica* (= Deusdedit 1.244) and JL 3442 in Anselm has a lacuna in the text that is also to be found in Gratian C.9 q.3 c.20, but the passage is present in *Britannica* Ep. Stephen 23, *Tripartita* 1.63.3, and Ivo's *Decretum* 5.13.[195] It must remain an open question whether Anselm's joining of JL 3450 and 3442 was his work or whether he took his text from an older compilation.

VII. Conclusion

If we review once more the papal letters from Boniface IV (608–615) to Stephen V (885–891), we see that only the letters of Nicholas I (858–867) found an important place in the canonical collections and in Gratian's *Decretum*. To illustrate this fact in numerical terms: there are eleven extracts

192. Edited, with reference to other canonical collections, by E. Caspar, MGH Epp. 7.334ff. They bear the heading 'ex registro Stephani' before the first excerpt in the *Britannica;* cf. Ewald, NA 5 (1880) 399ff.

193. They are edited by G. Laehr, MGH Epp. 7.354ff., and PL 129.785ff.; cf. on this Santifaller, *Saggio* 271ff.

194. *Tripartita* 1.63.1–9 corresponds with *Collectio Britannica* Ep. Stephani 11, 12, 23, 24c, 25a.b, 27, 28, 15; cf. Ewald, 'Papstbriefe' NA 5 (1880) 595 and Fournier, 'Collections canoniques' 660 (repr. *Mélanges* 1. 466). Ivo *Decretum* 4.232 (ep. 24a), 7.131 (ep. 20), 8.59 (ep. 9a) 10.117 (ep. 6b), and 10.186 (ep. 26a) occur only in the *Britannica*, whereas *Tripartita* 1.63.1, 2, 6, and 7 were not taken into the *Decretum*. The parallels between the *Collectio Britannica* and Gratian's *Decretum* are listed by Landau, 'Wandel und Kontinuität' 233.

195. Cf. MGH Epp. 7.346.23 with variant h. This lacuna in Anselm was noticed by the *Correctores Romani*, who printed Ivo's complete text in their note on C.9 q.3 c.20; cf. Friedberg, col. 612.

from the letters of Pope Honorius in pre-Gratian collections and three excerpts from Pope Martin in Deusdedit and Gratian. The letters of Gregory II and Gregory III appear ten and eleven times respectively, while Pope Zacharias' letters occur nineteen times in the canonical collections.

Nicholas I's letters enjoyed a much wider circulation. 232 texts from his letters were included in the collections, and of these, 116 appear in Gratian's *Decretum*.[196] The reception of so many of Nicholas's letters was certainly a result of their large numbers, but even more important was their widespread circulation. In the end, however, the decisive factor for the reception of these letters was their content. The reception occurred in three phases. The first was the work of Regino, Burchard, the *Collectio Duodecim Partium,* and a few isolated collections, which used Nicholas' letters to give instruction for questions of ecclesiastical adminsitration, especially marriage law and jurisdictional claims. A second wave of reception occurred in Gregorian canonical writings, whose authors were interested in quite different questions and who searched Nicholas' letters for texts on 'de potestate et primatu apostolicae sedis' (Anselm Book 1), or 'de libertate ecclesiae' (Deusdedit Book 4). They found rich material, as shown by the extract from Nicholas' summary of papal authority and power in Letter 88 to Emperor Michael III, which takes up more than nine pages in Thaner's edition of Anselm.[197] The third phase of reception was Ivo of Chartres' canonical works and the *Collectio Tripartita,* which partially incorporated, in addition to new canons, the material used in the first two waves of reception. After the beginning of the twelfth century, hardly any new letters of Nicholas turn up in the collections. The canonists only juggled the order and the choice of their texts.[198]

Unlike the history of the letters of Nicholas I, the discovery by the canonists of the decretals of Leo IV, John VIII, and Stephen V, and also the papal letters in Boniface's correspondence did not occur until the second half of the eleventh century. The sources seem largely to have been collections of canonistic material that have now been lost or subsumed into other collections. The compilers of these collections turned to the registers for papal letters, though it is not clear whether they did this directly or indirectly. A prime example of such a collection must be the *Collectio Britannica* in London, British Library Add. 8873. In spite of all reservations about the genuineness of its material and in spite of all the uncertainties about when and where it was compiled, the *Britannica* remains a primary source of papal letters from the ninth century.

196. Perels, 'Briefe' NA 39 (1914) 140ff.
197. Anselm 1.72 ; also in Deusdedit 4.159–73.
198. Perels, 'Briefe' NA 39 (1914) 135f.

Besides the *Collectio Tripartita*, Ivo of Chartres used a collection of papal letters closely related to the *Britannica*, not only for ninth-century letters but also for fifth- and sixth-century letters (Gelasius and Pelagius) and for letters of Alexander II and Urban II.[199] Moreover, the *Britannica* was a collection that was confused both chronologically and thematically. We may draw some conclusions about the other lost collections from the *Britannica*'s lack of organization.

From the selection of papal letters in the *Britannica* we can make the following conjectures: the easily accessible letters of Leo I and Gregory I—those most often cited in canonical literature—are completely lacking in the *Britannica*, both in the register extracts and in the Variae. Further, the well-documented letters of Nicholas I are only occasionally included in the Variae. Perhaps compilers of such collections wished to conserve materials not readily accessible or those threatened with extinction. Thus the letters of Leo IV, John VIII, or Stephen V owe their incorporation into the law of the Church to this aim.[200] The remaining papal letters of this period that circulated before Gratian were primarily forgeries,[201] falsely attributed texts,[202] or texts from sources that cannot be clearly identified as Pope Agatho's dictum (JE 2108).

199. Ewald, 'Papstbriefe' NA 5 (1880) 350f. and 370ff., and Brett, 'Urban II' 43 and Somerville, *Pope Urban II* 14ff.

200. On the letters of Pope John VIII, and in general on this point, see A. Esch, 'Überlieferungs-Chance und Überlieferungs-Zufall als methodisches Problem des Historikers', *Historische Zeitschrift* 240 (1985) 529ff (repr *Zeitalter und Menschenalter: Der Historiker und die Erfahrung vergangener Gegenwart* [Munich 1994] 39ff.).

201. Pseudo-Boniface JE † 1996, Pseudo-Deusdedit JE † 2003.

202. *Capitula Martini* to Pope Martin I, *Capitula Angilramni* to Hadrian I, Wido of Arezzo to Paschal I.

The Pseudo-Isidorian Forgeries

Horst Fuhrmann

I. The Extent of the Forgeries

The name of 'Pseudo-Isidore' is associated with a series of collections[1] that are heavily interlaced with forgeries; consequently the entire set of collections containing these forgeries is called 'Pseudo-Isidorian Forgeries' or 'False Decretals', even though the collections contain authentic materials as well. The primary work of the Pseudo-Isidorian forger(s) was the eponymous Pseudo-Isidorian Decretals that were put together around the middle of the ninth century. The origins and purpose of the Decretals were intricately intertwined. The name 'Pseudo-Isidore' was popularized by David Blondel in his book of 1628 directed against the False Decretals, *Pseudo-Isidorus et Turrianus vapulantes* (Geneva 1628), and Bernhard Simson († 1915) applied the term of Pseudo-Isidorian, used for the decretals, to the entire group of writings as the 'Pseudo-Isidorian Forgeries'.[2]

The eponym 'Pseudo-Isidore' is derived from the putative collector of the 'False Decretals', who called himself 'Isidorus Mercator' (variations in more recent traditions include 'Mercatus', 'Peccator'). The collection consists of mostly non-genuine papal letters and genuine councils from Clement I (c.90–101) or Anacletus I (c.79–90), who is here placed after Clement, through Gregory I (590–604) or Gregory II (715–731), whose council of 721 is the final piece. The Middle Ages usually thought this Isidore was St. Isidore of Seville († 636),[3] and even the earliest manuscripts are provided with a heading which refers to a St. Isidore: 'Incipit praefatio sancti Isidori libri huius'.[4]

1. Among surveys of the Pseudo-Isidorian collections, these should be mentioned: E. Seckel, 'Pseudoisidor', RE 16 (3rd ed. Leipzig 1905) 265–307, and the definitive section 'Les recueils pseudo-isidoriens', Fournier-Le Bras, *Histoire* 1.127–233; H. Fuhrmann, 'False Decretals (Pseudo-Isidorian Forgeries)', NCE 5 (1967) 820ff. A history of the research is found in Fuhrmann, *Einfluß und Verbreitung* 1.5ff.; the Pseudo-Isidorian works are described 137ff.; more recent literature in H. Fuhrmann, 'Pseudoisidorische Fälschungen', HRG 4 (1985) 80ff. and 'Pseudoisidorische Dekretalen', LMA 7 (1994) 307ff.

2. B. Simson, *Die Entstehung der Pseudo-isidorischen Fälschungen in Le Mans* (Leipzig 1886), cf. E. Seckel in his article, 'Pseudo-Isidorian Decretals and Other Forgeries', *The New Schaff-Herzog Encyclopedia of Religious Knowledge* (New York 1911) 9.343–344.

3. For example, Hincmar of Reims (PL 126.379A–C), Rufinus in his *Summa*, Huguccio on D.16 c.1 (Vat. lat. 2280, fol. 13v), Johannes Teutonicus on D.16 c.1 (Vat. lat. 1367, fol. 7v), and even the *Correctores Romani*, cf. Schulte, *Geschichte der Quellen* 1.42, 73 n. 34. The error that the forger is, in fact, Isidor of Seville is perpetuated by modern textbooks. The theories over the pseudonym, some of them quite imaginative, will not be further investigated here.

4. Hinschius, *Decretales* 17. On the origins and association of the invocation and introductory rubric, cf. E. Seckel, *Die erste Zeile Pseudoisidors: Aus dem Nachlaß mit Ergänzungen*, ed. H. Fuhrmann (SB Berlin Heft 4; Berlin 1959).

Usually included among the Pseudo-Isidorian forgeries are:

1. The *Collectio Hispana Gallica Augustodunensis.*
2. The so-called *Capitula Angilramni.*
3. The Capitulary Collection of Benedictus Levita, and
4. The Pseudo-Isidorian Decretals, from which all these forgeries (1–4) derive their name.

It is unlikely that this exhausts all the witnesses of Pseudo-Isidorian activity, since even the scope of the decretals is not yet clarified beyond any doubt,[5] just as writings exist whose relationship with the whole body of the forgery must still be analyzed. E. Seckel did not regard it as impossible that 'Pseudo-Isidore himself may have prepared the Gallican *Hispana,*the *Dionysio-Hadriana* (Codd. Paris. [B.N.] 1453, 3838) in advance for his purposes', and he found the question worth posing whether the forger was working with a 'prepared *Quesnelliana'.* The Codex Phillippicus 1764 of the Berlin Staatsbibliothek, for example, contains a copy of the *Capitula Angilramni* that seems to lie between the original source and the vulgate version and deserves as much attention as the *Collectio Hispana Gallica Augustodunensis,* for example.[6] The same codex preserves the fragment of a letter, probably by Pope Leo I, which cannot be found among the False Decretals, yet which conveys a totally Pseudo-Isidorian spirit; it could very well have come from the workshop of the Pseudo-Isidorian

5. For example, Hinschius found the letter of Bishop Felix of Messina and the response of Pope Gregory I (JE † 1334) only in one of the A2 manuscripts known to him; he published the correspondence (Hinschius, *Decretales* 747–753; PL 130.1132ff.). David Blondel, *Pseudo-Isidorus et Turrianus vapulantes* (Geneva 1628) 675, included in his analysis the Deusdedit letter JE † 2003 (Burchard, *Decretum* 17.44, but also traceable to the tenth century, cf. Hoffmann and Pokorny, *Burchard von Worms* 158–159 n. 129), which, for example, also appears in Vat. lat. 3829, fol. 255, heavily interspersed with Pseudo-Isidorian items, and in its derivative manuscripts; Hinschius did not choose to use it. In the same way, Blondel, *Pseudo-Isidorus* 645–646 includes ('Stylus . . . Mercatorem artificem probat') the letter of Pelagius II, JK † 1065 (on its canonistic tradition, cf. Friedberg on De con. D.1 c.71), which is also included in Vat. lat. 3829, fol. 178; in canon law collections, the letter appears to emerge first in Burchard, *Decretum* 3.69, cf. Fournier, 'Études critiques' 62 (repr. *Mélanges* 1.268) and particularly Hoffmann and Pokorny, *Burchard von Worms* 97–98; this letter was also omitted by Hinschius. The four writings of Pope Vitalian (657–672) JE 2090–2093 appear in the A1, A2 and C manuscripts, yet they are missing in Hinschius (in contrast, PL 130.1141ff.); on the Vitalian letters, cf. Schieffer, 'Kreta' 15ff. (with a critical edition of these genuine letters transmitted only in the Pseudo-Isidorian collection). Hinschius was accused of incompleteness by his reviewer F. X. Kraus (*Theologische Quartalschrift* 48 [1866] 493ff., esp. 498), improperly as it happened in the case cited. Kraus had investigated the manuscript Bernkastel-Kues 52 and established, for example, that the two letters listed there, JK 188 and JK 228, were lacking in Hinschius.

6. Cf. Seckel-Fuhrmann, *Die erste Zeile Pseudoisidors* 8, and Fuhrmann, *Einfluß und Verbreitung* 3.696ff., 749–750.

forgers.[7] A canonical collection in Codex 442 of the Bern Burgerbibliothek derives from a Pseudo-Isidorian setting; texts from the early stages of the forgery process appear to be preserved here.[8] This manuscript also includes a shortened version of the Council of Chalcedon (451), which is found in the long version of the Pseudo-Isidorian Decretals in many cases, but which is not included in any editions of Pseudo-Isidore.[9] The impression arises that Pseudo-Isidorian collections did not always derive from a single, precisely defined exemplar. The works appear to have been sent out in various forms and to have been of heterogeneous composition.[10]

In later times papal letters appear which are at least produced in a manner analogous to Pseudo-Isidorian decretals.[11] All of these writings

7. Berlin, Staatsbibl. Phill. 1764, fol. 100–100v: 'In decretalibus sancti Leonis papae. Metropolitanus igitur episcopus propter reverentiam idcirco competenter honorandus est, eo quod ad ipsum pertineat electio episcoporum cum ceteris coepiscopis et ordinatio et synodalis convocatio et rerum facillimarum in synodo discussio, non ut in alterius parroechiam ullas administrationes faciat aut proprio episcopo aliquid sui iuris aut potestatis minuat; sed sicut ille suam, sic unusquisque commissam sibi regat parroecchiam'. The text, which has echoes of canon 9 of the Synod of Antioch, shares with Pseudo-Isidore a predisposition against the autonomous rights of metropolitans, cf. Fuhrmann, *Einfluß und Verbreitung* 3.679–680, 734.

8. Cf. H. Hagen, *Catalogus codicum Bernensium* (Bern 1875) 385; this manuscript of the early tenth century originates in France; the collection, which has not been analyzed, is the first section of the codex (fol. 1r–36v), followed by the *Lex Salica,* cf. Mordek, *Kirchenrecht und Reform* 154–155.

9. Printed in J. B. Pitra, *Spicilegium Solesmense complectens Sanctorum Patrum scriptorumque ecclesiasticorum anecdota hactenus opera* (Paris 1858) 4.166a–179a; the links were uncovered by K.-G. Schon, 'Exzerpte aus den Akten von Chalkedon bei Pseudoisidor und in der 74-Titel-Sammlung', DA 32 (1976) 546ff.

10. The problem was dealt with in an essay by H. Fuhrmann, 'Reflections on the Principle of Editing Texts: The Pseudo-Isidorian Decretals as an Example', BMCL 11 (1981) 1ff.

11. The number of such papal letters prepared in the Pseudo-Isidorian style is not small. Some examples should be given. In the eleventh century a forgery under the name of Pope Clement I (JL † 5340) circulated and dealt with the treatment of baptismal and holy water, see H. Fuhrmann, 'Eine Fälschung im Stile der Pseudo-Clemensbriefe', *Variorum munera florum: Latinität als prägende Kraft mittelalterlicher Kultur: Festschrift für H. F. Haefele zu seinem 60. Geburtstag* (Sigmaringen 1985) 157ff. (with edition of the text). The situation is similar with another Clementine forgery on the 'Twelve Golden Fridays', analyzed and edited by D. Jasper, 'Inveni in canonibus apostolorum . . . Zu einer mittelalterlichen Fälschung auf Papst Clemens I.', *Papsttum, Kirche und Recht im Mittelalter: Festschrift für H. Fuhrmann zum 65. Geburtstag* (Tübingen 1991) 201ff.; Jasper mentions, p. 210 n. 51, two more textual witnesses to the Pseudo-Clement letter JL † 5340. There is a letter attributed to Pope Alexander I which discusses marriage as a sacrament: 'Alexander papa et martir in epistola decretali ad Sisunnum Antiocenum patriarcham. Si de universis . . .' It is to be found, among other places, as an insert in *Collectio Lipsiensis* Tit. 59.6, ed. W. Deeters, *Die Bambergensisgruppe der Dekretalensammlungen des 12. Jahrhunderts* (Diss. Bonn 1956) 262f. A late-medieval forgery composed in Dutch in the name of Pope Alexander, relying on the Pseudo-Isidorian decretal JK † 24, has been published by W. Diekamp, 'Die neuere Literatur zur päpstlichen Diplomatik', *Historisches Jahrbuch* 4 (1883) 222, 387 (after Vienna, Österreichische National-

belonging to the narrower and broader circle of Pseudo-Isidore will be put aside for now and will not be discussed: their historical role is small, and this survey will restrict itself to the Pseudo-Isidorian Forgeries conventionally so called. We shall retain the name 'Pseudo-Isidore', although the vast extent and skilled preparation make it unlikely that a single person created the forgeries. Instead, we must assume a circle of forgers with access to a rich library, producing and distributing products of highly various types.

II. *The Purpose of the Forgeries*

One speaks of the period after Charlemagne as that of the 'dissolution of the Empire'.[12] The central authority dwindled, fragmentary realms

bibliothek 13843, saec. XV). The falsified synodal records for the abbey of Massay might also be attributed to Pseudo-Isidorian influence, where it describes Archbishop Radulf of Bourges (843–866) as the 'prime sedis Aquitanie Bituricensium archiepiscopus', corresponding perhaps to the falsified version of JE 2765, cf. MGH Concilia 2.2 p. 854ff. (The letter of Leo I, JK 460, mentioned on p. 856 n. 2, is, contrary to Werminghoff, not spurious and is not one of the forgeries of Pseudo-Isidore.) C. Berardi, *Dissertatio de variis sacrorum canonum collectionibus ante Gratianum* (Turin 1752), speculates that D.19 c.4 (Pope Stephan) arose in emulation of Pseudo-Stephan, ep. 1, Hinschius, *Decretales* 180ff. (cf. Friedberg here), yet it would require a special investigation, going back to the particular cases, to investigate the Pseudo-Isidorian items in collections of canon law since the time of Burchard's *Decretum*, such as Burchard, *Decretum* 7.21 (= C.35 q.6 c.1, cf. Friedberg here), which circulated under the name of Fabian and shows Pseudo-Isidorian tendencies. A glance in the Jaffé-Kaltenbrunner, *Papstregesten*, with the additions in 2.689ff. and 731ff., shows how numerous such forgeries are. Pilgrim of Passau (971–991) takes the same position as Pseudo-Isidore against the 'chorepiscopi' in his forgery JL † 3614, cf. T. Gottlob, *Der abendländische Chorepiskopat* (Kanonistische Studien und Texte 1; Bonn 1928) 135. A series of falsified conciliar canons of Carthage, Laodicea, Ancyra, and Toledo conformed to the Pseudo-Isidorian model; Fournier, who edited them in: *Annales de l'Université de Grenoble* 11 (1899) 358ff., assumed that they came from the end of the ninth or the start of the tenth century; E. Seckel, 'Benedictus Levita decurtatus et excerptus: Eine Studie zu den Handschriften der falschen Kapitularien', *Festschrift der Berliner Juristenfakultät für H. Brunner* (Munich-Leipzig 1914) 400 n. 6, provides additions to the tradition; Mordek, *Kirchenrecht und Reform* 175–176 with n. 372, found that the canons 'might prove on closer investigation to be another work of . . . Pseudo-Isidore'. The miscellaneous codex of Salzburg, St. Peter, a. IX.32, also contains Pseudo-Isidorian pieces (cf. G. Phillips, SB Wien 44; Vienna 1863, 12ff.). J. von Pflugk-Harttung (*Zeitschrift für Kirchenrecht* 19 [1884] 361ff.) was of the opinion concerning a collection in the Turin manuscript E. V. 44, that 'we . . . are dealing with an extensive forgery in the style of Pseudo-Isidore'. Pflugk-Harttung's later dating of it to the early thirteenth century has been rejected by Fournier-Le Bras, *Histoire* 2.221, in favor of locating it at the beginning of the twelfth century. This attribution is confirmed by Mordek's further analysis, *Kirchenrecht und Reform* 141ff. Cf. also G. Motta, 'Una silloge canonistica del sec. XII tra Deusdedit ed Anselmo di Lucca (Torino, Biblioteca Nazionale E.V.44)', SG 27 (1996) 415ff.

12. Cf. F. L. Ganshof, 'La fin du règne de Charlemagne: Une décomposition', *Zeitschrift für schweizerische Geschichte* 28 (1948) 433–452, also in English in his collection, *The Carolingians and the Frankish Monarchy* (Ithaca 1971) 240–255. W. Schlesinger, 'Die Auflösung des Karlsreiches', *Karl der Große: Lebenswerk und Nachleben*, ed. W. Braunfels (Düsseldorf 1965) 1.792–857; repr. idem, *Ausgewählte Aufsätze 1965–1979*, ed. H. Patze and F. Schwind (Vorträge und Forschungen 34; Sigmaringen 1987) 49–124.

arose, the insecurity of rights became a preoccupation, and legal structures were increasingly being destroyed by the incursions of the Northmen. Powerful secular rulers on all levels ('potentes') intervened rigorously in ecclesiastic organization, alienating the property of the Church. Between 818 and 845, bishops in significant numbers were deposed or driven from their sees, and secular judges tried clerics in criminal trials.[13] Reforming synods (Paris 829; Aachen 836; Meaux-Paris 845–846) achieved little with their calls for reform, and no improvement could have been expected after the breakup of the Empire in 843. Even the chief instrument of secular legislation, the capitularies, which were supposed to have effect in the entire Empire, had grown weak. Abbot Ansegis of Fontenelle († 833) in his collection[14] of the capitularies of the previous fifty years comprehended a mere 30 percent of the whole, an abridgement that Benedictus Levita, a member of the Pseudo-Isidorian circle of forgers, sought to fill in his own way through his capitulary collection, which was presented as a continuation of Ansegis' work.[15]

The Pseudo-Isidorian Forgeries are often placed in the context of a reform effort arising from a world awash with legal uncertainty. Hans von Schubert[16] found that at the end of the rule of Louis the Pious, 'a canon law grew up that was a discipline committed to struggle, resorting to the most daring means' (precisely the forgeries of Isidore) to achieve 'freedom from the secular power'. Gerhart Ladner[17] saw in them 'only the "illegal" continuation of the "legal" reform of canon law collections which had taken place under Charlemagne, which had been inadequate from the point of view of their own concept of the Church as self-sufficient'. But it is obvious that the Pseudo-Isidorian Forgeries did not wish to work openly, or at least not primarily. They concerned themselves with far more than ecclesiastical jurisdiction; they wrote about the liturgy, the sacraments, and marital law, further sketching an image of the 'vita primitiva', which has been called a 'vision of a Church in a golden age'.[18] This

13. Other than hierarchical questions, the Pseudo-Isidorian Decretals deal with no matter as frequently as trial and accusation. A useful listing of the criminal trials in the Frankish period is given by A. Nissl, *Der Gerichtsstand des Clerus im fränkischen Reich* (Innsbruck 1886) 63ff. n. 4, though Nissl has specifically excluded the question of the influence and effect of Pseudo-Isidore.

14. On the capitulary collection of Ansegis, see *History of Medieval Canon Law*, volume three (to be published).

15. See below, p. 151.

16. H. von Schubert, *Der Kampf des geistlichen und weltlichen Rechts* (SB Heidelberg Heft 2; Heidelberg 1927) 30–31.

17. G. Ladner, *Theologie und Politik vor dem Investiturstreit* (Veröffentlichungen des Österreichischen Instituts für Geschichtsforschung 2; Vienna 1936) 45.

18. That is the title of the dissertation supervised by Ernst Kantorowicz, written by Schafer Williams, who dedicated his life to research on the Pseudo-Isidorian Forgeries. Vi-

vision, however, was not simply a product of imagination, since it built on what had already been discovered. The very breadth of the Pseudo-Isidorian Decretals was one reason for their success; it is the most extensive collection of canon law arranged in a historical, chronological order.

A significant goal of the forgeries[19] was to protect suffragan bishops from intervention by the metropolitans, the provincial synods, or the secular power.[20] Trial procedure and the possibility of deposing bishops, who themselves are heaped with panegyric and flattering titles ('oculi [domini], columnae, summi sacerdotes, servi dei, throni dei, dii, sancti'), are rendered immeasurably difficult. For example, no layman, no subject, no alien or freedman, no one who is an enemy of the bishop, no one infamous,[21] could accuse the bishop, particularly not before a secular court. If such an accusation occurred, the accused is to regain full possession of all rights, and if the accused, who can reject suspect judges, makes no confession, then 72 witnesses are needed to condemn him, and at any moment of the trial (not just at the end, as the Council of Sardica, c. 4, decreed) he can appeal to the primate or the pope. In order to strengthen the position of the bishops, the 'chorepiscopi',[22] conceived as rivals, were

---

sio aetatis aureae Ecclesiae Pseudo-Isidoriana (Ph. D. Dissertation, Department of History, University of California, Berkeley 1951). On the life work of Williams (1910–1982), whose scholarly legacy was bequeathed to the Institute of Medieval Canon Law, cf. S. Kuttner in his memorial essay, *In Iure Veritas: Studies in Canon Law in Memory of Schafer Williams*, ed. S. Bowman and B. Cody (Cincinatti 1991) ixff. On the Williams legacy, cf. K. Christensen, 'The Schafer Williams Papers at the Institute of Medieval Canon Law', BMCL 16 (1986) 101ff.

19. The Church imagined by Pseudo-Isidore, primarily in the Decretals, has been repeatedly reconstructed: cf. Seckel, 'Pseudoisidor' 279.21ff. and 305.47ff.; R. Seeberg, *Lehrbuch der Dogmengeschichte, 3: Die Dogmenbildung des Mittelalters* (4th ed. Leipzig 1930) 82ff. Particularly instructive is H. Jäger, *Das Kirchenrechtssystem Pseudoisidors* (Jur. Dissertation; Würzburg 1908), though it should be recalled that not only are the individual forgeries not without contradictions, but also that within the forgeries there are inconsistencies. An example of this can be seen in the hierarchical level of primate invented by Pseudo-Isidore: it is only in the first part of the Decretals that the assertion is made that primate and patriarch are synonymous, and while the possibility of raising a new primacy or patriarchate is foreseen in that part, it is excluded in the third part, cf. ZRG Kan. Abt. 40 (1954) 17–18.

20. Cf. A. Marchetto, *Episcopato e Primato pontificio nelle decretali pseudo isidoriane: Ricerca storico-giuridica* (Rome 1971); idem, 'In partem sollicitudinis' 269ff., who has pursued the later influence of the Pseudo-Isidorian organizational scheme; F. Yarza, *El Obispo en la organización eclesiástica de las Decretales pseudoisidorianas* (Pamplona 1985); on that DA 44 (1988) 660 and R. Weigand, AKKR 155 (1986) 301–302. The extensive older literature is summarized in Fuhrmann, *Einfluß und Verbreitung* 1.41ff.

21. The role of infamy, first introduced to canon law by Pseudo-Isidore, is dealt with by G. May, 'Die Infamie bei Benedikt Levita', ÖAKR 11 (1960) 16–36; idem, 'Die Bedeutung der pseudoisidorianischen Sammlung für die Infamie im kanonischen Recht', ÖAKR 12 (1961) 87–113 and 191–207.

22. Cf. R. Kottje, 'Chorbischof', LMA 2 (1983) 1884ff.; a tractate published by R. Reynolds 'A Ninth-Century Treatise on the Origins, Office, and Ordination of the Bishop', RB 85 (1975) 321ff., shows that there were polemics against the 'chorepiscopi' in the Pseudo-Isidorian spirit and at the same time as the forgeries.

suppressed to the status of priests. Metropolitans, who were supposed to make their decisions together with their fellow bishops in their province, were limited by Pseudo-Isidore's establishment of a new superior authority for primates or patriarchs. In keeping with the distribution of the ancient *Notitia provinciarum,* the chief city (metropolis) of the 'first (prima) province' should also be the place of residence of the primate or patriarch.[23]

In Pseudo-Isidore, the growth of papal power served to protect the position of bishops. Indeed, it was not the pope but the bishops who were called the 'keys' of the Church—according to an understanding of Cyprian—and for whose invulnerability all were to cooperate. The Lord had granted to them the power of binding and loosing.[24] Accusations against them were no longer to be handled by provincial and national synods. Cases that touched upon their prerogatives were called 'causae maiores' and reserved to the pope, who alone had the right to confirm the decisions of the councils. Papal rights were stressed when used to defend the suffragan bishops.

The purpose and the making of the Pseudo-Isidorian Forgeries betray the marks of a common literary workshop. The False Decretals as well as the Capitularies of Benedictus Levita are presented as supplements to genuine works, and they draw extensively from common sources. Individual forgeries do demonstrate different redactions of their sources[25] and also different purposes in their intent. For example, in Benedictus Levita the 'chorepiscopi' are still tolerated in part, but in the False Decretals Pseudo-Isidore tries to eliminate them from the hierarchy. The class of primate/patriarch invented by Pseudo-Isidore is found fully articulated only in the Decretals. Nevertheless, the range of sources used, their connections with one another, and their basic attitudes are similar or identical, so that there can be no doubt that they all originated from kindred spirits. They were probably not from one workshop, since the texts of individual forgeries differ in sophistication and type of source. 'The Pseudo-Isidorian Forgeries are all, so to speak, wound up in one another' (Seckel), and the sequence of the Forgeries is not yet clarified either in detail or in the degree of their mutual influence. It is quite possible that there were links and adoptions of forgeries that were not yet fully formed, and cer-

---

23. H. Fuhrmann, 'Studien zur Geschichte mittelalterlicher Patriarchate', ZRG Kan. Abt. 40 (1954) 14ff.; 41 (1955) 95ff.; idem, *Einfluß und Verbreitung* 1.42, 197ff.

24. Hinschius, *Decretales* 41.30–31, 243.22ff.

25. Examples: *Capitula Angilramni* 5 and Pseudo-Victor c.6, Hinschius, *Decretales* 760 and 128. *Capitula Angilramni* 4, Hinschius, *Decretales* 758 and Benedictus Levita 3.156, MGH Leges 2.2.112, and Pseudo-Felix I c.9, Hinschius, *Decretales* 201.

tainly the *Hispana Gallica Augustodunensis* could be a product used in the Pseudo-Isidorian Decretals and in the False Capitularies. The Decretals presupposed the existence of the *Capitula Angilramni* and the perhaps unfinished Capitularies of Benedictus Levita, and yet the author of *Additio IV* of the Capitularies also knew the False Decretals.

III. The Individual Forgeries

1. The *Collectio Hispana Gallica Augustodunensis*

The *Collectio Hispana Gallica Augustodunensis*, which has never been edited, contains readings and additions from the hand of the Pseudo-Isidorian forgers.[26] 'Augustodunensis' is named after Autun, the place of origin of the sole complete manuscript of the collection, Vat. lat. 1341 (tenth century).[27] The same version is to be found in a supplement from the middle of the ninth century in the codex Hamilton 132 of the Staatsbibliothek Berlin (beginning of the ninth century). From the information of the Maurist P. Coustant († 1721), we know of the existence of three further manuscripts, now lost, in the libraries of Beauvais, Noyon, and Laon,

26. On the formation and distribution of the collection, which reached substantially further than had hitherto been assumed, cf. J. Richter, 'Stufen pseudoisidorischer Verfälschung' 1ff.

27. Due to an oath of Abbot Theotard before Bishop Agano of Autun († 1098), entered at the front of this manuscript, it is assumed that it is from Autun, originating there in the tenth century, cf. G. Le Bras, 'Autun dans l'histoire du droit canon', *Mémoires de la Société Eduenne* 48 (1937) 161–174, esp. 165. J. Tarré, 'L'influence des Écoles dans la transmission des canons médiévaux', *Études Le Bras* 1.354, believes that the codex came from the cathedral chapter of Autun. Even this manuscript is defective; between fol. 115 and fol. 116 text has been lost, the Third Council of Braga is lost from c.6 on, the First Council of Seville is missing entirely and the second through c.13. The fragment of a letter of Sidonius Apollinaris to Domnolus (MGH Auctores antiquissimi 8.76. 10–28), added to the codex in a hand of the twelfth century (fol. 130) was published by S. Williams, *Manuscripta* 11 (1967) 48ff. Reproductions of fol. 160v (cf. Hinschius, *Decretales* 580–581) of the manuscript are in the *Enciclopedia Cattolica* 10 (1953) 242 and NCE 5 (1967) 821. The manuscript was already analyzed by the Ballerini brothers, 'De antiquis . . . collectionibus et collectoribus', Pars III, c. IV § 5 n. 13ff. (PL 56.231ff.). They held the collection in the manuscript Vat. lat. 1341 to be a Hispana 'originis Gallicanae', in which interpolations from the Pseudo-Isidorian Decretals were added later, though the Ballerini do express the suspicion that Pseudo-Isidore could have had a hand in *Hispana* manuscripts of Gallican origins. G. Martínez Díez included the collection *Hispana Gallica Augustodunensis* under the sigla F in his investigation of the *Collectio Hispana* and in his edition carried out with F. Rodríguez, which has reached the Tenth Toledan Council: *La Colección canónica Hispana* (Madrid 1966) 1.355ff. and 3–5 (Madrid 1982–1992). A corrector from as early as the eleventh century entered variants from Burchard's *Decretum* into Vat. lat. 1341. An example is that in the Fourth Toledan Council c. 55, the *Hispana*, the *Hispana Gallica*, the *Augustodunensis* and Pseudo-Isidore, with the exception of the manuscripts of Novara and S. Amand, all read 'si reverti non possunt', Burchard 8.27, 'si reverti nolunt', and an improvement of his model by Regino of Prüm, *De synodalibus causis*, *App.* 2.31, 'si reverti non volunt'. In Vat. lat. 1341, fol. 76, Burchard's text is placed between the lines.

all episcopal sees in the ecclesiastical province of Reims, in which the monastery of Corbie also lies, where Hamilton 132 was written. Three further codices can be added, so that we have a total of eight witnesses to the text, no small success for a Carolingian legal collection.[28]

The *Hispana Gallica Augustodunensis* is taken from the Spanish canon law collection *(Collectio Hispana)* in the form in which it circulated in Frankish Gaul *(Collectio Hispana Gallica)*. There are only a few witnesses to the Gallican *Hispana,* which also has never been edited. It contains a text still unfalsified, but a text that is corrupt and confused. The most important witness is the Codex 411 of Vienna, Österreichische Nationalbibliothek (end of eighth or beginning of the ninth century)[29] since the *Hispana Gallica* manuscript, prepared at the order of Bishop Rachio in 787, was destroyed during the bombardment of Strasbourg in 1870.[30] The Rachio Codex cannot have been used by the Pseudo-Isidorian forgers. Rather the evidence points to their having used a manuscript of the Vienna type.[31]

28. On the general tradition cf. Richter, 'Stufen pseudoisidorischer Verfälschung' 21ff. and Fuhrmann, *Einfluß und Verbreitung* 1.151ff. On the Laon manuscript, cf. J. J. Contreni, 'A New Description of the Lost Laon Manuscript of the "Collectio Hispana Gallica",' BMCL 7 (1977) 85ff. (repr. in *Carolingian Learning, Masters and Manuscripts* [Aldershot 1992] no. xiv).

29. According to E. A. Lowe, *Codices Latini Antiquiores* (Oxford 1963) 10.12 no. 1477 with illustrations of fol. 136v and p. 47 (bibliography), the manuscript derives from eastern France, near the Rhineland. On the content, cf. Maassen, *Geschichte* 668 no. 5 and p. 710ff. The manuscript was done in facsimile: *Wiener Hispana-Handschrift: Vollständige Faksimile-Ausgabe im Originalformat des Codex Vindobonensis 411,* introduction by O. Mazal (Codices selecti 41; Graz 1974).

30. Several illustrations of the Codex have come down to us through reproductions of Count A. de Bastard (Paris 1835ff.), cf. E.A. Lowe, *Codices Latini Antiquiores* (Oxford 1953) 6.34 no. 835 with illustrations, and p. 48 (bibliography), J. B. Pitra did a description, *Analecta novissima Spicilegii Solesmensis, Altera continuatio* 1 (Paris 1885) 87ff., which P. Séjourné, *Le dernier père de l'Église, Saint Isidore de Séville* (Paris 1929), published. Why C. Vogel and R. Elze, *Le Pontifical romano-germanique du dixième siècle* (Studi e testi 226; Vatican City 1963) 1.269 on Ordo LXXIX, refers to Pitra's description in particular cannot be determined. A short summary of what one can still say about the Codex is given by B. Franck, 'Recherches sur le manuscrit de l'Hispana de l'évêque Rachio', *Archives de l'église d'Alsace,* N.S. 7 (1956) 67ff.; on 74–75, Franck gives a collation of the prologue as published by Grandidier (1778), Koch (1804), and Maassen (1870). The writing was done according to the year of the incarnation 788, according to the regnal years of rulers and popes 786–787. E. Ewig, 'Saint Chrodegang et la réforme de l'église franque', *Saint Chrodegang: Communications présentées au colloque tenu à Metz à l'occasion du XIIe centenaire de sa mort* (Metz 1967) 52 (repr. *Spätantikes und fränkisches Gallien: Gesammelte Schriften (1952–73)* (Beihefte zu Francia 3.2; Munich [1979] 2.258), wants to use the existence of the Rachio-Codex and the *Augustodunensis* to draw conclusions about relations between Strasbourg and Autun: 'It seems to us probable that the collection [the *Hispana*] was transmitted from Autun to Strasbourg', B. Bischoff, 'Panorama der Handschriftenüberlieferung aus der Zeit Karls des Großen', *Karl der Große: Lebenswerk und Nachleben, 2: Das geistige Leben,* ed. B. Bischoff (Düsseldorf 1965) 243, holds the Rachio Codex to have been created in Strasbourg.

31. Characteristics of a *Hispana Gallica,* varying from the Vienna type, are also shown in the manuscripts Vat. Pal. lat. 575 (saec. IX/X) and Rome, Bibl. Vallicelliana D.18 (s. X), cf. Richter, 'Stufen pseudoisidorischer Verfälschung' 8ff.

At first scholars held that the Pseudo-Isidorian elements of the *Hispana Gallica Augustodunensis* were added to the text, even though the Ballerinis and particularly F. H. Knust († 1841) raised doubts about this.[32] Paul Hinschius completely disproved Knust's theory. He thought that the Pseudo-Isidorian Decretals were an augmented *Hispana,* but in a premature conclusion he held that the forgers did not use the *Hispana* form of Autun but a *Hispana* such as is preserved in the manuscript Vienna 411. To him the Rachio Codex was a proof that such a form of Gallican origins, (Gallicanae originis), was available to the Frankish forgers of decretals. He thought that the councils contained in the Pseudo-Isidore were genuine and taken from the *Hispana.* He printed the corresponding portions, to his mind untouched by Pseudo-Isidore, from the *Hispana* edited by F. A. Gonzalez.[33] He concluded that the manuscript of Autun was a product of forgery by emendation. In 1884–1885, 'Maassen, in a methodologically irrefutable demonstration' (Seckel) showed that the *Collectio Hispana Gallica Augustodunensis* had been edited by the Pseudo-Isidorian forgers themselves and had been the direct source for the False Decretals in their 'genuine portions', particularly the councils.

The reworking of the *Hispana Gallica Augustodunensis* had proceeded in various ways. In many places, incomprehensible passages of the *Hispana Gallica* were rendered into a Latin more capable of being under-

32. F. H. Knust, *De fontibus et consilio Ps.-Isidorianae collectionis* (Göttingen 1832), particularly p. 7; cf. the review associating it with historical questions, *Freimüthige Blätter über Theologie und Kirchenthum* 5 (1833) 246ff.

33. *Collectio canonum ecclesiae Hispanae ex probatissimis ac pervetustis codicibus nunc primum in lucem edita a publica Matritensi Bibliotheca,* ed. Francisco Antonio Gonzalez (Madrid 1808–1821). See Hinschius, *Decretales* lxxxiiff.; on the plan of his edition, ccxxxviii; p. 438–439 is canon 7 of the Second Council of Seville, which Hinschius believed to be the only part falsified by Pseudo-Isidore, and he edited it according to Pseudo-Isidorian manuscripts. Martínez Díez, *Hispana* 1.218ff., 359ff., attributes the *Hispana Gallica,* the *Hispana Gallica Augustodunensis* and the Codices Vat. Pal. lat. 575 and Rome, Bibl. Vallicelliana D. 18 (see above, n. 31) to the Gallican branch of a redaction begun under Archbishop Julian of Toledo († 680) and completed in 681, an assertion made throughout the edition, but which deserves closer investigation. Some items belonging to the *Collectio Hispana,* its manuscript transmissions and edition, are listed by M. C. Díaz y Díaz, *Index scriptorum latinorum medii aevi Hispanorum* (2 vols. Madrid 1959): cf. the entries and the bibliography in Clavis 583ff. no. 1790. Díaz y Díaz expressed himself on the distribution of Hispana manuscripts, 'La circulation des manuscrits dans la Péninsule Ibérique du VIIe au XIe siècle', *Cahiers de la civilisation médiévale* 12 (1969) 386ff. Special mention should be made of the edition of the confession of the First Toledo Council by J. A. de Aldama, *El símbolo Toledano* (Analecta Gregoriana 7; Rome 1934) 26ff., where the *Hispana* tradition is considered up to and including the Pseudo-Isidorian Decretals. J. Vives, in collaboration with T. Marín Martínez and G. Martínez Díez, *Concilios visigótos e hispano-romanos* (España Cristiana, Textos 1; Barcelona 1963), has edited the Spanish councils from that of Elvira (300–306) to Toledo XVII. He used only one manuscript for each council.

stood.[34] The forgers clearly intended to improve the Latinity of the text. With this goal in mind, the editor altered many passages that the *Hispana* shares with its Gallican derivative: 'abstinent a carnibus' (Council of Ancyra, c.14) becomes 'abstinent se a carnibus'; 'conaverit' (Twelfth Council of Toledo, c.4) becomes 'conatus fuerit', and so on. Tortured syntax is avoided: 'Quicumque ex his qui lapsi sunt' (Nicaea, c.10) becomes 'Quicumque ex lapsis'. Conversely, in order to increase clarity, additions were made: 'canonicum' is added to 'ordinem recognoscat' (Council of Orange, c.10); 'de singulis' is expanded to 'de singulis ipsius regionis causis' (Council of Antioch, c.9), and so on. Unusual words or words capable of being misunderstood are changed, so that in the place of 'internuptarum' there is 'viduarum' (Fourth Council of Arles, c.3); the 'dressed up dwarves' and 'hair-curlers' of the Council of Elvira, c. 67: 'aut comatos aut viros cinerarios' become simply jokesters and actors, 'aut comicos aut viros scenicos', from the 'limpor evidens' we get the 'norma' (Eleventh Council of Toledo, preface), and so on.

'The emendations are in part the free imagination of their creator; in part they stem from the *Dionysio-Hadriana*'.[35] In fact the adaptation to the *Hadriana* that Maassen failed to describe completely is quite extensive.[36] Thus certain introductory pieces are taken from the *Dionysio-Hadriana*: the first two annotations, in abridged form, the *Canones apostolorum*, and the metric preface to the Nicene Council.[37] A reader of the collection is reminded all the more of the *Dionysio-Hadriana*, since its concluding piece, the synod of Pope Gregory II of 721 also went into the *Hispana Gallica Augustodunensis*. The textual parallels to the *Dionysio-Hadriana* are considerable, even if lacking in uniformity. Hence the rubrics of the canons for the African councils are modeled after the *Hadriana*, but here as well the skill with which the changes are made is astounding. A rubric whose intent is advantageous ('Si quis presbyter contra episcopum suum

34. Examples in Fuhrmann, *Einfluß und Verbreitung* 1.156–157.

35. Seckel, 'Pseudoisidor' 293.44–45.

36. He restricts himself 'to report only such examples in which the alteration is the product of the free invention of the author of the recension' (thus 'Pseudoisidor-Studien 1' [SB Wien 108; Vienna 1885] 1077, similarly p. 1066). It remains to be seen what texts were added as corrections. Seckel, 'Pseudoisidor' 293.53ff., considered the Irish canonical collections which the forger of the Decretals used.

37. This shows that the *Dionysio-Hadriana* used by the redactor of Autun could have been of the same form as that used by the forger of the Pseudo-Isidorian Decretals. For the pieces cited in the text and a few other prologue pieces are the characteristic marks of a special form of the *Hadriana* which also provided the invocation and introductory words for the Pseudo-Isidorian Decretals: 'In nomine domini. Incipit praefatio libri huius', cf. Seckel-Fuhrmann, *Die erste Zeile Pseudoisidors* 24ff.

schisma fecerit, anathema sit') is placed between two canonical texts and formed with them into a unity, and the new creation is given a canonical number from both the *Hispana* and the Gallican *Hispana,* where the text is actually only one canon (Carthage II, c.8).

The specifically Pseudo-Isidorian elements of the *Augustodunensis* appear in various ways. It is manifested in the addition of entirely forged letters:[38] one by Archbishop Stephen to Pope Damasus, as well as in the pope's response, which contains several Pseudo-Isidorian programmatic points,[39] as well as in a tractate-like letter of Pope Damasus, 'De vana superstitione chorepiscoporum vitanda'.[40] Further, creative interpolations were not taken from the *Dionysio-Hadriana,* and it is astonishing in how many heterogeneous subject areas the forgers made these tendentious alterations and additions. They dealt with the entire hierarchy, from the lowest grade of ordination through the priests, bishops, metropolitans through the primates/patriarchs (a level of authority first introduced by Pseudo-Isidore) all the way to the pope.

The content as well as the style of the forgery mirrors the Pseudo-Isidore Decretals. The position of the bishop (which was 'the apple of Pseudo-Isidore's eye' [Seckel]), is elevated through calculated alterations: 'ad hoc ut vilescat nomen episcopi et summi honoris auctoritas' (Council of Serdica, c.6, 'summi honoris' added to the *Augustodunesis*). 'Huius vero temerator edicti prout aetas [*Hispana Gallica:* 'aeas'] permiserit aut flagris aut abstinentiae subiacebit': the penalty should not be determined by the age of the person defying the law, but by the bishop, and hence 'prout episcopus' is put in the place of 'prout aetas' (Ninth Council of Toledo, c.17). The *Augustodunensis* interpolator clearly thinks that the rule that the metropolitan and the bishops of a province must invite a foreign bishop before he may enter is injurious to episcopal rights. In addition, he demands that the metropolitan must be bound to the decision of the bishops of his province, so that the request must come from all the suffragans: 'nisi forte per litteras rogatus abierit, non solum autem a metropolitano, sed ab his qui cum eo sunt ('omnibus ipsius' addition of the *Hispana Gallica Augustodunensis*) provinciae episcopis' (Council of Antioch, c. 13).

The intent and complexity of the objectives covered by the alterations can be found elsewhere only in the False Decretals themselves, and one might accurately speak of *Augustodunensis* as an early example of the forg-

---

38. Cf. the listing of differences between the *Gallican Hispana* on the one hand and the Augustodunensis and False Decretals on the other in Maassen, 'Pseudoisidor-Studien 2' (SB Wien 109; Vienna 1885) 838ff.

39. Hinschius, *Decretales* 501ff.

40. Ibid. 509ff.

ers' entire program. For this reason Fournier thought that the *Hispana Gallica Augustodunensis* was compiled at about the same time as the False Decretals and that the compiler knew the general plan of Pseudo-Isidore.[41] Seckel established that the redactor of the *Augustodunensis* 'developed or indicated a system which, in a nutshell, already contains the general basic ideas . . . of Pseudo-Isidore'.[42] More precise comparisons of the *Augustodunensis* with two of the oldest manuscripts of the False Decretals (Vat. lat. 630 and Vat. Ottoboniani lat. 93) showed that the *Augustodunensis* belongs to the contemporary milieu of the process of forgery.[43] The completed Vat. lat. 630 was later reworked using an *Augustodunensis*, and Vat. Ottoboniani lat. 93, which in its *Constitutum Constantini* still bears traces of a preparatory stage,[44] carries in part readings of the unfalsified *Hispana Gallica*. It is possible to imagine, then, that a *Hispana Gallica* was altered into a *Hispana Gallica Augustodunensis,* and the Pseudo-Isidorian collection of decretals was being compiled and written at the same time. The *Augustodunensis'* influence is found in the False Decretals and in the Capitularies of Benedictus Levita. Consequently, the forgers must have used it, at least in part, from the start of the 850s at the latest. When it left the workshop of the forgers is hard to say.

2. The *Capitula Angilramni*

'No question so vitally occupied the circle of the Pseudo-Isidorian canonists as accusations against bishops and clerics of lower degrees'.[45] This general theme of the Pseudo-Isidorian forgers is exhibited in the so-called *Capitula Angilramni:* it consists of 71 (another tradition has 72) short and lightly altered maxims of law, almost all dealing with the process of accusation against clerics, particularly bishops, 'a small treatise of criminal procedure for the prosecution of bishops'.[46] The *Capitula* usually appear in manuscript together with the longer version of the Pseudo-Isidorian Decretals (A1 or A/B and their derivations), and Hinschius edit-

41. P. Fournier, 'Étude sur les Fausses Décrétales', RHE 7 (1906) 311 n. 4 (repr., *Mélanges* I.112 n. 4), not so pointedly in Fournier-Le Bras, *Histoire* I.140–141, 167.

42. Seckel, 'Pseudoisidor' 294.20ff.

43. Richter, 'Stufen pseudoisidorischer Verfälschung' 46ff., made precise comparisons. The following assertions rest on his results.

44. Cf. H. Fuhrmann, 'Konstantinische Schenkung und abendländisches Kaisertum', DA 22 (1966) 88ff.

45. Thus Fournier-Le Bras, *Histoire* I.142.

46. Thus E. Seckel, 'Studien VIII', NA 40 (1916) 63. An evaluation of the substance of the *Capitula Angilramni* stressing the restriction of accusations is given by G. May, 'Zu den Anklagebeschränkungen, insbesondere wegen Infamie, in den Capitula Angilramni', ZKG 72 (1961) 106–112; still ever instructive is A. Hauck, *Kirchengeschichte Deutschlands* (6th ed. Berlin 1952) 2.539ff.

ed the two together in 1863.[47] It purports to have been sent by Pope Hadrian I (772–795) to Bishop Angilram of Metz (768–791) (hence it is sometimes called the *Capitula Hadriani* or, after *Capitula Angilramni* 4: 'synodus Romana'). In many manuscripts, Pope Hadrian is the recipient, but the chapters have nothing to do with either man, and it is at best risky to conclude, as some have, that Angilram of Metz was in Rome at this time.[48] The notions that Metz has any special relationship with the *Capitula Angilramni* or that the vicariate of Drogo of Metz was specifically combatted in them—a favorite thesis of F. Lot—are equally unlikely.[49] A major source of the *Capitula Angilramni* is Roman law, specifically in its Visigothic redaction (among others, the *Breviarium Alaricianum* and its *Epitomai Parisiensis* and *Aegidii, Sententiae Pauli*), but other sources are the *Dionysio-Hadriana*, Cassiodorus' *Historia Tripartita,* and other sources also drawn upon in the False Decretals. The *Capitula* could have been compiled directly from the sources without the mediation of the Pseudo-Isidorian Decretals, though the question of a common intermediary source for both has not yet been fully clarified.[50] In many places they give a text with little sense for practical application. There are cross-connections between the *Capitula Angilramni* and the Capitularies of Benedictus Levita (see, for example, Benedictus Levita 1.36, where there is perhaps an allusion to the *Capitula*[51]), but the filiation is not yet clarified in all cases:

47. Hinschius, *Decretales* 757ff.; see also Fuhrmann, *Einfluß und Verbreitung* 1.26 and below, p. 154ff. A reprint, revised but without variants, of Hinschius is given by P. Ciprotti, *I capitula Angilramni con appendice di documenti connessi* (Università degli studi di Camerino, Istituto giuridico, testi per esercitazioni sezione 7.1; Milan 1966); appendices include the parallels of the *Capitula Angilramni* in Pseudo-Julius, Pseudo-Felix, and in the Capitularies of Benedictus Levita, 2.381; to these pieces, Ciprotti adds the letter of Gregory IV to Aldrich of Le Mans of 833, printed by Hinschius from Mabillon (JE † 2579); Ciprotti holds it to be bogus; W. Goffart holds it to be genuine, 'Gregory IV for Aldric of Le Mans (833): A Genuine or Spurious Decretal?' *Mediaeval Studies* 28 (1966) 22–38, but Goffart's thesis has been convincingly contradicted by D. Lohrmann, in his review QF 48 (1968) 403f.

48. Most recently O. G. Oexle, 'Die Karolinger und die Stadt des heiligen Arnulf', *Frühmittelalterliche Studien* 1 (1967) 296. To the present day, some of the historical references of the *Capitula* to Angilram have not been uncovered. On Angilram of Metz, cf. J. Fleckenstein, *Die Hofkapelle der deutschen Könige* (MGH Schriften 16; Stuttgart 1959) 1.48ff. and N. Häring, 'Angilram', LMA 1 (1977–1980) 635.

49. F. Lot, *Études sur le règne de Hugues Capet* (Paris 1903) 370f. Lot supported his theory on *Capitula Angilramni* 22 (Hinschius, *Decretales* 762–763); Seckel already opposed him in 'Pseudoisidor', 296.21ff., and Fournier-Le Bras, *Histoire* 1.142–143 n. 3. Lot sought to defend his position on new grounds, 'Textes manceaux et Fausses Décrétales II', BEC 102 (1941) 33–34 (repr. *Recueil des travaux historiques de F. Lot* [Hautes Études médiévales et modernes 4; Geneva 1968] 1.606–607).

50. A version of its own is represented by Phill. 1764 of the Berlin, Staatsbibliothek, cf. Fuhrmann, *Einfluß und Verbreitung* 3.696ff.; without a doubt there exist other preliminary forms and redactions that have not yet been investigated.

51. Cf. Seckel, 'Studien VI', NA 31 (1906) 70. Benedictus Levita mentions that one could

'between Benedict and Angilram, interrelations back and forth appear to have taken place on various levels'.[52] The *Capitula Angilramni* are recapitulated to a large degree as Benedictus Levita 3.307–374[53] and Benedictus Levita 2.381,[54] and parallel formulations are given in the False Decretals as canons of the Council of Nicaea.[55]

3. The Capitulary Collection of Benedictus Levita

The collection consists of three books and four 'additiones',[56] and it was intended to be understood as a supplement to the capitulary collection of Abbot Ansegis of Fontenelle, with which it is often transmitted and whose numeration of books it continues (Ansegis 1–4, Benedictus Levita 5–8).[57] The impact of the work must be understood in the context of capitulary legislation, whose effectiveness is, to be sure, in dispute. The three books and four 'additiones' of the capitulary collection of Benedic-

---

find more about the procedure of accusation 'in canonibus'. Seckel has proposed that this is a play on the *Capitula Angilramni*. Indeed the *Capitula Angilramni* do appear under the name of the *Canones Angilramni*, such as (if the edition corresponds to the text of the manuscript) in the collection of the manuscript Turin D IV 33 analyzed by P. Fournier, *Mélanges P. Fabre* (Paris 1902) 213, (repr. *Mélanges* 1.229); cf. also Fournier-LeBras, *Histoire* 2.166. On the Turin collection, but not on the *Capitula Angilramni* contained in it, see R. E. Reynolds, 'The Turin Collection in Seven Books: A Poitevin Canonical Collection', *Traditio* 25 (1969) 508–514, who holds a provenance from Poitiers to be not unlikely.

52. Seckel, 'Pseudoisidor' 292.2–3.

53. Seckel, 'Studien VIII', NA 40 (1916) 55ff., demonstrated that Benedictus Levita was here using the *Capitula Angilramni*, not that the *Capitula Angilramni* depend upon the False Decretals. Seckel demonstrated in his irrefutable and penetrating investigation that the *Capitula Angilramni* were incorporated as a 'mass' in sequence, cf. his conclusion, 129–130.

54. Cf. Seckel, 'Studien VII', NA 35 (1910) 491ff.

55. Pseudo-Julius, Hinschius, *Decretales* 467ff. and Pseudo-Felix II, Hinschius, *Decretales* 485ff.

56. Of the many surveys, cf. particularly F. Baix, 'Benoît le Lévite', DHGE 8 (1935) 213–218; W. A. Eckhardt, 'Benedictus Levita', HRG 1 (1965) 362–364, and as an introduction, especially, G. Schmitz, 'Die Waffe der Fälschung zum Schutz der Bedrängten? Bemerkungen zu gefälschten Konzils-und Kapitularientexten', *Fälschungen im Mittelalter* 2.79ff., who mentions that many items seen as ungenuine are actually under the 'suspicion of being genuine'.

57. Fundamental on all questions of the tradition, E. Seckel, 'Benedictus Levita decurtatus' 377ff. Corresponding to the combination of Ansegis and Benedictus Levita is an *Abbreviatio Ansegisi et Benedicti Levitae*, which was produced shortly thereafter and which had some circulation, cf. Mordek, *Kirchenrecht und Reform* 181 with n. 394, 194–195 n. 495, and G. Schmitz, 'Die Überlieferung der sog. "Abbreviatio Ansegisi et Benedicti Levitae",' DA 40 (1984) 176ff. Further additions, an *Epitome Ansegisi et Benedicti Levitae*, were made by H. Mordek and G. Schmitz, 'Neue Kapitularien und Kapitulariensammlungen', DA 43 (1987) 378ff. The current edition of the capitulary collection of Benedictus Levita is that by G. H. Pertz, MGH Leges 2.2.39–158 (repr. PL 97, first printing 1851), although Pertz saw the edition as only a stopgap; a critical introduction on the sources is given by F. H. Knust († 1841), who died young, p. 19–39. A new edition was being prepared for decades by E. Seckel (1864–1924); on Seckel's efforts at an edition and the fate of his efforts, cf. Fuhrmann, *Einfluß und Verbreitung* 1.164–165 n. 52.

tus Levita comprehend 1721 chapters. In his first Prologue of seven distichs, the collector calls himself 'Benedictus Levita' (=deacon)[58] and declares that he did the work at the command of Archbishop Otgar of Mainz (826–847),[59] claiming to have found the materials primarily in the archives of the church of Mainz. The forger tried to suggest a Mainz provenance to his reader.

At the start of the first book he placed three genuine pieces from the correspondence of Boniface normally connected with Mainz (JE 2275; *Concilium Germanicum* of 743; Council of Estinnes of 743). He also tried to present himself to the reader as writing on the right bank of the Rhine (although Mainz lies on the left!): 'Hludowicus enim fluvii cis litora Reni / imperat et gentes comprimit ecce feras'. Varying credence is given to the prologue, and authorship in Mainz has been considered, both for the entire forgery and for one part: 'a certain confidence can be imparted' to the writer of the prologue.[60] Yet the many cross-connections among the forgeries support a theory that they originated in one place and within one and the same circle of persons. The evidence points to the Western Frankish realm and the enemies of Hincmar of Reims, that is, the friends and followers of Ebo of Reims. The 'terminus post quem' for the creation is 21 April 847, the day of the death of Otgar of Mainz, who is mentioned in the perfect sense in the prefatory poem. A more certain 'terminus ante quem' is 14 February 857, the date of the Capitulary of Quierzy, which cited false capitularies in its 'Capitula domni Karoli et domni Hludowici imperatorum'.[61]

Although Benedict called his products 'capitularies', using 'capitularies' more intensively than the forger of the Decretals (a quarter of his collection consists of genuine capitularies), he still drew from the same body of sources as Pseudo-Isidore[62] (the Bible, councils, decretals, Roman law,

58. Cardinal Deusdedit (see Fuhrmann, *Einfluß und Verbreitung* 2.522ff.) understood Benedict to be the monastic father of Nursia: V. Wolf von Glanvell, *Die Kanonessammlung des Kardinals Deusdedit* (Paderborn 1905) 4.19–23 (Prologue).

59. Cf. A. Gerlich, 'Die Reichspolitik des Erzbischofs Otgar von Mainz (826–847)', *Rheinische Vierteljahrsblätter* 19 (1954) 315; J. Hannig, 'Zentrale Kontrolle und regionale Machtbalance: Beobachtungen zum System der karolingischen Königsboten am Beispiel des Mittelrheingebiets', *Archiv für Kulturgeschichte* 66 (1984) 15, imagines Otgar assigning Benedict to compose a collection 'for the practical needs of the mission of a missus'.

60. Cf. B. Krusch, *Neue Forschungen über die drei oberdeutschen Leges: Bajuvariorum, Alamannorum, Ribuariorum* (Abh. Göttingen N.S. 20.1; Berlin 1927) 53ff.; Fuhrmann, *Einfluß und Verbreitung* 1.166.

61. MGH Concilia 3.394–396.

62. Basic for any analysis of the sources and their reworking remains Seckel, 'Studien I–VIII', NA 26 (1901) 37–72 (individual 'source masses'); NA 29 (1904) 275–331 (individual 'source masses'); NA 31 (1906) 59–139, 238–239 (sources of Book I); NA 34 (1909) 319–381

Germanic codes, penitentials, writings of Fathers of the Church, more recent theological writings, the *Dionysio-Hadriana,* Irish canon collections, and so on). On the whole, the circle of sources is smaller, but in some cases he used a broader body of material than the forgers of the Pseudo-Isidorian Decretals drew upon; for example, besides a series of synods that are not exploited in the False Decretals, he used the *Breviatio canonum* of Fulgentius Ferrandus, the *Collectio Vetus Gallica,'* from which he took early Frankish councils,[63] extensive Roman legal sources,[64] and *Capitula episcoporum,*[65] which were, surprisingly, omitted by the Pseudo-Isidorian Decretals. Benedict was reluctant to mix his sources; a single chapter frequently gives an excerpt from only one source, and many chapters are repeated time and again. Hence in the third book, more than a hundred chapters are repeated. Benedict also does not integrate the texts as energetically as does Pseudo-Isidore, but takes factual incoherence in his stride; he is linguistically more restrained. For example, he emulates the straightforward style of the Frankish royal chancery rather well.

4. The Pseudo-Isidorian Decretals

The False Decretals comprehend primarily papal letters and councils from Clement I (roughly 90–101) and Anacletus I (roughly 79–90) through Gregory I (590–604), whose letters are followed by the Roman council of Gregory II in 721.[66] Of all the medieval canon law collections arranged in chronological order, the Pseudo-Isidorian Decretals were the most widely distributed work, being even more widely distributed than the *Dionysio-Hadriana.*

(sources of 2.1 to 2.161); NA 35 (1910) 105–191, 433–537 (sources of 2.162 to 2.436); NA 39 (1914) 327–431 (sources of 3.1 to 3.254); NA 40 (1916) 15–130 (sources of 3.255 to 3.374); NA 41 (1917–1919) 157–263 (sources of 3.375 to 3.429); supplemented and edited from his papers by J. Juncker, 'Studien zu Benedictus Levita (Studie VIII, Schlußteil IV)', ZRG Kan. Abt. 23 (1934) 269–377 (sources of 3.430 to 3.446); 24 (1935) 1–112 (sources of 3.447 to 3.478). Seckel and Juncker never made an investigation of the additions. Among Seckel's source-critical investigations of Benedict's capitularies there was also his contribution, 'Die ältesten Canones von Rouen', *Historische Aufsätze: K. Zeumer zum sechzigsten Geburtstag als Festgabe dargebracht von Freunden und Schülern* (Weimar 1910) esp. 617ff.

63. Precisely handled by H. Mordek, 'Une nouvelle source de Benoît le Lévite', RDC 20 (1970) 241–251, and in summary, *Kirchenrecht und Reform,* 190ff.

64. Cf. F. L. Ganshof, *Droit romain dans la collection de Benoît le Lévite* (IRMAe, pars I, 2bccß; Milan 1969) 23–24.

65. R. McKitterick, *The Frankish Church and the Carolingian Reforms, 789–895* (Royal Historical Society, Studies in History 2; London 1977); P. Brommer, 'Benedictus Levita und die "Capitula episcoporum"',' *Mainzer Zeitschrift* 70 (1975) 145ff.

66. The extensive literature is listed in Seckel, 'Pseudoisidor' 265ff. and in Fuhrmann, *Einfluß und Verbreitung* 1.41ff. (questions of influence in various specialties), 168ff. (questions of sources).

a. Breadth and Form of the Manuscript Tradition

The critical editor of the False Decretals, Paul Hinschius, counted 65 manuscripts,[67] though at least 50 more manuscripts of the Pseudo-Isidorian Decretals can now be counted, primarily thanks to the discoveries of F. Schulte, F. Maassen, E. Seckel, P. Fournier, Z. N. Brooke, J. H. Erickson, and H. Mordek. This does not include the many collections of Pseudo-Isidorian excerpts,[68] some of them quite extensive, as well as an abundance of manuscripts known earlier but now lost or destroyed. S. Williams investigated 80 codices of Pseudo-Isidore (not including excerpts), and he established that an astonishing number of manuscripts were written in the first half-century after the time when the False Decretals were composed.[69]

67. In his listing of 64 manuscripts (Hinschius, *Decretales* xi–xvi) Hinschius does not count four excerpt manuscripts (xii, a–d); there were 54 manuscripts available to Hinschius, not including the excerpt traditions he listed. During printing Hinschius discovered the manuscript Codex 113 of Köln, Erzbischöfliche Diözesan- und Dombibliothek (s.x–xi), cf. his addendum, 770.

68. The work of S. Williams laid a good foundation for the manuscript tradition of the Decretals: *Codices Pseudoisidoriani: A Palaeographico-Historical Study* (MIC Series C: Subsidia 3; New York 1971), reviews, cf. H. Mordek, QF 51 (1971) 630 n. 8; R. E. Reynolds, *Speculum* 47 (1972) 818ff.; J. Gilchrist, TRG 92 (1974) 130ff.; A. García y García, REDC 28 (1972) 434–435. Further additions are given by Fuhrmann, *Einfluß und Verbreitung* 1.168ff. n. 61; J. H. Erickson, 'New Pseudo-Isidore Manuscripts', BMCL 5 (1975) 115ff. More than just a review of Williams is H. Mordek, 'Codices Pseudo-Isidoriani: Addenda zu dem gleichnamigen Buch von Schafer Williams', AKKR 147 (1978) 471ff., enumerating on 475–476 n. 19 the manuscripts that became known after the appearance of William's book. Despite this achievement, by no means all the Pseudo-Isidorian manuscripts have been discovered; cf., for example, Cathedral Library of York, Add. 8, a manuscipt of class B of 1469, N. R. Ker and A. J. Piper, *Medieval Manuscripts in British Libraries* (Oxford 1992) 4.795ff. There is also the gray area of references to earlier codices. The monastery of Montserrat harbors a manuscript of the eighteenth century with excerpts from Pseudo-Isidore: A. Olivar, *Catàleg dels manuscrits de la Biblioteca del Monestir de Montserrat* (Scripta et documenta 25; Montserrat 1977) 1.129ff., manuscript number 605; in the Bibliothèque municipale of Dijon lie remnants of a Pseudo-Isidore manuscript of the second half of the twelfth century, probably from the Cistercian house of Pontigny; the codex fell into the hands of a private family at the time of the storming of the monastery, 'where it served to cover jam-pots', cf. Y. Zaluska, *Manuscrits enluminés de Dijon* (Paris 1991) 170–171, Cod. 2975. The temporal specification of the codices and their ordering in manuscript classes as done by Hinschius was extensively corrected by Williams' manuscript analyses. Drawing a line between what should still be seen as a Pseudo-Isidorian manuscript and what must be seen as a collection of excerpts is difficult. The *Capitula* of Pseudo-Remedius, for example, are quite an extensive work of excerpts in the entourage of the forgery, but it could hardly be called a shortened Pseudo-Isidorian collection as is the case with the *Collectio Lanfranci*, the Pseudo-Isidorian collection of decretals obtained by Archbishop Lanfranc of Canterbury (1070–1089) in the monastery of Bec and later spread in England.

69. S. Williams, 'Pseudo-Isidore from the Manuscripts', CHR 53 (1967) 62ff. New discoveries have made the findings even more surprising than Williams had assumed.

b. The Misleading Texts of the Editions

Today we have to use a partially critical edition of the Pseudo-Isidorian Decretals edited by the jurist Paul Hinschius.[70] Hinschius divided the manuscripts of the Pseudo-Isidorian Decretals into five classes according to their extent, redaction, and the age of the tradition contained in them: A1, A2, A/B, B, C.

Class A1, seen by Hinschius as the oldest, contains all three parts, which are:

1. After some introductory and explanatory pieces, decretals from Clement I to Melchiades († 314);[71]

2. Councils beginning with Nicaea I (325) and closing with Seville II (although chronologically the last should have been Toledo XIII of 683, which had been entered earlier);[72]

3. Primarily decretals from Silvester I († 335) to Gregory II (715–731).[73]

If one overlooks some additions and interpolations, the conciliar portion in the middle of Class A1 manuscripts corresponds to the first part of the *Hispana Gallica Augustodunensis;* the third part, the decretals from Silvester to Gregory II, to a large extent corresponds in its organization to the second part of the same collection. If one wished to have a brief definition of Pseudo-Isidore, which is generally correct, one could say that Pseudo-Isidore is a *Hispana* expanded by adding false papal letters. However, one should not forget that the entire work is supplemented with pieces from Hadrian's collection. In his edition, Hinschius was determined to reproduce his Class A1, which he judged the oldest.

Class A2 did not contain the conciliar portion, but only the decretals from Clement to Damasus (366–384). The central section is completely lacking. In A2 the text of Confessio of the *Constitutum Constantini* is immediately followed by that of 'Excerpta quaedam ex synodalibus gestis sancti Silvestri papae',[74] and manuscripts in this class end in the middle of the decretals of Damasus.[75] Consequently A2 does not include the letter of Damasus against the 'chorepiscopi' already incorporated in the *Augustodunensis.*[76] It is a peculiarity of this class that the chapters are provided with rubrics and that all the decretals of the individual popes are numbered. These items were adopted by Hinschius in his edition.

---

70. Hinschius, *Decretales;* on his biography, cf. H. Liermann, *Neue Deutsche Biographie* (1972) 9.190–191.

71. Hinschius, *Decretales* 1–254.   72. Ibid. 254–444.

73. Ibid. 445–754.   74. Ibid. from 252.14 to 449.1.

75. Ibid. 508.29 n. 24.   76. Ibid. 509–515.

Hinschius significantly undervalued Class A/B, because he misdated the best manuscript of this class, Vat. lat. 630. As the Ballerini brothers long ago proposed, this version was one of the oldest of the Pseudo-Isidorian tradition.[77] In its structure and text A/B actually stands closer to the *Hispana* tradition, particularly to the *Augustodunensis* form, than classes A1 and A2 do. Hinschius recognized this fact, but he ascribed this difference to the efforts of scribes of a later time to improve A/B: (the writer of Vat. lat. 630 or the author of its source) 'videtur collectionem Pseudo-Isidorianam secundum Hispanam expurgare voluisse'.[78] The later Class B and Class C both derive from A/B.

A manuscript of the C-class, Codex no. 27 of the Bibliothèque de l'Assemblée Nationale in Paris, which Williams judged to be a codex written in a Cistercian house in 1191,[79] was the basis for the first complete Pseudo-Isidore edition, by Jacques Merlin († 1541), edited in the course of his edition of the councils (Paris 1524). Certainly there had been partial editions of the Pseudo-Isidorian Decretals made before this and there were others afterwards, but to this day it is the sole complete printing of a codex of Pseudo-Isidore. Fragments had been printed before; for example, in 1494 the *Constitutum Constantini* was published in the form found in the Pseudo-Isidore manuscripts, and in 1504 Lefèvre d'Étaples supplemented the introductory letter with some Pseudo-Isidorian decretals in his edition of the *Recognitiones* of Clement. In 1526 some decretals of Isidore Mercator were published in two small editions by Johannes Cochlaeus, but it was Merlin, whose work quickly reprinted twice (Cologne 1530; Paris 1535), who laid the basis for the many republications of the councils, which the Observant Franciscan Peter Crabbe († 1554) improved but did not significantly change. Despite its considerable circulation, Merlin's edition was early recognized as inadequate. The Benedictine scholar Pierre Coustant, a Maurist well-versed in Pseudo-Isidore, wanted to do a volume of the false papal decretals of Isidore as a second volume of his *Epistolae Romanorum Pontificum* (Paris 1721), but he died in

77. Ballerini, 'Disquisitiones de antiquis collectionibus et collectoribus canonum', P. III c. VI § 5, PL 56.251ff. Hinschius built his entire argumentation to reject the thesis of the Ballerinis, cf. the first chapter of his introduction, xvii.

78. Hinschius, *Decretales* lxiii.

79. Williams, *Visio aetatis* 40–41. Williams, 'Pseudo-Isidore from the Manuscripts' 59 calls this tradition the 'Reims version'; it was composed about the middle of the twelfth century, if not in Reims itself then 'certainly somewhere between Reims and Clairvaux'. That applies to the group of manuscripts from which the Merlin model derives; Hinschius' Class C, however, is older, for the author of the *Collection of 74 Titles* and Ivo of Chartres appear to have known it; the basic form of the C-class was formed at the latest by the eleventh century.

1721 before being able to carry out his plan.[80] The University of Göttingen established a prize for a treatment of the theme of Pseudo-Isidore in 1832, which Friedrich Heinrich Knust won for his *De fontibus et consilio Ps.-Isidorianae collectionis*. Knust, who soon came into contact with the Monumenta Germaniae Historica and with J. F. Böhmer, worked on an edition but died young (1841). Mysterious is the report of Johann Adam Möhler († 1838) that he knew of the plan for an edition which would be 'supplied with sharply critical notes . . . to demonstrate the fraud in the work of everyone'.[81] These plans came to nothing, obviously, and in 1860 J. Weizsäcker complained in view of Migne's reprint of Merlin's work,[82] 'how little the major question about this ever curious creation . . . can so be resolved with the current state of [edition] materials'.[83] Three years later, in 1863, appeared what is today seen as the standard edition of P. Hinschius. He was twenty-eight years old, and he had completed his work alone and by his own means ('itineris sumptus nisi pater nemo mihi suppeditabat') after only two years of work—an enormous accomplishment in view of the state of technology and the amount of labor required.

Hinschius' achievement was bought with concessions. He followed the advice of his teacher A. L. Richter (1808–1864) and simply took over texts 'ex editionibus vulgatis' of the 'genuine parts' of the Pseudo-Isidorian Decretals, in the sections where it was believed that the forger had left them virtually untouched. This uncritical approach to the text was particularly marked in the conciliar section, where Hinschius reprinted long parts of the conciliar texts from the *Hispana* edition of F. A. Gonzalez.[84] Certainly by 1885, through Maassen's 'Pseudoisidor-Studien',[85] it had become clear that Hinschius had edited his own Pseudo-Isidore, not the original. Maassen proved that those parts of the *Hispana* taken by Hinschius from Gonzalez had been reworked by Pseudo-Isidore in the

80. Collations of Pseudo-Isidore by Coustant can be found in Vat. lat. 9857; A. Thiel, who used Coustant's material in his *Epistolae Romanorum pontificum genuinae* (Braunsberg 1868), did not try to revive the plan.

81. J. A. Möhler, 'Fragmente aus und über Pseudo-Isidor', *Theologische Quartalschrift* (1829) 479; repr. *Gesammelte Schriften und Aufsätze*, ed. J. J. I. von Döllinger (Regensburg 1839) 1.284.

82. PL 130; Paris 1853 (but often reprinted) duplicates the second edition of Merlin in Cologne, 1530, with the prolegomena of H. J. Denzinger, who oversaw the edition.

83. J. Weizsäcker, 'Die pseudo-isidorische Frage in ihrem gegenwärtigen Stande', *Historische Zeitschrift* 3 (1860) 43–44.

84. *Collectio canonum ecclesiae Hispanae.*

85. F. Maassen, 'Pseudo-Isidor Studien, 1: Die Textesrecension der ächten Bestandtheile der Sammlung', 2: 'Die Hispana der Handschrift von Autun und ihre Beziehungen zum Pseudoisidor' (SB Wien 108; Vienna 1885) 1061ff. and 109 (1885) 801ff.

Hispana Gallica Augustodunensis. Consequently, Hinschius' edition had printed a version alien to that of Pseudo-Isidore. Although the utterly uncritical Merlin had published a more recent manuscript, his edition was truer to the tradition than the split image of Hinschius.

The inadequacies of Hinschius' edition were extensively noted by Maassen himself, and there were efforts to improve the text. The great Emil Seckel planned to 'edit Pseudo-Isidore completely anew'. But Seckel was consumed by his studies of Benedictus Levita. To the present day, we are left with the mixed edition of Hinschius, 'a fundamentally incorrect edition'.[86]

In addition to the misleading shape of the edition, Hinschius made serious paleographic errors.[87] He had accused the Ballerini brothers of dating their manuscripts too early, while he persisted with incorrigible decisiveness to date an entire series of codices two centuries too late. Hinschius placed Vat. Ottoboniani lat. 93, which originated about 860, as 'saec. XI ex./XII in.'; Hinschius did not set a single A2 manuscript in the second half of the ninth century, although fully nine of the twenty A2 codices (Aosta, Biblioteca Capitolare 102, Brescia, Biblioteca Civica Queriniana B.II.13, Ivrea, Biblioteca Capitolare 83, Lucca, Biblioteca Capitolare Feliniana 123, Monza, Biblioteca Capitolare H.3.151, Pistoia, Archivio Capitolare C.130 (olim 102), Rome, Biblioteca Vallicelliana D.38, St. Gallen, Stiftsbibliothek 670, Vercelli, Biblioteca Capitolare LXXX) might have been written in the brief period before the beginning of the tenth century. Paleographic evidence impelled Hinschius to ascribe Vat. lat. 630 to the turn of the eleventh or beginning of the twelfth century, instead of the third quarter of the ninth century. In this way he dated a mixed class, A/B, whose primary representative was Vat. lat. 630, written in Corbie, about two and a half centuries too late.[88] Hinschius placed his trust in the

86. S. Williams, 'The Pseudo-Isidorian Problem Today', *Speculum* 29 (1954) 706–707, developed a four-stage plan: (1) A catalogue of the manuscripts of Pseudo-Isidore; (2) A critical edition of the *Hispana Gallica* including the Pseudo-Isidorian interpolations; (3) A critical edition of the Capitularies of Benedictus Levita; (4) A critical edition of the Pseudo-Isidorian Decretals. With his catalogue, Williams had largely achieved his first stage. From the philological side, the judgment on Hinschius' edition is negative, cf. F. Chatillon, 'Le verset biblique le plus souvent cité par les Fausses Décrétales', *Revue du Moyen Age Latin* 15–18 (1969–1972) 17–18 n. 5. Through the readings which vary from the outset, the editing of the Pseudo-Isidorian Decretals would be 'an enormous task': S. Kuttner, 'Universal Pope or Servant of God's Servants: The Canonists, Papal Titles, and Innocent III', RDC 31 (1981) 136 (repr. *Studies in the History of Medieval Canon Law* [Aldershot 1990] no. VIII).

87. On his paleographic misjudgments, cf. Fuhrmann, *Einfluß und Verbreitung* 1.176–177.

88. Cf. the argumentation resting specifically on the dating of Vat. lat. 630 by Hinschius in his introduction, *Decretales* lxiff.; on this, Williams, 'The Pseudo-Isidorian Problem Today', 705, and idem, 'Pseudo-Isidore from the Manuscripts' 62ff. On the manuscript, see B. Bischoff, 'Hadoardus and the Manuscripts of Classical Authors from Corbie', *Didascaliae:*

manuscript Modena, Biblioteca Capitolare O.I.4., dated shortly before 881, a fragmentary and textually not even very good exemplar.[89]

c. The Sources and Their Editing

Through considerable portions, Pseudo-Isidore did not forge his materials freely, but rather composed them of highly varied, often heavily edited excerpts. The number of these excerpts, pieced together like a mosaic, could have amounted to more than ten thousand. Among the sources he extensively exploited were:[90] the Bible, extensively, partly in the Vulgate form, partly the *Vetus Latina,* partly even in a version of his own, varying from all known traditions[91] (the overwhelming number of agreements of passages from the *Liber Ecclesiasticus* with a text also found in Corbie is remarkable); rulings of councils; decretals; sources of Roman law; the Germanic codes; capitularies; penitentials; writings and letters of Fathers of the Church,[92] bishops and private persons; the edict *De recta fide*

Studies in Honor of A. M. Albareda (New York 1961) 51 n. 27 (repr. *Mittelalterliche Studien* [Stuttgart 1966] 1.57 n. 27). According to S. Williams, 'Le Ms. Saint-Omer 189 des Fausses Décrétales d'Isidore Mercator', *Bulletin trimestriel de la Société Académique des Antiquaires de la Morinie* 381 (1964) 257ff., Bishop Jean Jouffroy of Arras (1453–1462) brought the manuscript to Rome. In any case, a notice on fol. 323 indicates that Hieronymus Aleander, after 1519 librarian of the Vatican Library, worked on the book 'Die ultima Maii MDXX', before he went as 'nuntio' to the Worms Diet of 1521. Cf. Kuttner-Elze, *Catalogue* 20ff. and J. Ruysschaert, 'Les Décrétales du Ps.-Isidore du Vat. Lat. 630', *Miscellanea Bibliothecae Apostolicae Vaticanae* (Studi e testi 329; Vatican City 1987) 1.111ff. On Jouffroy and this manuscript, cf. C. Märtl, *Kardinal Jean Jouffroy († 1473): Leben und Werk* (Beiträge zur Geschichte und Quellenkunde des Mittelalters 18; Sigmaringen 1996) 287f.

89. Some of the misleading readings are listed in Fuhrmann, *Einfluß und Verbreitung* 1.177–178.

90. Cf. Hinschius in his 'tabula fontium' on the edition, *Decretales* cxiff.; Hinschius based his efforts above all on the preparatory work of Blondel, *Pseudo-Isidorus* and Knust, *De fontibus.* Seckel made an additional summary in 'Pseudoisidor' 273.10ff. and 270.42ff.

91. On the use of the Bible by the Pseudo-Isidorian forgers, cf. Hinschius, *Decretales* cxxxix ff. The version used by Pseudo-Isidore often cannot be identified with the Vulgate or with any others, P. Sabatier, *Bibliorum sacrorum latinae versiones (1743–1751)* (3 vols. Reims 1743). An entire series of biblical citations is indirect, via the *Liber contra Varimadum* (still ascribed by Hinschius to Idacius Clarus), which is now available in a new critical edition: *Florilegia Biblica Africana saec. V,* ed. B. Schwank (CCL 90; Turnhout 1961). Schwank gives the passages adopted by Pseudo-Isidore on p. xiv; they agree with the Paris, B.N. lat. 12217 (saec. VIII) from Corbie. How misleading Hinschius' edition can be is shown on p. 706.7 (John II); there he reads Vat. lat. 630 as 'caro' instead of 'spiritus', which further confuses the image of the tradition in *Contra Varimadum* 1.5.15–16, ed. Schwank, p. 21. The Bible version of the Pseudo-Isidorian papal letters is taken account of in the Beuron *Vetus latina* edition, cf. for example, on 1 John 5:7, *Vetus Latina* 26.1: *Epistulae Catholicae* (Freiburg 1966) 5.364–365. F. Chatillon, 'Le verset' 14ff., contends that a sign of Pseudo-Isidorian influence is that the most frequently used biblical verse in the False Decretals, Zechariah 2:8, is found elsewhere, such as at the Synod of Quierzy (November 858) MGH Concilia 3.426.3–4.

92. R. E. Reynolds, 'Basil and the Early Medieval Latin Canonical Collections', *Basil of Caesarea: Christian, Humanist, Ascetic, a Sixteen Hundredth Anniversary Symposium,* ed. P. J. Fedwick (Toronto 1981) 513ff., shows that the Church Father Basil, principally in the Latin

of Emperor Justinian I;[93] the *Constitutum Constantini;* the *Liber Pontificalis,* and rules of monastic orders. He used only a very few of these sources in their original form. In terms of breadth, he drew the most pieces from the *Hispana* tradition; the second part of the False Decretals, the councils, was taken largely from the first part of the *Hispana Gallica Augustodunensis,* and the third part of Pseudo-Isidore corresponded to the second part of *Augustodunensis.* Things were done differently in the *Capitula Angilramni* and in the False Capitularies of Benedictus Levita. He also used canonical collections such as the *Collectio Quesnelliana,* the Irish canonical collection,[94] and above all the *Collectio Dionysio-Hadriana,* which by 880 had become the preferred and most widely circulated collection of canon law of the Carolingian period.[95] Pseudo-Isidore might have adopted the title and surname of Mercator from the anti-Nestorian translator of the fifth century,[96] and he might have imitated a form of the *Hadriana,* which begins with almost the same invocation and the clumsy transposition of 'libri huius': 'In nomine domini. Incipit praefatio libri huius', from which Pseudo-Isidore made, 'In nomine domini nostri Iesu Christi. Incipit praefatio sancti Isidori libri huius'. The borrowed beginning of the *Hadriana* might also have given the idea to the forger 'of baptizing his little monster Isidore' (Seckel). The historical Isidore of Seville had written the first section of the *Hadriana*'s preface, and it was the rubric to this text that Pseudo-Isidore stole. Consequently, the name of Isidore was not taken from the *Hispana* and given to the False Decretals—the *Hispana* tradition is not associated with Isidore at least until the era of Pseudo-Isidore—but rather

---

translation of Rufinus of Aquileia, was more significant in early-medieval canon law, and hence in Pseudo-Isidore, than usually assumed. The same might hold true for other Fathers of the Church as well.

93. Cf. H. Fuhrmann, 'Justinians "Edictum de recta fide" (551) bei Pseudoisidor: Nach Notizen von Emil Seckel (†)', *Mélanges G. Fransen* (SG 19; Rome 1976) 1.217ff., in conjunction with R. Schieffer, 'Nochmals zur Überlieferung von Justinians Edictum de recta fide', *Kleronomia* 4 (1972) 280ff.

94. This model was not yet known by Hinschius. From it comes the influential sentence on the creation of an ecclesiastical province, 'scitote certam provinciam esse' (Pseudo-Pelagius II, Hinschius, *Decretales* 724.22ff.), cf. ZRG Kan. Abt. 41 (1955) 122–123 with nn. 92 and 93. On the influence of the Hibernensis, cf. R. E. Reynolds, 'Unity and Diversity in Carolingian Canon Law Collections: The Case of the Collectio Hibernensis and Its Derivations', *Carolingian Essays,* ed. U.-R. Blumenthal (Washington, D.C. 1983) 99ff.

95. On the status of the *Collectio Dionysio-Hadriana,* cf. Fuhrmann, 'Das Papsttum und das kirchliche Leben' 431–432, and the summary of H. Mordek, 'Dionysio-Hadriana', LMA 3 (1985) 1074–1075.

96. Cf. P. Hinschius, 'Der Beiname: Mercator in der Vorrede Pseudo-Isidor's', *Zeitschrift für Kirchenrecht* 6 (1866) 148–152; F. von Schulte, 'Marius Mercator und Pseudo-Isidor' (SB Wien 147;Vienna 1904) 167–172, who found many Marius Mercator excerpts in the Pseudo-Isidorian manuscript Grenoble 473, cf. the forms of greeting of Marius Mercator in Schwartz, ACO 1.5 (Berlin 1924–1925) 23 and 28.

from the *Dionysio-Hadriana*.[97] At the end of the work stands a typical element of the *Dionysio-Hadriana,* the Roman synod of Gregory II of 721; also, rubrics and text in the council section were significantly altered to conform with the Hadrianic collection. Thus a user of the False Decretals would be aware of the core of the *Hispana* and would also recognize the well-known *Dionysio-Hadriana*. The combination of *Hadriana* and *Hispana* appears to have corresponded with Carolingian concepts of reform. In the same way, the greatest systematic collection of the Carolingian reform, the *Dacheriana,* was also drawn from the same two collections.

In other respects, however, the user of the Pseudo-Isidorian Decretals was largely deceived about the author and scope of the work. In the preface 'Saint Isidore' writes that he wishes to continue the 'decreta praesulum Romanorum usque ad sanctum Gregorium', hence to Pope Gregory I (590–604). If one reads this passage literally, St. Isidore of Seville († 636) could indeed appear as author if the collection had actually ended with the items of that pope. But since Pseudo-Isidore included among the councils the canons of Toledo XIII of 683 and placed at the end the Roman synod of Pope Gregory II (715–731) of 5 April 721, an attentive reader would have to exclude the bishop of Seville as a possible author, although his phrases are extensively used in the preface by Pseudo-Isidore.

d. Structure of the Pseudo-Isidorian Decretals and the
Origin of Individual Pieces

For this brief survey, which is intended to indicate the role of forgery and adaptation, as well as to indicate newer partial editions, the following abbreviations will be used: PS = Pseudo-Isidore; H = *Hispana;* HG = *Hispana Gallica;* HGA = *Hispana Gallica Augustodunensis;* D-H = *Dionysio-Hadriana;* Q = *Quesnelliana.* Page numbers refer to the Hinschius edition

Preface, p. 17–20, PS: The beginning, consisting of an invocation and an announcement ('In nomine domini nostri Iesu Christi. Incipit praefatio sancti Isidori libri huius'),[98] relies on a special recension of D-H, which

97. Cf. Seckel-Fuhrmann, *Die erste Zeile Pseudoisidors* 39–40; H. Mordek, 'Dionysio-Hadriana und Vetus Gallica—historisch geordnetes und systematisches Kirchenrecht am Hofe Karls des Großen', ZRG Kan. Abt. 55 (1969) 39–63, has demonstrated that at least a part of the *Adnotationes* were combined with the *Dionysio-Hadriana* at the court of Charlemagne.

98. Seckel-Fuhrmann, *Die erste Zeile Pseudoisidors* 11ff.; Hinschius left out the invocation with no justification; Pseudo-Isidore did not adopt the invocation of the West Frankish King Charles the Bald ('In nomine sanctae et individuae trinitatis') but that of the ruler of the Middle Kingdom, Emperor Lothar I ('In nomine domini nostri Iesu Christi [dei aeterni]')

could also be the case with c.3 of the preface.[99] The beginning of the text is a topos: 'Compellor a multis tam episcopis quam reliquis . . .' (p. 17.4ff.).[100]

I. Decretals from Clement I to Melchiades, p. 20–247.

    A. Introductory items (p. 20–30)

        1. (p. 20–21) Correspondence between Bishop Aurelius of Carthage († between 427 and 430) with Pope Damasus I (366–384), PS.

        2. (p. 22–24) *Ordo de celebrando concilio,* HG.[101]

        3. (p. 25–26) Table of contents according to HG, expanded by PS.

        4. (p. 26–30) 50 *Canones apostolorum,* found both in the D-H (cf. Turner, EOMIA 1.1 p. 1ff.) and in the HGA,[102] and a letter of Jerome to Pope Damasus, all of them pre–Pseudo-Isidorian fictions.

    B. 60 decretals from 30 popes, beginning with Clement I, Anacletus I, Evarist to Melchiades (310–314), p. 30–247. Most of the letters are Pseudo-Isidorian inventions; a few, such as the first two Clement letters (p. 30–52; JK † 10, † 11), were, at least in their foundations, pre–Pseudo-Isidorian forgeries.[103] Many letters actually show a certain historical content,[104] and on closer analysis of a Pseudo-Isidori-

99. With item 1 of the special recension of D-H, which adopts § 1–13 of Isidore's *Etymologies* 6.16, also used in the H (Martínez Díez, *Hispana* 3.43ff.).

100. Compare this perhaps with the linguistically quite peculiar prologue in Paris, B.N. lat. 12444 (saec. IX in., Sangermanensis 938, from the library of Corbie, written in Fleury according to B. Bischoff, a special form of the Irish canonical collection), fol. 75v: 'Stimulatus quorundam quaerillis multitudinem exemplariorum diversam et turbulentem eorundem inordinata detestantiam hec de infinito scripturarum pelago velut pauca de multis brevitate ordinate et luculentiae fulgenti per singula operam dans . . .' Cf. Maassen, 'Bibliotheca' (SB Wien 54; Vienna 1866) 283; idem, *Geschichte* 836–837; H. Wasserschleben, *Die irische Kanonensammlung* (2nd ed. Leipzig 1885) xxvii. On the *Collectio Sangermanensis,* which is bound with this 'excerpt from the Irish collection', cf. Mordek, *Kirchenrecht und Reform* 144ff.

101. The *Ordo de celebrando concilio,* originating in Spain in the seventh century, lived a life of its own within which the original version of the Pseudo-Isidorian Decretals was only one stage, though one of great influence. In the MGH edition of the *Ordines de celebrando concilio,* ed. H. Schneider (Hannover 1996), the Pseudo-Isidorian is listed as Ordo 2 (142ff.). Cf. also Schneider's comments on p. 19ff.

102. H. Mordek, 'Canones apostolorum', LMA 2 (1981–1983) 1437–1438.

103. For the question of the influence of the first epistle of Clement, in whose distribution Pseudo-Isidore was decisively involved, the analyses of W. Ullmann are very instructive: 'The Significance of the Epistola Clementis in the Pseudo-Clementines', JTS 11 (1960) 295ff., esp. 303–304 (reorganized into a lecture, it appears under the title, 'Some Remarks on the Significance of the Epistola Clementis in the Pseudo-Clementines', *Studia Patristica* (Texte und Untersuchungen zur Geschichte der altchristlichen Literatur 79; Berlin 1961) 4.330ff. (repr. in his selected studies *The Church and the Law in the Earlier Middle Ages* [London 1975] no. II). On the forming of the first, second, and fifth epistles of Clement and the use of the *Recognitions* of Rufinus of Aquileia, cf. H. Fuhrmann, 'Kritischer Sinn und unkritische Haltung. Vorgratianische Einwände zu Pseudo-Clemens-Briefen', *Aus Kirche und Reich: Studien zu Theologie, Politik und Recht im Mittelalter: Festschrift für F. Kempf,* ed. H. Mordek (Sigmaringen 1983) 86ff.

104. Cf., for example, J. E. Weis, 'Die historische Grundlage der pseudoisidorianischen

an papal letter of the sixth century (JK † 883), E. Caspar declared: 'This example demonstrates that the forger worked carefully and with measured judgment, for all his unscrupulousness and errors; in his forgeries there always remains a kernel of historical truth'.[105] The *Liber Pontificalis* in particular is exploited as a historical guide, insofar as PS 'creates decretals for popes on the basis of the entries which he finds here on the activities of individual popes'[106] and fills those decretals with his constructions.

II. Councils, p. 247–444

    A. Introductory pieces (p. 247–257):

        1. (p. 247–249) Treatise 'De primitiva ecclesia et sinodo Nicena', PS, but a pre–Pseudo-Isidorian model is not impossible.[107]

        2. (p. 249–254) *Constitutum Constantini*, pre–Pseudo-Isidorian forgery, lightly and poorly reorganized by PS.[108]

---

epistola Callisti "ad omnes Galliarum urbium episcopos",' AKKR 78 (1898) 167ff. The question of whether Pseudo-Isidore knew material from the conflict between Calixtus and Hippolytus continued to be considered without Weis' work making any impact, cf. the discussion in A. M. Koeniger, 'Prima sedes a nemine iudicatur', *Beiträge zur Geschichte des christlichen Altertums und der Byzantinischen Literatur: Festgabe A. Ehrhard*, ed. A. Koeniger (Bonn-Leipzig 1922) 288–289, who cites O. Bardenhewer, *Geschichte der altkirchlichen Literatur* (2nd ed. Freiburg 1914) 2.637–638: 'one might well reach the conclusion that Pseudo-Isidore was informed of the conflict between Calixtus and Hippolytus', at 289 n. 2. The historicity of various liturgical directions from the *Liber Pontificalis* that also appear in the False Decretals is tested by T. Schermann, 'Liturgische Neuerungen der Päpste Alexander I. (c. 110) und Sixtus I. (c. 120) in der römischen Messe nach dem liber pontificalis', *Festgabe A. Knöpfler* (Freiburg 1917) 276ff., esp. 288–289. According to B. Leeming, 'The False Decretals, Faustus of Riez and the Pseudo-Eusebius', *Studia Patristica*, ed. K. Aland and F. L. Cross (Texte und Untersuchungen zur Geschichte der altchristlichen Literatur 64; Berlin 1957) 2.122ff., Pseudo-Melchiades, c.6–7, and Pseudo-Urban, c.9 (Hinschius, *Decretales* 245–246 and 146) derive from writings of the semi-Pelagians, probably from Faustus of Riez († before 500). The content and influence of the two decretals of Pseudo-Zephyrin (131–135 JK † 80, † 81) is reviewed by J. C. Besse, 'Zephyrin (St.)', DDC 7 (1965) 1670–1671.

105. Caspar, *Papsttum* 2.214 n. 1.

106. M. Buchner, *Historisches Jahrbuch* 57 (1937) 193. This exploitation of the historical data has repeatedly, into our own century provoked the opinion or interpretation that the False Decretals were perhaps genuine after all, as in E. Dumont, 'Les Fausses Décrétales', *Revue des questions historiques* 1 (1866) 392ff.; 2 (1867) 97ff. (cf. the review by F. Schulte in *Theologisches Literaturblatt* 2 [1867] 597ff., esp. 600); or P. Hergenröther, *Lehrbuch des katholischen Kirchenrechts* ed. J. Hollweck (2nd ed. Freiburg 1905) 178: 'Is it really unthinkable that the decretals contained there of which information exists from another source [in the *Liber Pontificalis*, for example] might really have existed and been used by ecclesiastical writers without reference to their source, as so often happens?'

107. The pontifical of Sens (St. Petersburg, Publichnaia biblioteka im M.E. Saltykova Shchedrina Q I no. 35) contains a corresponding text, cf. Fuhrmann, *Einfluß und Verbreitung* 2.370 n. 40.

108. C. Silva-Tarouca (1936) and S. Williams (1964) have actually declared the *Constitutum Constantini* to be the work of Pseudo-Isidore, the latter describing it as the 'masterpiece' of the False Decretals ('Le Ms. Saint-Omer' 257ff.), but there can be no doubt that it originated before Pseudo-Isidore, cf. *Constitutum Constantini*, MGH Fontes iuris 10 (Hannover 1968) 10ff. Without doubt, however, the Pseudo-Isidorian Decretals contributed de-

3. (p. 254) The brief treatise 'Quo tempore actum sit Nicenum concilium', HG.

4. (p. 254–257) 'Epistola vel praefatio Niceni concilii', Q (cf. Maassen, *Geschichte* 40–41 no. 40). The Epistola, which is closely coordinated with Pseudo-Anaclete, cc. 30–34, was edited by Turner, EOMIA 1.2.155–63, excluding the insert of Rufinus (p. 256.17–257.29). Because of its close connection with c. III of the *Decretum Gelasianum,* von Dobschütz 85ff., edits the excerpt p. 255.4–35, according to the edition of Hinschius, placing the Anacletus piece in a parallel column.

5. (p. 257) 'Alia praefatio eiusdem sancti concilii metrice composita', D-H and HGA (cf. Maassen, Geschichte 45–46 no. 48).[109]

B. Canons of 54 councils (p. 258–444); the Greek councils through Chalcedon (451), the African and Gallic councils to Arles IV (524), Spanish to Toledo XIII (683),[110] the latest piece of this section, which closes with Pseudo-Isidore's strong interpolation of the canons of Seville II (619). In between is a small collection of primarily Gallic and Spanish conciliar canons (p. 394–397) and the *Capitula* of Martin of Braga (p. 426–433).[111] This conciliar section largely corresponds to the first part of HG, in sections strongly reworked by PS (see above of the HGA, p. 146–147). The letter of the African bishops Aurelius, Mizonius, and their fellow bishops is inserted and reworked (from Q).[112]

---

cisively to the distribution of the *Constitutum Constantini;* on the impact of the Pseudo-Isidorian versions in canon law collections, cf. J. Petersmann, 'Die kanonistische Überlieferung des Constitutum Constantini bis zum Dekret Gratians', DA 30 (1974) 360ff.

109. On the distribution of the poem, cf. the summary of D. Schaller and E. Könsgen, *Initia carminum Latinorum saeculo undecimo antiquiorum* (Göttingen 1977) 120 no. 2510.

110. Cf. Martínez Díez and F. Rodríguez' edition of the *Hispana,* volume 5 of which has now reached the Tenth Synod of Toledo (A.D. 656) (Madrid 1992).

111. In the edition by C. W. Barlow, *Martini episcopi Bracarensis opera omnia* (Papers and Monographs of the American Society in Rome 12; New Haven 1950) the Pseudo-Isidorian tradition is considered, if with problems, cf. the review of S. Williams, *Speculum* 29 (1954) 256. Along with the *Capitula Martini,* Barlow also edited the councils of Braga I and Braga II by consulting Pseudo-Isidorian manuscripts; on these two synods, cf. G. Martínez Díez, 'La colección canónica de la Iglesia sueva: Los capitula martini', *Actas do Congresso de estudos da Comemoraçao do XIII centenário da morte de S. Frutuoso* (Bracara Augusta 21; Braga 1967) 224ff.

112. There are differences among the various classes of manuscript. The so-called Cluny version of class A1 preserves a Latin version of the conciliar canons of 649 which could have been written in the seventh century, cf. Schon, 'Redaktion' 503 and R. Riedinger, 'Griechische Konzilsakten auf dem Wege ins lateinische Mittelalter', AHC 9 (1977) 253ff., particularly 262ff. and the edition, *Concilium Lateranense a. 649 celebratum,* ed. R. Riedinger, ACO, series 2.1 (Berlin1984) xv.

III. Primarily decretals and conciliar decrees from Silvester I to Gregory II,
p. 444–754.
A. Introductory items (p. 444–448)
1. (p. 444) Transitional passage from the conciliar to the decretal
portion ('Hactenus digestis conciliis sanctorum patrum sequun-
tur decreta praesulum Romanorum—intendit'), HG.
2. (p. 445–448) Index of contents of the third part, largely from
HGA.
B. Decretals and conciliar decrees of 33 popes, reaching from Silvester
I (314–335) to Gregory II (715–731) (p. 449–754), depending on the second part of HGA.

The basic material is, compared with H, increased by the following
items:[113]

1. (p. 449–451) 'Excerpta quaedam ex synodalibus gestis S. Silvestri papae', earlier forgeries *(Constitutum Silvestri)* from the circle of Symmachus, reworked by PS.[114]

2. (p. 451–498) Correspondence, falsified by PS, of the popes Marcus
(JK † 181), Julius I (JK † 195, † 196), Liberius (JK † 222), Felix II (JK † 230, †
231) with various partners, among others, Athanasius.[115]

3. (p. 498–499) Correspondence of Pope Damasus I (366–384; JK † 242)
with Jerome, pre–Pseudo-Isidorian forgery.[116]

113. In his comprehensive analysis of the origin of the first decretal collections, Wurm,
Studien included the Pseudo-Isidorian tradition. It is thoroughly recommended. As models,
Wurm edited two decretals (JK 293, 402: Hinschius, *Decretales* 531ff., 614–615) using Pseudo-
Isidorian manuscripts (Vat. lat. 630 and 3791; Vat. Ottoboniani lat. 93): 'Decretales selectae'
40ff. (also separate). In contrast, G. Malchiodi, *La lettera di S. Innocenzio I a Decenzio vescovo
di Gubbio* (1921), simply repeated the Coustant edition (JK 311; Hinschius, *Decretales* 527ff.),
rendered obsolete by Cabié, *Lettre.*

114. Cf. Duchesne, *Liber Pontificalis* i.cxxxiv–cxxxv, cxl, and E. Wirbelauer, 'Zum Umgang mit kanonistischer Tradition im frühen Mittelalter: Drei Wirkungen der Symmachianischen Documenta', *Schriftlichkeit im frühen Mittelalter,* ed. U. Schäfer (ScriptOralia 53;
Tübingen 1993) 221–222; on the canonistic reception of the *Excerpta* and the *Constitutum Silvestri,* cf. S. Kuttner, 'Cardinalis: The History of a Canonical Concept', *Traditio* 3 (1945)
204ff. (repr. *The History of Ideas and Doctrines of Canon Law in the Middle Ages* [London 1980;
repr. with additional notes Aldershot 1992] no. IX).

115). On the Pseudo-Nicaean canons in JK † 196, cf. H. J. Sieben, 'Sanctissimi Petri apostoli memoriam honoremus: Die Sardicenischen Appellationskanones im Wandel der
Geschichte', *Theologie und Philosophie* 58 (1983) 501ff.

116. As early as W. Diekamp, 'Die neuere Literatur zur päpstlichen Diplomatik', *Historisches Jahrbuch* 4 (1883) 222–223, reference was made to the fact that this correspondence
existed in the *Psalterium Karoli Magni* (Vienna Österreichische Nationalbibliothek 1861, cf.
Lowe, *Codices Latini Antiquiores* 10.19, with bibliography, p. 49), written before 795, editing
both pieces from this codex, p. 387–388. On the origins, cf. G. Mercati, *Note di letteratura biblica e cristiana antica* (Studi e testi 5; Vatican City 1901) 115–116, and P. Blanchard, 'La corre-

4. (p. 501–508) Letter of Archbishop Stephen and three African synods to Pope Damasus, and his response (JK † 243), after HGA (i.e. by Pseudo-Isidore).

5. (p. 509–515) Pope Damasus I, 'De vana superstitione chorepiscoporum vitanda' (JK † 244), from HGA (i.e. by PS).

6. (p. 516–519) Letter of Pope Damasus I and his confession of faith (JK 235, 232) from Cassiodorus, *Historia Tripartita*, IX.15–16 and V.29 (CSEL 71 p. 516–522 and 257–259; cf. Turner, EOMIA 1.2.1 284ff).

7. (p. 519–520) Letter of Pope Damasus I to the Italian bishops (JK † 245), PS.

8. (p. 525–527) Two letters of Pope Anastasius I (JK † 277, † 278), PS.

9. (p. 533–544) In the corpus of letters of Innocent I in H, 7 letters from Q are inserted (JK 321–324 and 3 letters of African councils and bishops).

10. (p. 561–565) Letter of Pope Sixtus III (JK † 397), PS.

11. (p. 565–580) 16 letters of the correspondence of Pope Leo I (440–461), including two episcopal letters to Leo and JK 496, 514, 423 (cf. Hinschius, *Decretales* 570b), 425, 447, 500, 398, 429, 424, 490, 531, 539, 540, 509; except for the first letter of Leo (JK 496) all from Q. On these borrowings from Q by PS., cf. Schwartz, ACO 2.4.xxxff., who rejects the derivation of JK 496 from Q (cf. in opposition, Maassen, *Geschichte* 268 no. 58); Schieffer, 'Der Brief Papst Leos d. Gr.' 81ff., holds the middle portion of JK 496 to be a forgery of Northern Italian opponents to the condemnation of the Three Chapters from the second half of the sixth century; the letter appears in slightly shorter form in Q and in PS.; for JK 496, Schwartz notes the readings of the Pseudo-Isidorian version in Vat. lat. 3791 saec. XII (= Class A1) and describes the C-class, considerably expanded by a number of Leonine letters, supported on Vat. lat. 1340 (saec. XIII), which he also draws upon in his edition of the letters. Chavasse has investigated the Leo letters which entered the Pseudo-Isidorian Decretals, 'Les lettres du pape Léon' 28ff.; on the Leonine letters in the so-called Cluny version, cf. Schon, 'Redaktion' 501–502.

---

spondance apocryphe du Pape S. Damase et de S. Jérome', *Ephemerides Liturgicae* 63 (1949) 376ff., who holds both letters to be the work of the sixth century, already known by Gregory I. Hinschius held both were Pseudo-Isidorian (Hinschius, *Decretales* 498 on c.4 and introduction, xcvii), and it is possible that the conclusion of the Jerome letter was added by a scribe. Here, once again, his opinion depends upon his false dating of Vat. lat. 630. Seckel ('Pseudoisidor' 271.34–35) holds the first letter to be Pseudo-Isidorian. The literature is listed by Clavis 222 no. 633, on epist. 43–47, and R. Kottje, *Studien zum Einfluß des Alten Testamentes auf Recht und Liturgie des frühen Mittelalters* (Bonner Historische Forschungen 23; Bonn 1964) 59 n. 16. The manuscript distribution for both items is given by B. Lambert, *Bibliotheca Hieronymiana Manuscripta* (Instrumenta Patristica 4; Steenbrugge 1970) 190ff. nos. 346–347. With the somewhat frivolously presented assertion that exchanges of letters were cheerfully forged in the sixth century, A. Ferrua, *Epigrammata Damasiana* (Sussidi allo studio delle antichità cristiane 2; Vatican City 1942) 224, attributes the Damasus-Jerome correspondence to that century.

12. (p. 621–625) Letter of Pope Leo I (JK 410) from HGA, enriched by PS.

13. (p. 628) Forged letter of Pope Leo I, *De privilegio chorepiscoporum* (JK † 551), pre-PS (?).[117]

14. (p. 628–629) The apocryphal *Damnatio Vigilii* of Pope Silverius (536–537) (JK † 899), pre-PS (?).[118]

15. (p. 637–649) Four letters of Pope Gelasius I (492–496) (JK 622, 632, 664, 665), from Q.[119]

16. (p. 657–664) Roman synods from 499, 502, and 501 under Pope Symmachus (498–514), from D-H (there in the same sequence); T. Mommsen edited the acts of the three synods without use of the Pseudo-Isidorian tradition, MGH Auctores antiquissimi 12.399ff.

17. (p. 664–675) *Libellus apologeticus* of Ennodius of Pavia († 521), framed as a synod and circulating in later tradition under the name of Pope Symmachus (for example, in the *Dictatus papae* of Gregory VII, c.23 or Gratian, D.83 pr., C.8 q.4 c.1), with a typical Pseudo-Isidorian insert.[120]

---

117. Seckel regarded the Leo letter as well as the *Damnatio Vigilii* following it to be forgeries done before the Pseudo-Isidorian Decretals ('Pseudoisidor' 271.45ff.), while Hinschius believed himself secure in opposition to the Ballerinis that the forger of the Decretals was the author, 'a cuius ceteris decretalibus nulla in re abhorret' (Hinschius, *Decretales* civ). The Leo letter on the 'chorepiscopi' is preserved outside the False Decretals in at least two manuscripts of the D-H in the form which provided the model for the beginning of the Pseudo-Isidorian Decretals (Paris, B.N. lat. 1453, 3838), cf. Seckel-Fuhrmann, *Die erste Zeile Pseudoisidors* 29–30. For that reason Seckel weighed the possibility, 'did Pseudo-Isidore himself prepare the Gallic *Hispana*, as well as the *Dionysio Hadriana*, in advance for his purposes?' The question cannot be answered affirmatively from the age of the two *Hadriana* manuscripts (s. IX/X; X). A similar problem is embodied in establishing the provenance of the *Damnatio Vigilii*, see the following note.

118. On the question of the origin of the *Damnatio Vigilii* prior to the *False Decretals*, see the previous note. The *Damnatio Vigilii* is found outside the *False Decretals* in a pair of manuscripts of Q (Paris, B.N. lat. 1454, 3842A), cf. Maassen, *Geschichte* 416; Maassen, 'Bibliotheca' 192, 232. Seckel considered the possibility of a 'prepared *Quesnelliana* [by Ps.]?' ('Pseudoisidor' 271.49–50). Schwartz, ACO 2.4 p. xxxi, believes it a settled matter that this item was placed in Q from the Pseudo-Isidorian corpus: (Damnatio Vigilii) 'quam . . . ex corpore Pseudoisidoriano desumptam esse constat'. Schieffer, 'Dreikapitel-Schisma' 182–183, places its origin in Upper Italy after the middle of the sixth century, parallel to the forgery of the Leo letter JK 496. A. von Harnack, 'Der erste deutsche Papst (Bonifatius II., 530/32) und die beiden letzten Dekrete des römischen Senats' (SB Berlin 1924, Abh. 5) p. 36 n. 2, was of the opinion that the *Damnatio Vigilii* was an 'old forgery' drawing from a 'good source'; this was opposed by Caspar, *Papsttum* 2.198 n. 2: 'Pseudo-Isidore was simply basing himself on the *Vita Bonifatii II*', cf. also ibid. 230 n. 7.

119. JK 622, 632 and 665 have been edited by Schwartz, including Quesnelliana manuscripts, *Publizistische Sammlungen* 16ff. nos. 7, 8, 10; JK 664 was already edited by O. Guenther in his edition of the *Collectio Avellana* (CSEL 35, 2) 774ff. (appendix I), drawing on the *Quesnelliana* and Pseudo-Isidorian traditions.

120. On Pseudo-Isidore's forgery of the defense of Ennodius, cf. E. Seckel, 'Studien VII' 493–494, 530–531. Placing the Pseudo-Isidorian Ennodius in the context of its tradition, R. H. Rouse and M. A. Rouse, 'Ennodius in the Middle Ages: Adonics, Pseudo-Isidore, Cistercians, and the Schools', *Popes, Teachers and Canon Law in the Middle Ages*, ed. J. R. Sweeney and S. Chodorow (Ithaca 1989) 91ff., esp. 95ff.

With the inclusion of the Pseudo-Isidorian tradition, the *Libellus apologeticus* was edited by F. Vogel (MGH Auctores antiquissimi 7, no. 49 p. 48ff.; the insert, p. 50.12), and by W. Hartel (CSEL 6.287ff.; the insert, p. 291.1).

18. (p. 675–684) The so-called fifth and sixth synods of Symmachus, probably by PS;[121] on the source for the subscription list of the two assemblies cf. W. von Pölnitz, 'A propos des synodes apocryphes du pape Symmaque', RHE 32 (1936) 81ff.

19. (p. 684–686) Two letters of Ennodius of Pavia, ascribed by PS to Pope Symmachus (JK † 760, 752); edited by F. Vogel, comprehending the Pseudo-Isidorian tradition, MGH Auctores antiquissimi 7 nos. 214, 174, p. 171–172, 153–154, and by W. Hartel, CSEL 6, dict. III and epist. V.1, p. 433–435, 123–124.

20. (p. 694–709) Eight letters of the Popes John I (JK † 872, † 873), Felix IV (JK † 878, † 879), Boniface II (JK † 883, see above, p. 163), John II (JK † 889), Agapetus I (JK † 895), Silverius (JK † 901), together with the enquiry of a Bishop Amator to Pope Silverius,[122] all by PS.

21. (p. 710–712) The letter of Pope Vigilius (JK 907) is expanded by PS by a seventh chapter.[123]

22. (p. 712–732) Six letters of Pope Pelagius I (JK † 973), John III (JK † 1042), Benedict I (JK † 1045), and Pelagius II (JK † 1051, † 1049, † 1050), all by PS.[124]

23. (p. 735–747) Three letters and a synodal decree of Pope Gregory I.

a. Gregory I to the 'inclusus' Secundinus in the interpolated form found in the *Collectio Pauli* of the letters of Gregory I (Gregory I, Reg. IX.147; cf. MGH Epistolae 2.146ff. with p. 143, note; JE 1673). This manipulation of the text could have taken place in the eighth century; the possibility of a Pseudo-Isidorian origin was once considered but rejected.[125]

b. The genuineness of the so-called *Responsiones Gregorii I*, questions posed by Augustine of Canterbury with Gregory's re-

121. Cf. Caspar, *Papsttum* 2.106 n. 3, who notes that both synods are still treated as genuine in Hefele and Leclercq; H. Zimmermann, 'Papstabsetzungen des Mittelalters', MIÖG 69 (1961) 286 n. 8 (cf. the collected essays on this question by Zimmermann, *Papstabsetzungen des Mittelalters* [Graz 1968] 3–4).

122. On the historical background of the Silverius letter (JK † 901), cf. Caspar, *Papsttum* 2.233 n. 2.

123. Cf. Caspar, *Papsttum* 2.234 n. 1. Ullmann, *Growth of Papal Government* 184.

124. The letters of Pelagius I and II are regarded as Pseudo-Isidorian by Gassó and Batlle, *Pelagii I epistulae* 237ff.

125. The pre-Pseudo-Isidorian origin is reviewed by Kottje, *Die Bußbücher Halitgars von Cambrai* 217ff.

sponses (Gregory I, Reg. XI.56a; MGH Epistolae 2.331ff.; JE 1843), is still in dispute; they first appear in Bede's *English Church History* and are possibly genuine in their nucleus.[126]

c. JE 1817 (Gregory I, Reg. XI.27; MGH Epistolae 2.290 ff.).

d. Roman synod of Gregory I of 7 July 595 (Gregory I, Reg. V.57a; MGH Epistolae 1.362ff.).

24. (p. 747–753) Letter of Bishop Felix of Messina with the response of Gregory I (JE † 1334; cf. MGH Epistolae. 2 xxii, where two traditions within the Gregorian letters are named), doubtful whether it is from PS; Hinschius happened to find the text once in a manuscript of his Class A2 (Cologne 114, saec. XI), but otherwise only in codices of the Class C. An earlier tradition might exist in the collection of Fécamp (Paris, B.N. lat. 3182, saec. X),[127] whose items (other than the Felix/Gregory I correspondence) are older than PS. The existence of the item in 860 or 873/875 is guaranteed by a citation of Hincmar of Reims and John the Deacon.[128]

25. (p. 753–754) Roman synod of Gregory II of 721, from D-H, already adopted in HGA.

To reiterate, all remaining items in part 3 (p. 449–754) not mentioned in nos. 1 to 25 are in the *Hispana*.

Hinschius called the form found here A1 and declared it to be the oldest class; as we have seen, that led him into a major error in his evaluation of Class A/B. There appear to have been variant versions in circulation even in the era of the forgery.[129] The breadth and appearance of the individual manuscript classes as well as the stages of text development still pressingly need investigation.

126. From the rich literature, the review of research by P. Meyvaert, 'Le libellus responsionum à Augustin de Cantorbéry: Une oeuvre authentique de saint Grégoire le Grand', *Grégoire le Grand: Chantilly 15–19 septembre 1982. Actes*, ed. J. Fontaine et al. (Paris 1986) 543ff., and H. Chadwick, 'Gregory the Great and the Mission to the Anglo-Saxons', *Gregorio Magno e il suo tempo: XIX Incontro di studiosi dell antichità cristiana in collaborazione con l'École française de Rome, Roma 9–12 maggio 1990* (Studia Ephemeridis Augustinianum, 33; Rome 1991) 199ff. R. von Scherer, *Handbuch des Kirchenrechtes* (Graz 1898) 2.298 n. 27 (from p. 297), held the *Responsiones* to be the work of Pseudo-Isidore.

127. Cf. Maassen, *Geschichte* 416, 786; *Bibliothèque Nationale: Catalogue général* (Paris 1958) 4.316. On the letter of Gregory I to Felix, cf. L. Machielsen, 'Les spurii de S. Grégoire le Grand en matière matrimoniale, dans les collections canoniques jusqu'au Décret de Gratien', *Sacris Erudiri* 14 (1963) 260. P. R. McKeon, 'A Note on Gregory I' 305ff., lists the extraordinarily frequent use of the letter between 860 and 881 in the conflict of the two Hincmars.

128. Cf. L. Böhringer, Hinkmar von Reims, *De divortio Lotharii regis et Theutbergae reginae*, MGH Concilia 4 Suppl. 1 (Hannover 1992) 84 with the documentation; Johannes Diaconus cites the letter in his biography of Gregory the Great, *Vita Gregorii Magni* 2.38; PL 75.101C–102. Both passages were dealt with by Hinschius, *Decretales* cviii.

129. The problem is discussed by H. Fuhrmann, 'Reflections' 1ff.

IV. The Origin of the Forgery and Its Immediate Influence

The questions surrounding the identity of the forgers or forger of Pseudo-Isidore will be briefly considered here. They or he finished the work between 847 and 852. These dates can be determined because the work incorporates the Capitularies of Benedictus Levita, which were finished after April 847, and because the False Decretals are cited in the writings of Hincmar of Reims, perhaps in 852, certainly in 857 (see below, at n. 174ff.). Furthermore, in the argument for the primacy of Trier made by Thietgaud of Trier, the clear influence of Pseudo-Isidore is evident. Yet it is not impossible that the forgers did not end their activities suddenly, but rather fabricated or circulated other items later.

Of the many proposals for the place and person of the forger, some fantastic, only the most recent suggestions will be mentioned.[130]

(1) The bishopric of Le Mans in the ecclesiastical province of Tours. According to this argument, the forgery was intended to create jurisdictional protection for the bishop of Le Mans against the attacks of the duke of Brittany. Linguistic similarities between the Pseudo-Isidorian Decretals and the *Gesta Domini Aldrici* and the *Actus pontificum Cenomannis in urbe degentium* provide the principle evidence for this suggestion. Walter Goffart is the most vigorous supporter of the Le Mans thesis. He has argued for the unity of the forgeries (acts, *gesta*, poems of various saints' legends) and for their common origin, which he sets after 857 (the death of Aldrich) and before 863, the Synod of Verberie, or, perhaps, shortly afterwards. Goffart deals with a possible connection of Le Mans to the False Decretals only marginally but stresses that the forgeries of Le Mans as well as the Pseudo-Isidorian Decretals took shape in different contexts and around different issues: the former dealt primarily with the situation in the diocese of Le Mans, and the latter with the organization of the entire Church. He also stresses the differing attitudes of the two forgery circles to the institution of 'chorespiscopi'. Consequently, on the 'chorepiscopus' Merolus' claims to be the legitimate bishop of Le Mans, Goffart notes, 'Pseudo-Isidore would have gnashed his teeth at the drawing of such a consequence from his utterances'. Goffart would argue that Pseudo-Isidore might actually have been used, since the False Decretals had demanded that three colleagues be present for an effective episcopal consecration. This was asserted by Merolus, so that Pseudo-Isidore was

---

130. Documentation for the various theses is detailed in Fuhrmann, *Einfluß und Verbreitung* I.191ff., with nn. 122–140.

checkmated. Future scholarship will decide whether Goffart put too much care and calculation into the forgeries with his energetic, imaginative explanations.[131]

(2) The court chapel of Charles the Bald, more precisely Hilduin the Younger, Lupus of Ferrières, Wenilo of Sens, and Wulfad of Bourges, but this thesis has found no adherents.[132]

(3) The circle of the opponents of Hincmar of Reims and the adherents of Ebo of Reims. There is much to support this conjecture: Ebo's deposition, which would have been almost impossible according to Pseudo-Isidore, the struggle against the 'chorepiscopi' and the confrontation between the suffragan bishops and their metropolitan all support the assumption that the forgers were embroiled in the controversy between Hincmar and Ebo.

The question of place and author has remained unanswered, but the most widely accepted opinion today holds that the forger or forgers are to be sought in the circle of the adherents of Ebo or the opponents to Hincmar of Reims (845–882), and that all so-called 'Pseudo-Isidorian Forgeries' originated in one place in the Western Frankish realm or in connection with it.

The manuscript and textual evidence provides much support for the thesis that the ecclesiastical province of Reims was the geographical cen-

131. The thesis was first advanced by B. Simson, 'Pseudo-Isidor und die Geschichte der Bischöfe von Le Mans', *Zeitschrift für Kirchenrecht* 21 (1886) 151–169, and his *Die Entstehung* (cf. the reviews listed by Seckel in 'Pseudoisidor' 267.2ff.); Simson persisted in this opinion until his last utterance, 'Pseudoisidor und die Le Mans-Hypothese', ZRG Kan. Abt. 4 (1914) 1–74. His primary argument consists of parallels of language and similar working procedures in the Pseudo-Isidorian Forgeries and the forgeries of Le Mans. P. Fournier made Simson's opinion his own and advocated it forcefully in 'Étude sur les Fausses Décrétales', RHE 7 (1906) esp. 303ff., 761ff. (repr. *Mélanges* 1.140ff.), arguments briefly taken up in Fournier-Le Bras, *Histoire* 1.183ff. Goffart's arguments can be found in *The Le Mans Forgeries: A Chapter from the History of Church Property in the Ninth Century* (Harvard Historical Studies 76; Cambridge 1966). Goffart also argued that the letter of Pope Gregory IV of 833 to Aldrich of Le Mans (JE † 2579) was genuine, removing the item from the complex of Pseudo-Isidorian Forgeries (Goffart, 'Gregory IV for Aldric of Le Mans (833)' 22ff.). His thesis has been energetically contradicted by D. Lohrmann in a review in QF 48 (1968) 403–404, and Fuhrmann, *Einfluß und Verbreitung* 2.241–242 n. 13. Goffart focused his views once again when he review J. van der Straeten, 'Hagiographie du Mans', *Analecta Bollandiana* 85 (1967) 473ff., proposing as patron, if not author, Bishop Robert of Le Mans (857–883), 'The Literary Adventures of St. Liborius: A Postscript to the Le Mans Forgeries', *Analecta Bollandiana* 87 (1969) esp. 54ff. Of the reviews of Goffart, the most important for our question are S. Williams, CHR 54 (1968–1969) 672, and J. M. Wallace-Hadrill, *Speculum* 43 (1968) 719ff.

132. This thesis was presented by M. Buchner, 'Pseudoisidor und die Hofkapelle Karls des Kahlen', *Historisches Jahrbuch* 57 (1937) 180–181; cf. the sharp rejection by W. Holtzmann's review in the *Historische Zeitschrift* 157 (1938) 402; Buchner's thesis was adopted by G. Oesterle, 'De Pseudo-Isidoro et cappella aulica Caroli Calvi', *Ius pontificium* 18 (1938) 142ff., 219ff.

ter of Pseudo-Isidore. A total of three lost exemplars of the *Hispana Gallica Augustodunensis,* an early form of Pseudo-Isidorian forgery, came from the province. From the house of Corbie (also in the ecclesiastical province of Reims) came two witnesses, both written about 860: the Leipzig fragment (Universitätsbibliothek II.7) and the Vat. lat. 630 of the Pseudo-Isidorian Decretals. In the False Decretals, a *Vetus Latina* version of the Old Testament book *Ecclesiasticus* is used which is found among the manuscripts in Corbie. Also from Corbie is the *Liber contra Varimadum,* a version of which was used by the Pseudo-Isidorian forger. A *Dionysio-Hadriana* codex of the Corbie type 'ab' from the time around 800 was reworked using Pseudo-Isidorian materials around the middle of the ninth century (Berlin, Staatsbibliothek, Hamilton 132). In a papal charter issued for Corbie in 863 (JE 2717) there are certain linguistic affinities to the Pseudo-Isidorian Decretals. Richard and Mary Rouse have given further evidence in their study of the Ennodius materials exploited by Pseudo-Isidore that also come from Corbie. In addition the first explicit references to Pseudo-Isidore are to be found in the ecclesiastical province of Reims: Archbishop Hincmar, 852 and 857, in the circle of his suffragan Rothad. Within the same ecclesiastical province Hincmar of Laon was adept at using the Pseudo-Isidorian materials, and he obviously received forgeries straight from the Pseudo-Isidorian workshop. In sum, the case for Reims is compelling.[133]

Of the Pseudo-Isidorian Forgeries, only the decretals of Isidor Mercator achieved great influence: the Gallican *Hispana* of Autun found little circulation, though more than was long assumed; the *Capitula Angilramni* was only a small work and also not thoroughly saturated with Pseudo-

---

133. Seckel, 'Pseudoisidor' 278–279 and 286ff. assembled some of the main arguments for the Reims thesis. Cf. also the review by K.-U. Betz, *Hinkmar von Reims, Nikolaus I., Pseudo-Isidor. Fränkisches Landeskirchentum und römischer Machtanspruch im 9. Jahrhundert* (Ev.-theol. Diss.; Bonn 1965) 101ff.; E. Ewig, 'Das Trierer Land im Merowinger- und Karolingerreich', *Geschichte des Trierer Landes,* ed. R. Laufner (Trier 1964) 301 n. 101, discusses the issue of episcopal and metropolitan authority in Pseudo-Isidore, which worked to the disadvantage of Hincmar of Reims. The Ennodius evidence is presented by R. A. Rouse and M. A. Rouse, 'Ennodius in the Middle Ages' 95ff. Further possible evidence for the province of Reims can be found in Vat. lat. 630, but it is complicated. A scribe wrote on fol. 1 an 'epistola formata' of Bishop Liutad of Vence (c. 835–868), probably dated 853 to Archbishop Wenilo of Rouen (ed. by Zeumer, MGH Formulae 562 no. 19; J. Sirmond, whom Zeumer reprints, probably published out of Vat. lat. 630). Was this a transcription error for Wenilo of Sens (ca. 837–865) instead of Wenilo of Rouen (ca. 858–869), as the older research has assumed without examination? But Wenilo of Rouen was the chief recipient of Hincmar's petition 'pro causa Vulfadi' 866 (MGH Epp. 8.174, 182, 185). If Wenilo of Rouen is the recipient, and the indiction is correct, then the beginning of his episcopacy will have to be set earlier (858?–869); the 'epistola formata' is for Wulfad, the most respected Reims cleric from the group of clergy consecrated by Ebo and prosecuted by Hincmar; the content is partly confirmed by the *Narratio clericorum Remensium.*

Isidorian themes; and the False Capitularies never found a large circulation, which Ulrich Stutz explained as 'due also to the rapid collapse of
Carolingian rule'.[134] Whoever wants to pursue the Pseudo-Isidorian Forgeries has to concentrate on the False Decretals.

1. The Earliest Traces

The first evidence that the Pseudo-Isidorian Decretals or that any of
the Pseudo-Isidorian Forgeries were used is surprisingly weak. The first
person to use the forgery for the purposes for which it was made appears
to have been the metropolitan of the province bordering Reims, Archbishop Thietgaud of Trier (847–863, † 868). Thietgaud claimed to be the
primate of the neighboring province of Reims. He justified his demand
with the position of his see within the province of *Belgica,* which, according to the division of provinces in late antiquity, consisted of *Belgica prima*
(Trier) and *Belgica secunda* (Reims). Trier as the metropolis of *Belgica prima* outranked Reims as the capital of *Belgica secunda.* Until the time of
Thietgaud of Trier, no one had sought to assert primatial rights on the basis of late-antique provincial order, with its first, second, third, and even
fourth provinces, as listed in the *Notitia Galliarum.* Provinces with the
same name were distinguished by means of number, such as was the case
with *Lugdunensis*/Lyon: there was *Lugdunensis prima* (the eponymous
Lyon itself), *Lugdunensis secunda* (Rouen), *Lugdunensis tertia* (Tours), and
Lugdunensis quarta (Sens). The metropolitan of Lyon could, consequently,
claim precedence as a patriarch or primate over the other archbishops of
the *Lugdunensis* provinces. The position of 'primate' as an equivalent for
'patriarch' was a pure invention of Pseudo-Isidore; only in Pseudo-Isidore
is primatial precedence of a 'metropolis' over other 'metropoles' with the
same name advocated: 'primas est, qui primam civitatem tenet'.[135]

We cannot know when Thietgaud of Trier first stepped forward with
his primatial claim. It probably happened in the years 852/853.[136] There is

134. U. Stutz's review of Fournier-Le Bras, *Histoire* in ZRG Kan. Abt. 21 (1932) 380; cf.
also Fournier-Le Bras, *Histoire* 1.202–203.

135. On primacy in Pseudo-Isidore, cf. E. Lesne, *La hiérarchie épiscopale: Provinces, métropolitains, primats en Gaul et Germanie depuis la réforme de saint Boniface jusqu'à la mort de
Hincmar, 742–882* (Paris 1905) 240ff.; H. Schmidt, 'Trier und Reims in ihrer verfassungs-
rechtlichen Entwicklung bis zum Primatialstreit des neunten Jahrhunderts', ZRG Kan. Abt.
18 (1929) 77ff.; W. Levison, 'Die Anfänge rheinischer Bistümer in der Legende', *Annalen des
historischen Vereins für den Niederrhein* 116 (1930) 22–23 (repr. idem, *Aus rheinischer und
fränkischer Frühzeit* [Düsseldorf 1948] 22–23); H. Fuhrmann, 'Studien zur Geschichte mittelalterlicher Patriarchate, II', ZRG Kan. Abt. 40 (1954) 12ff., 23ff.; finally E. Ewig, 'Kaiserliche
und apostolische Tradition im mittelalterlichen Trier', *Trierer Zeitschrift* 24–26 (1956–1958)
169ff. (repr. *Spätantikes und fränkisches Gallien* [Beihefte der Francia 3.2; Munich 1979] 2.73ff.).

136. H. Schrörs, *Hinkmar, Erzbischof von Reims* (Freiburg 1884) 519, dated Thietgaud's
first efforts toward primacy from the first year of his pontificate, 847, but according to

no formal citation in Thietgaud's materials, which probably is due to the fact that we know of the claim only through chronicles.[137]

The first direct reference to the existence of the Pseudo-Isidorian Decretals is unclear and disputed. On 1 November 852 Archbishop Hincmar of Reims gathered the clergy of his diocese at his residence and promulgated statutes.[138] At two places in these statutes reference is made to the False Decretals. The first seventeen chapters of the Reims diocesan statutes deal with the priests. The eleventh statute forbids priests to use the 'sacred vessels of the church' as pledges for loans, for someone who is not permitted to enter taverns also cannot pawn sacramental vessels, 'sicut Stephanus sanctus papa et martyr ad sanctum Hilarium in suis decretalibus docuit'. This is a reference to the first Pseudo-Isidorian letter of Pope Stephen, which forbade in general that any liturgical clothing be touched or worn by non-consecrated persons.[139]

Following the *Capitula presbyteris data* are instructions for rural deacons, which normally were included with the chapters for priests. Here,

Lesne, *La hiérarchie épiscopale* 240 n. 2, H. Schmidt, 'Trier und Reims' 87ff., could convincingly show that the years 852–853 were the likely dates, which has been followed by Levison, 'Anfänge' 22 (reprinted in his essays, p. 22) and E. Perels, MGH Epp. 8.33 no. 58; on the further literature cf. ZRG Kan. Abt. 40 (1954) 12–13 with n. 43.

137. The report derives from an excerpt of a letter recorded by Flodoard of Reims (*Historia Remensis ecclesiae* 3.21, MGH Scriptores 13.514), cf. MGH Epp. 8.33 no. 58. The entry in the Codex Reims, Bibl. mun. 671, fol. 1r, a *Dionysio-Hadriana* written at the beginning of the ninth century, appears to belong to the discussion concerning the Trier-Reims primacy relationship: 'primatus id est Treveris / archiepiscopus in Magontia / metropolitanus Remis / episcopus Suessionis'. Bernhard Bischoff is inclined to place the writing 'not past the middle of the ninth century', and considers it 'not of Reims origin'. In evaluating the script, the content was left disregarded. The Trier claim of primacy, based on Pseudo-Isidore, emerges shortly after the middle of the ninth century, and a slight differentiation between archbishops and metropolitans can be found in the False Decretals, in which context it is interesting to observe that Hincmar of Reims, during whose service these four lines were probably written, never signed himself as a metropolitan, even in autograph, but as 'archiepiscopus', 'episcopus' or 'praesul'. The fact that the bishop of Mainz was termed 'archiepiscopus' could have something to do with his position in the *Notitia Galliarum*, where the place is carried as metropolitan of *Germania prima*. The notice shows a promotion of Trier and an aversion to Reims. For a variant position on this entry, see G. Schneider, *Erzbischof Fulco von Reims (883–900) und das Frankenreich* (Münchener Beiträge sur Mediävistik und Renaissance–Forschung 14; Munich 1973) 186ff., on p. 262 he discusses B. Bischoff's view.

138. The text of Hincmar's synodal statute of 852 is placed on a secure foundation by the new edition of R. Pokorny and M. Stratmann, MGH Capitula episcoporum (Hannover 1995) 2.8ff. On the contents of the four synodal statutes composed by Hincmar of Reims, cf. M. Stratmann, *Hinkmar von Reims als Verwalter von Bistum und Kirchenprovinz* (Quellen und Forschungen zum Recht im Mittelalter 6; Sigmaringen 1991). On the discussion of this first reception of Pseudo-Isidore, cf. Fuhrmann, *Einfluß und Verbreitung* 1.200ff.

139. Cf. MGH Capitula episcoporum 2.40.1f. and Pseudo-Stephan, c.3, Hinschius, *Decretales* 183; the passage is not a forgery of Pseudo-Isidore, but rather a borrowing from the *Liber Pontificalis* (ed. Duchesne 1.154).

at the end of these chapters, a second reference to Pseudo-Isidore appears. Along with the introduction of the falsified letter of Gregory I to the 'inclusus' Secundinus, it reads: 'Et beatus Gregorius, quod et praedecessor eius sanctus Calixtus scripserat, de lapsis in ordine ecclesiastico, sed non detectis interroganti se respondit'. The citation that immediately follows is taken from the Gregorian letter interpolated prior to Pseudo-Isidore, which had been briefly used in the false decretal of Pseudo-Calixtus, c.20.[140]

In addition to these references by Hincmar to Pseudo-Isidore in 852, scholars have tried to discover Pseudo-Isidorian citations at the Council of Soissons of April 853. In Soissons, the bishops of the ecclesiastical provinces of Reims, Tours, and Sens gathered under the leadership of King Charles the Bald, and here the clergy consecrated by Ebo and suspended by Hincmar presented themselves, asking for readmission.[141] But Hincmar compelled the petitioners to enter a formal complaint, which could then be heard and judged. The synod decided that Ebo's deposition and Hincmar's elevation were valid and that the consecrations of the plaintiffs were invalid. The deposed clerics of Reims wrote their own report concerning their fate and that of Ebo, from the end of the reign of Louis the Pious to the Synod of Soissons; in that report a specific reference is made to the Pseudo-Isidorian 'decreta sacrosanctorum patrum'. But it is likely that this *Narratio clericorum Remensium* is not from the Synod of Soissons of 853, but from a considerably later time, since, on the command of Nicholas I (866), their case was again referred to a council, and the pope specifically chose Soissons once more as the place of meeting.[142]

We encounter the first exact citation of a text from Pseudo-Isidore in 857, again in conjunction with Hincmar of Reims. To win support in a critical moment from the church of his realm, the West-Frankish King

140. What Hincmar cites (MGH Capitula episcoporum 2.68.11–69.3) is taken from the conclusion of the falsified letter of Gregory I, Reg. IX 147 (as p. 168) (MGH Epp. 2.146, 10ff.), in which a gentle treatment of 'lapsi' is ordered. The forged letter of Gregory is cited as a whole in the final portion of the Pseudo-Isidorian Decretals, Hinschius, *Decretales* 735ff. On the discussion concerning Hincmar's position and his relation to Pseudo-Isidore, cf. Fuhrmann, *Einfluß und Verbreitung* 1.204ff.

141. On the procedure at the synod, cf. Hartmann, *Synoden der Karolingerzeit* 245ff.; on the character of the written items presented in Soissons, cf. idem, 'Fälschungsverdacht und Fälschungsnachweis im früheren Mittelalter', *Fälschungen im Mittelalter* 112ff.

142. The *Narratio clericorum Remensium*, a title probably invented by its first editor, A. Duchesne (1636), was edited by A. Werminghoff, MGH Concilia 2.806ff. In the course of the editing he adopted the dating suggested by F. Maassen, 'Notiz zur pseudoisidorischen Frage', *Anzeiger der Wiener Akademie der Wissenschaften* (Vienna 1882) no. 24.73ff. (repr. AKKR 50 [1883] 174ff.).

Charles the Bald held an assembly of the bishops and of his realm in Quierzy on 14 February 857. Charles issued a capitulary directed, among other things, against the robbers and alienators of ecclesiastical property. Included in the capitulary were an *Admonitio synodalis,* which J. Sirmond entitled *Collectio de raptoribus,* and 'capitula regia', excerpts from capitularies, 'which all bishops were to announce in their dioceses and the royal emissaries in their missatica'.[143] In both the *Admonitio* and the 'capitula regia', Pseudo-Isidore is quoted verbatim, the False Decretals for the bishops and Benedictus Levita for the 'missi'.[144]

Beyond the fact that these are the first literal quotes of Pseudo-Isidore, the *Admonitio* deserves particular attention. This is because it contains a series of excerpts from canon law in a special form that made it possible for V. Krause to show that the *Admonitio* of the Capitulary of Quierzy was the work of Hincmar of Reims.[145] Krause could show that the same combination of citations was to be found in a series of other writings of Hincmar in slightly modified form.[146] Hincmar of Reims was obviously drawing upon the Pseudo-Isidorian Forgeries. In his own writings, putting aside official documents composed by him, Hincmar cited Pseudo-Isidore rather later, first of all in the *Collectio de ecclesiis et capellis* of 857 or early 858,[147] which circulated separately from his letters. In the same year of 858 Lupus of Ferrières asked Pope Nicholas I about the validity of a decretal of Melchiades that was a Pseudo-Isidorian fabrication.[148] Hincmar used

143. Cf. the critical edition and prefatory remarks by W. Hartmann, MGH Concilia 3.383ff.; the quotation on p. 389.18f.; see on this his narrative, *Synoden der Karolingerzeit* 251ff.

144. MGH Concilia 3.392ff.; cf. Schrörs, *Hinkmar* 409 with n. 105; F. Maassen, 'Zwei Excurse zu den falschen Capitularien des Benedictus Levita', NA 18 (1893) 295 n. 1; Seckel, 'Pseudoisidor' 303.8ff.; idem, 'Benedictus Levita decurtatus', 405 n. 1.

145. V. Krause, 'Hincmar von Reims der Verfasser der sog. Collectio de raptoribus im Capitular von Quierzy 857', NA 18 (1893) 303–308. Devisse, *Hincmar* 1.296ff., doubts the authorship of Hincmar of the *Collectio de raptoribus;* the combination of excerpts would have been presented by Hincmar only at the Synod of Tusey in 860. Devisse had overlooked the partial echoes to be found in Hincmar's *Collectio de ecclesiis et capellis* of 857–858 ed. M. Stratmann (MGH Fontes iuris 14; Hannover 1990), as well as in his letter to Louis the German of November 858 (MGH Epp. 8.57 no. 115).

146. Cf. the still expandable combination in Fuhrmann, *Einfluß und Verbreitung* 1.212ff.; on that also Hincmar of Reims, *Collectio de ecclesiis et capellis* 120.14 ff.; G. Schmitz, 'Das Konzil von Trosly (909)', DA 33 (1977) 429ff.; MGH Concilia 3.387; Hartmann, *Synoden der Karolingerzeit* 252–253.

147. Cf. *Collectio de ecclesiis et capellis* 41ff. with p. 120.

148. The question was whether the mentally ill Bishop Hermann of Nevers (841, † c. 860) could be deposed without the approval of the pope; they had heard of a decretal of Melchiades and asked for its wording, 'as it was preserved at your place'. The question is preserved in a single manuscript outside the corpus of the letters of Lupus (Orléans, Bibl. mun. 191, end of the ninth century, certainly from the area of Fleury), cf. *Servati Lupi epistulae,* ed. P. K. Marshall (Leipzig 1984) 128–129, no. 132 and p. ix. There is no question that this refers to a Pseudo-Isidorian Melchiades decretal (Hinschius, *Decretales* 243.19–20). Pope Nicholas I did not say a word about the request in his reply: JE 2674, MGH Epp. 6.611–612 no. 103.

that decretal in his third work, *De praedestinatione* (859),[149] in the canonical counsel concerning the marital separation of King Lothar II (860),[150] and in its sequel, which lasted until the end of the 860s. The Pseudo-Isidorian Decretals never provide the central proofs for Hincmar's arguments. Even in his treatise on the 'Pseudo-Isidorian' Rothad of Soissons (863), Hincmar obviously preferred the *Dionysio-Hadriana,* as he did in most cases.[151] There has never been a study of 'Pseudo-Isidore in Hincmar of Reims'. Completing such a study would not be easy, since in many cases citations or references have been significantly altered or turned around to defend his own point of view.[152] The matter is further complicated by Hincmar's use of other collections of canonistic materials in addition to Pseudo-Isidore, which he may have gathered together earlier.

2. The Struggle between the Metropolitan Hincmar of Reims and His Suffragan Bishop Hincmar of Laon over the Effect of Pseudo-Isidorian Legal Citations

Hincmar of Reims' use of Pseudo-Isidore in the polemic against his own nephew, Bishop Hincmar of Laon, is a special case. Hincmar of Laon virtually bombarded his metropolitan, Hincmar of Reims, with collections of excerpts from Pseudo-Isidore. During the period of his conflict with his suffragan, in 869–871,[153] Hincmar of Reims wrote his *Opusculum*

149. On the date, cf. Schrörs, *Hinkmar* 141–142 n. 47, and Perels, MGH Epp. 8.68. On the question of content, cf. D. Ganz, 'The Debate on Predestination', *Charles the Bald: Court and Kingdom,* ed. M. T. Gibson and J. L. Nelson (2nd ed. Aldershot 1990) 283ff. Cited are Pseudo-Anacletus, c.29–30, Hinschius, *Decretales* 83.2–14 (PL 125.212D–213B). In c.11 of the text (PL 125.413C) Hincmar hints darkly that he desires to compose something to enlighten the 'simplices' on the 'formae canonum: 'De canonum autem formis, quas quidam non attendentes solertius ecclesiasticas regulas inter se autumant discordare, quae et quot sint et quas singulae canonum complectantur sententias, quia sagaces et studiosi non indigent, devotis atque simplicibus . . . scribere temporis processu disponimus'. Did Hincmar intend at that time to combat uncertainty that Pseudo-Isidore had brought about concerning the correct form of ecclesiastical laws?

150. Cf. the edition of Böhringer, *De divortio,* MGH Concilia 4, Suppl. 1, the register of sources, p. 274 and the introduction, p. 83–84.

151. Cf. E. Perels, 'Eine Denkschrift Hinkmars von Reims im Prozeß Rothads von Soissons', NA 44 (1922) 43–100; MGH Epp. 8.122ff. no. 160. Hincmar still supports himself here on the Pseudo-Isidorian canons, which he later, in his letter of 55 chapters, sought to brand a forgery, cf. Perels, 'Eine Denkschrift' 62 with n. 4. It was only Hincmar's memorial discovered by Perels which brought a proof that was more than a mere suspicion that Rothad of Soissons and his supporters made use of Pseudo-Isidore.

152. Opinions are divided on Hincmar's 'modus operandi' and desire to forge. While Devisse, *Hincmar* is convinced of Hincmar's honesty, other authors are inclined to assume that the Reims archbishop was not averse to cutting corners, cf. H. Fuhrmann, 'Fälscher unter sich: Zum Streit zwischen Hinkmar von Reims und Hinkmar von Laon', *Charles the Bald: Court and Kingdom,* ed. M. T. Gibson and J. L. Nelson (2nd ed. Aldershot 1990) 224–225.

153. On this conflict, cf. Schrörs, *Hinkmar* 315ff.; Devisse, *Hincmar* 2.728ff.; McKeon, 'Toward a Reestablishment of the Correspondence of Pope Hadrian II' 169ff.; and Fuhrmann, *Einfluß und Verbreitung* 1.217ff. and 3.627ff. An exhaustive biography of Hincmar of Laon is

LV capitulorum (870) against Hincmar of Laon, in which he demonstrated an intensive use of Pseudo-Isidore. His employment of Pseudo-Isidore was provoked by the attacks of the younger Hincmar, also based on the False Decretals. It was then, at the very latest, that the archbishop of Reims completed his Pseudo-Isidorian library. For the references and citations of the 50s and 60s, a knowledge of the shorter form A2 of the False Decretals would have sufficed, which Hincmar perhaps already had in a special version. His knowledge of the False Decretals was already clear in the Assembly of Quierzy in 857. Now, in 870, citations in his *Opusculum* appear and are taken from the long form of the Pseudo-Isidorian Decretals, together with the *Capitula Angilramni*,[154] after both Pseudo-Isidorian works had been exploited by Hincmar of Laon shortly before, in 869.

Personalities aside, this conflict between the two Hincmars from 869 to 871 is a struggle over the validity and circulation of Pseudo-Isidorian canonical norms. Hincmar of Laon, as H. Schrörs believes,[155] was won

lacking. McKeon, *Hincmar,* consists more of specialized essays. A supplementary volume, *Die Streitschriften Hinkmars von Reims und Hinkmars von Laon 869–871,* ed. R. Schieffer, will appear as Suppl. 2 to vol. 4 of MGH Concilia, comprising the synods of the years 860 to 874 and edited by W. Hartmann.

154. Cf. Böhringer in the introduction to her edition of *De divortio* (MGH Concilia 4, Suppl. 1) 83–84; the analysis of Hinschius, *Decretales* liv–lv, lxiv n. 1, lxxviii, ciii, cviii, is still valuable. In comparison to Hinschius, the conclusions of Schrörs, *Hinkmar* 398 n. 38, are a step backward. The use of A1 is already visible in the excerpt from Pseudo-Pelagius II, p. 724.19–37 (PL 126.333C–334A), which lies beyond the limits of the A2 version. Hinschius (*Decretales* lxiv n. 1, ciii) takes as a further indication the citation from the letter of Leo I (JK 410), which is garbled in the Gallic *Hispana,* improved in the *Augustodunensis,* and at least supplemented with the *Hadriana* version in the False Decretals (Hinschius, *Decretales* 621–625) (thus the Paris, B.N. lat. 3852 printed by Hinschius). In many A1 manuscripts, parts of the Leo letter to Dioscoros (JK 406) have been incorporated into the letter; cf. Hinschius, *Decretales* xxvii–xxviii, cii and esp. Maassen, 'Pseudoisidor-Studien' 2.846ff. and above, p. 55. From the form in which Hincmar recasts this letter 'ad episopos per Caesariensem Mauritaniam' (PL 126.306C–D 'Lege decretalem epistolam'), Hinschius rightly concluded that the Reims metropolitan must have had that mixed product before his eyes as it is found in the manuscripts of the long form. From the same letter there is in Hincmar's writing *De praedestinatione* of 859 with the same introduction, 'ad episcopos per Caesariensem Mauritaniam constitutos' (PL 125.388D; MGH Concilia 3.290.7ff.), a citation of Bishop Theoderich of Cambrai from the Synod of Soissons in 853, which could have been taken from the *Dionysio-Hadriana* (in Pseudo-Isidore, Hinschius, *Decretales* 624.43–46). It is not impossible that Hincmar was already using an A1 manuscript before 870 while he was citing passages that also are found in A2 exemplars. Betz, *Hinkmar* 330–331 (nn. 150–153), comments on the bold assertion of Hincmar of Reims that he has known the False Decretals before his nephew Hincmar of Laon was born (about 840), with the words, 'In any case, from the statements of Hincmar it can be concluded that he had long been in possession of a complete copy of the forgeries of Angilram and of Pseudo-Isidore'.

155. Schrörs, *Hinkmar* 315–353; the citation is on p. 318. Precise in his estimation of the contemporary position of the metropolitan and of his suffragan is Lesne, *La hiérarchie épiscopale* esp. 212ff.

over by 'the chiefs of the Pseudo-Isidorian party', and 'the fact that they found in him a loyal pupil is shown not only by the rapidly unfolding conflicts but also from the citations of the falsified papal letters in the writings of the bishop of Laon, reflecting attentive study of the collection'.

Hincmar of Laon did indeed make repeated use of the writings of Pseudo-Isidore at the end of the 60s. In April 869 he imposed Pseudo-Isidorian principles on his clergy; in July 869 he had his diocesan clerics subscribe to a collection of excerpts from Pseudo-Isidore in order to bind them solidly to these rules. In November 869 he presented to the Assembly of Gondreville a work taken from the forgeries, and at the Council of Attigny in June 870 he dared to offer the same document that the clergy of his diocese had subscribed to the year before.[156] All of these examples can be added to the Pseudo-Isidore citations in his letters. Here as well the younger Hincmar shows the degree of his understanding of the forgeries, exceeding anything found before. No one had yet come out so openly and to such an extent on behalf of the application of Pseudo-Isidorian canonical norms.

Yet of the Pseudo-Isidorian collections that Hincmar of Laon made during his feud with his metropolitan, only one has come down to us, the work presented in Gondreville (November 869), which the author gave the Pseudo-Greek title of *Pittaciolus*.[157] Charles the Bald had summoned to Gondreville the magnates of Lotharingia to do homage, since he had arbitrarily occupied a considerable portion of the Middle Kingdom after the death of Lothar II (8 August 869). Now he wanted to secure his new possession through formal allegiance. The assembly knew of the conflict between Hincmar of Reims and Hincmar of Laon and called upon the suffragan to present his archbishop with the legal foundation for his hostility to him. Hincmar of Laon could no longer resist the pressure and surrendered the *Pittaciolus*. Following a preface consisting of ten distichs ('Iste pitatiolus plane depromit et apte / . . .') there are texts, primarily from the decretals of Isidore Mercator and the *Capitula Angilramni*, but also from the letters of the popes Leo I, Gelasius, Gregory I, and Nicholas I. At the close of his collection, Hincmar of Laon remarks that what was presented consists only of excerpts from a more comprehensive work

156. More detailed on the individual steps is Fuhrmann, *Einfluß und Verbreitung* 3.627ff., esp. 651ff.

157. On the manuscript tradition and the current edition situation, cf. Fuhrmann, 'Zur Überlieferung des Pittaciolus' 517ff., and Schieffer, 'Der Pittaciolus Hinkmars von Laon' 137ff. On the content of the *Pittaciolus*, cf. Fournier-Le Bras, *Histoire* 1.215–216; M. Manitius, *Geschichte der lateinischen Literatur des Mittelalters* (Munich 1911) 1.347, 352, 354; R. Naz, 'Pittaciolus' DDC 6 (1957) 1508.

which he had gathered 'in alio codicello'. This larger collection of which he speaks ('in alio codicello') has been lost. If it is not the Pseudo-Isidorian 'codicellus' itself, then a good alternate possibility would be the canon law material that is contained in the Berlin Phillipps Manuscript 1764, a collected codex from Soissons of the tenth and eleventh centuries.[158] With this manuscript we are dealing with the oldest canonical collection drawing on Pseudo-Isidore. It is older than the *Pittaciolus*, with which Hincmar of Laon went to war to establish and protect his rights. But the younger Hincmar and his *Pittaciolus* fell victim to the most influential and politically most experienced scholar of his time. Hincmar of Reims composed a response, the *Opusculum LV capitulorum*, which he presented at the national Synod of Attigny in June 870, rejecting Pseudo-Isidorian pretensions. In it, for example, Hincmar rejected the Pseudo-Nicaean canons invented by the forger with a brilliantly critical eye, calling them ungenuine and invalid. The younger Hincmar saw that his cause was lost and departed the synod by dark. The first effort to gain acceptance for Pseudo-Isidorian law had failed. What did the failure of Hincmar of Laon mean for the introduction of the Pseudo-Isidorian Decretals? Let us recall the Pseudo-Isidorian forgers' primary intentions: they wanted to prevent metropolitans from intervening in the affairs of suffragan bishops and to remove suffragans from the jurisdiction of the provincial synod as well as from the authority of secular power. The fact that these protections were reinforced by the newly created office of primate as well as through an extensive strengthening of papal power can only be understood from the desire of the forger to restrict the privileges of the metropolitan with papal authority, to the advantage of the bishops, 'a guideline of his own [Pseudo-Isidore's] construction', as A. Hauck put it.

Hincmar of Laon was a faithful partisan of the Pseudo-Isidorian opinion; he used the forgeries to combat the metropolitan rights of the archbishop of Reims. Yet he failed in his conflict with Hincmar of Reims. The main reason for the defeat was certainly not only the strangeness of the new Pseudo-Isidorian law, but in the end the political ineptness of the bishop of Laon. He had alienated a large portion of the clergy, and a bit

158. A precise analysis of Codex Phillipicus 1764 of the Berlin Staatsbibliothek is in Fuhrmann, *Einfluß und Verbreitung* 3.627ff. Contreni, 'Codices Pseudo-Isidoriani' 1ff., indicates that the manuscript Paris, B.N. lat. 9629 belongs together as a unity with Paris, B.N. lat. 1557, making it probable that the entire codex comes from the 'scriptorium' of Laon in the time of Hincmar. Also valuable is Contreni's attempt to assemble the canonistic manuscripts in the cathedral library of Laon, 'A New Description of the Lost Laon Manuscript' 85ff., and 'Two Descriptions of the Lost Laon Copy of the "Collection of Saint-Maur",' BMCL 10 (1980) 45ff. The essays reprinted in Contreni's collection, *Carolingian Learning*, supplement Contreni's book, *The Cathedral School of Laon*.

later he made King Charles the Bald into a deadly enemy, when he fell unjustly under the suspicion of plotting with political rebels. At the Synod of Douzy (August 871), he was deposed, primarily on the basis of royal accusation, and a short time later he was blinded, and finally the pope, to whom he had appealed, abandoned him. In 876 he had a successor, in 878 he was partly rehabilitated, and he died in 879 or 880.

Hincmar of Laon's fall also meant a decisive defeat for the new Pseudo-Isidorian norms favoring the suffragan bishops. Only in the middle of the eleventh century did the collection achieve greater influence, but then it did not protect the immunity of bishops. Rather it provided legal arguments for centralizing papal power.

3. Reception in Other Realms: Lotharingia, Eastern Francia, Italy, Spain, England

To sum up, E. Seckel wrote: 'The Western Frankish realm was the first homeland for its [the Pseudo-Isidorian Decretals'] spread'. What was the situation in the other Frankish realms? In the middle kingdom of Emperor Lothar I († 855), whose invocation, 'In nomine domini nostri Iesu Christi (dei aeterni)'[159] Isidore Mercator placed at the head of his decretals, Thietgaud of Trier emerges as the first certain user of Pseudo-Isidore when he argued for the primacy of Trier in 852–853. In the following years, evidence of a knowledge of the Pseudo-Isidorian Decretals is not apparent until Bishop Rothad of Soissons, attacked by his Metropolitan Hincmar of Reims, wrote to the bishops of Lotharingia around the beginning of 863. Archbishops of the earlier middle kingdom—Thietgaud, with his provocative title of 'Belgicae Galliae primas' (847–863), Gunthar of Cologne (850–863), Hartwig of Besançon (859–871), Rotland of Arles (852–869), Tado of Milan (860–868)—sent this letter that included a collection of sentences with Pseudo-Isidorian elements, joined with a letter of information, to the 'bishops in the realm of the splendid King Louis [the German]'. It is likely that the letter reached the Eastern Frankish episcopate.[160] In 863 Pseudo-Isidorian sentences were making their way into the realm of Louis the German from Lotharingia, even though the Eastern synods began to make sparing use of the False Decretals only later:[161] Cologne in

159. See above, p. 161, n. 97.

160. Mansi 15.645ff. Hartwig of Besançon was, by the way, a close friend and protector of the 'Pseudo-Isidorian' Hincmar of Laon, cf. McKeon, *Hincmar* 106ff., 111–112. The letter of information is preserved in a Mainz manuscript, Vat. Pal. lat. 576, saec. IX ex., cf. Fuhrmann, *Einfluß und Verbreitung* 2.255–256, 268ff.

161. The Council of Worms of 868, mentioned by Seckel, 'Pseudoisidor' 291.20–21 and by Fuhrmann, *Einfluß und Verbreitung* 1.226 and 2.599 with n. 63, is to be eliminated, according to Hartmann, *Das Konzil von Worms* 46 with n. 94. The source here was the *Hispana*.

887, Mainz in 888, Metz in 893, Tribur in 895, and Hohenaltheim in 916. The oldest textual witness of the Pseudo-Isidorian *Capitula Remedii* originated in the scriptorium of Bishop Anno of Freising (854/855–875), a collection of excerpts from a manuscript of the Class A2.[162]

So far as the acceptance of Pseudo-Isidore in Italy goes, there is a dramatic difference between Rome and the rest of Italy. The False Decretals appear to have reached Rome and the papacy during the pontificate of Nicholas I (858–867), probably in 863/864.[163] Tado, archbishop of Milan (860–868), who sent the Sentences of Rothad to the Eastern Frankish realm in 863, appears not to have known anything of the Pseudo-Isidorian collection.[164] Consequently, in Northern Italy Pseudo-Isidore appears quite late. The slight resonance of Pseudo-Isidore in the ecclesiastical life of Italy contradicts the discovery that an entire series of cathedral libraries of Northern Italy obtained copies of Pseudo-Isidore, usually in the A2 version. The scribe Agifred presented his manuscript of the 'dicta priscorum' (the Pseudo-Isidorian Decretals) to Bishop Azo of Ivrea, who flourished around 876, with a dedication in golden letters.[165] Around 880 Bishop Leodoin of Modena (869/871–892/898) reminded Abbot Theodorich of Nonantola of the limits of his rights in a letter made up almost entirely of citations from Pseudo-Isidore. This letter is inserted into the Pseudo-Isidore codex O.I.4 of the Cathedral Library of Modena from the start of the 80s.[166] It was probably at the end of the 70s that Pope

162. Cf. H. John, *Collectio canonum Remedio Curiensi episcopo perperam ascripta* (MIC Series B, 2; Vatican City 1976) 32–33, 120; the Pseudo-Isidore fragment of the Munich Clm 2940 from the library of Altomünster probably came from northern Italy, 'certainly from the third quarter of the ninth century', cf. Bischoff, *Die südostdeutschen Schreibschulen* 2.230.

163. See below, p. 186ff., Pseudo-Isidore in Rome.

164. It continues to surprise that, of the seven Italian A2 manuscripts of the ninth century that have survived (Aosta, Bresica, Ivrea, Lucca, Monza, Pistoia, Vercelli), four belong to suffragans of the ecclesiastical province of Milan (Brescia, Ivrea, Monza, Vercelli), who were summoned by Tado in 863 (cf. Hartmann, *Synoden der Karolingerzeit* 297–298), that Rothad and clerics of the church of Soissons were entered in the *Liber memorialis* of S. Giulia in Brescia, and that an early Milan collection of excepts exists, related to those in West Francia (Milan, Bibl. Ambrosiana A. 46 inf.). In addition, there is the *Collectio Anselmo dedicata*, which could have arisen from materials in the ecclesiastical province of Milan and which is dedicated to an archbishop of Milan.

165. Entered on the penultimate and on the last folio of the Pseudo-Isidorian copy contained in Ivrea, Bibl. Cap. 83; cf. *Colophons de manuscrits occidentaux des origines au XVIe siècle*, ed. Benedictines of the Abbey of Le Bouveret (Spicilegii Friburgensis Subsidia 2; Fribourg 1965) 1.40–41 no. 315. Löwe, *Deutschlands Geschichtsquellen im Mittelalter* 4.402 n. 70, considers a connection between Azo of Ivrea and Leodoin of Modena, who are both acquainted with Pseudo-Isidore in this period; on the other hand, the differing versions of the decretals in the manuscripts Ivrea, Bibl. Cap. 83 and Modena, Bibl. Cap. O.I.4 give room for doubt.

166. Cf. H. Fuhrmann, 'Der angebliche Brief des Erzbischofs Hatto von Mainz an Papst Johannes IX.', MIÖG 78 (1970) 53ff.; on this manuscript, the model codex for Hinschius in his edition, cf. Fuhrmann, 'Reflections' 3ff.

Hadrian II (872–882) warned against the overly hasty deposing of a bishop named Antonius, who may have been Bishop Antonius of Brescia. A little later (between 882 and 896) the *Collectio Anselmo dedicata* originated in Milan or its environs, in which the larger part of the chapters are transcribed from the short form of the False Decretals. For the first stage of the spread of Pseudo-Isidore, the other parts of Europe are as good as invisible. It is unclear whether the False Decretals were known and respected in the remnant of Christian Spain before the *Reconquista* of the eleventh century. England is a problem in its own right: not a single manuscript of Pseudo-Isidore survives or is mentioned in catalogues from the Anglo-Saxon period.[167] There is no doubt that it was Archbishop Lanfranc of Canterbury (1070–1089) who systematically introduced and applied the False Decretals after the Norman Conquest.[168] A weak and obviously local knowledge of Pseudo-Isidore is in evidence around 1000, possibly with Aelfric, later the abbot of Eynsham († before 1020),[169] and certainly in an episcopal manual in the Cathedral Library of Worcester.[170] The legal relations on the island did not compel the bishops to seek support from decretals: 'Such power had the bishops in all public affairs, that they had little to gain from decretals forged or genuine' (F. W. Maitland).[171] It is only

167. There is no Pseudo-Isidorian manuscript until after the Norman Conquest in N. R. Ker, *Medieval Libraries of Great Britain* (Royal Historical Society, Guides and Handbooks 3; 2nd ed. London 1964); cf. also J. D. A. Ogilvy, *Books Known to the English, 597–1066* (Mediaeval Academy of America 76; Cambridge 1967) 122.

168. Z. N. Brooke, *The English Church and the Papacy from the Conquest to the Reign of John* (Cambridge 1931) laid the foundation for this conclusion. He showed that Lanfranc brought along a shortened version of the False Decretals to the island, today Cambridge, Trinity College B 16.44 (405), and he had copies distributed. Cf. Fuhrmann, *Einfluß und Verbreitung* 2.419ff.; R. Schieffer, *Die Entstehung des päpstlichen Investiturverbots für den deutschen König* (MGH Schriften 28; Stuttgart 1981) 64ff.; R. Somerville, 'A Parisian Fragment of the Collectio Lanfranci', BMCL 16 (1986) 86ff.; M. Brett, 'The Collectio Lanfranci and Its Competitors', *Intellectual Life in the Middle Ages: Essays Presented to M. Gibson,* ed. L. Smith and B. Ward (London 1992) 157ff.

169. M. Förster, *Über die Quellen von Aelfric's Homiliae Catholicae,* 1: *Legenden* (Dissertation; Berlin 1892) 12–13, was the first to observe that Aelfric could have had a Pseudo-Isidorian text before him, and B. Fehr, *Die Hirtenbriefe Aelfrics in altenglischer und lateinischer Fassung* (Hamburg 1914) cvi–cvii, cxff., sought to reinforce this with new documentation.

170. Announced by M. Bateson, 'A Worcester Cathedral Book of Ecclesiastical Collections Made c. 1000 A.D.', EHR 10 (1895) 712–731. Few conciliar canons from the Pseudo-Isidorian Decretals were transcribed into the Worcester manuscript; there was at least, directly or indirectly, *Capitula Angilramni* 71, 72 (Bateson, p. 723–724). N. R. Ker, *Catalogue of Manuscripts Containing Anglo-Saxon* (Oxford 1957) 92 no. 53, dates the manuscript (Cambridge, Corpus Christi College, 265) in the middle of the eleventh century. On the manuscript, cf. L. Bieler, 'Towards an Interpretation of the So-called "Canones Wallici",' *Medieval Studies presented to A. Gwynn* (Dublin 1961) 387ff.; idem, *The Irish Penitentials* (Scriptores Latini Hiberniae 5; Dublin 1963) 15; H. Gneuss, *Hymnar und Hymnen im englischen Mittelalter* (Tübingen 1968) 119–120.

171. F. Pollock and F. W. Maitland, *The History of English Law before the Time of Edward I* (2nd ed. Cambridge 1898) 1.21.

under the Norman lordship that more rigid forms of political organization were introduced that suited the strictly hierarchically articulated ecclesiology of Pseudo-Isidore.

4. The Contradiction: Many Manuscripts, Little Effect

When one asks about the immediate influence of Pseudo-Isidore, the answer is that it was meager. The volume of the total forgeries and falsifications of Pseudo-Isidore might amount to several thousand pages of text when transformed into normal octavo book format, and the decretals themselves amount to over 750 pages. In view of this mass, the traces are slight: until the 860s, a few sentences of Hincmar of Reims, Lupus of Ferrières, Rothad (only indirect in the latter two cases); other than Thietgaud's more rhetorical claim of the primacy there was no resonance in Lotharingia and none whatsoever in Eastern Francia. In Italy outside of Rome the first certain trace appears only after 869/871 (the beginning of Bishop Leodoin of Modena's pontificate). The great exception in this panorama is the duel between Archbishop Hincmar of Reims and Bishop Hincmar of Laon, 869–871.

In contrast to the slight immediate impact of the False Decretals there was an almost explosive expansion of the manuscripts themselves: even today there are at least 30 complete or almost complete manuscripts, fragments or excerpt series from the period through 900.[172] Added to this are

---

172. Williams, 'Pseudo-Isidore from the Manuscripts' 62–63, counted 11 codices, but new discoveries have considerably increased the number. The amazing thing is that the tradition of several classes of manuscripts begins in the time near that of the forgery. It is probable that the False Decretals were distributed from the very beginning in various forms and composition (cf. Fuhrmann, 'Reflections' 1ff.). The manuscripts are without precise differentiation, even when there are clear connections in their traditions, as is the case with the Italian codices of the A2 class: Aosta, Biblioteca Capitolare C.102 (A2); Bern, Burgerbibliothek 451 (fragment); Brescia, Biblioteca Civica Queriniana B.II.13 (A2); Freiburg im Breisgau, Universitätsbibliothek 8 (excerpt); Ivrea, Biblioteca Capitolare 83 (A2); Leiden, Bibliotheek der Rijksuniversiteit Voss. lat. octavo 29 (excerpt), lat. quarto 108 (excerpt); Leipzig, Universitätsbibliothek II.7 (A/B); Lucca, Biblioteca Capitolare Plut. II 123 (A2); Merseburg, Archiv des Domkapitels 104 (excerpts); Modena, Biblioteca Capitolare O.I.4 (A1?); Monza, Archivio Capitolare (Biblioteca Capitolare) H.3.151 (A2); Munich, Bayerische Staatsbibliothek lat. 2940 (excerpt)(A2); New Haven, Yale University, Beinecke Library 442 (Cluny version); Paris, B.N. Baluze 271 (fragment), Paris, B.N. lat. 2449 (excerpt), lat. 3877 (excerpt), lat. 9629, with lat. 1557 (A1), lat. 12445 (excerpt); Pistoia, Archivio Capitolare del Duomo C. 130 (A2); Rennes, Bibliothèque Municipale 134; Rome, Biblioteca Vallicelliana D.38 (A2); Sankt Gallen, Stiftsbibliothek 670 (A2); Vat. Ottoboniani lat. 93 (A1), Vat. Reginensis lat. 994 (excerpt), Vat. lat. 630, lat. 1341 (excerpt); Vercelli, Biblioteca Capitolare LXXX; Würzburg, Universitätsbibliothek M. p. th. f. 70 (excerpt); Zürich, Zentralbibliothk Z XIV 10 (excerpt). In this listing, the Pseudo-Isidorian texts used by the two Hincmars are left out, such as the *Pittaciolus* (Metz, Bibliothèque municipale 351; Paris, B.N. lat. 5095). Also the 'Address of Pope Hadrian II' (Milan, Biblioteca Ambrosiana G 58 sup.) is not included. See now the listing in L. Kéry, *Canonical Collections of the Early Middle Ages (ca. 400–1140): A Bibliographical Guide to the Manuscripts and Literature* (History of Medieval Canon Law; Washington, D.C. 1999) 100–108.

four manuscripts of Pseudo-Remedius, which originated in the third quarter of the ninth century,[173] and many manuscripts of the *Collectio Anselmo dedicata*, dedicated to Archbishop Anselm II of Milan (882–896), which took on extensive items from Pseudo-Isidore, and which is supposed to have been composed before the turn of the tenth century.[174] The image of a strong tradition of Pseudo-Isidore setting in from the beginning is reinforced by the report from 868. Bishop Aeneas of Paris (856–870) repeats some points of the Donation of Constantine and refers anyone who wishes to read the full text to the privilege itself, 'whose copies are found in full in the libraries of the churches of Gaul'. This assertion of the copies whose existence is assumed in all West Frankish church libraries could be applied to codices of Pseudo-Isidore in those days, for the *Constitutum Constantini* was not solidly incorporated in any other collection, and there were virtually no genuine individual traditions.[175] There is some truth in the thesis of C. de Clercq (1958) that in the first period the Pseudo-Isidorian Decretals were spread less by literary activity than by the mechanical distribution of manuscripts.[176]

There have been repeated questions about the basis for the hesitant acceptance of Pseudo-Isidore. F. Maassen, who stumbled upon the glosses of the *Dionysio-Hadriana* originating after the appearance of the False Decretals, gave the following explanation for the small use of the Pseudo-Isidorian Forgeries:[177]

> The forgery was too monstrous; if it had been recognized and exposed, it would nevertheless have befuddled readers at the time. . . . The Pseudo-

173. Also belonging to the ninth century: Munich, Bayerische Staatsbibliothek Clm 6245 (excerpt); Cologne, Erzbischöfliche Diözesan-und Dombibliothek 118 (fragment); St. Gallen, Stiftsbibliothek 614 (excerpt); cf. John, *Collectio* 29ff. In addition to that is a fragment of a codex, St. Gallen, Stiftsbibliothek 1398a, p. 1–12 (formerly 343–354), cf. Hoffmann and Pokorny, *Burchard von Worms* 76 n. 39.

174. U. Fiorina has found some on parchment leaves in Pavesan notarial protocols, which he thinks are from the late ninth century, and B. Bischoff would like to set fragments from the Archives départementales du Bas-Rhin in Strasbourg 'perhaps even before the turn of the century', cf. Fuhrmann, 'Fragmente' 539ff.

175. Cf. Fuhrmann, 'Abendländisches Kaisertum' 98ff. The rare exception of separate preservation is treated by H. Fuhrmann, 'Ein in Briefform verschicktes Constitutum Constantini aus der Zeit des Investiturstreits', *Geschichtsschreibung und geistiges Leben im Mittelalter: Festschrift für H. Löwe*, ed. K. Hauck and H. Mordek (Cologne 1978) 346ff.

176. C. de Clercq, *La législation religieuse franque, 2: De Louis le Pieux à la fin du IXe siècle (814–900)* (Antwerp 1958) 404; see also Fuhrmann, *Einfluß und Verbreitung* 2.411.

177. 'Die Fälschung war zu ungeheuer, als daß, wenn nicht sofort erkannt und aufgedeckt, sie anders denn verblüffend hätte wirken sollen, . . . Die pseudoisidorischen Typen mußten erst über das Leben Macht gewinnen, aus ihm gewissermaßen wiedergeboren werden; sie mußten mit den Schöpfungen der ächten Quellen zu einem einheitlichen practischen System zusammenwachsen um als integrirender Bestandtheil des geltenden Rechts ihre wissenschaftlichen Pflege zu finden. Daß aber dies eintrat, das hat nicht weniger als drei Jahrhunderte erfordert'. F. Maassen, 'Glossen des canonischen Rechts aus dem karolingischen Zeitalten' (SB Wien 84; Vienna 1876) 241–242.

Isidorian view of the Church first had to become reality; only then could Pseudo-Isidorian ideas become part of canon law. It had to grow together with new doctrines from genuine sources to find its scholarly expression as an integrated part of the law. By the time this process took place, however, no less than three centuries had passed.

One could hardly call this beginning phase of weak influence 'The Age of Pseudo-Isidore',[178] whose 'hierocratic ideas' transformed ecclesiological self-perception. First ecclesiastical understanding had to be altered in order that Pseudo-Isidore could be received.

5. Pseudo-Isidore in Rome[179]

For Flacius Illyricus and the Magdeburg centuriators in the sixteenth century,[180] it was certain that the Pseudo-Isidorian Decretals originated in Rome, since the pope was the prime beneficiary of the forgery. When it became clear that Rome could be acquitted of forgery, the new thesis arose that the False Decretals were 'eagerly and immediately seized by Pope Nicholas I (858–867)' (I. von Döllinger).[181] The judgment of Paul Fournier was more nuanced. To be sure, the Pseudo-Isidorian Decretals had been known to Pope Nicholas I, but his conduct had not been influenced by the forgery. Pope Nicholas showed 'great reserve vis-a-vis this new and unknown element'.[182]

178. Ullmann, *Growth of Papal Government* 167, has a chapter with the title 'The Age of Pseudo-Isidore'.

179. The question is thoroughly dealt with and documented for the period through the middle of the eleventh century in Fuhrmann, *Einfluß und Verbreitung* 2.237–353. On the disposition of the papal primacy in the False Decretals and its later influence, cf. Marchetto, *Episcopato e Primato pontificio* and idem, 'La "fortuna" di una falsificazione: Lo spirito dello Pseudo-Isidoro aleggia nel nuovo Codice di Diritto Canonico?', *Fälschungen im Mittelalter* 2.393ff.

180. 'Ecclesiastica historia . . . congesta . . . per aliquot studiosos et pios viros in urbe Magdeburgica', Cent. II c. VII (Basel 1560) 147.59ff.

181. Döllinger asserted this several times. The most influential was his book drawn from a series of newspaper articles and translated into French, English, and Italian within the first year of its appearance: *Der Papst und das Concil, von Janus* (Leipzig 1869). It appeared after his death in an expanded version responding to the discussion it had aroused: I. von Döllinger, *Das Papstthum: Neubearbeitung von Janus,* ed. J. Friedrich (Munich 1892) 36.

182. P. Fournier, 'Étude sur les Fausses Décrétales', part 5: 'Les Fausses Décrétales.—Le Saint-Siège. 1. Le Pontificat de Nicolas Ier', RHE 8 (1907) 19–56, cf. esp. the summary, p. 49 (repr. *Mélanges* 1.164ff., esp. p. 194); in his collaboration with Le Bras, *Histoire* 1.227–228, the problem is only lightly touched upon. On Nicholas I, cf. K. Herbers, LMA 6 (1993) 1168ff. A spirited explanation was given by A. Lapôtre, *De Anastasio bibliothecario sedes apostolicae* (Paris 1885) (repr. *Études sur la papauté au IXe siècle,* ed. A. Vauchez, P. Droulers and G. Arnaldi [Vol. 1; Torino 1978]), who ascribed to the archivist Anastasius a knowledge of Pseudo-Isidore not shared by Nicholas I; G. Arnaldi, *Natale 875: Politica, ecclesiologia, cultura del papato altomedievale* (Istituto Storico Italiano per il Medio Evo, Nuovi studi storici 9; Rome 1990), deals with the situation of the papal archives during the time (77ff.) and stresses the conclusion that the ecclesiastical presumptions of the papacy had to have been thoroughly and expansively developed before Pseudo-Isidore would have been valued in Rome.

Pope Nicholas I is thought to be the first pope who came into contact with the False Decretals. We can no longer be sure that the papacy learned of the Pseudo-Isidorian Forgeries before his papacy.[183] No certain citation of Pseudo-Isidore has yet been discovered in his writings. The use of Pseudo-Isidore was 'consciously covered up', thought Ernst Perels, the editor of the letters of Nicholas I.[184]

The influence of Pseudo-Isidore could be read from the varied treatment of legal cases. In 858 the question of the deposition of a mentally ill bishop was brought before him. The petitioners asked the pope for the whole text of the Pseudo-Isidorian decretal. Nicholas did not respond to their request for the text of the decretal and did not yet claim authority over episcopal depositions. One might assume that Pseudo-Isidore is not yet in the pope's hands.

The transmitter of the Pseudo-Isidorian Decretals to Rome is thought to be Bishop Rothad II of Soissons (832–862, 865–869). Rothad was persistently persecuted by his metropolitan, Hincmar of Reims, at the beginning of the 60s. Hincmar defended his own conduct in a treatise. The case, which culminated in Rothad's deposition in 862, came to Nicholas I's attention, and in the end Rothad was allowed to travel to Rome to present his case. The trial, at which no one was present to represent Hincmar of Reims, demonstrated Rothad's guiltlessness in the eyes of the pope, and Rothad was formally rehabilitated. In his acquittal, Nicholas accused the Frankish bishops of wrongdoing, saying that they were not allowed to act 'against so many and such weighty decretals' ('contra tot . . . et tanta decretalia . . . statuta') by deposing a bishop without asking the pope.[185] In

183. Popes from Hadrian I (772–795) to Leo IV (847–855) have been mentioned as receiving Pseudo-Isidore, cf. Fuhrmann, *Einfluß und Verbreitung* 2.241ff. and Herbers, *Leo IV.* 350ff.

184. E. Perels, *Papst Nikolaus I. und Anastasius Bibliothecarius* (Berlin 1920) 112 in connection with the Rothad affair; p. 112 n. 1, Perels declared, 'I intend to dedicate a special study to the question of the reception of the Pseudo-Isidorian Decretals at the curia' (cf. also his reference from 1912: MGH Epp. 6.381 n. 1). The work never appeared.

185. The reservation that a bishop could be deposed only with papal approval first appears in the Roman synod of 24 December 864 (MGH Epp. 6.380.24ff.): 'quamvis et ipse sedem apostolicam nullatenus appellasset, contra tot tamen et tanta decretalia se efferre statuta et episcopum inconsultis nobis nequaquam deponere, sicut vos bene nostis, debuerunt. . . . Quamquam etsi numquam provocasset, numquam nos appellasse constaret, quod saepe dicendum est, numquam omnino praeter scientiam nostram deponi debuerit quia sacra statuta et veneranda decreta episcoporum causas utpote maiora negotia nostrae diffiniendas censurae mandarunt'. Until then, Nicholas had been supported by a very extensive explication of c.3 of Sardica. Even if the accused bishop did not appeal, the judge was to report the case to Rome. Now, with Pseudo-Isidore, every deposing procedure of a bishop became a 'causa maior', which had to be handled in Rome, cf. A. V. Müller, 'Zum Verhältnisse Nicolaus' I. und Pseudo-Isidors', NA 25 (1900) 652–663; on interpreting the canons of Serdica, p. 657, and the literature cited by Perels, *Papst Nikolaus I.* 103 n. 6. The passage with the 'tot . . . et tanta decretalia . . . statuta' is repeated in a letter to the West

858, Nicholas I had accepted a bishop's deposition, and in 862 he still referred the Rothad case to a provincial synod.[186] Now he held any dealings concerning a bishop to be a papal matter, just as Pseudo-Isidore saw it. We find other Pseudo-Isidorian peculiarities in the Rothad proceedings: that during an ongoing and not yet completed court case, the accused might appeal to the apostolic see at any time, and that the calling of a general synod, as Nicholas declared, was reserved to the apostolic see.[187] The two episcopal basic rights repeatedly asserted in Pseudo-Isidore can be used as an indicator that Nicholas knew the False Decretals: that 'causae episcoporum' were reserved to the apostolic see as 'maiora negotia',[188] and that, in keeping with the principle of the 'exceptio spolii' asserted by Pseudo-Isidore, the accused, particularly the bishop, remained in or was to be restored to full possession of his rights and goods until such time as judgment was pronounced.[189] Yet Nicholas did not simply assert the 'tot et tanta decretalia statuta', from which one could suspect any collection of decretals. He described its authors in more detail.[190] They were those 'who have persisted in the Catholic faith unto the last days of their lives', whose decretals must always be preserved by the Roman Church, 'and

---

Frankish episcopate at the end of January 865: JE 2785, MGH Epp. 6.393.24ff. Further writing on the restitution of Rothad (JE 2781, 2782, 2783, 2784, 2786) are edited in MGH Epp. 6.381ff.

186. JE 2708, MGH Epp. 6.620–621.

187. Cf. MGH Epp. 6.380.3f.; ('facto concilio generali'), 'quod sine apostolicae sedis praecepto nulli fas est vocandi'. Perels remarks on this passage (p. 380 n. 2) by referring to the fact that Nicholas is speaking of a right of convoking, not of confirming, such as is often ascribed to the Roman see in many passages by Pseudo-Isidore. Cf. the analysis by Seckel on Benedictus Levita 2.381 and 3.153, 'Studien VII' 492–493 and 'Studien VIII' 381.

188. It had been a demand even of the early papacy that 'causae maiores' be reported to the Roman bishop or his vicar. Among the 'maiora negotia', the 'causae episcoporum' was reserved for the apostolic see alone, cf. Perels, *Papst Nikolaus I.* 273 with n. 3; G. Hartmann, *Der Primat des Römischen Bischofs bei Pseudo-Isidor* (Stuttgart 1930) 59–60; J. Haller, *Nikolaus I. und Pseudo-Isidor* (Stuttgart 1936) 178; Betz, *Hinkmar* 141–142.

189. Nicholas does not yet appear to insist on the 'exceptio spolii' in 862 in his letter JE 2708 to King Salomon III of Brittany (857–874); he only demands a just trial of deposed bishops (MGH Epp. 6.622). At the earliest in the letter of 19 January 865 (JE 2781), with which he orders the restitution of Rothad to the church of Soissons, he makes use of this legal principle by citing Pseudo-Damasus, c.13, Hinschius, *Decretales* 503.24ff. (MGH Epp. 6.383–384, with n. 6; Pseudo-Damasus is cited at least once more by Nicholas in December, 866, in connection with the Synod of Soissons in which the clerics consecrated by Ebo are rehabilitated: MGH Epp. 6.420 nn. 4, 5). The essay by H. Schrörs, 'Die pseudo-isidorische Exceptio spolii bei Papst Nikolaus I.', *Historisches Jahrbuch* 26 (1905) 275ff., is shot through with numerous errors. In addition to the principle of the 'exceptio spolii', other Pseudo-Isidorian demands are touched on in the letter JE 2781, such as the demand that the accuser be present ('quem [Rothad] praesentialiter nemo accusat') or the pause before the beginning of the trial. Formulations are within range of the Pseudo-Isidorian text, without agreeing verbatim.

190. MGH Epp. 6.393.26ff.

which the Church has rightfully venerated in her archives and old monuments'.

Without doubt Nicholas is speaking of the decretals of martyr and confessor popes, whose respect he demands in words bordering on a hymn. Papal decrees from the time of persecution did not exist in the most widely distributed genuine chronological-historical collections, either in the *Dionysio-Hadriana* or in the *Hispana*. The oldest decretal in either of these is the letter of Pope Siricius (384–399) to the Metropolitan Himerus of Tarragona (JK 255). Decrees by martyred popes—and indeed 'tot et tanta decretalia statuta'—were to be found only in the decretal collection of Pseudo-Isidore. We can infer from the same letter that the West Frankish episcopate sought to oppose the validity of Pseudo-Isidorian norms, since these papal decretals of the early Church were not contained in the 'codex canonum', which probably meant the *Hadriana*. Nicholas did not heed this objection, and he formulated the principle that later reached Gratian's *Decretum* (D.19 c.1) via Ivo of Chartres: 'The decretals of the Roman bishops are to be accepted, even if they do not stand in the 'codex canonum' ('decretales epistolae Romanorum pontificum sunt recipiendae, etiamsi non sunt canonum codici compaginatae').[191] With that papal statement the way was cleared for the reception of the Pseudo-Isidorian Decretals by the entire Church.

For a long time scholars thought that Rothad of Soissons brought the False Decretals to Rome in the summer of 864; this thesis won greater probability when direct evidence was discovered that the group around Rothad of Soissons cited from Pseudo-Isidore.[192] A memorial of Hincmar of Reims of February/March 863, published by Perels in 1924, reveals the connections. It says that 'many who would restore Rothad' called on decretals of Julius and Victor demanding approval by the Roman bishop for the deposing of a bishop,[193] which was a fundamental principle demand-

---

191. Cf. C. Duggan, *Twelfth-Century Decretal Collections and Their Importance in English History* (University of London Historical Studies 12; London 1963) 27–28.

192. The notion that Rothad had contact with Pseudo-Isidore has been disputed by an expert of the stature of Lesne, *La hiérarchie épiscopale* 216ff., but he contradicts himself, cf. Perels, 'Eine Denkschrift' 69 n. 4.

193. Cf. Hincmar's remarks of February–March 863, b, c.10 (MGH Epp. 8.139.15ff., and Perels, 'Eine Denkschrift' 50, 62, 69 n. 4, 99): 'Nec perfunctorie transeundum est, quod quidam volentes Rothadum statuere, qui nesciunt quae locuntur neque de quibus adfirmant, testimonia ex decretis Iulii papae atque Victoris et quorundam antiquorum apostolicae sedis pontificum ad suum confirmandum errorem adsumunt, dicentes, quod nullus episcopus sine auctoritate Romani pontificis possit deponi, cum saepenumero iudicia depositionis de episcopis in canonibus et in decretis Romanae sedis pontificum relegantur'. There is an allusion to Pseudo-Julius, c.12, Hinschius, *Decretales* 467.20ff., and Pseudo-Victor, c.4–5 p 128 9ff., two passages that are largely in harmony.

ed by Pope Nicholas in the Rothad case. Here it is obvious that Rothad's friends were calling on Pseudo-Isidore.

Rothad himself appears to have sought refuge in the episcopal privileges of Pseudo-Isidore when he composed his complaint, sent by the archbishops of Trier, Cologne, Besançon, Arles and Milan and their suffragan bishops to the Eastern Frankish episcopate.[194] As examples of canonical norms that were found 'in decretalibus', Rothad states that no bishop could restrain the members of another diocese and that a metropolitan could act autonomously only in matters pertaining to his own archdiocese. This doctrine and language can be found only in the Pseudo-Isidorian Forgeries. Rothad's sentences were further distributed in the realm of Louis the German.[195]

194. Mansi, 15.645ff.; cf. Fuhrmann, *Einfluß und Verbreitung* 2.255–256, with n. 47; 268–269.

195. This witness to the distribution of Pseudo-Isidore is usually overlooked, and Perels, 'Eine Denkschrift' 68 rightly speaks of a 'regarded work'. Rothad's assertions are not easy to verify in detail, and Perels, 'Eine Denkschrift' 69 n. 4 writes generally of 'Pseudo-Isidorian influences'. I will choose two passages as examples. Among the chief points of his complaint, Rothad inserts, 'Si [a negation missing here?] debeat quilibet episcopus alterius ordinatum retinere, quanto minus capere vel in carcerem trudere, cum de hoc in decretalibus ita statuatur: Nullus episcopus alterius parochianum praesumat retinere etc.' (Mansi 15.647b). The full form of the citation should read: 'Nullus episcopus alterius parochianum praesumat retinere aut ordinare absque eius voluntate vel iudicare, quia sicut irrita erit eius ordinatio, ita et diiudicatio, quoniam censemus nullum alterius iudicis nisi sui sententia teneri: nam qui eum ordinare non potuit, nec iudicare ullatenus poterit'. It can be drawn from *Capitula Angilramni* c.15 (Hinschius, *Decretales* 761), Pseudo-Julius c.12, p. 468.6ff., Pseudo-Sixtus II c.6, p. 192.22–23, Benedictus Levita, Add. 4.23, less likely from Benedictus Levita 3.308; since the excerpt is introduced with the information that it had been decreed in the decretals, the source is either in the *Capitula Angilramni* or in passages of Pseudo-Isidore. The sources of the chapter, entirely assembled from Pseudo-Isidore, is analyzed by Seckel, 'Studien VIII' 81ff. The citation, which is broken off with an 'etc.', continues, 'Et post aliquanta: Si quis metropolitanus episcopus, nisi quod ad suam solummodo propriam pertinet parochiam, etc.' The continuation probably reads: 'sine consilio et voluntate omnium comprovintialium episcoporum extra aliquid agere tentaverit, gradus sui periculo subiacebit et quod egerit, irritum habeatur et vacuum'. Thus *Capitula Angilramni* c.43 (p. 765), agreeing with Pseudo-Calixtus, c.13, p. 139.9ff., Pseudo-Lucius, c.3, p. 176.8ff., Pseudo-Julius, c.12, p. 470.5ff. and Benedictus Levita 3.358. On their composition, cf. Seckel, 'Studien VIII' 117–118. Since the second citation is put into a relation with the first through the words 'Et post aliquanta', only the *Capitula Angilramni* and Pseudo-Julius can be the source, where the two passages occur in sequence. The expression 'in decretalibus' appears to suit the Pseudo-Julius letter better. In the other case, the earliest use is of the *Capitula Angilramni*. This letter to the Eastern Frankish bishops is preserved in a remarkable place: in the Vat. Pal. lat. 576 (saec. IX ex.), fol. 11v–13v from St. Martin in Mainz, a manuscript that perhaps originated in the environs of Reims. Together with some items by Hrabanus (MGH Epp. 5.444–445), it contains, among other things, the *Apologeticum Ebonis* (MGH Concilia 2.2.794ff.) and Ebo's declaration of resignation (MGH Concilia 2.2.701ff.), cf. E. Stevenson and J. B. De Rossi, *Codices Palatini Bibliothecae Vaticanae* (Vatican City 1886) 190–191. The publication by Mansi derives from the transcription in the notes of Lucas Holste († 1661), and it is not without error.

It is possibly a result of Rothad's transmission of the Pseudo-Isidorian Decretals to Rome that today there is a manuscript of the Pseudo-Isidorian short form A2, composed in the second half of the ninth century in the ecclesiastical province of Reims, though not in Reims itself, and that it contains the most important letters of the pope in the 'causa Rothadi', the *Libellus proclamationis* of Rothad of Soissons, and the Christmas address of Nicholas I on the rehabilitation of the bishop of Soissons.[196] The fact that Rothad cultivated connections with Italy is shown by the entry of the clergy of Soissons in the *Liber memorialis* of S. Giulia in Brescia.[197] Perhaps it is no accident that a short time later another adept of Pseudo-Isidore and decided enemy of Archbishop Hincmar of Reims, Bishop Hincmar of Laon, recalled the efforts of Nicholas I on behalf of Rothad in the midst of his own Pseudo-Isidorian compilation.[198]

A question in its own right, often posed, is whether Pope Nicholas himself knew the False Decretals or whether it was the Papal Librarian Anastasius who introduced the pope to Pseudo-Isidore as the scribe of the letters in question,[199] or whether Anastasius communicated his knowl-

196. It is a matter of the D. 38 of the Biblioteca Vallicelliana in Rome, which no longer reflects the entire A2 form: the Pseudo-Isidorian Decretals end (fol. 187v) at 'spernit et' (Hinschius, *Decretales* 508.17) immediately before the conclusion of the A2 version; on the manuscript, cf. Fuhrmann, 'Konstantinische Schenkung' 87 with n. 62. On the content, cf. E. Perels, 'Die Briefe Papst Nikolaus I.', NA 37 (1912) 548ff. The same items connected with the 'causa Rothadi' are contained in the manuscript Paris, B.N. lat. 3854 (saec. XII), derived from Rome, Vallicelliana D.38 and Vat. lat. 1344. On this 'Rothad tradition', cf. Schieffer, 'Kreta' 15ff.

197. In the *Liber memorialis* of the house of S. Giulia in Brescia, ten named members of Rothad's following are listed as having died during their stay in Rome: 'Hęc sunt Nomina de hominibus rothadi episcopi, qui defuncti sunt romam [sic] tempore Nicolai papę'. Seventy-four other names follow. On this entry, cf. K. Schmid, 'Religiöses und sippengebundenes Gemeinschaftsbewußtsein in frühmittelalterlichen Gedenkbucheinträgen', DA 21 (1965) 54 n. 138, repr. in his selected studies *Gebetsgedenken und adliges Selbstverständnis im Mittelalter* (Sigmaringen 1983) 570 and Fuhrmann, *Einfluß und Verbreitung* 2.256–257 n. 52.

198. Berlin, Staatsbibl. Phill. 1764, fol. 135v; cf. Fuhrmann, *Einfluß und Verbreitung* 2.270 n. 81 and 3.690–691. An insert by the author of the collection, Hincmar of Laon, reads: 'Quod et Nicolaus memorabilis papa pro Rothado venerabili episcopo eodem statuit atque roboravit tenore intemerabili inquiens: Ita ut secundum—procul amovimus' (JE 2783; MGH Epp. 6.388.23–31). After the citation of c.7 of the Council of Gangra and of sermon 10 of Leo I, it is assured (fol. 136–136v): 'Quorum auctoritatem a sepę nominando apostolico Nicolao exanclatam omnibus sanctae dei ecclesię filiis suffragari et verissime s[c]imus et certissime unum cum tanto capite nostro sencientes sequimur / nosque secutores fore fatemur; non enim latebant hunc tantum virum tanta reverentia venerabilem sanctorum praedecessorum suorum convulsa summe auctoritatis praecepta ac inrefragabilia divinę sanctionis instituta'. Cf. Fuhrmann, *Einfluß und Verbreitung* 3.691ff.

199. This view is most consistently supported by Lapôtre, *De Anastasio bibliothecario*. Lapôtre believed, for example, that Anastasius presented to the trusting Pope Nicholas the False Decretals brought by Rothad or a transcription of them, 'as if they had come from the Roman archives' (p 170); cf. the general opinion of Lapôtre's efforts by G. Arnaldi,

edge of the forgeries to Nicholas.[200] A decision in this matter is difficult, and it does not contribute much. As Ernst Perels, the editor of the letters of Nicholas, says, 'the policy of Pope Nicholas and the writings issued under his name, when taken as a whole, form a unity'.[201] For our question, which is the acceptance of Pseudo-Isidore in Rome, the significance of the pontificate of Nicholas I consists of the circumstance that the False Decretals were probably brought to Rome then. It was essentially more significant that Nicholas' own concept of the Church and the mission of the bishop of Rome created assumptions that prepared the way for many of the principles of Pseudo-Isidore. The core of the ecclesiological consciousness of Nicholas I was the responsibility of the Roman bishop for the entire Church. 'The pope is the apostolic see, and this is the *ecclesia Romana*, the summary of the Universal Church. The body is summarized in its head and must follow its direction'.[202] To document his attitude and his decisions, Nicholas did not need to resort to the forgeries, but it was precisely due to their congruence with his concepts that the Pseudo-Isidorian Decretals entered Rome not as a stranger but as a confirmation of many of the papacy's own convictions.

The Pseudo-Isidorian Decretals, 'which Nicholas I . . . claimed for his own, began to operate under Hadrian II', writes a biographer of Pope Hadrian II.[203] The character and rank of the possible crown witness to the 'operation' of Pseudo-Isidore under Hadrian II is uncertain: it is an address by an unknown person before an otherwise unknown assembly, probably held on 1 July 869 in Montecassino or on 9 July 869 in Rome. The speech itself, dealing with the marriage affair of King Lothar II (855–869) and the excommunication of the two deposed bishops, Gunthar of Cologne (850–863, † 871) and Zacharias of Anagni (860–863, later restored), had as an appendix a collection of examples including 38 Pseudo-Isidorian excerpts, although Pseudo-Isidorian texts do not literally appear in the speech. Friedrich Maassen interpreted the collection of excerpts and the speech as 'the first comprehensive use of the False Decretals to

---

'Anastasio Bibliotecario', DBI 3 (1961) 36–37. His degree of participation remains unclear in N. Ertl, 'Diktatoren frühmittelalterlicher Papstbriefe', *Archiv für Urkundenforschung* 15 (1937) 105: 'Anastasius was not uninvolved in the unofficial reception of the Pseudo-Isidorian Decretals by the curia under Nicholas I. The degree of his participation cannot be established with certainty'.

200. That is, for example, the opinion of Haller, *Nikolaus I. und Pseudoisidor* 187ff.; Anastasius would have been active as dictator from letter JE 2703 of 23 November 862.

201. Perels, *Papst Nikolaus I.* 316.

202. Y. Congar, *L'ecclésiologie du haut moyen-âge* (Paris 1968) 216.

203. H. Grotz, *Erbe wider Willen: Hadrian II. (867–872) und seine Zeit* (Vienna 1979) 314.

document the plenitude of power of the Roman See'.[204] Maassen assumed that the speaker was Pope Hadrian II, but the question of the identity of the speaker, and the further question of whether the Pseudo-Isidorian addition belongs to the speech, cannot be decisively answered, though much speaks for the authorship of Hadrian.[205] It is probable that Hadrian II in 868 was the first pope to send a Pseudo-Isidorian work as an instruction on canonical norms. To prevent bishops in Brittany from submitting themselves in the future to secular courts rather than presenting such cases to the metropolitan or the pope, he gave the *Capitula Angilramni* to Bishop Actard of Nantes (later Tours) († 875). The accompanying letter to King Salomon III of Brittany (857–874) was a clear indication how the secular ruler was to conduct himself in the future.[206]

In 871 we finally find the first certain, literal citation of Pseudo-Isidore in a papal letter, and its genuineness is not doubted even by those who hold that papal knowledge of the False Decretals can be accepted only from the middle of the eleventh century:[207] 'It is more than doubtful if they [the False Decretals] were used by any Pope before Leo IX, except once by Hadrian II'. This supposedly lone exception stands in a response by Hadrian II to the Synodal Acts of Douzy that had been sent to him

204. That was the subtitle of F. Maassen, 'Eine Rede des Papstes Hadrian II. vom Jahre 869: Die erste umfassende Benutzung der Falschen Decretalen zur Begründung der Machtfülle des römischen Stuhles' (SB Wien 72; Vienna 1872) 521ff. Maassen gave a short review of the research; cf. H. Fuhrmann, 'Ein Bruchstück' 373 n. 7. It is possible that the manuscript Milan, Biblioteca Ambrosiana G 58 sup. comes from the scriptorium of Bobbio in the time of Abbot Agilulf (c. 887–896), cf. P. Engelbert, 'Zur Frühgeschichte des Bobbieser Skriptoriums', RB 78 (1968) 256 n. 3, based on the research of P. Colluras, *Studi paleografici. La precarolina e la carolina a Bobbio* (Fontes Ambrosiani 22; Milan 1943) esp. 123–124, 132–133.

205. The research discussion is to be found in Fuhrmann, *Einfluß und Verbreitung* 2.273ff.

206. This letter fragment is transmitted together with two manuscripts of the *Capitula Angilramni*: Salzburg, St. Peter, a. IX. 32; Trier, Stadtbibliothek 927 (1362). Besides these two manuscripts, the announcement of the transmission exists in the Angilram tradition Münster, Staatsarchiv VII. 5201 from Corvey, saec. X; cf. P. Lehmann, *Corveyer Studien* (Abh. München 30, Heft 5; Munich 1919) 46; repr. in his selected essays, *Erforschung des Mittelalters* (Stuttgart 1962) 5.144; H. Hoffmann, *Buchkunst und Königtum im ottonischen und frühsalischen Reich* (MGH Schriften 30.1; Stuttgart 1986) 1.128–129, and Pokorny, 'Triburer Synodalakten' 492ff. This Corvey manuscript could have been written around 945 in Corvey and soon afterward, at the latest in the eleventh century, it was placed in its current home, cf. G. Theuerkauf, *Lex, Speculum, Compendium iuris* (Forschungen zur deutschen Rechtsgeschichte 6; Cologne 1968) 67ff. J. Sirmond knew of a tradition which is today unknown, cf. the editions in Hinschius, *Decretales* 769 and by Perels, MGH Epp. 6.712 no. 11.

207. See, among others, H. K. Mann, *The Lives of the Popes in the Early Middle Ages, 3: The Popes during the Carolingian Empire, 858–891* (2nd ed. London 1925) 143, relying on the judgment of Ch. de Smedt, 'Les fausses décrétales, l'épiscopat franc et la cour de Rome du IXème siècle au XIème siècle', *Études religieuses, historiques et littéraires publiées par les Pères de la Compagnie de Jésus*, ser. 4, 6 (1870) 77–101 and P. Fournier, 'Étude sur les Fausses Décretales', RHE 8 (1907) 49ff. (repr. *Mélanges* 1.194ff.).

(August–September 871). One bishop had been translated and another deposed, both central Pseudo-Isidorian themes. The pope approved the transfer and cited a text of Pope Anterus that a change of bishops could take place in response to pressing necessity and the desire of the congregation.[208] Hadrian did not succeed in bringing the deposition of the bishop under his jurisdiction, and he had to accept the autonomy of the West Frankish episcopate.

The fragment of a papal letter preserved in an obscure place is probably also to be attributed to Hadrian II: in the formula book of Notker the Stammerer († 912) there is a warning against overhastily deposing a Bishop Antonius; one must observe the principle of the 'exceptio spolii'. The name of the pope is not given, but the perspective of the letter suggests Hadrian II, and the Antonius could have been that bishop of Brescia who was certainly in office in the 870s.[209]

Under Pope John VIII (872–882), the Pseudo-Isidorian Decretals seem to be handled with a certain obviousness. In this pope's letters are found some citations of Pseudo-Isidore,[210] but something else is more important: many of the legal concepts that are formed or stressed in the False Decretals are clearly expressed by John VIII. Hence the principle of 'exceptio spolii' is played upon. In a trial the accused and the accuser should be present, infamous persons should not be admitted, and the episopal dignity should not suffer damage.[211] As Pseudo-Isidore had proclaimed

208. JE 2945, MGH Epp. 6.738ff. Cited is Pseudo-Anterus c.2, Hinschius, *Decretales* 152. On the tradition of the letter, cf. Contreni, 'Codices Pseudo-Isidoriani' 12–13.

209. MGH Formulae, ed. K. Zeumer, 433–434. The item is preserved in the Rheinau manuscript 131 (saec. X; cf. *Katalog der Handschriften der Zentralbibliothek Zürich, 1: Mittelalterliche Handschriften*, ed. L. C. Mohlberg [Zürich 1951] 223–224) in the middle of a running text between c.42 and c.43, and placed at the end as an addendum only by Zeumer. The latest date is Notker's death; according to W. von den Steinen, 'Notkers des Dichters Formelbuch', *Zeitschrift für schweizerische Geschichte* 25 (1945) 485ff. (repr. *Menschen im Mittelalter* [Bern 1967] 115ff.), the final redaction is to be set at 890, although Notker could have 'happened to add something' to his personal copy 'after 890 as well' (p. 486). E. Dümmler, *Das Formelbuch des Bischofs Salomo III von Konstanz aus dem neunten Jahrhundert* (Leipzig 1857) xxix, considers it possible 'that [the letter] originally belonged to the collection and was left out by other copiers'. Zeumer (Formulae, 433f. n. 1; 'Über die alamannischen Formelsammlungen', NA 8 [1883] 539) appears to have accepted that proposal: the letter is placed after the letter of Liutbert of Mainz (863–889) to Hadrian II (867–872), so that Zeumer thought of the pontificates of Nicholas I and Hadrian II. However, Nicholas can be eliminated because of his obvious reluctance to cite Pseudo-Isidorian passages verbatim. Perels (MGH Epp. 6.684–685 no. 61, with n. 5) also doubts Nicholas' authorship. On the person of Bishop Antonius of Brescia, cf. V. De Donato, DBI 3 (1961) 533–534.

210. JE 3298, MGH Epp. 7.210.24–25. This is an excerpt from the first epistle of Clement, which was fabricated before the False Decretals and was transmitted together with the *Recognitiones* of Rufinus.

211. Cf. JE 2976, MGH Epp. 7.283.23ff.; JE 3002, ibid., p. 299.

the equivalency and equal rank of the primate and the patriarch, so too John VIII proclaimed that 'primatibus, quos alias patriarchas novimus appellari'. This is an obvious reference to Pseudo-Anacletus, c.29.[212] Such a handling of the text, which included a citation without identification, makes it hard to identify Pseudo-Isidorian excerpts. Yet it is clear that the papacy gradually put aside its reluctance and cited the forgeries often, thoroughly, and literally.[213]

212. JE 2986, MGH Epp. 7.290.31–32 (= Epp. 7.314.20–21 = Epp. 6.256.11–12); after Pseudo-Anacletus c.29, Hinschius, *Decretales* 82.26–27: 'primates . . . qui in quibusdam locis patriarchae a nonullis vocantur'.

213. For John VIII (872–882) and the following pontificates through the Gregorian Reform, cf. Fuhrmann, *Einfluß und Verbreitung* 2.281ff.

Selected Bibliography

Primary Sources

Alger of Liège. Ed. R. Kretzschmar. *Alger von Lüttichs Traktat "De misericordia et iusti-tia": Ein kanonistischer Konkordanzversuch aus der Zeit des Investiturstreits: Unter-suchung und Edition.* Quellen und Forschungen zum Recht im Mittelalter 2. Sig-maringen 1985.

Ambrose of Milan. *Sancti Ambrosii opera X: Epistulae et acta III: Epistularum liber de-cimus, Epistulae extra collectionem, Gesta concilii Aquileiensis (Sancti Ambrosii Opera X).* Ed. M. Zelzer. CSEL 82, 3. Vienna 1982.

Anselm of Lucca. *Anselmi episcopi Lucensis collectio canonum una cum collectione minore.* Ed. F. Thaner. Regensburg 1906 and 1915.

Bede. *Bede's Ecclesiastical History.* Ed. B. Colgrave and R. A. B. Mynors. Oxford Medieval Texts. Oxford 1969.

Boniface, Saint. *Die Briefe des heiligen Bonifatius und Lullus.* Ed. M. Tangl. MGH Episto-lae selectae 1. Berlin 1916. *See also* Rau, R.

Bonzio of Sutri. *Bonizo Liber de vita christiana.* Ed. E. Perels. Texte zur Geschichte des römischen und kanonischen Rechts im Mittelalter 1. Berlin 1930.

Burchard of Worms. *Burchardi Wormaciensis ecclesiae episcopi Decretorum libri viginti.* PL 140.499–502, 541–1058.

———. *Decretorum libri XX. Ergänzter Neudruck der Editio princeps Köln 1548.* Ed. G. Fransen and Th. Kölzer. Aalen 1992.

Codex Carolinus. Ed. W. Gundlach. MGH Epistolae 3.469–657. Berlin 1892.

Collectio Avellana. Ed. O. Guenther. *Epistulae imperatorum pontificum aliorum inde ab a.367 usque ad a.553 datae Avellana quae dicitur collectio.* CSEL 35.1.2. Vienna 1891–1898.

Collectio canonum ecclesiae Hispanae ex probatissimis ac pervetustis codicibus nunc primum in lucem edita a publica Matritensi Bibliotheca. Edited by Francisco Antonio Gonza-lez. Vol. 2: *Epistolae decretales et rescripta Romanorum pontificum.* Madrid 1808–1821.

———. *Collectio Hispana.* Ed. G. Martínez Díez and F. Rodríguez. *La Colección canóni-ca Hispana.* 5 vols. Monumenta Hispaniae Sacra, Serie canónica 1–5. Madrid 1966–1992.

Collectio Cassinensis. Ed. E. Schwartz. ACO 1.3. Berlin 1929.

Collectio Dionysio-Hadriana. PL 67.135–346.

Collectio Thessalonicensis. Ed. C. Silva-Tarouca. *Epistularum Romanorum pontificum ad vicarios per Illyricum aliosque episcopos Collectio Thessalonicensis.* Textus et documen-ta 23. Rome 1937.

Collectio Veronensis (Verona Cod. XXII [20]). Ed. E. Schwartz. *Publizistische Sammlungen zum acacianischen Schisma*. Abh. München N.S. 10. Munich 1934.

Collectio Veronensis (Verona Cod. LVII [55]). Ed. E. Schwartz. ACO 1.2. Berlin 1926.

Collection in 74 Titles. Ed. J. T. Gilchrist. *Diversorum patrum sententie sive Collectio in LXXIV titulos digesta*. MIC Series B, 1. Vatican City 1973.

Collection in 183 Titles. Ed. J. Motta. *Liber canonum diversorum sanctorum patrum sive Collectio in CLXXXIII titulos digesta*. MIC Series B, 7. Vatican City 1988.

Collection in Two Books. Ed. J. Bernhard. *La collection en deux livres (Cod. Vat. lat. 3832)*. RDC 12 (1962) 1–601.

Concilia Africae A.345 –A.525. Ed. C. Munier. CCL 149. Turnhout 1974.

Concilia Galliae A.314 –A.506. Ed. C. Munier. CCL 148. Turnhout 1963.

Concilia aevi Merovingici. Ed. F. Maassen. MGH Concilia 1. Hannover 1893.

Concilia aevi Karolini 1. *Ed*. A. Werminghoff. MGH Concilia 2.1.2. Hannover 1906/ 1908.

Concilia aevi Karolini DCCCXLIII–DCCCLIX. Ed. W. Hartmann. MGH Concilia 3. Hannover 1984.

Concilios visigóticos e hispano-romanos. Ed. J. Vives. España Cristiana, Textos 1. Barcelona-Madrid 1963.

Constitutum Constantini. Ed. H. Fuhrmann. MGH Fontes iuris Germanici antiqui 10. Hannover 1968.

Coustant. See *Epistolae Romanorum pontificum*.

Cresconius. *Die Concordia canonum des Cresconius: Studien und Edition*. Ed. K. Zechiel-Eckes. 2 vols. Freiburger Beiträge zur mittelalterlichen Geschichte. Studien und Texte 5. Frankfurt 1992.

Deusdedit, cardinal. *Die Kanonessammlung des Kardinals Deusdedit, 1: Die Kanonessammlung selbst*. Ed. V. Wolf von Glanvell. Paderborn 1905.

Epistolae Romanorum pontificum . . . a S. Clemente I usque ad Innocentium III. Tomus I ab anno Christi 67 ad annum 440. Ed. P. Coustant. Paris 1721. Repr. Farnborough 1967.

Epistolae Romanorum pontificum genuinae . . . a S. Hilaro usque ad Pelagium II., 1: a S. Hilaro usque ad Hormisdam Ann. 461–523. Ed. A. Thiel. Braunsberg 1868.

Das Decretum Gelasianum de libris recipiendis et non recipiendis. Ed. E. von Dobschütz. Texte und Untersuchungen zur Geschichte der altchristlichen Literatur 38, 4. Leipzig 1912.

Gratian. *Decretum Magistri Gratiani*. Ed. Ae. Friedberg. Corpus Iuris Canonici 1. Leipzig 1879.

Gregory I, pope. *Gregorii I papae Registrum epistolarum*. Ed. P. Ewald and L. M. Hartmann. MGH Epistolae 1 and 2. Berlin 1887–1899.

———. *Registrum epistolarum libri I–XIV*. Ed. D. Norberg. CCL 140, 140A. Turnhout 1982.

Gregory VII, pope. *Das Register Gregors VII. (Gregorii VII Registrum)*. Ed. E. Caspar, MGH Epistolae selectae 2.1.2. Berlin 1920/ 1923.

Hadrian II, pope. *Hadriani II. papae epistolae*. Ed. E. Perels. MGH Epistolae 6.691–765. Berlin 1902/ 1925.

Hincmar of Laon. *Pittaciolus*. PL 124.993–1026.

Hincmar of Reims. *Capitulare 1 and 2*. Ed. R. Pokorny and M. Stratmann. MGH Capitula episcoporum 2.38–45. Hannover 1995.

————. *Collectio de ecclesiis et capellis.* Ed. M. Stratmann. MGH Fontes iuris Germanici antiqui 14. Hannover 1990.

————. *Collectio de raptoribus.* Ed. W. Hartmann. MGH Concilia 3.392–394. Hannover 1984.

————. *De divortio Lotharii regis et Theutbergae reginae.* Ed. L. Böhringer. MGH Concilia 4, Supplement 1. Hannover 1992.

————. *Epistolae,* Ed. E. Perels. MGH Epistolae 8. Berlin 1939.

Ivo of Chartres. *Ivonis Carnotensis episcopi Decretum.* PL 161.47–1022.

————. *Panormia.* PL 161.1041–1344.

John VIII, pope. *Registrum Johannis VIII. papae.* Ed. E. Caspar. MGH Epistolae 7.1–333. Berlin 1912–1928.

John the Deacon. *Joannis Diaconi Vita sancti Gregorii Magni.* PL 75.59–242.

Leo I, pope. *Leonis Papae I epistolarum collectiones.* Ed. E. Schwartz. ACO 2.4. Berlin 1932.

————. *S. Leonis Magni Tomus ad Flavianum episc. Constantinopolitanum (ep. XXVIII) additis testimoniis patrum et eiusdem S. Leonis M. epistula ad Leonem imp. (ep. CLXV).* Ed. C. Silva-Tarouca. Textus et documenta. Series theologica 9. Rome 1932.

————. *S. Leonis epistulae contra Eutychis haeresim.* Ed. C. Silva-Tarouca. Textus et documenta. Series theologica 15 and 20. Rome 1934/1935.

————. *Sancti Leonis Magni Romani Pontificis Tractatus septem et nonaginta.* Ed. A. Chavasse. CCL 138. Turnhout 1973.

Leo IV, pope. *Epistolae selectae . . . Leonis IV.* Ed. A. de Hirsch-Gereuth. MGH Epistolae 5.585–614. Berlin 1899.

Liber auctoritatum Arelatensis ecclesiae. Ed. W. Gundlach. MGH Epistolae 3.1–83. Berlin 1892.

Le Liber Pontificalis. Ed. L. Duchesne. 2 vols. Paris 1884–1892. Vol. 3: *Additions et corrections de Mgr. L. Duchesne,* published by C. Vogel. Paris 1957.

Martin of Braga. *Martini episcopi Bracarensis opera omnia.* Ed. C. W. Barlow. Papers and Monographs of the American Academy in Rome 12. New Haven 1950.

Narratio clericorum Remensium. Ed. A. Werminghoff. MGH Concilia 2.806–814. Hannover 1908.

Nicolaus I, pope. *Nicolai I. papae epistolae.* Ed. E. Perels. MGH Epistolae 6.257–690. Berlin 1902/1925.

Pelagius I, pope. *Pelagii I papae epistulae quae supersunt (556–561).* Ed. P. M. Gassó and C. M. Batlle. Scripta et documenta in abbatia Montisserrati 8. Montserrat 1956.

Decretales Pseudo-Isidorianae et Capitula Angilramni. Ed. P. Hinschius. Leipzig 1863.

Regino of Prüm. *Reginonis abbatis Prumiensis libri duo de synodalibus causis et disciplinis ecclesiasticis.* Ed. F. G. A. Wasserschleben. Leipzig 1840.

Pseudo-Remedius of Chur. *Collectio canonum Remedio Curiensi episcopo perperam ascripta.* Ed. H. John. MIC Series B, 2. Vatican City 1976.

Stephan V, pope. *Fragmenta registri Stephani V. papae.* Ed. E. Caspar and G. Laehr. MGH Epistolae 7. 334–365. Berlin 1912/1928.

Thiel. See *Epistolae Romanorum pontificum genuinae.*

Pseudo-Vigilii Thapsensi opus contra Varimadum. Ed. B. Schwank. CCL 90.1–134. Turnhout 1961.

Vives. See *Concilios.*

Secondary Literature

Arens, H. *Die christologische Sprache Leos des Großen: Analyse des Tomus an den Patriarchen Flavian*. Freiburger theologische Studien 122. Freiburg im Breisgau 1986.

Babut, E. C. *La plus ancienne décrétale*. Paris 1904.

Ballerini, P. and H. Ballerini. 'Disquisitiones de antiquis collectionibus et collectoribus canonum', PL 56.11–354.

Batiffol, P. *Cathedra Petri: Études d'histoire ancienne de l'Église*. Unam Sanctam 4. Paris 1938.

Benson, R. L. 'Plenitudo potestatis: Evolution of a formula from Gregory IV to Gratian'. *Collectanea S. Kuttner*. SG 14, 4.193–218. Rome 1968.

Berschin, W. *Bonizo von Sutri: Leben und Werk*. Beiträge zur Geschichte und Quellenkunde des Mittelalters 2. Berlin 1972.

Besse, J.-C. *Histoire des Textes du Droit de l'Église au Moyen-Age de Denys à Gratien: Collectio Anselmo dedicata: Étude et Texte* (Extraits). Paris 1960.

Betz, K.-U. *Hinkmar von Reims, Nikolaus I., Pseudo-Isidor: Fränkisches Landeskirchentum und römischer Machtanspruch im 9. Jahrhundert*. Ev.-theol. Diss. Bonn 1959.

Bischoff, B. *Die südostdeutschen Schreibschulen und Bibliotheken in der Karolingerzeit*, 1: *Die bayerischen Diözesen*. Leipzig 1940. 2: *Die vorwiegend österreichischen Diözesen*. Wiesbaden 1980.

———. 'Panorama der Handschriftenüberlieferung aus der Zeit Karls des Großen'. *Karl der Große: Lebenswerk und Nachleben*, 2: *Das geistige Leben*. Ed. B. Bischoff, 233–254. Düsseldorf 1965.

Blondel, D. *Pseudo-Isidorus et Turrianus vapulantes*. Geneva 1628.

Bock, F. 'Bemerkungen zu den ältesten Papstregistern und zum "Liber diurnus Romanorum pontificum".' *Archivalische Zeitschrift* 57 (1961) 11–51.

Brett, M. 'The Collectio Lanfranci and Its Competitors'. *Intellectual Life in the Middle Ages: Essays Presented to M. Gibson*. Ed. L. Smith and B. Ward, 157–174. London 1992.

———. 'Urban II and the Collections Attributed to Ivo of Chartres'. *Proceedings San Diego*. MIC Subsidia 9.27–46. 1992.

Buchner, M. 'Pseudoisidor und die Hofkapelle Karls des Kahlen'. *Historisches Jahrbuch* 57 (1937) 180–208.

Cabié, R. *La lettre du pape Innocent Ier à Décentius de Gubbio (19 mars 416): Texte critique, traduction et commentaire*. Bibliothèque de la RHE 58. Louvain 1973.

Caspar, E. 'Studien zum Register Johanns VIII.' NA 36 (1911) 77–156.

———. *Geschichte des Papsttums von den Anfängen bis zur Höhe der Weltherrschaft*, 1: *Römische Kirche und Imperium Romanum*; 2: *Das Papsttum unter byzantinischer Herrschaft*. 2 vols. Tübingen 1930–1933.

———. 'Hadrian I. und Karl der Große'. ZKG 54 (1935) 150–214. Repr. separately in *Das Papsttum unter fränkischer Herrschaft*, 35–113. Darmstadt 1965.

Chatillon, F. 'Le verset biblique le plus souvent cité par les Fausses Décrétales'. *Revue du Moyen Age Latin* 15–18 (1969–1972) 14–86.

Chavasse, A. 'Les lettres de Saint Léon le Grand dans le supplément de la Dionysiana, et de l'Hadriana et dans la Collection du manuscrit du Vatican'. *Revue des Sciences religieuses* 38 (1964) 154–176.

———. 'Les lettres du pape Léon le Grand (440–461), dans l'Hispana et la collection dite des Fausses Décrétales'. RDC 25 (1975) 28–39.

Chodorow, S. 'Decretals'. DMA 4 (1984) 122–124.

Classen, P. *Kaiserreskript und Königsurkunde: Diplomatische Studien zum Problem der Kontinuität zwischen Altertum und Mittelalter.* Byzantina Keimena kai meletai 15. Thessaloniki 1977.

Constable, G. 'The Treatise "Hortatur nos" and Accompanying Canonical Texts on the Performance of Pastoral Work by Monks'. *Speculum Historiale: Geschichte im Spiegel von Geschichtsschreibung und Geschichtsdeutung.* Ed. C. Bauer, 567–577. Freiburg and Munich 1965.

Conte, P. *Chiesa e primato nelle lettere dei papi del secolo VII.* Pubblicazioni dell'Università Cattolica del S. Cuore. Saggi e ricerche, ser. 3, Scienze storiche 4. Milan 1971.

———. *Il sinodo Lateranense dell'ottobre 649: La nuova edizione degli atti a cura di Rudolf Riedinger: Rassegna critica di fonti dei secoli VII–XII.* Collezione teologica 3. Vatican City 1989.

Contreni, J. J. 'A New Description of the Lost Laon Manuscript of the "Collectio Hispana Gallica".' BMCL 7 (1977) 85–89. Repr. in his *Carolingian Learning.*

———. *The Cathedral School of Laon from 850 to 930: Its Manuscripts and Masters.* Münchener Beiträge zur Mediävistik und Renaissance-Forschung 29. Munich 1978.

———. 'Codices Pseudo-Isidoriani: The Provenance and Date of Paris, B. N. MS lat. 9629'. *Viator* 13 (1982) 1–14. Repr. in his *Carolingian Learning.*

———. *Carolingian Learning, Masters and Manuscripts.* Aldershot 1992.

Devisse, J. *Hincmar: Archevêque de Reims 845–882.* 3 vols. Travaux d'histoire éthico-politique 29. Geneva 1975–1976.

Drobner, H. R. *Lehrbuch der Patrologie.* Freiburg im Breisgau. 1994.

Duchesne, L. 'La première collection romaine des décrétales'. *Atti del II° Congresso Internazionale di archeologia cristiana tenuto in Roma nell'aprile 1900,* 159–162. Rome 1902.

Duggan, C. 'Decretals (epistolae decretales, litterae decretales); Decretals, Collections of'. NCE 4 (1967) 707–711.

Dvornik, F. *The Photian Schism: History and Legend.* Cambridge 1948.

Ewald, P. 'Studien zur Ausgabe des Registers Gregors I.' NA 3 (1878) 433–625.

———. 'Die Papstbriefe der Brittischen Sammlung'. NA 5 (1880) 275–414, 503–596; 6 (1881) 451–454.

Feine, H.E. *Kirchliche Rechtsgeschichte, I: Die Katholische Kirche.* 4th ed. Weimar-Cologne 1964.

Fournier, P. 'Une forme particulière des Fausses Décrétales d'après un manuscrit de la Grande-Chartreuse'. BEC 49 (1888) 325–349.

———. 'Les collections canoniques attribués à Yves de Chartres'. BEC 57 (1896) 645–698; 58 (1897) 26–77, 293–326, 410–444, 624–676. Repr. in his *Mélanges* 1.451–678.

———. 'Étude sur les Fausses Décrétales'. RHE 7 (1906) 33–51, 301–316, 543–564, 761–784; 8 (1907) 19–56. Repr. in his *Mélanges* 1.83–201.

———. 'Études critiques sur le Décret de Burchard de Worms'. RHD 34 (1910) 41–112, 213–221, 289–331, 564–584. Repr. in his *Mélanges* 1.247–391. Also published as a monograph with the same title: Paris 1910.

———. 'Un tournant de l'histoire du droit 1060–1140'. RHD 41 (1917) 129–180. Repr. in his *Mélanges* 2.373–424.

———. 'Les sources canoniques du "Liber de vita christiana" de Bonizo de Sutri'. BEC 78 (1917) 117–134. Repr. in his *Mélanges* 2.667–684.

————. 'Les collections canoniques romaines de l'époque de Grégoire VII'. *Mémoires de l'Académie des inscriptions et belles-lettres* 41 (1920) 271–397. Repr. in his *Mélanges* 2.425–550.

————. *Mélanges de droit canonique*. Ed. Th. Kölzer, with foreword by J. Gaudemet. 2 vols. Aalen 1983.

———— and G. Le Bras. *Histoire des collections canoniques en Occident depuis les Fausses Décrétales jusqu'au Décret de Gratien*. 2 vols. Paris 1931–1932.

Fransen, G. Les décrétales et les collections de décrétales. Typologie des sources du Moyen-Age occidental 2. Turnhout 1972; updated 1985.

Freisen, J. *Geschichte des kanonischen Eherechts bis zum Verfall der Glossenliteratur.* 2nd ed. Paderborn 1893.

Fuhrmann, H. 'Studien zur Geschichte mittelalterlicher Patriarchate'. Part II and III. ZRG Kan. Abt. 40 (1954) 1–84; 41 (1955) 95–183.

————. 'Ein Bruchstück der Collectio ecclesiae Thessalonicensis'. *Traditio* 14 (1958) 371–377.

————. 'Ein Papst Ideo (zu Collectio Lipsiensis, tit. 27,5)'. *Études Le Bras.* 1.89–98.

————. 'Konstantinische Schenkung und abendländisches Kaisertum'. DA 22 (1966) 63–178.

————. 'Zur Überlieferung des Pittaciolus Bischof Hinkmars von Laon'. DA 27 (1971) 517–524.

————. *Einfluß und Verbreitung der pseudoisidorischen Fälschungen: Von ihrem Auftauchen bis in die neuere Zeit.* 3 vols. Schriften der MGH 24.1–3. Stuttgart 1972–1974.

————. 'Zu kirchenrechtlichen Vorlagen einiger Papstbriefe aus der Zeit Karls des Großen'. DA 35 (1979) 357–367.

————. 'Das Papsttum und das kirchliche Leben im Frankenreich'. *Nascita dell'Europa ed Europa carolingia*. Settimane di studio del Centro italiano di studi sull'alto medioevo 27.419–456. Spoleto 1981.

————. 'Reflections on the Principle of Editing Texts: The Pseudo-Isidorian Decretals as an Example'. BMCL 11 (1981) 1–7.

————. 'Fragmente der Collectio Anselmo dedicata'. DA 44 (1988) 539–544.

————. 'Fälscher unter sich: Zum Streit zwischen Hinkmar von Reims und Hinkmar von Laon'. *Charles the Bald: Court and Kingdom*. Ed. M. T. Gibson and J. L. Nelson, 224–234. 2nd ed. Aldershot 1990.

————. *See also* Seckel, E.

Gaudemet, J. *La formation du droit séculier et du droit de l'Église aux IVe et Ve siècles*. Institut de droit romain de l'Université de Paris 15. Paris 1957.

————. 'Patristique et Pastorale: La contribution de Grégoire le Grand au "Miroir de l'Évêque" dans le Décret de Gratien'. *Études Le Bras* 1.129–139. Repr. in his *La société ecclésiastique dans l'Occident médiéval*. London 1980.

————. *Les Sources du droit de l'Église en Occident, du IIe au VIIe siècle*. Initiations au christianisme ancien 1. Paris 1985.

————. '"Traduttore, traditore"—Les Capitula Martini'. *Fälschungen im Mittelalter* 2.51–65.

————. *L'Église dans l'Empire Romain (IVe–Ve siècles)*. Histoire du Droit et des Institutions de l'Église en Occident 3. 2nd ed. Paris 1990.

————. 'L'héritage de Grégoire le Grand chez les canonistes médiévaux'. *Gregorio Magno e il suo tempo: XIX Incontro di studiosi dell'antichità cristiana in collaborazione* con *l'École française de Rome, Roma, 9–12 maggio 1990*. Studia Ephemeridis *Augustinianum* 34.199–221. Rome 1991.

———. *Église et Cité. Histoire du droit canonique* (Paris 1994).

Getzeny, H. *Stil und Form der ältesten Papstbriefe bis auf Leo d. Gr.: Ein Beitrag zur Geschichte des römischen Primats*. Günzburg 1922.

Gilchrist, J. 'The Influence of the Monastic Forgeries attributed to Pope Gregory I (JE † 1951) and Boniface IV (JE † 1996)'. *Fälschungen im Mittelalter* 2.263–287.

Girardet, K. M. 'Gericht über den Bischof in Rom: Ein Problem der kirchlichen und der staatlichen Justiz in der Spätantike (4.–6. Jahrhundert)'. *Historische Zeitschrift* 259 (1994) 1–38.

Goffart, W. 'Gregory IV for Aldric of Le Mans (833): A Genuine or Spurious Decretal?' *Mediaeval Studies* 28 (1966) 22–38.

Günther, O. *Avellana-Studien*. SB Wien 134, Abh. 5. Vienna 1896.

Gundlach, W. 'Der Streit der Bisthümer Arles und Vienne um den Primatus Galliarum'. NA 14 (1889) 251–342; 15 (1890) 11–102, 235–292. An enlarged edition appeared as a book, *Der Streit der Bisthümer Arles und Vienne um den Primatus Galliarum: Ein philologisch-diplomatisch-historischer Beitrag zum Kirchenrecht*. Hannover 1890.

Hageneder, O. 'Papstregister und Dekretalenrecht'. *Recht und Schrift im Mittelalter*. Ed. P. Classen, 319–347. Vorträge und Forschungen 23. Sigmaringen 1977.

Haller, J. *Nikolaus I. und Pseudo-Isidor*. Stuttgart 1936.

———. *Das Papsttum: Idee und Wirklichkeit*. 2nd ed. Urach 1950.

Hampe, K. 'Hadrians I. Vertheidigung der zweiten nicänischen Synode gegen die Angriffe Karls des Großen'. NA 21 (1896) 83–113.

Hartmann, G. *Der Primat des Römischen Bischofs bei Pseudo-Isidor*. Stuttgart 1930.

Hartmann, W. *Das Konzil von Worms 868: Überlieferung und Bedeutung*. Abh. Göttingen, 3rd ser., 105. Göttingen 1977.

———. 'Fälschungsverdacht und Falschungsnachweis im früheren Mittelalter'. *Fälschungen im Mittelalter* 2.111–127.

———. *Die Synoden der Karolingerzeit im Frankenreich und in Italien*. Konziliengeschichte Reihe A: Darstellungen. Paderborn 1989.

———. 'Autoritäten im Kirchenrecht und Autorität des Kirchenrechts in der Salierzeit'. *Die Salier und das Reich, 3: Gesellschaftlicher und ideengeschichtlicher Wandel im Reich der Salier*. Ed. S. Weinfurter, 425–446. Sigmaringen 1991.

Hauck, A. *Kirchengeschichte Deutschlands*, 2. 3rd–4th ed. Leipzig 1912. 6th ed. Berlin 1952.

Heckel, R. von. 'Das päpstliche und sicilische Registerwesen in vergleichender Darstellung mit besonderer Berücksichtigung der Ursprünge, 2: Der Ursprung des päpstlichen Registerwesens und seine Entwicklung bis zur Mitte des 13. Jahrhunderts'. *Archiv für Urkundenforschung* 1 (1908) 394–445.

Herbers, K. *Leo IV. und das Papsttum in der Mitte des 9. Jahrhunderts: Möglichkeiten und Grenzen päpstlicher Herrschaft in der späten Karolingerzeit*. Päpste und Papsttum 27. Stuttgart 1996.

Hiestand, R. *Initienverzeichnis und chronologisches Verzeichnis zu den Archivberichten und Vorarbeiten der Regesta pontificum Romanorum*. MGH Hilfsmittel 7. Munich 1983.

Hoffmann, H., and R. Pokorny. *Das Dekret des Bischofs Burchard von Worms: Textstufen—Frühe Verbreitung—Vorlagen*. MGH Hilfsmittel 12. Munich 1991.

Horst, U. *Die Kanonessammlung Polycarpus des Gregor von S. Grisogono: Quellen und Tendenzen*. MGH Hilfsmittel 5. Munich 1980.

Jäger, H. *Das Kirchenrechtssystem Pseudoisidors*. Würzburg 1908.

Jasper, D. 'Romanorum pontificum decreta vel gesta: Die pseudoisidorischen Dekretalen in der Papstgeschichte des Pseudo-Liudprand'. AHP 13 (1975) 85–117.

Juncker, J. *See* Seckel, E.

Kerner, M., F. Kerff, R. Pokorny, K.G. Schon, and H. Tills. 'Textidentifikation und Provenienzanalyse im Decretum Burchardi'. *Mélanges G. Fransen*. SG 20, 2.17–63. Rome 1976.

Knust, Friedrich Heinrich. *De fontibus et consilio Ps.-Isidorianae collectionis*. Göttingen 1832.

Kottje, R. *Die Bußbücher Halitgars und des Hrabanus Maurus: Ihre Überlieferung und Quellen*. Beiträge zur Geschichte und Quellenkunde des Mittelalters 8. Berlin 1980.

Kuttner, S. 'Urban II and the Doctrine of Interpretation: A Turning Point ?' *Post Scripta: Essays on Medieval Law and the Emergence of the European State in Honor of G. Post*. Ed. J.R. Strayer and D.E. Queller. SG 15, 55–86. Rome 1972. Repr. in his *The History of Ideas and Doctrines of Canon Law in the Middle Ages*. London 1980.

—————. 'Auctor noster beatus Petrus apostolus: Pope Agatho on the Papal Office'. *Studia in honorem eminentissimi Cardinalis A. M. Stickler*. Ed. R. J. Castillo Lara, 215–224. Studia et Textus Historiae Iuris Canonici 7. Rome 1992.

————— and R. Elze. *A Catalogue of Canon and Roman Law Manuscripts in the Vatican Library*, 1: *Codices Vaticani Latini 541–2299*. Studi e testi 322. Vatican City 1986.

Landau, P. 'Neue Forschungen zu vorgratianischen Kanonessammlungen und den Quellen des gratianischen Dekrets'. *Ius Commune* 11 (1984) 1–29.

—————. 'Gefälschtes Recht in den Rechtssammlungen bis Gratian'. *Fälschungen im Mittelalter* 2.11–49.

—————. 'Kanonisches Recht und römische Form: Rechtsprinzipien im ältesten römischen Kirchenrecht'. *Der Staat* 32 (1993) 553–568.

—————. 'Wandel und Kontinuität im kanonischen Recht bei Gratian'. *Sozialer Wandel im Mittelalter: Wahrnehmungsformen, Erklärungsmuster, Regelungsmechanismen*. Ed. J. Miethke and K. Schreiner, 215–233. Sigmaringen 1994.

—————. 'Das Register Papst Gregors I. im Decretum Gratiani'. *Mittelalterliche Texte: Überlieferung—Befunde—Deutungen: Kolloquium der Zentraldirektion der MGH am 28./29. Juni 1996*. Ed. R. Schieffer, 125–140. Schriften der MGH 42. Hannover 1996.

Lapôtre, A. *De Anastasio bibliothecario sedis apostolicae*. Paris 1885. Repr. in *Études sur la papauté au IXe siècle*. Ed. P. Droulers and G. Arnaldi. Vol. 1. Torino 1978.

Le Bras, G. 'Notes pour servir à l'histoire des collections canoniques III: Un moment décisif dans l'histoire de l'Église et du droit canon: la Renaissance gélasienne'. RHD 9 (1930) 506–518.

Lesne, E. *La hiérarchie épiscopale. Provinces, métropolitains, primats en Gaul et Germanie depuis la réforme de Saint Boniface jusqu'à la mort de Hincmar, 742–882*. Mémoires et travaux publ. par des professeurs des Facultés catholiques de Lille 1. Paris 1905.

Löwe, H. *Deutschlands Geschichtsquellen im Mittelalter: Vorzeit und Karolinger, 4: Die Karolinger vom Vertrag von Verdun bis zum Herrschaftsantritt der Herrscher aus sächsischem Hause: Italien und das Papsttum*. Weimar 1963.

Lohrmann, D. *Das Register Papst Johannes' VIII. (872–882)*. BDHI 30. Tübingen 1968.

Lorenz, R. *Das vierte bis sechste Jahrhundert (Westen)*. Die Kirche in ihrer Geschichte 1.4. Göttingen 1970.

Maassen, F. 'Bibliotheca latina iuris canonici manuscripta I. Theil: Die Canonensammlungen vor Pseudoisidor'. SB Wien 53. Vienna 1866: 373–437; 54 (1866) 157–288; 56 (1867) 157–212.

———. 'Eine Rede des Papstes Hadrian II. vom Jahre 869: Die erste umfassende Benutzung der Falschen Decretalen zur Begründung der Machtfülle des römischen Stuhles'. SB Wien 72. Vienna 1872: 521–554.

———. 'Eine römische Synode aus der Zeit von 871 bis 878'. SB Wien 91. Vienna 1878: 773–792.

———. 'Pseudoisidor—Studien, 1: Die Textesrecension der ächten Bestandtheile der Sammlung'. SB Wien 108. Vienna 1885: 1061–1104; 2: 'Die Hispana der Handschrift von Autun und ihre Beziehungen zum Pseudoisidor'. SB Wien 109. Vienna 1885: 801–860.

Maccarrone, M. '"Sedes Apostolica—Vicarius Petri": La perpetuità del primato di Pietro nella sede e nel vescovo di Roma (Secoli III–VIII)'. *Il primato del vescovo di Roma nel primo millennio: Ricerche e testimonianze: Atti del symposium storico-teologico Roma, 9–13 ottobre 1989*. Ed. M. Maccarrone. Pontificio comitato di scienze storiche. Atti e documenti 4.275–362. Vatican City 1991.

Machielsen, L. 'Les spurii de S. Grégoire le Grand en matière matrimoniale, dans les collections canoniques jusqu'au Décret de Gratien'. *Sacris Erudiri* 14 (1963) 251–270.

McKeon, P. R. 'Toward a Reestablishment of the Correspondence of Pope Hadrian II: The Letters Exchanged between Rome and the Kingdom of Charles the Bald regarding Hincmar of Laon'. RB 81 (1971) 169–185.

———. *Hincmar of Laon and Carolingian Politics*. Urbana 1978.

———. 'A Note on Gregory I and the Pseudo-Isidore'. RB 89 (1979) 305–309.

McShane, P. A. *La Romanitas et le Pape Léon le Grand: L'apport culturel des institutions impériales à la formation des structures ecclésiastiques*. Recherches 24. Tournai-Montréal 1979.

Marchetto, A. *Episcopato e Primato pontificio nelle decretali pseudo isidoriane: Ricerca storico-giuridica*. Rome 1971.

———. 'In partem sollicitudinis . . . non in plenitudinem potestatis: Evoluzione di una formula di rapporto Primato—Episcopato'. *Studia in honorem eminentissimi Cardinalis A. M. Stickler*. Ed. R.J. Castillo Lara. Studia et Textus Historiae Iuris Canonici 7.269–298. Rome 1992.

———. 'La "fortuna" di una falsificazione: Lo spirito dello Pseudo-Isidoro aleggia nel nuovo Codice di Diritto Canonico?' *Fälschungen im Mittelalter* 2.397–411.

Massigli, R. 'La plus ancienne collection de décrétales'. *Revue d'histoire et de littérature religieuses* N.S. 5 (1914) 402–424.

May, G. 'Die Bedeutung der pseudoisidorianischen Sammlung für die Infamie im kanonischen Recht'. ÖAKR 12 (1961) 87–113, 191–207.

Mazal, O., ed. *Wiener Hispana-Handschrift: Vollständige Faksimile-Ausgabe im Originalformat des Codex Vindobonensis 411*. Codices selecti phototypice impressi 41. Graz 1974.

Meyvaert, P. 'Les "Responsiones" de S. Grégoire à S. Augustin de Cantorbéry'. RHE 54 (1959) 879–894.

Michel, A. *Die Sentenzen des Kardinals Humbert, das erste Rechtsbuch der päpstlichen Reform*. Schriften der MGH 7. Leipzig 1943.

Mor, C. G. 'Una piccola collezione di testi gregoriani del secolo VIII'. *Études Le Bras* 1.283–291.

Mordek, H. *Kirchenrecht und Reform im Frankenreich. Die Collectio Vetus Gallica, die älteste systematische Kanonessammlung des fränkischen Gallien. Studien und Edition.* Beiträge zur Geschichte und Quellenkunde des Mittelalters 1. Berlin 1975.

———. 'Kirchenrechtliche Autoritäten im Frühmittelalter'. *Recht und Schrift im Mittelalter.* Ed. P. Classen. Vorträge und Forschungen 23.237–255. Sigmaringen 1977.

———. 'Codices Pseudo-Isidoriani: Addenda zu dem gleichnamigen Buch von Schafer Williams'. AKKR 147 (1978) 471–478.

———. 'Der römische Primat in den Kirchenrechtssammlungen des Westens vom IV. bis VIII. Jahrhundert'. *Il primato del vescovo di Roma nel primo millennio: Ricerche e testimonianze: Atti del symposium storico-teologico Roma, 9–13 ottobre 1989.* Ed. M. Maccarrone. Pontificio comitato di scienze storiche: Atti e documenti 4.523–566. Vatican City 1991.

———. 'Spätantikes Kirchenrecht in Rätien: Zur Verwandtschaft von Tuberiensis und Weingartensis als Tradenten des ältesten lateinischen Corpus canonum'. ZRG Kan. Abt. 79 (1993) 16–33.

———. *Bibliotheca capitularium regum Francorum manuscripta: Überlieferung und Textzusammenhang der fränkischen Herrschererlasse.* MGH Hilfsmittel 15. Munich 1995.

Morin, G. 'Les Statuta ecclesiae antiqua sont-ils de S. Césaire d'Arles ?' RB 30 (1913) 334–342.

Müller, J. *Untersuchungen zur Collectio Duodecim Partium.* Münchener Universitätsschriften. Juristische Fakultät. Abh. zur rechtswissenschaftlichen Grundlagenforschung 73. Ebelsbach 1989.

Nautin, P. *Lettres et écrivains chrétiens du IIe et IIIe siècles.* Patristica 2. Paris 1961.

Norberg, D. *In Registrum Gregorii Magni studia critica* 2. Uppsala Universitets Årsskrift 7. Uppsala 1939.

Omont, H. 'Recherches sur la Bibliothèque de l'église cathédrale de Beauvais', *Mémoires de l'Académie des inscriptions et belles-lettres* 40 (1916) 1–93.

Peitz, W. *Das Register Gregors I.: Beiträge zur Kenntnis des päpstlichen Kanzlei-und Registerwesens bis auf Gregor VII.* Ergänzungshefte zu den Stimmen der Zeit. Zweite Reihe: Forschungen, 2. Heft. Freiburg im Breisgau. 1917.

Perels, E. 'Die Briefe Papst Nikolaus' I. A. Die Handschriften'. NA 37 (1912) 535–587; 'B. Die kanonistische Überlieferung'. NA 39 (1914) 43–153.

———. *Papst Nikolaus I. und Anastasius Bibliothecarius.* Berlin 1920.

———. 'Zur Wiederauffindung verschollener Handschriften der Biblioteca Vallicelliana'. NA 43 (1922) 605–609.

———. 'Eine Denkschrift Hinkmars von Reims im Prozeß Rothads von Soissons'. NA 44 (1922) 43–100.

Pietri, C. *Roma christiana: Recherches sur l'Église de Rome, son organisation, sa politique, son idéologie de Miltiade à Sixte III (311–440).* 2 vols. Bibliothèque des Écoles Françaises d'Athènes et de Rome 224. Rome 1976.

Pitz, E. *Papstreskripte im frühen Mittelalter: Diplomatische und rechtsgeschichtliche Studien zum Brief-Corpus Gregors des Großen.* Beiträge zur Geschichte und Quellenkunde des Mittelalters 14. Sigmaringen 1990.

Pokorny, R. 'Die drei Versionen der Triburer Synodalakten von 895: Eine Neubewertung'. DA 48 (1992) 429–511.

———. *See also* Hoffmann, H.

Pontal, O. *Die Synoden im Merowingerreich.* Konziliengeschichte Reihe A: Darstellungen. German translation by I. Schröder. Paderborn 1986.

Posner, E. 'Das Register Gregors I.' NA 43 (1922) 243–315.

Rau, R. *Briefe des Bonifatius: Willibalds Leben des Bonifatius.* Freiherr vom Stein-Gedächtnisausgabe 4b. Darmstadt 1968.

Richards, J. *The Popes and the Papacy in the Early Middle Ages, 476–752.* London 1979.

Richter, J. 'Stufen pseudoisidorischer Verfälschung: Untersuchungen zum Konzilsteil der pseudoisidorischen Dekretalen'. ZRG Kan. Abt. 64 (1978) 1–72.

Riedinger, R. 'Griechische Konzilsakten auf dem Wege ins lateinische Mittelalter'. AHC 9 (1977) 253–301.

Roethe, G. 'Zur Geschichte der römischen Synoden im 3. und 4. Jahrhundert'. *Geistige Grundlagen römischer Kirchenpolitik.* Forschungen zur Kirchen- und Geistesgeschichte 11. Stuttgart 1937.

Rouse, R. H. and M. A. Rouse. 'Ennodius in the Middle Ages: Adonics, Pseudo-Isidore, Cistercians, and the Schools'. *Popes, Teachers, and Canon Law in the Middle Ages.* Ed. J. R. Sweeney and S. Chodorow, 91–113. Ithaca 1989.

Santifaller, L. *Saggio di un Elenco dei funzionari, impiegati e scrittori della Cancelleria Pontificia dall'inizio all' anno 1099.* 2 vols. BISM 56 (1940).

Scharnagl, A. 'Die kanonistische Sammlung der Handschrift von Freising'. *Wissenschaftliche Festgabe zum zwölfhundertjährigen Jubiläum des heiligen Korbinian.* Ed. J. Schlecht, 126–146. Munich 1924.

Schieffer, R. 'Zur Beurteilung des norditalischen Dreikapitel-Schismas: Eine überlieferungsgeschichtliche Studie'. ZKG 87 (1976) 167–201.

———. 'Spätantikes Kirchenrecht in einer rätischen Sammlung des 8. Jahrhunderts'. ZRG Kan. Abt. 66 (1980) 164–191.

———. 'Der Brief Papst Leos d. Gr. an Theodoret von Kyros (CPG 9053)'. *Antidoron: Hulde aan Dr. M. Geerard bij de voltooiing van de Clavis Patrum Graecorum* 1.81–87. Wetteren 1984.

———. 'Redeamus ad fontem: Rom als Hort authentischer Überlieferung im frühen Mittclalter'. *Roma—Caput et Fons.* 45–70. Opladen 1989.

———. 'Kreta, Rom und Laon: Vier Briefe des Papstes Vitalian vom Jahre 668'. *Papsttum, Kirche und Recht im Mittelalter: Festschrift für H. Fuhrmann zum 65. Geburtstag.* Ed. H. Mordek, 15–30. Tübingen 1991.

———. 'Der Pittaciolus Hinkmars von Laon in einer Salzburger Handschrift aus Köln'. *Aus Archiven und Bibliotheken: Festschrift für R. Kottje zum 65. Geburtstag.* Ed. H. Mordek. Freiburger Beiträge zur mittelalterlichen Geschichte: Studien und Texte, 3.137–147. Frankfurt 1992.

Schmitz, G. 'Die Waffe der Fälschung zum Schutz der Bedrängten? Bemerkungen zu gefälschten Konzils- und Kapitularientexten'. *Fälschungen im Mittelalter* 2.79–110.

Schon, K.-G. 'Exzerpte aus den Akten von Chalkedon bei Pseudoisidor und in der 74-Titel-Sammlung'. DA 32 (1976) 546–557.

———. 'Eine Redaktion der pseudoisidorischen Dekretalen aus der Zeit der Fälschung'. DA 34 (1978) 500–511.

Schrörs, H. *Hinkmar, Erzbischof von Reims.* Freiburg im Breisgau. 1884.

Schulte, Johann F. von. *Vier Weingartner jetzt Stuttgarter Handschriften.* SB Wien 117 Heft 11. Vienna 1889.

———. 'Marius Mercator und Pseudo-Isidor'. SB Wien 147. Vienna 1904: 167–172.

Schwartz, E. *Der Prozeß des Eutyches.* SB München Heft 5. Munich 1929.

———. 'Zum Decretum Gelasianum'. *Zeitschrift für die neutestamentliche Wissenschaft* 29 (1930) 161–168.

———. 'Die sog. Sammlung der Kirche von Thessalonich'. *Festschrift R. Reitzenstein.* Ed. E. Fraenkel et al. 137–159. Leipzig-Berlin 1931.

———. 'Die Kanonessammlungen der alten Reichskirche'. ZRG Kan. Abt. 25 (1936) 1–114. Repr. in his *Gesammelte Schriften* 4.159–275. Berlin 1960.

Seckel, E. 'Studien zu Benedictus Levita': I, NA 26 (1901) 37–72; II–V, NA 29 (1904) 275–331; VI, NA 31 (1906) 59–139, 238–239; VII.1, NA 34 (1909) 319–381; VII.2 and 3, NA 35 (1910) 105–191, 433–539; VIII.1, NA 39 (1914) 327–431; VIII.2, NA 40 (1916) 15–130; VIII.3, NA 41 (1917/1919) 157–263;

———. (Juncker, J.), 'Studien zu Benedictus Levita VIII.4: Ergänzt und aus dem Nachlaß hg. von J. Juncker'. ZRG Kan. Abt. 23 (1934) 269–377; 24 (1935) 1–112.

———. 'Pseudoisidor'. RE 16 (3rd ed. Leipzig 1905) 265–307.

———. 'Benedictus Levita decurtatus et excerptus: Eine Studie zu den Handschriften der falschen Kapitularien'. *Festschrift der Berliner Juristenfakultät für H. Brunner,* 377–464. Munich-Leipzig 1914.

———. *Die erste Zeile Pseudoisidors, die Hadriana Rezension In nomine domini incipit praefatio libri huius und die Geschichte der Invokation in den Rechtsquellen: Aus dem Nachlaß mit Ergänzungen.* Ed. H. Fuhrmann (SB Berlin Heft 4; Berlin 1959).

Silva-Tarouca, C. 'Beiträge zur Überlieferungsgeschichte der Papstbriefe des IV., V. u. VI. Jahrhunderts'. *Zeitschrift für katholische Theologie* 43 (1919) 467–481, 657–692.

———. C. 'Le antiche lettere dei papi e le loro edizioni'. *La Civiltà Cattolica* 72 (1921) 14–22, 323–336.

———. 'Die Quellen der Briefsammlung Papst Leos des Großen'. *Papsttum und Kaisertum: Forschungen zur politischen Geschichte und Geisteskultur des Mittelalters: P. Kehr zum 65. Geburtstag dargebracht.* Ed. A. Brackmann, 23–47. Munich 1926.

———. 'Nuovi studi sulle antiche lettere dei Papi'. *Gregorianum* 12 (1931) 1–56, 349–425, 547–598. Published under the same title as a monograph. Rome 1932.

———. 'Originale o Registro ? La tradizione manoscritta del Tomus Leonis'. *Studi dedicata alla memoria di P. Ubaldi.* Pubblicazioni della Università Cattolica del Sacro Cuore, Serie quinta: Scienze storiche 16.151–170. Milan 1937.

Silvestre, H. 'Notices et extraits des manuscrits 5413–22, 10098–105 et 10127–44 de la Bibliothèque Royale de Bruxelles'. *Sacris Erudiri* 5 (1953) 174–192.

Simson, B. 'Pseudo-Isidor und die Geschichte der Bischöfe von Le Mans'. *Zeitschrift für Kirchenrecht* 21 (1896) 151–169.

———. *Die Entstehung der Pseudo-isidorischen Fälschungen in Le Mans.* Leipzig 1886.

———. 'Pseudo-Isidor und die Le Mans-Hypothese'. ZRG Kan. Abt. 4 (1914) 1–74.

Somerville, R. 'The Letters of Pope Urban II in the Collectio Britannica'. *Proceedings Cambridge.* MIC Subsidia 8.103–114. Vatican City 1988.

———. *Pope Urban II, The Collectio Britannica, and the Council of Melfi (1089).* With the collaboration of Stephan Kuttner. Oxford 1996.

Steinacker, H. 'Die Deusdedithandschrift (Cod. Vat. 3833) und die ältesten gallischen libri canonum'. MIÖG Ergänzungsband 6 (1901) 113–144.

———. 'Ueber das älteste päpstliche Registerwesen'. MIÖG 23 (1902) 1–49.

Stickler, A. *Historia Iuris Canonici Latini: Institutiones academicae,* 1: *Historia fontium.* Torino 1950.

Studer, B. 'Les pontifes romains de Sirice à Léon le Grand'. *Initiations aux Pères de l'Église IV: Du concile de Nicée au concile de Chalcédoine (451): Les Pères latins,* 735–777. Paris 1986.

Tangl, M. 'Studien zur Neuausgabe der Briefe des hl. Bonifatius und Lullus'. NA 40 (1916) 639–790; 41 (1917–1919) 23–101. Repr. in his selected studies *Das Mittelalter in Quellenkunde und Diplomatik*, 1. Forschungen zur mittelalterlichen Geschichte 12.1.60–240. Berlin 1966.

————. 'Gregor-Register und Liber Diurnus: Eine Kritik'. NA 41 (1919) 741–752. Repr. in his selected studies *Das Mittelalter in Quellenkunde und Diplomatik*, 2. Forschungen zur mittelalterlichen Geschichte 12.2.709–718. Berlin 1966.

Tarré, J. 'Sur les origines de la collection canonique, dite "Hispana".' *Mélanges P. Fournier*, 705–724. Paris 1929.

Turner, C. H. 'Chapters in the History of Latin MSS of Canons II: A Group of MSS of Canons at Toulouse, Albi, and Paris'. JTS 2 (1901) 266–273.

————. 'The Collection of the Dogmatic Letters of St Leo'. *Miscellanea Ceriani: Raccolta di scritti originali per onorare la memoria di Mr. A. M. Ceriani*, 687–739. Milan 1910.

————. 'Latin Lists of Canonical Books III: From Pope Innocent's Epistle to Exsuperius of Toulouse (A.D. 405)'. JTS 13 (1911/1912) 77–82.

————. 'Arles and Rome: The First Developments of Canon Law in Gaul'. JTS 17 (1916) 236–247.

————. 'The Organisation of the Church'. *The Cambridge Medieval History*, 1: *The Christian Roman Empire and the Foundation of the Teutonic Kingdoms*, 143–182. 2nd ed. Cambridge 1924.

————. 'Chapters in the History of Latin MSS of Canons IV: The Corbie MS(C), now Paris. lat. 12097'. JTS 30 (1929) 225–236.

————. 'Chapters in the History of Latin MSS of Canons VII: The Collection named after the MS of St Maur (F), Paris Lat. 1451'. JTS 32 (1931) 1–11.

Ullmann, W. 'Nos si aliquid incompetenter . . . (Some Observations on the Register Fragments of Leo IV in the Collectio Britannica)'. *Ephemerides iuris canonici* 9 (1953) 3–11. Repr. in his selected studies *The Church and the Law in the Earlier Middle Ages*, no. VII. London 1975.

————. 'The Significance of the Epistola Clementis in the Pseudo-Clementines'. JTS N.S. 11 (1960) 295–317. Repr. in his selected studies *The Church and the Law in the Earlier Middle Ages*, no. II. London 1975.

————. *The Growth of Papal Government in the Middle Ages: A Study in the Ideological Relation of Clerical to Lay Power*. 3rd ed. London 1970.

————. *Gelasius I. (492–496): Das Papsttum an der Wende der Spätantike zum Mittelalter*. Päpste und Papsttum 18. Stuttgart 1981.

Unterkircher, F., ed. *Codex Epistolaris Carolinus: Österreichische Nationalbibliothek Codex 449*. Codices selecti phototypice impressi 3. Graz 1962.

Van der Speeten, J. 'Quelques remarques sur la collection canonique de Weingarten'. *Sacris Erudiri* 29 (1986) 25–118.

Van Hove, A. *Prolegomena ad Codicem iuris canonici*. Commentarium Lovaniense in Codicem iuris canonici 1.1.2 nd ed. Mechelen-Rome 1945.

Vollmann, B. *Studien zum Priszillianismus: Die Forschung, die Quellen, der fünfzehnte Brief Papst Leos des Großen*. Kirchengeschichtliche Quellen und Studien 7. St. Ottilien 1965.

Wallach, L. 'The Greek and Latin Versions of II Nicaea, 787, and the Synodica of Hadrian I (JE 2448)'. *Traditio* 22 (1966) 103–125. Repr. in his *Diplomatic Studies in Latin and Greek Documents from the Carolingian Age*, 3–26. Ithaca 1977.

Wenger, L. *Canon in den römischen Rechtsquellen und in den Papyri*. SB Wien 220 Abh. 2. Vienna 1942.

———. *Die Quellen des römischen Rechts*. Akad. Wien, Denkschriften 2. Vienna 1953.

Williams, S. *Visio aetatis aureae Ecclesiae Pseudo-Isidoriana*. Ph.D. Dissertation, Department of History, University of California, Berkeley 1951.

———. 'The Pseudo-Isidorian Problem Today'. Speculum 29 (1954) 702–707.

———. 'Le Ms. Saint-Omer 189 des Fausses Décrétales d'Isidor Mercator'. *Bulletin trimestriel de la Société Académique des Antiquaires de la Morinie* 20 (Fasc. 381) (1964) 257–266.

———. 'Pseudo-Isidore from the Manuscripts'. CHR 53 (1967) 58–66.

———. *Codices Pseudo-Isidoriani: A Paleographico-Historical Study*. MIC Series C. Subsidia 3. New York 1971.

Wirbelauer, E. *Zwei Päpste in Rom: Der Konflikt zwischen Laurentius und Symmachus (498–514): Studien und Texte*. Quellen und Forschungen zur antiken Welt 16. Munich 1993.

———. 'Zum Umgang mit kanonistischer Tradition im frühen Mittelalter. Drei Wirkungen der Symmachianischen Documenta'. *Schriftlichkeit im frühen Mittelalter*. Ed. U. Schäfer. ScriptOralia 53.207–228. Tübingen 1993.

Wojtowytsch, M. *Papsttum und Konzile von den Anfängen bis zu Leo I. (440–461)*. Päpste und Papsttum 17. Stuttgart 1981.

Wurm, H. *Studien und Texte zur Dekretalensammlung des Dionysius Exiguus*. Kanonistische Studien und Texte 16. Bonn 1939.

———. 'Decretales selectae ex antiquissimis Romanorum Pontificum epistulis decretalibus'. *Apollinaris* 12 (1939) 40–93.

Index of Manuscripts

Aosta, Biblioteca Capitolare
C. 102: 158, 182 n. 164, 184
n. 172

Bamberg, Staatsbibliothek
Can. 9 (P.I.9): 118 n. 135
Fragment IX: 94 n. 25

Berlin, Staatsbibliothek–
Preussischer Kultur-
besitz
Hamilton 132: 144 f., 172
Ms. 79 (Phillipps 1776):
60–62
Ms. 91 (Phillipps 1764): 83
n. 362, 92, 138f., 150 n.
50, 180, 191 n. 198

Bern, Burgerbibliothek
442: 139
451: 184 n. 172
611: 74

Bernkastel-Kues, Bibliothek
des St. Nikolaus Hospi-
tals
52: 138 n. 5

Brescia, Biblioteca Civica
Queriniana
B. II. 13: 158, 182 n. 164, 184
n. 172

Bruxelles (Brussels), Bibliothèque Royale Albert
Ier
5413–22 (Gheyn 2606): 112
n. 100, 113 n. 108

Cambridge, Library of Corpus Christi College
265: 183 n. 170

Cambridge, Library of
Trinity College
B. 16. 44 (405): 183
n. 168

Carpentras, Bibliothèque
municipale Inguimber-
tine
1856 (Peiresc 74. 1): 86 n.
378

Chartres, Bibliothèque
municipale
41: 74

Dijon, Bibliothèque municipale
2975: 154 n. 68

Engelberg, Stiftsbibliothek
52: 94 n. 25

Firenze, Biblioteca
Nazionale Centrale
Conv. soppr. D. 2. 1476: 66

Firenze (Florence), Biblioteca Medicea Lauren-
ziana
Conv. soppr. 91: 102 n. 58
Fiesole 46: 49 n. 200

Freiburg (Breisgau), Universitätsbibliothek
8: 184 n. 172

Fulda, Hessische Landes-
bibliothek
Cod. Bonifatianus 2: 51

Göttweig, Stiftsbibliothek
53 (56): 96

s'Gravenhage (The Hague),
Museum Meermanno-
Westreenianum
10. B. 4 (prev. 9): 29 n. 117

Grenoble, Bibliothèque
municipale
473: 41 n. 172, 56, 160 n. 96

Ivrea, Biblioteca Capitolare
83 (Mazzatinti 29): 158,
182 nn. 164f., 184 n. 172

Karlsruhe, Badische
Landesbibliothek
Rastatt 22: 97

Köln (Cologne), Erzbis-
chöfliche Diözesan-
und Dombibliothek
113: 154 n. 67
114: 76 n. 332, 169
117: 83 n. 362
118: 185 n. 173
212: 86
213: 35 n. 144

Laon, Bibliothèque municipale
122: 45 n. 185
407: 111, 113 n. 108, 126

La Rochelle, Bibliothèque
municipale
387: 111 n. 99

Leiden, Bibliotheek der
Rijksuniversiteit
Voss. lat. oct. 29: 184 n.
172
Voss. lat. qu. 108: 184 n.
172

Leipzig, Universitätsbibliothek
836: 96, 98 n. 41
II. 7: 172, 184 n. 172

Livorno, Biblioteca Comu-
nale Labronica
sin. num. (prev. 10): 77 n.
333

London, British Library
Add. 8873: 6 n. 9; 61,
64–66, 100, 122, 123 n.
156, 132

Lucca, Biblioteca Capito-
lare Feliniana

Index of Papal Letters

Anaclet
JK † 4: 177 n. 149, 195 n.
212
Clement I
JK † 10: 162
JK † 11: 162
JL † 5340 (not Clement
III): 139 n. 11
Alexander I
JK † 24: 139 n. 11
Soter
JK *58: 18 n. 65
Victor I
JK † 74: 189 n. 193
Zephyrin
JK † 80: 163 n. 104
JK † 81: 163 n. 104
Calixtus I
JK † 86: 190 n. 195
Urban I
JK † 87: 163 n. 104
Anterus
JK † 90: 194 n. 208
Lucius
JK † 123: 190 n. 195
Stephen I.
JK † 130: 174
Melchiades
JK † 171: 163 n. 104
Silvester I
JK † 174: 69 n. 293
JK † 175: 69 n. 293
Marcus
JK † 181: 165
Julius I
JK 188: 138 n. 5
JK † 195: 165

JK † 196: 126, 165, 189
n.193, 190 n. 195
Liberius
JK † 222: 165
JK 223: 12 n. 33
JK 228: 138 n. 5
Felix II
JK † 230: 165
JK † 231: 165
Damasus I
JK 232: 166
JK 235: 166
JK † 242: 165
JK † 243: 31 n. 130, 148, 155,
166, 188 n. 189
JK † 244: 31 n. 130, 148, 155,
166
JK † 245: 166
Siricius
JK 255: 9, 11f., 16 f., 21–24,
26 n. 102, 27, 32, 35, 40,
59 n.245, 189
JK 258: 10, 14, 17, 31 n. 130,
34f., 40, 59 n. 245
JK 260: 34f., 40 n. 168
JK 261: 34 n. 143
JK 263: 20 n. 77, 31 n. 130,
35
Anastasius I
JK † 277: 166
JK † 278: 166
Innocent I
JK 285a: Canones synodi
Romanorum: 11 n. 32,
28–32
JK 286: 10 n. 24, 14f., 17,
22, 25f., 31 n. 130,
34f.
JK 288: 19 n. 73

JK 292: 19 n. 73, 20 n. 76,
36
JK 293: 17, 19 n. 73, 22f.,
25–27, 31 n.130, 35, 59
n. 245
JK 294: 19 n. 73
JK 297: 36
JK 299: 36
JK 301: 36
JK 302: 36
JK 303: 9 n. 23, 19 n. 73,
22f., 25f., 35, 59 n. 245
JK 304: 36
JK 308: 19 n. 71
JK 310: 19 n. 73
JK 311: 15, 19, 22, 27 f., 59
n. 245
JK 312: 17, 36
JK 313: 36
JK 314: 36f.
JK 315: 19 n. 71, 36
JK 316: 19 n. 73, 36
JK 317: 36
JK 318: 36
JK 321–324: 36, 166
JK 321: 10 n. 24, 38
JK 323: 84
JK 325–327: 84
Zosimus
JK 328: 16 n.52, 40
JK 329: 84
JK 330: 84
JK 331–334: 40
JK 331: 16 n. 52
JK 332: 13 n.38
JK 337: 16 n. 52
JK 339: 16 n. 52, 19 n. 71,
22–26, 40
JK 340: 40
JK 341: 40

General Index

Acacius, patriarch of Constantinople, Acacian Schism 44 n. 183, 46, 61–63, 84f.
Actard, bishop of Nantes 193
Adalard, abbot of Corbie 72
Admonitio synodalis 110 n. 95
Ado, bishop of Vienne 111
Adrianople, Battle of (378) 7
Adventius, bishop of Metz 117
Aelfric, abbot of Eynsham 183
Aeneas, bishop of Paris 185
Africa 84
Agano, bishop of Autun 144 n. 27
Agapetus I, pope 84, 168
Agatho, pope 93, 133
Agifred, scribe 182
Agilulf, abbot of Bobbio 193 n. 204
Agobard, archbishop of Lyon 67
Aldrich, bishop of Le Mans 79, 102, 170, 171 n. 131
Aleander, Hieronymus, cardinal 159 n. 88
Alexander I, pope 139 n. 11
Alexander II, pope 66 n. 279, 100, 110, 124, 133
Alexandria 9
Alfred the Great 110
Alger of Liège 95
Altinum 42 n. 177
Amandus, bishop of Tongeren 92, 95, 126
Amator, bishop 168
Ambrose, St. 34f., 78 n. 342
Anacletus I, pope 137, 162, 195
Anastasius Bibliothecarius 115, 186 n. 182, 191
Anastasius I, pope 166
Anastasius II, pope 61 n. 255, 63
Anastasius, metropolitan of Thessalonika 58
Anatolius, patriarch of Constantinople 37, 57 n. 237, 81
Andalusia 68 n. 290
Angilram, bishop of Metz 150
Anno, bishop of Freising 182
Ansegis, abbot of Fontenelle 151

Anselm II, archbishop of Milan 117, 185
Anselm, bishop of Limoges 130
Anselm of Lucca, Collectio canonum 57 n. 237, 60, 63 n. 265, 64, 66, 67 n. 285, 78, 85, 99, 102 n. 57, 103 n. 61, 107, 108 n. 88, 120f. 131f.
Anterus, pope 194
Antioch 9, 46, 69 n. 294
Antonius, bishop of Brescia 183, 194
Apulia 16, 22, 25, 38
Aquileia 42 n. 177
Arianism 12
Aribert, archbishop of Milan 102
Arles 32f., 47 n. 193, 67, 86
Athanasius of Alexandria, St. 165
Augustine of Canterbury, St. 72, 168
Augustine of Hippo, St. 78, 82
Aurelius, African bishop 164
Aurelius, bishop of Carthage 17, 36 n. 152
Autun 144, 145 n. 30
Azo, bishop of Ivrea 182

Babut, Charles E., historian 28
Ballerini, Pietro and Girolamo, canonists 41f., 48 n. 198, 81 n. 355, 83, 144 n. 27, 146, 156, 158, 167 n. 117
Baronio, Cesare, cardinal 86 n. 378
Basilius I, Byzantine emperor 130
Beauvais 144
Bede 72, 169
Belloni, Antonio, notary 47 n. 195
Benedict I, pope 168
Benedict II, pope 90f.
Benedict III, pope 113f.
Benedictus Levita, Collectio capitularium 97f., 101 n. 53, 141, 143f., 149–152, 170, 173, 176, 190 n. 195
Bernold of Constance 67 n. 285, 120
Bible 19, 152, 159
Bithynia 62

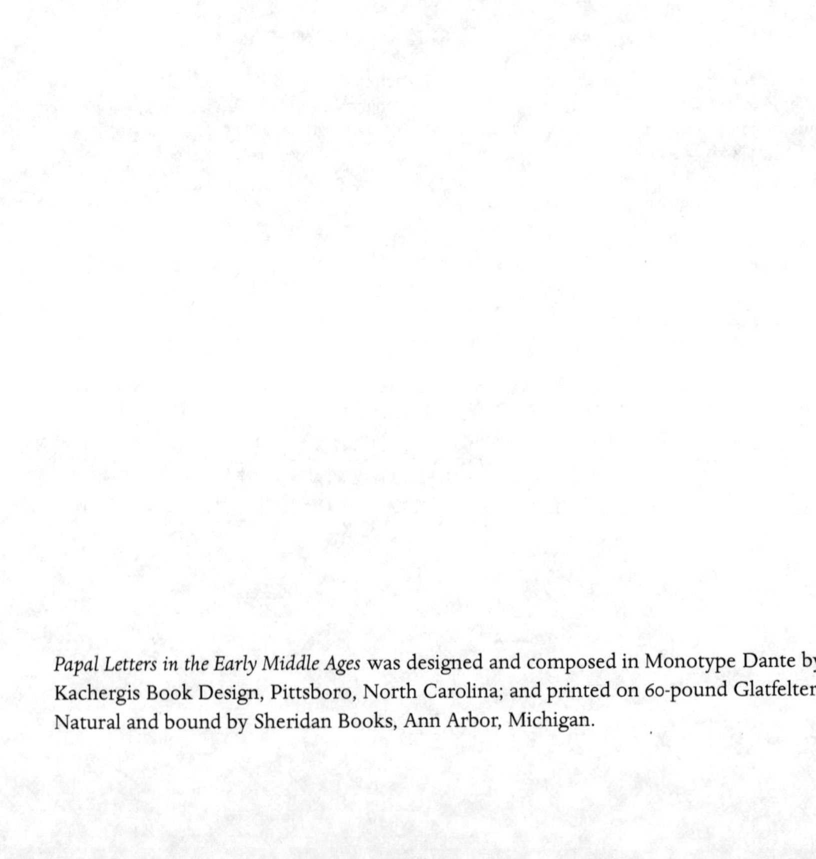

Papal Letters in the Early Middle Ages was designed and composed in Monotype Dante by Kachergis Book Design, Pittsboro, North Carolina; and printed on 60-pound Glatfelter Natural and bound by Sheridan Books, Ann Arbor, Michigan.